The Random House Personal Finance Library

How to Avoid a Personal Financial Crisis

Richard Eisenberg

RANDOM HOUSE
ELECTRONIC PUBLISHING

New York

Originally published as "How to Avoid a Mid-Life Financial Crisis"
by Scott Foresman and Company in 1987. An updated
edition was published by Penguin Books in 1988.
Manufactured in the United States of America
Revised edition

ISBN: 0-679-74288-3

New York, Toronto, London, Sydney, Auckland

*For my parents
and Liz*

HOW TO AVOID A PERSONAL FINANCIAL CRISIS

Richard Eisenberg is a Senior Editor for *Money* magazine, where he specializes in personal finance. He has written about a variety of topics, including articles about Individual Retirement Accounts, insurance you don't need, real estate investing, retirement and pension planning, and television's get-rich gurus.

In addition to being lead writer or contributor to several Money guides, his articles have appeared in such magazines, as *Ladies Home Journal, Home Office*, and others.

He and his wife, Elizabeth, live in Westfield, New Jersey. This is his first book.

"If the lessons explained here are heeded, they offer to all the pursuers of the American dream the means to reap its rewards."

From the Foreword by Landon
Jones, managing editor, *Money* magazine

"Richard Eisenberg has captured the essence of financial planning in basic no-nonsense terms. This should be must reading for everyone—certainly anyone who needs to really chart their financial course for life."

Charles B. Lefkowitz, CFP, president,
Financial Blueprints, Inc.

"Good, sound consumer advice to home sellers and home buyers"

Willard Gourley, Jr., vice president,
The Mortgage Bankers Association of America

"... does an extraordinary job in demonstrating how to juggle short-term financial needs with long-term retirement and estate planning goals. ... Eisenberg's presentation is also fun to read."

William G. Brennan, publisher and editor,
*Brennan Reports on Sophisticated
Tax and Investment Strategies*

"Here is a marvelous book, filled with information, worksheets, ideas, and peace of mind. The strategies can transform life's potential breakdowns into financial breakthroughs."

Herb Cohen, author,
You Can Negotiate Anything

CREDITS

CONTENTS

CHAPTER 6

CHAPTER 7

CHAPTER 8

FOREWORD

Middle age, once that tranquil sea between the storms of youth and old age, is rapidly becoming the most turbulent stage of American life. Millions of Baby Boomers are now crossing 40 and are encountering the unique set of life-cycle problems and rewards that we identify with middle age. As they do, they are changing the nation's mood dramatically. For 30 years the needs of the young have set the nation's agenda. But for the rest of this century, power will move to the middle-aged and our attention will increasingly move to the phenomenon of the mid-life financial crisis.

In the past we thought of the mid-life crisis as something that happens primarily in people's personal lives: longtime married people abruptly divorce, executives leap off into unexpected new careers, parents wrestle with the rebellion of their teenage children. In the future, however, the most grave mid-life crisis is just as likely to show up in people's financial lives.

That is because dramatic financial transitions are increasingly made in middle age today. Previous generations typically had settled many of their financial choices—career, spouse, family—before they left their 30s. But now all of these decisions remain open questions for Baby Boomers dealing with a whole new set of rules in middle age. Families are being started later; divorces arrive earlier and more often. The dream of home ownership seems possible only if two incomes are available. Mothers who used to be wed to the kitchen are now struggling to move ahead in careers. Both men and women face middle-management squeezes on corporate ladders. The goal of providing a college education for children is increasingly elusive at a time of rising tuitions and diminishing federal support. At the same time, great longevity means that caring adequately for aging parents is a difficulty faced by more and more people in mid-life. Yet the middle-aged today have no guarantees as to their own security. Even the government admits that the Social Security system, which protected the retirement of the generation that created it, will not be so generous to the next.

These problems will be faced by almost everyone under 40 today. How can you survive a mid-life financial crisis? As Richard Eisenberg demonstrates in this book, it begins with taking stock of your situation, starting long-term planning, and disciplining yourself financially. The encouraging news made clear here is that the building of wealth and financial security is within the grasp of anyone reaching mid-life today. If the lessons explained here are heeded, they offer to all who pursue the American dream the means to reap its rewards.

Landon Y. Jones

Managing Editor, Money magazine and

Author of Great Expectations: America and

the Baby Boom Generation

ACKNOWLEDGENTS

My thanks to the following people who helped enormously:

Landon Y. Jones, who assigned me the *Money* magazine article that inspired this book.

My other present and former colleagues at *Money* magazine, especially Bill Banks, Eric Berk, Jerry Edgerton, Diane Harris, Bob Klein, Frank Lalli, Flora Ling, Randy Lynch, Eric Schurenberg, Denise Topolnicki, and Carrie Tuhy.

Financial planners Stanley Cohen of Moseley Hallgarten Estabrook & Weeden, William Freund of Prescott Ball & Turben, Robin Oegerle of Financial Strategies, Robert Preston, and Eileen Sharkey.

Students of the Baby Boom generation, including Dr. Kenneth Dychtwald, Dr. Lawrence Eisenstein, University of Maryland Professor Frank Levy, and gamesman Michael Stern.

A variety of consultants specializing in employee benefits, retirement, and the workplace, including Philip Alden of Towers Perrin Forster & Crosby, Dennis Bunder of Handy Associates, David Carboni and Fred Munk of Retirement Counseling Associates, Karen Ferguson of The Pension Rights Center, Lloyd Kaye of William M. Mercer-Meidinger, Harry Levinson of The Levinson Institute, and Christine Seltz of Hewitt Associates.

Robert Hunter of the National Insurance Consumer Organization and Murray Rosen of The College of Insurance.

Cathy Guisewite, Heloise, and Jerry Mathers.

Pamela Dorman, my original editor.

Stuart Krichevsky, my agent.

And, most of all, my wife and in-house editor, Liz Sporkin.

INTRODUCTION

You need money to participate in Mid-Life
Crisis. *It's just like real life. It takes money to
do it right.*
*Michael Stern, co-inventor of the popular
new game* Mid-Life Crisis

How are your finances?

Chances are, that question has made you feel a little weak, whether
your family's annual income is $20,000 or $200,000. You might have a
sinking feeling, the kind that comes when you know something just isn't
right. Or you might suffer from the jitters because you're in a job you
can't stand and wonder whether you can afford to make a job switch right
now. You might be gloomy, worried about future expenses such as your
child's college tuition, your mother's medical bills, or your retirement but
unsure how you will scrape up the money to pay for them. You may fret
that you didn't pay close enough attention to the 1987 tax reform law or
that you didn't sell your stocks before the October 1987 crash. You may
even feel that your financial life is out of control—more money is going
out than coming in, bills are piling up, your closets are bursting with shoe
boxes full of receipts and old tax returns.

Cheer up. You're anything but alone in the time of your life that *New
York Times* columnist Russell Baker calls "middlescence." As you probably know all too well, there are 76 million Baby Boomers, born between
1946 and 1964, who are or soon will be turning 40. So, over the next 15
years, a third of Americans will also be suffering some pangs. A more
important reason for optimism about your finances is that you have realized that it's time to finally get serious about money and you are ready to
take action.

Mid-life, which these days means the years around age 40 (a century
ago the average *life expectancy* was 40), is a particularly opportune time to
take inventory of your finances. You are probably reasonably settled, with
a family and a career. The biggest purchases of your life—your house,
your cars—are probably behind you. You are about to enter the period of your life when your earnings will be at their peak, as will your
expenses and financial responsibilities.

At age 40 or thereabouts, you are also old enough to appreciate the importance of making your money work for you. Now that you are in what psychologist Carl Jung called "the noon of life," you are getting close enough to your lifelong career and financial goals to determine what you must do to meet them. Attaining those goals takes work, time, and forethought. But with a little knowledge, some financial and tax planning, the right team of financial advisers, and some discipline, you can do it.

Until now, your major objectives have most likely been short term: Find a job. Hook up with a mate. Start a family. Buy a house. Get a VCR. By age 40, you may well have achieved most of these goals. Ten years from now, your planning horizons will again take on a short-term cast. Once you reach 50, your concern about funding a retirement account, which you might tap in a few years, assumes an immediacy absent until that age. Travel could also take priority and become an important source of fulfillment.

But between 40 and 50, for what is likely to be the first time, you must take a truly long view. Most of your goals quite suddenly become distant and grand: the financial security of your family (perhaps for 30 years or so) if you should die or become disabled; the education of your children; an Individual Retirement Account—not so much for immediate tax savings, as may have been the case before tax reform cut many IRA write-offs, but now for long-term security.

Shifting focus from the near term to the long term is always jarring, but it is especially difficult for today's 40-year-olds. Baby Boomers represent far more than a statistic. To borrow a '60s phrase, your generation shares the mind-set "Live For Today."

That's fine when you can get along without planning for the future, not so fine when the lack of saving and planning can spell financial chaos for you and your family.

While you are learning to pay more attention to the future, you must not forget to take care of the present. For many people around age 40, that means providing not only for yourself but for the well-being of your children or stepchildren and for your elderly parents.

This feeling of being caught in the middle has led some psychologists to call today's mid-lifers the "Sandwiched Generation." With so many people depending on you, it is terribly important to have your financial life in order. Otherwise, you could be harming some of the people who matter most to you.

At age 40, it isn't too late to correct bad habits and start disciplining yourself financially. But there is not much time left to delay. This book will help you establish your financial objectives and provide the strategies that will enable you to attain them.

- Chapter 1 discusses who you are and where you have been, financially.

- Chapters 2 and 3 tell you how to put your financial life in order, juggle debt, and begin thinking long term.

- Chapter 4 shows you how to protect your family by owning the right types of insurance.

- Chapter 5 explains how to keep your tax bill low in light of the recent significant tax reform changes.

- Chapters 6 and 7 review investment and savings options that will help make your money grow.

- Chapter 8 instructs you on handling IRAs, Keogh accounts, and pension funds like a professional money manager.

- Chapter 9 describes how to pay for your child's college education through both long-term and short-term techniques.

- Chapter 10 analyzes how to make the best financial use of your home and helps you decide whether to trade up or remodel.

- Chapter 11 plots your work future, compares the pros and cons of job and career switches, and discusses how to get a job if you haven't had one in years.

- Chapter 12 offers tips on the best retirement-planning and estate-planning strategies.

By putting the book's strategies to work, you can help yourself thwart a mid-life financial crisis.

CHAPTER

I

WHO ARE YOU AND WHERE HAVE YOU BEEN FINANCIALLY?

*I've always spent whatever I've made, and
I have ever since I started work at the
Washington Star making $44.25 a week. Now
that I'm 42, I think I do have to be a little more
prudent and have a budget and do all those
things and make sure the kids' school gets paid.
But at the same time, I don't think your money
should sit back and do nothing.*
—*Carl Bernstein, author and former* Time, Washington
Post *and* ABC-TV *reporter, in* GQ *magazine*

Before getting knee-deep in the thicket of financial advice, it will help to take a look at how you feel about money and what you've done with the income you have earned until now. Reviewing the way you have handled your finances should reveal the bad habits that most need correcting. It will also show what you've been doing right. Believe it or not, you've probably done a pretty good job of managing your money–at least not much worse than most of your peers.

WHY YOU HAVE EVERY RIGHT TO BE PERPLEXED

The subject of money may be a bit perplexing to you. That makes sense. After all, you have been an eyewitness to the most volatile economic times of this century:

- *Take interest rates.* Or more specifically, take the prime rate (the rate banks ostensibly charge their best borrowers). The prime rate barely moved from 1935 through 1955; its low was 1.5 percent and its high was 3.2 percent. Compare that with the 1970s: one year the prime rate was 5.25 percent, the next 10.8 percent. In 1981, the prime hit 18.9 percent! The roller-coaster interest rates hit home for you as a saver and as a borrower. In the late 1970s you could benefit from the rising interest rates by putting cash in a money-market mutual fund paying 10 percent or so. When rates fell in the mid-1980s, money-market funds were paying only about 6 percent. The late-1970s runup in rates may have delayed you from buying a car or making home improvements because of the exorbitant cost of financing. But once rates fell, borrowing became more affordable again.

- *Take inflation.* In the placid Eisenhower years, the Consumer Price Index rose less than 1 percentage point a year. Two decades later, in the early '70s, when OPEC jacked up the price of oil, inflation rocketed to 12 percent. "Double-digit" practically became inflation's prefix again in the late '70s and early '80s, when inflation was deemed the nation's number-one problem. And then, in the mid-1980s, inflation almost miraculously tiptoed away from the American scene. Sure, it was terrific to see 85 cents-a-gallon gasoline again. But lower inflation also meant that after having received annual raises of 7 percent, 8 percent, or 9 percent, you started getting increases of merely 3 percent or so. If you worked for a company in financial difficulty, you may have received no raise at all or even a pay cut in exchange for job security–if you could keep your job.

- *Take taxes.* You are part of the most highly taxed generation in U.S. history. According to a Washington, D.C.–based research group called Americans for Generational Equity, between 1960 and 1982 the average tax rate rose from 10 percent to 23 percent and Social Security tax rates quadrupled. As inflation raised your annual income, it also pushed you into a higher and higher tax bracket. So there was a strong incentive to find ways to shelter your income from taxes, legally and otherwise. Then, the tax cut legislation of 1981 reduced some of that incentive. But two years later, Congress hiked Social Security payroll taxes. That move, combined with inflation, pretty much negated any tax savings from the 1981 law.

Then in 1986 Congress passed sweeping tax reform legislation that cut the top tax rate from 50 percent to 28 percent (effective in 1988) and eliminated many deductions, credits, and other shelters. The motivation was admirable–to create a simpler and fairer tax system. But one effect was to throw a curve ball at the tax-planning strategies many people had used.

So it's no wonder that finance has you slightly confused. Of course, the U.S. government hasn't set a very good example for household budgeters either. While politicians have lectured the American public about not saving enough and the evils of debt, the U.S. federal budget deficit has grown astronomically. The annual budget deficits of the mid-1980s are larger than all the previous deficits put together. The national debt has more than doubled since 1980. And Congress is telling you to get your financial act together?

THAT OVERWHELMED FEELING

Efforts to take control of your finances may also have been stalled because you feel slightly overwhelmed by financial pressures. That is entirely understandable. You are probably being tugged in more directions than were earlier generations of Americans in their 30s or 40s. California psychologist Kenneth Dychtwald calls yours "the most highly stressed generation in history." That could be an over statement, but not by much.

Consider: Your parents, who are living longer than the elderly ever have, may need some financial assistance from you for the next 20 years or so. Your children's expenses are the highest they have been, and, with college fast approaching, they will get higher still. That is even more true if you have remarried and now have stepchildren to care for as well as children of your own. Then there are your personal outlays for expenses such as clothes, utility bills, and transportation. Discretionary income? The phrase is practically a joke. Indeed, just finding the money to cover expenses has become the biggest financial concern of most people in their 30s and 40s.

The world of personal finance may be virgin territory if you are a woman who is recently divorced or who expects to be divorced soon. In many marriages today, managing money (or in some cases mismanaging it) is still considered the husband's responsibility. That division of labor may work well while a marriage is stable. But if your marriage begins to unravel and you are in the dark about your family's finances, disaster can follow. Without a clue about how to invest or save on taxes, you could unknowingly end up reducing your net worth and raising your tax bill. Today, 32 percent of women between the ages of 35 and 39 are divorced or separated, and some studies predict that another 27 percent of women in that age group will divorce. Single mothers suffer most from ignorance about money; their lack of financial planning can spoil their children's future.

YOUR ATTITUDES ABOUT MONEY (AND A SHORT HISTORY LESSON)

The notion of caring for your money as a gardener would his vegetables may also be a little disconcerting. Having grown up in the 1960s, you might harbor some vague notions of money as, if not evil, at least distasteful. You might even think that investing in the stock market is unethical, particularly after the Ivan Boesky insider trading scandal of 1986. (Actually, there are a variety of ways to buy stocks without compromising your ethical standards. More about that in Chapter 7.) Perhaps you chose a low-paying career such as teaching or social work partly as a personal statement saying you wanted no part of "business."

Yet you are hearing stories of entrepreneurs about your age whose success hasn't made them sacrifice their personal values. Take the bushy-haired founders of Ben & Jerry's Homemade Ice Cream, Ben Cohen and Jerry Greenfield, both 40. Cohen is a former pottery teacher at a school for mentally disturbed adolescents, and his former high school pal Greenfield was a lab technician. After taking a $5 correspondence course in making ice cream, they opened an ice cream store in Burlington, Vermont, in 1978. Today, their company has annual sales of more than $5 million. Perhaps equally important is the company's history of donating about 15 percent of annual earnings, through The Ben & Jerry's Foundation, to local community service organizations and other charities. It is also company policy that the lowest-paid employee must earn at least 20 percent of the salary of the highest-paid employee.

Most of your attitudes about money derive instinctively from the financial history of your generation. At first glance, it might appear that you and others your age (a group sometimes called "leading edge" Baby Boomers) have had a cushy adulthood. The economy was strong and jobs were plentiful when you graduated from college in the late 1960s. You grew accustomed to substantial raises at work. Many people your age bought houses at an especially good time. In the early 1970s, mortgage rates for 30-year fixed-rate loans hovered around 8 percent. The median-priced house cost just over $15,000 (compared with over $80,000 today). Your housing costs, according to the National Association of Realtors, came to between 7 percent and 15 percent of your income, versus 33 percent of income for today's home buyers. Then, like a new Bruce Springsteen album, the value of your house took off. Home prices rose at the fastest rate in U.S. history: up 9.5 percent a year, on average, between 1968 and 1975 and then 12 percent annually between 1976 and 1980. What may wind up being the best investment of your life–buying your house–was actually a serendipitous accident of timing.

But in inflation-adjusted terms, you have been treading water. According to a recent Congressional study, salaries and house prices for people your age have gone up at only about the inflation rate over the past decade. As a result, some economists say that yours will be the first American generation who won't be able to maintain a better standard of living than their parents.

Decent raises are only half the story of your work history. You might well have earned more money if there had not been so many people your age competing for similar jobs. Many labor analysts believe that the large number of Baby Boomers has kept salaries 10 percent to 15 percent lower than if workers had belonged to a normal-sized generation. Even though women your age were the first spurred to work in record numbers, many married women have paying jobs primarily because they believe they must work to maintain what they view as an acceptable standard of living.

Regardless of your sex, after 20 or so years of working you may now be feeling a sense of "Is that all there is?" Even if you like your job, you will probably have to worry soon about job security for the first time in your life. Those 76 million younger members of the Baby Boom generation are elbowing ahead in the workplace, presumably eyeing the jobs held by people about your age.

So, the reality of your economic history may make you somewhat resentful. You are probably also more than a little cynical about money, as with life itself–and with good reason. Your expectations, and those thrust upon you, were so great that they couldn't help but be dashed eventually. Here is what *Time* magazine said when in 1966 it named you, then the "Under-25 Generation," its Man of the Year: "He is the man who will land on the moon, cure cancer and the common cold, lay out blight-proof, smog-free cities, enrich the underdeveloped world and, no doubt, write finish to poverty and war."

Today such expectations seem unfair and ridiculous. They didn't seem so outlandish at the time. After all, *Time* was describing an idealistic generation growing up in the greatest period of economic prosperity in U.S. history. How could anyone know that you would later be scarred by Vietnam, Watergate, the resignation of a president, the OPEC squeeze (twice), several recessions, and empty political promises such as ones about the health of the Social Security system?

That mixture of resentment and cynicism has manifested itself in the way you view financial advisers, investments, and advertising. If you are like many others your age, you distrust authority figures. So you are likely to be suspicious of financial planners or stockbrokers who say they will make you richer. When a broker you've never heard of makes a cold call and tries to sell you on a hot stock over the telephone, you are apt to slam down the receiver. You would be the first to agree with the saying, "If something sounds too good to be true, it probably is."

Such skepticism can be a genuine virtue when it comes to financial advice. In fact, when you combine skepticism with research, you have a knockout punch. That is especially true in the current deregulated era, when many types of financial institutions are selling similar types of investments, insurance policies, and savings accounts. By asking a lot of questions of a lot of people, you can come up with the best ways to meet your financial needs.

For instance, it is rare that one bank will be best for all your checking, savings, and borrowing needs. After comparison shopping, you may end up with your checking and day-to-day savings accounts at one bank, your CDs at another, your mortgage with a savings and loan, and your car loan with the finance division of an automobile manufacturer.

Trouble arises only when skepticism and cynicism turn into repulsion. That leads to rejection of all advice, legitimate or otherwise, and failure to plan for the future. That has sadly been the case for many people of your generation. For example, by margins approaching 2 to 1, survey after survey shows that people in their 30s and 40s doubt that Social Security will provide for them. But the same surveys show that the doubters aren't compensating by saving much for their own retirement.

Your feelings about investing may well border on contempt, especially if you bought stocks and bonds during the 1970s or just before the October 1987 crash. The stock market was abominable during much of the '70s, especially for shareholders in stocks known as Real Estate Investment Trusts, which suffered a major collapse. Bonds were an even worse investment. As interest rates rose, the value of bonds fell. If you tried to get more exotic and speculated in commodity futures or flaky tax shelters, you probably lost a bundle, too. Gold had a great run for investors who bought coins or bullion in the early 1970s. Problem is, plenty of investors missed the right time to get out of gold and are still holding on to coins that are worth less than half of what they cost.

It wouldn't be surprising if your attempts at "shrewd" investing backfired. Writer Digby Diehl reflected on his history as an investor in a personal essay called "Looking at Forty," published in *Esquire* magazine in March 1981: "During my adulthood of respectable earning power, I had managed to shovel my money down every shoddy investment rathole known to suckers: Broadway shows, porno movies, penny stocks, hydrofoil boats, bull jism, and reputedly precious stones."

Diehl's experience is hardly unique. Financial planner Stanley Cohen, of the New York–based brokerage firm Moseley, Hallgarten, Estabrook & Weeden, says he knows many investors in their 30s and 40s who say they "like to be where the action is." Translation: They invest in fads without knowing what they are buying, and they trade stocks too frequently, churning their accounts and racking up expensive brokerage commissions and tax bills.

THE MONEY HABITS YOU HAVE FORMED

Even if you hardly consider yourself an authority on personal finances, you have probably formed some good and bad money habits by now. While it is dangerous to generalize about a group of 40-year-olds who range from David Stockman to Dolly Parton, most financial analysts agree that Baby Boomers have been nursed on Instant Gratification. "When you want it NOW and you want it GOOD!" is a recent advertising campaign for Pillsbury's microwave dinners that aims directly at this craving.

You are, after all, a member of the first generation to have grown up with Visa and MasterCard (nee BankAmericard and Master Charge). The first BankAmericard was issued in 1959 and people began Master Charging in 1967. Apparently the card issuers made a big impression on the children of the '60s. Today, only a quarter of American adults have a Visa card but nearly half of people ages 25 to 44 do.

Products from Davy Crockett coonskin caps in the '50s to compact disc players in the '80s were also created just for you, a generation that now controls more than $80 billion in discretionary income. In a recent survey by the N.W. Ayer advertising agency that asked people ages 25 to 44 what they wanted, the most popular answers were purchases with immediate benefits, such as a pool (51 percent), a maid (45 percent), and a computer (45 percent). Purchases paying bigger long-term dividends, such as IRAs and bank certificates of deposit, were much farther down on the list: 24 percent for IRAs and 25 percent for CDs.

But you are most likely not the Big Spender that is often portrayed in unflattering discussions of the typical Baby Boomer—owning more shoes than Imelda Marcos, buying the very latest in computer gadgetry. A recent study from the U.S. Bureau of Labor Statistics shows that, as with the average American household, three-quarters of expenditures in a Baby Boomer household go for shelter, food, and cars. Contrary to the Yuppie myth that people your age feast regularly at the trendiest restaurants, Baby Boomer families spend the same percentage of their income on food away from home as the average household.

It is also often said that people your age are up to their eyeballs in consumer debt-credit cards, personal loans, revolving charge accounts. Well, yes and no. Yes, on average, families in their late 30s and early 40s have more outstanding debt than families in general ($31,000 versus $15,200, according to 1989 figures). But that is only half the story. Roughly 48 percent of those age 35 to 44 owe no installment debt. Zero. They are probably the ones whose parents told vivid tales about the Depression of the 1930s and scared them out of going into hock. The other 52 percent do, in fact, pay off more installment debt as a percentage of their income than families in general; for example, the debt level of more than one-third of those 35 to 44 is equal to between 1 and 9 percent of their income, while it is only that high for one-fourth of the general population.

As for saving money for a rainy day, the idea probably seems to you as outdated as a slide rule. Some evidence: A recent survey by Market Facts, a Chicago-based research company, found that although 86 percent of parents want their children to have a college education, only 54 percent have saved money for that purpose. While that statistic is a sad one, it can be defended somewhat. For much of your adult life, putting money in the bank wasn't very smart. If you kept a 5 percent passbook savings account in the 1970s while inflation was in double digits, you were actually losing money. At that time, the smart money was either buying expensive items before their prices went up or borrowing and paying the loans back with dollars that inflation had eroded. And now you're told to cut back on your charge cards and start squirreling away money that your family will need in 10, 15, 25 years? That's not so easy.

Whether you and your peers will save and invest more in your 40s and 50s is still very much an open question. The answer may well determine the health of the U.S. economy over the next several decades. If you start saving and investing regularly, there will be more money available for businesses to buy or maintain factories, equipment, machinery, and supplies and to hire more employees. Productivity would likely increase and the economy should then chug along nicely (with occasional recessions). But if saving and investing do not increase, businesses will either make do with what they have or raise money by selling bonds. The result could very well be higher interest rates, financially wobbly companies, increased bankruptcies, and bigger and longer recessions.

HOW YOUR FINANCES COMPARE WITH YOUR NEIGHBOR'S

To get an idea of how your finances stack up against those of others in your age group and the national averages, take a look at the table on pages 11 and 12, culled from the most recent Census Bureau survey called

"Household Wealth and Asset Ownership: 1988" and a similar study done by the Federal Reserve Board in 1989. (The asset figures come from the Census and the data on debt are from the Fed.) All dollar amounts represent the median figures. You might want to fill in your household's figures or circle "yes" or "no" where applicable for comparison's sake.

You might not be able to answer some of the "yes/no" questions because of a lack of up-to-date information about your current financial status. It's also quite likely that your figures are not as impressive as some of the averages. Not to worry. After getting your financial life in order and then filling out the table's blank lines again, you are sure to be more pleased with your revised answers.

Table 1.1. **Your Money Versus The Averages**

Assets and Debts	Age 35-44	You	National Average
Annual family income	$30,000	$_____	$23,796
Net worth (gross assets minus liabilities)	$33,183	$_____	$35,752
Home ownership 64%	67%	yes/no	
Home equity	$35,892	$_____	$43,070
Interest-bearing bank accounts and CDs 73%	72%	yes/no	
Amount in interest-bearing bank accounts and CDs	$2,438	$_____	$3,494
Amount in interest-free checking accounts	$466	$_____	$487
IRAs and Keoghs 24%	27%	yes/no	
Amount in IRAs or Keoghs	$7,272	$_____	$9,016
Stocks and mutual funds 22%	23%	yes/no	
Amount in stocks and mutual funds	$6,230	$_____	$4,510
U.S. Savings Bonds 18%	21%	yes/no	
Money-market funds and bonds	8%	yes/no	9%

Managing Your Money Tip

You can use Managing Your Money to compare your money versus the averages anytime you want. You can find your current checking, savings, and other money account balances by selecting Money Accounts from the Money submenu. You can look at a summary of all of your assets (including your money accounts and your investments) by selecting Your Net Worth from the Net Worth submenu, pointing to "Assets," and pressing F10. To look at a summary of all of your debts (including your mortgage, credit card, and other debts) select Your Net Worth from the Net Worth submenu, point to "Liabilities," and press F10.

As for debt, you can see the amount of debt you're carrying by selecting Budget Categories from the Money submenu. (Press F7 until you see "Annual Total" and "Tax Category" as column headings.) As for the level of debt payments you're carrying, press F9; the second pie chart graph will show the percentage of your income that goes to debt service (unless it's a relative minor item in your personal budget).

CHAPTER

2

GETTING YOUR FINANCIAL LIFE IN ORDER

When you're 40, you can't ride the fence anymore. You gotta make definite decisions about your life.
—Dolly Parton in People Weekly *magazine*

WHY THE MUNDANE MATTERS

If you are the impatient type, this is the chapter you will be most tempted to skip. Please resist the temptation. Sure, things like budgeting, record keeping, debt control, and assembling a quality team of financial professionals are less exciting than learning how to make money in the stock market. But they are at least as important to your financial well-being, not to mention to increasing your disposable income.

You wouldn't drive cross-country on vacation without first plotting out the trip, inspecting your car, and collecting the right maps. Okay, maybe you would. But you'd end up missing out on some sights by spending the time asking for directions and getting your car fixed. The same holds true for your finances. By taking the time to lay the groundwork now, as tiresome as it may be, you will save yourself having to patch up your finances down the road.

13

You should also establish financial priorities before you take any new courses of action with your money. By first determining your most important financial needs and desires, you can proceed to find ways to fulfill them. For example, which is more important to you:

- Increasing your monthly income?

- Saving money for your child's college tuition?

- Boosting your cash reserve for an upcoming purchase?

Each answer suggests a different financial strategy. It's a good idea to write down or at least keep track mentally of your financial goals every year or so and after major life events, such as marriage, divorce, birth of a baby, or move. As your life changes, so will your goals, and you will need to adjust your finances accordingly. The accompanying worksheet should get you off on the right foot. Use checkmarks to indicate the importance of each objective.

Managing Your Money Tip

> You can use Managing Your Money to plan your financial goals. If you select Goal Planning from the Analyze submenu, enter the data requested, and press F10, you can see what you need to have to pay for your goal, and how much you must save annually to reach that goal. If you're saving for tuition for a child, or for your retirement, select Tuition Planning or Retirement Planning from the Analyze submenu. Using Managing Your Money will allow you to account for inflation in finding your savings targets.

ADD SOME RECORDS TO YOUR COLLECTION

The biggest financial problem for many people in their 30s and 40s isn't making enough money, but keeping it. If you danced to The Supremes' song "Where Did Our Love Go?" in 1964, today you might very well be dancing to the tune "Where Did Our Money Go?" Paychecks, it seems, have an uncanny way of withering away. One reason is the take from federal, state, and local governments in the form of withholding taxes. Even after the most recent round of tax cuts, income taxes represent one of the biggest expenses of American families. Another reason is inflation. A third reason is the most pernicious: seepage. Cash unaccountably gets sucked out of your wallet, vanishing without a trace.

The best way to hold on to what you've got is to keep good financial records. That way, you won't have to hire a private detective agency to track down your missing earnings. Start by confronting the record keeper's nemesis: automatic teller machine (ATM) withdrawals and checks written to "cash." Both seem harmless enough. But they are the number-one cause of money seepage in America. Gaining such easy access to your money tempts you to spend the cash without accounting for the nickel-and-dime purchases. Whittle away $50 a week this way, as is all too common, and by the end of the year you will have lost $2,600 of after-tax earnings. If more than 30 percent of your after-tax income is spent on cash, you need to keep better records. When self-discipline is impossible, you might do yourself a favor and bank with an institution that doesn't offer ATMs.

Make this the year to begin keeping better tax records, too. Now that the tax reform law has taken away some popular deductions, claiming the remaining write-offs that are legally yours is more important than ever. If you have always just thrown every receipt, credit card statement, and paycheck into one drawer and then handed the contents over to a tax preparer in April, start using the manila envelope system. It isn't pretty, but it works. Buy a bunch of 81/2"x11" envelopes and label them:

Work	IRA, Keogh, Other Pensions
House	Bank, Broker, Mutual Funds
Medical Costs	Credit Cards
Charity	Major Purchases
Taxes	Miscellaneous

If applicable, also do envelopes for:

Alimony Received or Paid

Rental Property

Moving Expenses

Child Care Expenses

Casualty or Theft Losses

Whenever you receive a piece of paper that might be of use at tax preparation time, stick it in the appropriate envelope. You will make your life and your tax preparer's life simpler come April. Equally important, as the year progresses you will be able to get a handle on your tax bill and take the proper tax-planning steps. Keep the tax records for at least three

MY GOALS

Objective	Short Term	Medium Term	Long Term
Reduce debt			
Build an emergency reserve			
Increase insurance coverage			
Buy a house			
Make home improvements			
Buy a vacation house			
Buy a car			
Make another big purchase			
Have children			
Finance children's education			
Live more luxuriously			
Take an expensive vacation			
Take an unpaid leave from work			
Start a business			
Take early retirement			
Live well after retirement			
Other			

SOURCE: *Money Guide: Personal Finance.*

years in case the Internal Revenue Service decides to question you about your deductions in the future.

Managing Your Money Tip

Managing Your Money "puts your receipts in envelopes" automatically. As you spend or receive money, Managing Your Money records who you paid (or who paid you)

- how much
- the date the transaction occurred
- the budget category
- any other information you care to save

You can see a list of all of the transactions involved by selecting Money Accounts from the Money submenu, pointing to the account you wish to study, and pressing F10.

To track your spending habits, you'll want to set up accounts for cash (pocket money expenditures) and checking. If you haven't yet set up these accounts, here's how:

1. Select Money Accounts from the Money submenu.
2. Press F5 to add to your new account. If you need any HELP, just press F1.

Managing Your Money features an extensive list of budget categories. But you can add new ones, or delete ones that Managing Your Money provided to produce a list of budget categories that is right for you. To set up your budget categories:

1. Select Budget Categories from the Money submenu.
2. Press F1 and read HELP.
3. To delete budget categories that don't apply to you, arrow down to the category and press F3 to delete them. If you'd prefer a different name for a category that does apply, just press F2 and change it. Press F10 when you're done.
4. To add categories, just press F5.

You can specify whether a budget category is a tax category or not when you set up the category, or later, by editing the category. Categories set up as tax categories will be read into the Tax submenu for tax planning purposes.

After you have disciplined yourself enough to keep tax records in envelopes, move to the next level of sophistication: tax record books. Most good bookstores stock such books, which let you keep a running tab on your tax bill all year long. Some financial planning computer programs do the same.

A tax log is critically important if you run your own business or if you use a car, computer, or any other equipment partly for business. The IRS has stepped up its auditing of small businesses and home offices. At the same time, Congress has passed tax laws requiring detailed record keeping for people working from home. If you are audited about a home-based firm or the business use of a personal possession, you will need to provide evidence of the amount of business use and the cost. The better your records are, the stronger your case will be against the IRS.

You and your spouse should also collect all your other financial records and keep them together: insurance policies, wills and trust documents, company benefit literature, credit card numbers, Veterans papers, and the like. Make sure you also include a list of the names and addresses of the professionals in your life: your lawyer, doctors, accountant, insurance agents, stockbroker, financial planner, and whomever else you rely on for counsel. Keep all this material together in one drawer at home, give a copy of everything to your lawyer, and keep an extra copy of everything in a bank safe deposit box.

THE BENEFITS OF CHECKING YOUR BENEFITS

While amassing your records, you might want to refresh your memory about—and fill your spouse in on—your company benefits. Most people have only the vaguest notion about the benefits they receive at work; they are especially fuzzy about their company–provided health, life, and disability insurance coverage as well as their pension plans.

If you can't find literature from your employer about the firm's benefits, go to the personnel office (sometimes called "human resources" or "employee benefits"). Be sure to ask for the document that explains how your company's pension plan works, called "the summary plan description," and the document that tells you how much your own pension benefits are now worth, called "the personalized employee-benefit statement." A good primer to help explain pensions in detail is *A Guide to*

Understanding Your Pension Plan, available for $3 from Pension Rights Center, 1346 Connecticut Ave. N.W., Washington, D.C. 20036.

Your company probably provides a defined-benefit pension a retirement benefit employees will get on the basis of their earnings and length of service with the company. Benefits are paid out in monthly installments after retirement. In most cases, employers fund these plans without contributions from workers.

Defined-benefit plans don't pay pensions until an employee is vested, which typically has meant ten years after starting work for the company. The Tax Reform Act of 1986 requires employers to vest workers faster. As of 1989, employees are now fully vested after a minimum of five or seven years, depending on the company's pension plan.

Lately, companies have been supplementing their pension plans with savings and stock-purchase arrangements known as defined-contribution plans. Employee or employer or both put a specified amount of money into the plan each year—generally a percentage of the worker's pay. Investment earnings grow tax-deferred until they are withdrawn. Payouts from these plans are based on how well the investments perform. The most common types of defined-contribution plans are:

- *Profit-sharing plans.* If the company makes money, it can contribute an amount equivalent to as much as 25 percent of a worker's pretax pay or $30,000, whichever is less, to one of these programs. The employee can contribute, too, and that money vests immediately. Most companies let employees stuff as much as 10 percent of their pay into the plans. The employer's contributions are ordinarily vested within five years. Companies usually invest profit-sharing funds in a variety of stocks and bonds, although some buy only their own securities. Most businesses pay out cash from these plans only when an employee leaves or withdraws his or her contributions.

- *Thrift Plans.* These plans let employees contribute between and 6 percent of pay and the company matches a portion–typically 50 cents for every dollar an employee invests. A few businesses match dollar for dollar; some even put up twice the amount of worker contributions. The individual's payroll deductions vest immediately. The company share usually vests in about five years. Thrift plans offer a variety of investments that generally include a diversified stock portfolio, the company's own shares, and a fixed-interest account.

- *Salary-reduction or 401(k) plans.* The 401(k), named after the section of the tax code that created it, is a thrift plan that allows employees to invest with pretax dollars. The gross salary figure on the worker's W-2 form is cut by the payroll deductions, so less wages are taxed. By law, workers can shelter up to $8,728, although companies typically limit investments to 10 percent of pay. (Prior to the tax reform law, employees could legally shelter up to 25 percent of their pretax pay or $30,000.) Vesting and matching rules are the same as those for thrift plans.

- *Employee stock-ownership plans (ESOPs) and payroll-based employee stock-ownership plans (PAYSOPs).* Funded exclusively by employers, ESOPs and PAYSOPs are the fabled plans that buy company stock for their workers. Most ESOPs give employees stock worth up to 10 percent of pay. ESOP programs usually use either graded vesting or ten-year vesting, so employees can't get ownership of the stock fast. A PAYSOP is the stingy cousin of the ESOP. It provides stock worth as much as one-half of 1 percent of a worker's salary, up to $100,000. But PAYSOP stock vests immediately.

A TIME TO CONSOLIDATE

When you collect your assortment of financial records, you may be flabbergasted to discover how many different institutions you do business with. Your family might have savings and checking accounts at three different banks. You might have five different $2,000 IRAs, one for each of the past five years. If you are a mutual fund investor, perhaps you own a small number of shares of six different funds. Diversification is swell, but it often swells your paperwork, too. After 20-odd years of financial transactions, it is probably time for you to consolidate some accounts.

Don't be too hasty, though. Your family may have an excellent reason for keeping accounts at, say, three different banks. Members of step families, for example, often like to keep their finances separate. Try to justify each bank, brokerage, and mutual fund account your family owns. If you can't make a convincing case for keeping one, get rid of it or merge it with another.

An important factor to consider when consolidating your accounts is what is sometimes called "building a financial relationship." Some call it financial blackmail. Essentially, you can sometimes get a better deal by doing a lot of your financial business with the same institution rather than using several.

Bankers are very big these days on building relationships. Deregulation has increased costs for banks to the point where they often can't afford to keep customers with tiny accounts. So bankers frequently now give you this choice: Keep your $100 checking account with us and pay exorbitant charges, or keep a lot more money with us and avoid the fees. Many banks, savings and loans, and credit unions in large cities also pay savers with balances over $10,000 or so a half a percentage point more in interest than savers with smaller balances. They are saying that if you don't develop a financial relationship with them, you will pay dearly for that decision.

Financial relationships can come in handy, though. For instance, a growing number of lenders give familiar customers with steady balances better rates on loans than people who walk in off the street and apply. Your stockbroker might cut his commission charges on a big trade if you do business with him frequently. Mutual fund families, which consist of a variety of stock, bond, and money-market funds, allow shareholders the ability to switch at will from one fund to another simply by making a phone call.

CHECK ON YOUR CHECKING

Start consolidating by taking a serious look at your family's checking habits, which are probably the most ingrained and most out-of-date. If you have had the same no-interest checking account with the same bank for more than a decade, it is especially worthwhile to shop around. Things have changed.

Ten years ago, about the biggest difference between checking accounts was the color of the checkbook cover. Today, virtually no two accounts are alike. A recent survey by the Consumer Federation of America of roughly 150 banks and savings and loans showed that fees differ so much among institutions that customers with $300 to $500 in a NOW account paying 5 1/4 percent interest would earn as much as $11 a year or pay as much as $172 a year, after netting fees from interest earned, depending on where they banked. To see whether the group has recently studied checking account fees in your city, write to Consumer Federation of America, 1424 16th St. N.W., Suite 604, Washington, D.C. 20036.

As a rule, savings and loans offer better deals than banks on checking accounts. Credit unions also often offer a low-cost checking alternative on what they call share draft accounts. You will probably be better off with a no-interest checking account instead of an interest-bearing NOW account. Fees are usually higher on NOWs. When comparing checking charges from various local institutions, find out about their minimum balances and how those balances are calculated.

If you know you won't keep enough cash in checking to avoid paying fees, look for a no-frills account. You will pay a flat monthly fee regardless of your balance. There may be a catch: some banks restrict the number of checks you can write or the number of times you can see a teller each month.

Money-market mutual funds let you write checks, too. But there usually are restrictions. Most funds don't permit shareholders to write checks for less than $250 or $500. Many funds also won't let you withdraw deposited money for two weeks, longer than the check-hold period at many banks and savings and loans.

THE ASSET MANAGEMENT ACCOUNT SOLUTION

One tool created to help you consolidate your records is an asset management account. Created a decade ago by Merrill Lynch, this is a brokerage, free-checking, money-market, and credit account all wrapped up in one. Most brokerage houses offer asset management accounts, as do many banks and some insurance companies and mutual funds.

Here's how one works: Anytime you sell stock or mutual fund shares or earn cash dividends from your shares, the money is automatically held in the interest-bearing portion of your account. So the account eliminates the need to reinvest dividends that arrive in dribs and drabs. Your cash earns a market interest rate (tax-free if you so desire), and you can write free checks for any amount up to your available balance. Many firms help customers with their record keeping by noting on the checks whether they are for expenses that might be tax deductible. You can also use the account to borrow against up to half the value of your securities without having to fill out forms-usually paying about 1 to 2 percentage points above the prime rate. The accounts also often include a credit card or debit card. Each month, you receive one statement that keeps track of all your transactions.

The minimum initial deposit for an asset management account is usually between $10,000 and $25,000, and fees range from zero to $100 a year. Lately, though, a number of brokers have begun selling junior asset management accounts for people with less money. Merrill Lynch calls its junior account the Capital Builder Account and has a $5,000 minimum initial deposit. The Raymond James brokerage firm requires only $1,000 to open its junior account. Fees on junior asset management accounts are slightly less than those for the regular accounts.

If the idea of an asset management account appeals to you, call around and find out the answers to a few questions:

- How often is cash swept into the money-market account? (The most desirable answer is daily.)

- What is the interest rate charged to borrow money?

- What are my choices of money-market funds? Is there a tax-free fund? Is there a government-insured fund?

- Will I get my canceled checks returned?

- Who will service my account and answer my questions in the future?

- Is the Visa, MasterCard, or American Express card a credit card with monthly billing charges or a debit card whose charges are immediately deducted from the account?

- Can I see a copy of your monthly statement so I can determine whether I will understand it?

- How can I close the asset management account?

FIGURING WHAT YOU ARE WORTH

After determining your goals and getting your records in order, you can begin to figure out how realistic your objectives are. The best way to do that is to determine how much you now have, so you can then estimate how much more you will need to reach your goals. A net worth statement or personal balance sheet will do the trick. After filling it out, you will be able to tell—perhaps, for the first time in your life—what you own and what you owe. The difference between the two represents your net worth. You can calculate your net worth by filling out the accompanying worksheet now and then updating it once a year.

Managing Your Money Tip

Managing Your Money's Net Worth program summons everything in the other sections of Managing Your Money (such as saving accounts you own, and loans you owe), gives you a chance to add as many other items as you like (such as a room-by-room household inventory), and then tallies your net worth.

To look at your net worth, select Your Net Worth from the Net Worth submenu. Press F6 to update your net worth. To look at a summary of your assets (including your money accounts and your investments) by selecting Your Net Worth from the Net Worth submenu, point to "Assets," and press F10. To look at a summary of all of your debts (including your mortgage, credit card, and other debts) by selecting Your Net Worth from the Net Worth submenu, point to "Liabilities," and press F10.

To add a new item, after you've entered Assets or Liabilities, just press F5, enter the name, amount, and type of asset or liability, and then press F10 again to save what you've done. (An aggregate item will serve as a heading to house individual items; "bicycle collection" is an aggregate item; "bicycle" is an individual item.)

Note:
You can have Managing Your Money update Your Net Worth automatically. Select Optional Features from the File submenu, and then select Net Worth Options. Highlight the answer to "Should we update Your Net Worth automatically?", and press "Y."

If your net worth is a negative number—and that is a distinct possibility—your primary financial goal should be paying off some debts. If your assets are just a tad more than your liabilities, that is a danger sign, too. You could be in trouble if a financial emergency arises, and you may also have a tough time achieving some of your financial goals with little spare cash.

Take another look at the figures for your assets. Is most of your money tied up in clothes, cars, furniture, or other depreciating assets? You would be better off tilting your assets toward ones that are likely to appreciate in value, such as bank CDs, stocks, real estate, and company savings plans. If your balance sheet reveals that most of the lines for investments are blank, you need to work on diversifying your portfolio.

BUDGING YOUR BUDGET

Now for the part most people dread most: the family budget (or lack thereof). A budget, contrary to conventional wisdom, is not a form of financial flagellation. It is merely a useful way of keeping track of your family's money.

For a serious look at your family's cash flow, fill out the accompanying cash flow worksheet with figures from the preceding twelve months or calendar year.

Managing Your Money Tip

To see your personal cash flow, enter last year's figures for each budget category in Managing Your Money.

1. Select Budget Categories from the Money submenu.
2. Point to a budget category and press F10.
3. Point to the January cell in the left-hand column (i.e., January of the current year).
   a. To use last year's annual total as a basis, enter the annual total, and press F7. This will divide the annual amount by 12 and enter it on a monthly basis.
   b. To use last year's average monthly total as a basis, enter the amount and press F6. (You can account for rising prices by indicating the amount or percentage you want the monthly total to increase.)
   c. If costs will change in a given month, point to that month and enter the new amount. To copy that amount into subsequent months, press F6.
4. Press F10 to save what you've done.

After completing this exercise, you may have found that the final figure is negative. Now you have a firsthand look at the familiar term: deficit spending. Perhaps an emergency required you to borrow or to tap savings last year. But if your best estimate is that an annual family cash flow statement from any of the past five years would have shown a similar bottom-line loss, you need to go on a spending diet.

Start by making a similar cash flow statement for the next twelve months. Fill out the income and tax lines based on what you expect the figures to be for the coming year. Then do the same for your living expenses, making any adjustments you think seem necessary. If you've got a bad case of economic consumption, try putting in smaller, but realistic, figures for the least essential expenses: mealsout, recreation, entertainment, vacations, and hair styling.

You can use Cash Forecasting to display your current and future cash positions, based on your budget, so you can spot trouble well in advance. To see your Cash Forecast, select Forecasting from the Money submenu.

The Forecasting screen has three sections—your current cash; the cash Managing Your Money projects you'll have at the end of this month; and your cash at the end of each of the next 11 months. (If you've turned on the 5-year-forecasting Money Option on the FILE submenu, F6 will take you to see that too.)

If you want to exclude a budget item from your cash forecast (such as a savings account you're keeping for your kids, or any account whose balance doesn't really affect the amount of cash you can lay your hands on), include "XXX" anywhere in its name ("1st Federal XXX"). The item will still figure into your net worth, but it won't show up as ready cash.

For more information on this menu selection, select Forecasting from the Money submenu, and then press F1 for help.

With luck, your new cash flow statement will show a surplus. (If you still show a deficit, more serious action is necessary. Try cutting every line of living expenses by the same percentage, say 10 percent.) You can ensure that your family will keep operating in the black by adhering to the figures and disciplining yourself to save and invest regularly. (Some specific suggestions are offered in Chapters 6 and 7.) You will improve the chances of staying within the budget by dividing the figures in each living expense category by 12 to get your projected monthly outlay.

Ideally, you and your family will keep a running tab of your monthly income and outgo. That may be asking too much, however. At the very least, keep records for three months straight to compare your actual expenses with those projected. Think of yourselves as the financial equivalent of a Nielsen family. Instead of jotting down the TV shows you watch, you will track the flow of your family's money. The budget will let you know how well your family is controlling its spending.

It might help to see how much you ought to be spending for various things. Financial Strategies, Inc., a financial planning firm in Washington, D.C., recommends the benchmarks in the accompanying table.

Table 2.1. **Suggested Spending Ranges as a Percentage of Net Income**

Expense	Single No Children	Single with Children	Married with Children	Married No Children
Housing	20-25	20-25	30	25-30
Loan payments	13-15	13-15	13-15	15-17
Food	10-15	10-15	10-15	10-15
Hobbies and entertainment	9-16	9-14	8-14	9-14
Child care	0	8-10	8-10	0
Out-of-pocket	8-12	7-10	5-8	7-10
Transportation	7-10	7-10	7-10	7-10
Utilities and phone	5-10	6-11	6-11	8-12
Clothing	3-10	4-10	4-10	8-10
Savings	5-7	5-7	5-7	5-7
Pension	5-7	5-7	5-7	5-7
Medical	3-5	4-7	7-10	7-10
Education (including student loan payments)	3-5	5-7	5-7	3-5
Gifts and contributions	2-10	3-10	4-10	3-8
Vacation	3-7	3-7	3-7	3-7
Insurance	1-3	3-5	3-5	3-5
Personal care	1-3	2-4	2-4	2-4
Dues and subscriptions	1-3	1-3	1-3	1-3

SOURCE: Financial Strategies, Inc.

Some people think that the only way to rope in spending is to just stay home every night and eat Spam. Truth is, your family can probably reduce its living expenses through a series of small, painless maneuvers that add up to savings of thousands of dollars over the course of the year, as illustrated in the following table:

Table 2.2. Little Savings That Add Up

Strategy	Estimated Annual Savings
Subscribe to newspapers and magazines instead of buying them on newsstands	$100
Buy food in bulk and large sizes	$500
Shop at wholesale clubs, outlet stores, and department store sales	$500
Clip newspaper coupons	$100
Use a cut-rate phone company	$100
Conserve energy better	$200
When vacationing, stay in hotels and motels one rung less expensive than customary	$200
Raise insurance deductibles	$200
Fill up with self-serve gas	$100
Fill out your own taxes	$50 to $1,000
Hand-launder clothes when possible to avoid cleaning bills	$250
Pay off credit cards faster	$200
Mow your lawn and shovel your snow instead of paying for it	$200
Return recyclable bottles	$ 50
Bring lunch to work	$1,000
Quit smoking	$100 to $300
Total savings	approx. $4,500

MANAGING DEBT WISELY

Your net worth and cash flow statements also show precisely how well you are handling debt and credit. Rules of thumb are a bit dicey when it comes to a figure for a reasonable amount of debt. You might not lose a moment of sleep even though 40 percent of your family's income is used to repay debts. On the other hand, the idea of owing anybody money might give you the willies; you might own no installment credit cards and pay for all purchases (other than your house) with cash. That said, the current rule of thumb is that your annual mortgage payments should represent less than 30 percent of your family's income, and other loans, including credit card interest, should not amount to more than 15 to 20 percent of family income.

Tax reform has increased the cost of borrowing money. Before the new tax law passed, you could deduct all your interest payments. Every time you took out a car loan or owed money to MasterCard, Uncle Sam helped you pay back the debt. No longer.

Consumer interest is no longer fully deductible. You still are allowed to write off mortgage interest on your primary residence and a second home. But none of your other personal interest owed is deductible, not credit card interest, not student loans, not car loans.

By all means, don't take a lender's word for the amount of debt you can handle. The lender probably doesn't know your attitude about debt, your credit history, or your impulse buying habits. Nor does he know whether you will need to borrow money for another purpose in the near future. The lender's objective is to make a loan that has a good chance of being repaid on time and that will be profitable for the bank. So his objectives and yours are hardly identical.

A better way to estimate the amount of debt you can handle is to complete the accompanying worksheet. Don't include your mortgage in the loan category, but do include overdraft checking if you use that service. For revolving credit accounts, write down the minimum monthly payment due.

To give you an idea how this worksheet works, assume both you and your spouse work for pay, your family's monthly debt payments come to $400, and your monthly after-tax income is $2,500 (roughly $50,000 gross income). You can afford another $100 in debt payments each month. But if you are now spending $600 a month to pay

MY DEBT TOLERANCE

Loans and Charge Accounts	Monthly Payments
	$
	$
	$
	$
	$
	$
	$
	$
	$
	$
	$
	$

1. Total monthly payments: $ _____

2. Your monthly after-tax income: $ _____

3. Total monthly payments you can safely handle (if you are the sole wage earner or if line 2 is less than $2,000, take 10% of line 2; if you and your spouse both work or if you are under 35 or if line 2 is more than $2,000, enter 20% of line 2: $ _____

4. Amount of room in your budget for more debt (if negative, amount of current debt over danger limit—line 3 minus line 1): $ _____

SOURCE: Money Guide: Personal Finance

off loans, everything else being equal, you are about $100 per month over your head.

The temptation to borrow is unrelenting. You probably receive a letter from a bank, brokerage firm, mortgage lender, or credit card issuer once a week asking you to sign on the line for more debt. But the invitation usually comes with a high, if hard to read, price tag: 18 percent interest or thereabouts. When inflation is running at a 12 percent rate, as it was for a time in the 1970s, an 18 percent rate on credit isn't so bad. Your real interest rate, the amount over your other costs as measured by the inflation rate, is 6 percentage points. But when inflation is running at a rate of 3 percent and you're asked to pay 18 percent to borrow, as is currently the case, that is a real interest rate of 15 percent. And that is unreal.

So the combination of high borrowing rates and tax reform has made it essential to reevaluate every outstanding loan and charge card you have and decide whether you really need them anymore. You are also reaching the age when it becomes increasingly important to build up your assets and cut back on additional borrowing. That's typically the way people react as they reach their late 40s and early 50s. Today, people between the ages of 35 and 44 have outstanding debt (including mortgages) that equals, on average, 74 percent of income and 29 percent of their assets. But families headed by people ages 45 to 54 have much lower debt levels—equal to 45 percent of income and 16 percent of assets, on average.

Managing Your Money Tip

To enter a new or existing loan in Managing Your Money is easy.

1. Select Loan Records from the Money submenu.

2. Press F5 to add a new loan and fill in the blanks—except the interest rate, unless it's a special loan or an interest-only loan. Where Managing Your Money asks for the Payment, enter whatever monthly payment the bank demands, less any escrow payment for taxes or insurance, which are entered separately.

3. Now press F10. Managing Your Money will calculate the interest rate for a loan of this size, term, and monthly payments. This may vary slightly from your bank's figure because different banks use different methods of calculation.

4. If you're not happy with what you've entered, press F6 and make any changes you want. Otherwise, press F10 again to add this loan to your list. If, at that point, you decide to make a change, just point to the loan and press F2 to edit it, or F3 to delete it altogether and start again. Press F1 for HELP if you're having trouble.

5. Even if you are happy, as you likely will be, point at your new loan and press F2 to look at it. If it's a mortgage-type loan, you can change the "payments already made" (and anything else) to see what effect that has on the essay we write at the bottom of the screen. Just press F6 to recalculate. Be sure to press <esc> when you're through, so you don't accidentally save the bogus scenario you were playing with.

6. Back on the Loan Records screen, there's one last chore. Press F6 or F7 to link this loan with an Alert List transaction or a Quick List transaction. In order for Managing Your Money to keep track of your loan balances properly, you must record all loan payments with on of these liked transactions.

   For mortgage-type loans, choose Alert List: F6. For interest-only and special loans, choose Quick List: F7.

   When Managing Your Money creates your transaction, it will ask what bank account you ordinarily use to make the payment. An Alert transaction is linked to a specific bank account; a Quick List transaction can be used with any account (tag it "Global").

   Fill in the address and Memo if you like (you'll need an address if you plan to print checks and mail them with window envelopes). Fill in the loan escrows, if any. Press F7 if you're a Check Free customer and want to make loan payments that way.

   Now press F10. Managing Your Money will ask you to designate the budget categories into which you want Managing Your Money to record the Interest and Principal from this loan, along with the escrows, if any. Home mortgage interest gets special tax treatment, so it should go into its own category. For other loans, you might assign them all to a single "Other Loan Interest" category, or separate ones (such as one for each rental property you own).

   You might want to dump the Principal portion of your payments into categories like "Home Equity" and "Automobile" (since, by paying off the loan, you're essentially paying for the automobile), or generic ones like "Loan Repayment."

There's a lot more you can do with loans once you've entered them into Managing Your Money. For more information, see the Abridged Managing Your Money Manual in the Appendix.

GETTING CREDIT COUNSELING HELP

If managing credit is a big problem in your household, you may want to get some professional assistance. There are more than 200 non-profit credit counseling organizations around the country that provide such a service. You can find the one nearest you by writing to the National Foundation for Consumer Credit, 8701 Georgia Ave., Silver Spring, MD. 20910. The National Foundation for Consumer Credit is funded by banks, department stores, labor groups, legal organizations, and other businesses.

When you visit an NFCC office, you will fill out a confidential application attesting to your income and indebtedness. A credit counselor will guide you in managing cash flow and making up a budget. You may be put on a debt repayment plan that will require you to give the agency each month an amount equal to one-thirtieth of the total amount you owe. The counselor will also work with your creditors. If bankruptcy is necessary, the agency will help you through that process, too. An initial NFCC consultation costs between $10 and $50, and a debt payment plan will cost about $15 a month.

Be wary of for-profit credit counseling firms known as credit clinics that charge as much as $1,500 for a similar service. Many of these businesses advertise heavily and claim they will clean up your credit history in a flash. Such promises can't always be kept. These companies sometimes say they can solve your credit problems by consolidating your debts, but in reality they are just refinancing your debt at a higher interest rate.

SHOPPING FOR CREDIT CARDS

Odds are you have a wallet full of credit cards from the same issuers that first gave you the cards 15 years ago. But, as with checking accounts, charges and interest rates for credit cards now vary dramatically. If you think it sounds like a pain to shop around for a piece of plastic, join the club. A recent survey said that 76 percent of consumer leaders believe people don't compare interest rates or terms when selecting credit cards.

Most people don't compare credit cards because they think any savings will amount to peanuts. Actually, you can save more than $100 a year in interest and credit card fees by switching to cards that best reflect your shopping habits.

Before doing any card shopping, empty out your wallet or purse (your spouse's, too) and lay out all your cards on the table. If you have more than four or five each, you can probably stand to snip some of that plastic. By limiting your ability to charge, you will reduce impulse spending and the chance that someone will use your cards without your approval. (By law, you don't have to pay for unauthorized charges after you tell the card issuer your card is missing. But you are liable for up to $50 a card for any charges made before you gave notice.)

You ought to own a bank credit card such as Visa or MasterCard, if only because both are so widely accepted worldwide. Just be sure you make the minimum payments each month on these installment cards. There's little economic sense in getting a prestige card such as the American Express Gold or Platinum card or the premium versions of Visa or MasterCard. The prestige cards typically cost at least 50 percent more than their declasse kin. You do, however, receive a higher credit line and special check-cashing privileges that might be handy if you must use the cards often while on the road. Some monthly statements also note expenses that are tax-deductible, which might be helpful if you are a lousy record keeper. Otherwise, snub these status symbols.

If you do a lot of business traveling or entertaining, pack a travel-and-entertainment card such as American Express, Carte Blanche, or Diners Club. Keep in mind, however, that charges on these cards generally must be paid in full each month. If you drive a lot, fill up your wallet with one or two gasoline credit cards, too. Independently owned gas stations may not accept your bank or travel-and-entertainment cards. You probably don't need department store charge cards, since most of the biggest retailers now honor cards other than their own. One advantage to having store cards: you won't reach your bank card's credit limit by making a big purchase.

When shopping for a MasterCard or Visa card, consider the kind of charger you are. Some people are revolvers, paying a portion of their bills plus interest each month but letting the remainder spill over into the next billing period. Some use the cards for cash advances, which come with immediate finance charges. Others pay their entire bills within their 15-to 25- day grace period and never incur finance charges.

If you are a revolver or frequently get cash advances with your bank card, it will pay to search for a card with an interest rate lower than the typical 14 to 18 percent. If you use the bank card as a check substitute, never mind the interest rate but look for a card with no annual fee or a low one—less than $25. Be sure, also, that the bank will give you a grace period before the meter starts running; some assess interest from the day they get your charge from the merchant or the date of sale. You might want two cards, one for small purchases that can be paid off quickly and one for big-ticket items that require installments.

Regardless of your charging habits, don't pick a credit card primarily on the basis of perks such as travel insurance or a credit card registration service. One perk worth checking out is discount shopping. Many cards, most notably the Sears Discover card, now offer discounts on purchases if you charge with them. Many bank cards slap on an extra $25 annual fee for telephone-shopping privileges, however. Before paying for this perk, take a serious look at the merchandise selection and discounts. The prices may be no lower than those at discount stores where you live.

Before getting any card, find out what your credit limit will be. Typically, you can borrow as much as $500 to $3,500 for the regular bank cards and $5,000 to $50,000 for the prestige cards.

In bank cards, as in life, there is no free lunch. So it is next to impossible to find a Visa or MasterCard with both a low fee and a low interest rate. But it is becoming increasingly possible to get a card from an out-of-state bank with a good deal. You can get a list of banks that currently offer the best interest rates, lowest fees, and longest grace periods by getting the Credit Card Locator newsletter ($10, Consumer Credit Card Rating Service, Box 5219, Ocean Park Station, Santa Monica, Calif. 90405). Money magazine and some newspapers also publish names of these institutions from time to time.

Before applying for a card from an out-of-state bank, however, call the institution to be sure that the information you have is up-to-date and that any nonresident can obtain a card. Some credit card issuers with mouth-watering rates don't accept applications across state lines. Others require applicants to have checking accounts or loans with them before they will give out credit cards. Still others issue cards only to people with spotless credit ratings.

Your best credit card bargain today might be a variable-rate Visa or MasterCard. Hundreds of lending institutions have switched from the conventional fixed-rate card to one whose rate fluctuates with other interest rates. The interest rates on variable-rate cards are pegged a few percentage points above bellwethers such as the prime rate, three- and six-month Treasury bills, and the Federal Reserve Board discount rate. Even so, the rates on variable-rate cards are typically 1 to 3 percentage points lower than those for most flat-fee cards. Lenders offering variable-rate cards usually set minimum and maximum interest rates, so you will know in advance just how expensive or inexpensive your borrowing could be. Often, the minimum rate on a variable-rate card is lower than the national average on fixed-rate cards.

Workers who belong to the AFL-CIO can get an especially good variable-rate credit card deal. The AFL-CIO, in conjunction with the Bank of New York, now offers members two different cut-rate MasterCards called Union Privilege MasterCard. Local union leaders decide which card their members can get.

The first AFL-CIO card has no annual fee and charges a rate equal to the previous quarter's last prime rate plus 5 percentage points. That works out to a rate roughly 3 to 7 points lower than that of most other MasterCards. Finance charges begin as of the date of a sale. The second card charges no annual fee for the first year. After that, card holders escape paying a fee if they charge more than $3,600 during the year. If their purchases total more than $2,400 but less than $3,600, they will owe a $7.50 fee. Anyone charging less will pay $15 a year. The interest rate on this card is the prime rate plus 7.25 percentage points. The card has a 25-day grace period.

Managing Your Money Tip

It's easy to set up credit card payments in Managing Your Money. To set up a separate charge account for each of your cards, select Money Accounts from the Money submenu, press F5 to add a new one, and type cha in the Type field to show that it's a charge account. (Unless the bank owes you money, be sure to enter a negative balance.) Then, as you charge things, bring your receipts home and record the charges in their respective accounts (Visa, MasterCard, etc.) and allocate them to budget categories. You'll have a running balance for each account. When the statement comes each month, reconcile it as you would your checking account.

When you write a check to pay off or pay down one of your cards, you are spending money in your checking account and receiving it into your charge account. You can do it

- in two steps (record the check in your checking account, then go to your charge account to "receive" the same amount);
- or in one step (select Transfer Money from the Money submenu or Alt-T from the Check Register);
- or in one even faster step (set up a Quick List Transfer transaction so that, thereafter, you can just mark it off the list as you're running through your other payments).

However you do it, don't try to allocate the payment to budget categories because you'd be double counting. Under this "full detail method," you recorded your various charges throughout the month and allocated them to expense categories. Now, you're just transferring some cash from one of your accounts to the other. No additional expense has occurred, so there's nothing new to allocate.

There are other short cuts you can use in handling your credit cards. For more information, see the Abridged Managing Your Money Manual in the Appendix.

SHOPPING FOR LOANS

There hasn't been a better time to borrow in years. Interest rates are far lower than in the late '70s and early '80s, and deregulation has increased your choice of lenders. Just remember that not every loan is a bargain. Each lender can charge a different rate and set different terms on its loans. As a rule, you will pay a lower interest rate on a secured loan—one where you put up collateral—than on an unsecured loan; the difference is often 1 to 3 percentage points. Another rule: Finance companies usually charge the highest rates of all lenders but may be your only choice if you have a bad credit rating.

Certain types of lenders are best for certain types of loans. Credit unions often charge less for mortgages than banks and savings and loans, but brokerage firms are usually the cheapest on secured loans (with a broker's margin loan, your securities are his security).

Before going hat in hand to a lender pleading for a loan, be sure you have exhausted other potential sources of ready cash. For example:

- *Your family.* After all, who knows you better and is most apt to be forgiving of a late payment? You generally don't need any collateral to hit up your parents or a close relative, either. Borrowing casually from a relative can lead to a home version of Family Feud, however. You can try to thwart that possibility by drawing up an official loan agreement with a form from a stationery store. Treat the loan like any other: Arrange a repayment schedule and, if you will be paying back the loan with interest, specify the rate.

- *Your life insurance policy.* While it has become harder to obtain a super-cheap loan against the cash value of your life insurance, most whole-life policies allow borrowing at rates between 6 and 11 percent. The longer you have had the policy, the cheaper the interest rate and the more you can borrow. The beauty of borrowing against your life insurance is that you can repay the loan as quickly or as slowly as you like. The drawback, of course, is that if you die with an outstanding insurance loan, the principal and interest due will be deducted from the proceeds of the policy. So you could end up shortchanging your family or any other beneficiary.

- *Your company savings plan.* Many companies let employees borrow from their savings plans at below-market interest rates. Loans can be repaid fairly painlessly—by payroll deductions. But your company may have strict rules about the amount you can borrow and the time in which the loan must be repaid.

When you have exhausted those alternatives, you can compare rates and terms among banks, savings and loans, credit unions, brokerage firms, mortgage lenders, automobile dealers, and finance companies. It's usually best to start your search as a loan ranger by quizzing the lender where you do your checking and saving. You could very well qualify as a preferred borrower and get a discounted interest rate, flexible repayment terms, or both.

After exploring that avenue, where you go next depends on the type of loan you need. If it's a car loan and you belong to a credit union, ask about its auto financing. Lately, credit unions have been aggressively pursuing car buyers by offering cut-rate loans, waiving down payments, and allowing borrowers to pay off loans over six years rather than the standard four or five years.

Car buyers should also get the skinny on rates and terms from dealers—but cautiously. Chrysler, Ford, and General Motors have all offered enticing financing deals in recent times (pitching loans with rates as low as 0 percent), usually charging less in interest and in application fees than banks. A few words to the wise are in order, though. The carmakers aren't giving anything away. You might wind up paying a higher price for one of their cars in exchange for a cut-rate loan.

Before agreeing to a car loan from a dealer, check to see that the car hasn't been loaded with expensive extras that you don't want. Check, too, on the term of the dealer's car loan. While most lenders let you pay off car loans over forty-eight or sixty months, most car dealers demand repayment within thirty months. You could wind up paying an extra $300 or so per month by signing up for the abbreviated repayment schedule.

Interest rates for first and second mortgages don't vary a great deal among lenders, but it still pays to compare. A 1 percentage point difference on a mortgage can wind up costing $100 a month and more than $30,000 over the life of the loan. A pointed review of points will be in order as well, because a few extra points can cost a few extra thousand dollars at closing. Some newspapers publish weekly rundowns of mortgage rates and terms from local lenders. There also are a number of firms around the country that publish similar lists for a fee of $10 or so. Your real estate agent or a local mortgage lender should know whether such a service is available in your area.

SOME ADVICE ABOUT ADVISERS

After you've done all you can to get your financial life in order, it is time to call in the pros. A quality accountant, lawyer, stockbroker, financial planner, insurance agent, or money manager may be expensive, but the service will more than pay for itself over time.

A financial adviser, no matter how talented, is of no use unless he or she satisfies your precise needs and matches your temperament. You probably know someone who is conservative with his money but who was audited by the IRS because of an iffy tax deduction his aggressive tax preparer made him take. (For advice on choosing a tax pro, see Chapter 5.) Before hiring a professional, chat with him or her for a half hour to be sure you share similar views about money and financial risk taking.

As obvious as it may sound, it is quite important to hire an adviser for your precise needs. Not everyone does. A common mistake is having the wrong type of stockbroker. In a recent New York Stock Exchange poll, half the people surveyed said they didn't know how to go about picking a broker who would be right for them. (The stock market crash of October 1987 no doubt has left many brokerage customers skeptical about the advice they had been receiving from their brokers.) Full-service brokers from national firms such as Merrill Lynch or Paine Webber or regional firms such as Raymond James & Associates or Alex. Brown and Sons are great if you trade securities frequently or desire investment advice. But you might be far better off with a discount broker, charging commissions as much as 90 percent lower than those at full-service firms, if all you really need is someone to actually buy and sell the stocks or bonds of your choosing.

The stock market crash strengthened the case for full-service stockbrokers vs. discounters. State securities regulators heard horror stories from many discount brokerage customers who reported they either could not get through to the discounters to sell their stocks or the delay was so long that they were penalized with far lower share prices than if they had connected with the brokers immediately. Spokesmen for some discount brokers, such as Charles Schwab & Co., said after the crash that they planned to beef up their phone systems in 1988. But full-service brokers took their lumps, too. Securities regulators also received many post-crash complaints from people who said their full-service brokers had put them in speculative investments, such as options and futures, that they did not understand.

When selecting any financial professional, try to get names of three good candidates. The more precise you can be when narrowing down the initial search, the better. For example, if you want an accountant who specializes in working with small business people or a stockbroker who is aces on over-the-counter stocks, be sure to ask for someone with such experience. You are more likely to be satisfied if the adviser comes highly recommended by a friend or relative—preferably a friend or relative in good financial shape. (In the case of choosing an executor or guardian, your best choice could actually be your brother, sister, or best friend.)

Once you have the names of potential advisers, meet with each one. Ask them to tell you about their backgrounds and any specialties. If the adviser hasn't been in the business for at least five years, you probably don't want to use him or her. Let the person learn the ropes on somebody else's time. Try to find out how important a client you will be, so you can tell in advance the kind of treatment you will receive. Ask for names and phone numbers of references whom you can call.

Price isn't everything. In fact, value, not price, should be a primary consideration when hiring a financial adviser. Sometimes fees can be deceiving. For instance, discount stockbrokers are generally considered less expensive than full-service brokers. But it ain't necessarily so. Most discounters charge minimum commissions, and those rates on small trades may be costlier than those of full-service firms on the same trades. Many ads from discount brokers are less than honest, too. They sometimes use out-of-date fee schedules of full-service firms and thus give unfair comparison figures.

WEEDING OUT FINANCIAL PLANNERS

Perhaps the hardest financial adviser to pick, if indeed you need one at all, is a financial planner. There is no licensing requirement for this profession, so anyone can call himself or herself a financial planner. You wouldn't believe the inexperience and ineptitude of some of the 100,000+ people who have. If a planner has taken courses to become a Certified Financial Planner or a Chartered Financial Consultant, that is no guarantee of excellence. But at least it shows that the planner has taken the time to get educated.

Do you need a financial planner? Quite likely. Do you need to pay a lot for one? Not necessarily.

There are essentially four types of financial planners: those who charge only sales commissions, those who provide only computerized printouts, those who provide flat fees for advice and sales commissions on investments, and those who charge only flat fees. The cost of hiring an astute planner—usually $500 to $5,000 in the first year, about half that in subsequent years—will probably exceed the benefits you will get if your family's income is less than $50,000 or so. Consider only those planners who meet either of these criteria:

- They charge fees for advice and plans as well as commissions for investments and insurance they sell. Usually, 60 to 75 percent of such planners' income is from commissions.

- They do not sell anything and charge fees only for their advice and financial plans. Because they do not deal in investment products, fee-only planners are, by definition, more objective than fee-plus-commission planners. But they are also expensive—usually assessing annual charges of $3,000 and up. The clients of fee-only planners generally have annual incomes of at least $100,000.

For most people, a fee-plus-commission planner is the most economical choice. But make sure the planner is willing to justify his or her commissions by describing how each investment or insurance policy fits into your financial plans. Robert Wegner, a fee-only planner in Summit, New Jersey, says you should ask any prospective planner you interview: "What is an example of a problem or two you solved for a client in the past six months that you had not encountered before?" If the question leaves the planner dumbfounded, exit pronto. And if the problems the planner describes are ones you are unlikely to encounter, look for a planner whose most memorable recent triumphs are more closely related to the problems you are likely to face.

Evaluate your planner a year after you receive the written plan. If you have met your original short-term goals, are making progress toward your long-term ones—your net worth is going up at least as fast as inflation—and your planner and your other financial advisers get along well, congratulations. You have a winner. But if after a year you are disappointed or the meetings between your planner and your other advisers have been reminiscent of the relationship between Ross Perot and his professional campaign consultants, consider looking for a new planner.

You can get names of nearby financial planners or planners who will travel to see you by writing to the Institute of Certified Planners (2 Denver Highlands, 10065 E. Harvard Ave., Suite 320, Denver, Colo. 80231), The International Association for Financial Planning (Two Concourse Parkway, Suite 800, Atlanta, Ga. 30328), The International Association of Registered Financial Planners (4127 W. Cypress St., Tampa, Fla. 33607), or The National Association of Personal Financial Advisers, the trade group for fee-only planners (Leonetti & Associates, 125 S. Wilke Rd., Suite 204, Arlington Heights, Ill. 60005) . The International Association for Financial Planning also publishes a free directory of members who have met stringent qualifications and scored well on a written financial planning test. The directory, which lists names, addresses, and phone numbers, is called *The Registry of Financial Planning Practitioners.*

Now that you have done the throat-clearing part of financial planning, you can begin to talk and act with authority. The next exercise is primarily a mental one. After spending years thinking and planning only days or weeks ahead, you now need to start looking farther into the future. Switching from thinking short term to thinking long term may be one of the most important decisions of your life. Years from now, you will probably find it was one of your best and most lucrative decisions, too.

CHAPTER
3

THINKING LONG TERM

A mortgage, two or three kids, a couple of cars
and college to pay for make you sober up real fast.
Arthur Ashe in The New York Times Magazine

YOUR NEW GOALS TAKE TIME

When the Life Insurance Marketing and Research Association recently asked a cross-section of Baby Boomers to name their reasons for saving, short-term goals triumphed. The top three answers: major purchases, vacations, and an improved standard of living.

There is absolutely nothing wrong with wanting to have a better, more luxurious life *now*. In fact, until recently you had little need to think much farther ahead than the near future because your obligations were few. But now that you have growing family responsibilities and the word "retirement" no longer seems otherworldly, planning for the future is just as important as providing for the present.

For an illustration of the new importance of long-term goals in your life, check off the appropriate boxes in the accompanying worksheet. You will notice that the worksheet is similar to the one in Chapter 2, except this time the goals are broken down by time period rather than importance.

After completing the worksheet you may be surprised to see that you checked off "long term" for about half of the goals, such as buy a vacation

45

MY GOALS			
Objective	Short Term	Medium Term	Long Term
Reduce debt			
Build an emergency reserve			
Increase insurance coverage			
Buy a house			
Make home improvements			
Buy a vacation house			
Buy a car			
Make another big purchase			
Have children			
Finance children's education			
Live more luxuriously			
Take an expensive vacation			
Take an unpaid leave from work			
Start a business			
Take early retirement			
Live well after retirement			
Other			

SOURCE: *Money Guide: Personal Finance.*

house, finance children's education, live more luxuriously, take an expensive vacation, start a business, take early retirement, and live well after retirement. But if you had filled out the same worksheet five or ten years ago, chances are you would have left many of those items blank. The idea of starting a business or financing children's education most likely seemed too futuristic to get concerned about. What a difference a few years can make.

Managing Your Money Tip

> You can use Managing Your Money to plan your financial goals. If you select Goal Planning from the Analyze submenu, enter the data requested, and press F10, you can see what you need to have to pay for your goal, and how much you will have to save annually to reach that goal. If you're saving for tuition for a child, or for your retirement, select Tuition Planning or Retirement Planning from the Analyze submenu. Using Managing Your Money will allow you to account for inflation in finding your savings targets.

GO FOR GROWTH, TAX SAVINGS, AND DIVERSIFICATION

Achieving your long-term goals requires zeroing in on three investment objectives: growth of capital, tax savings, and diversification. These objectives will help make the money you earn work for you—both today and in the future.

Growth of capital simply means putting your money someplace where it will appreciate in value over the long haul. Your choices include investments with varying degrees of growth potential, such as stocks, bonds, mutual funds, options, real estate, savings accounts, certificates of deposit, annuities, and limited partnerships. Seeking capital growth also means trying not to spend much on depreciable assets, such as cars, clothes, and furniture.

Just how desirable is it to make your money grow? Look at it this way: invest your cash now to earn $7 \frac{1}{2}$ percent a year (a fairly conservative earnings assumption) and you will have nearly tripled your money by the year 2000; today's $25,000 ante will be worth almost $75,000 in fewer than 15 years.

The objective of tax savings can be summed up in a favorite expression of accountants and financial planners: It's not what you make that counts, it's what you keep. Tax savings takes on more importance in your financial life during your 30s and 40s than in your 20s because keeping the money you make has become a higher priority. Your present and future financial needs are greater now, so the more you can do to help satisfy them, the better. That means reducing the tax collector's take.

True, the need for deft tax-planning strategies is slightly diminished compared with a few years ago when tax rates were higher. But don't be lulled into thinking that tax reform has done away with the need for astute tax planning. Your tax rate may not be substantially lower than it was before tax reform. Your tax bill is not likely to drop much anytime soon, either, considering that your family's earnings will probably rise steadily for the next 20 or so years. Some of the deductions that may have lowered your tax bill in the past are no longer available.

Diversification of your investments is a worthy goal at any age, of course, but it is especially desirable for you now that your net worth has grown and is likely to continue doing so for the next few decades. Does diversification pay? You bet. A diversified investment index has consistently beaten the stock market and the typical professional portfolio manager over the past 20 years.

The importance of diversification is best explained by showing what would happen if you put all your family's spare cash into one investment, such as the stock of your company. What if the company suddenly lost its competitive edge because of another firm's new product or because your company's top executives were killed in a plane crash? The value of your shares—indeed a substantial portion of your net worth—would take a dive. Yet most of your financial needs wouldn't change. Sure, you could put off a vacation or buying a new car. But you would still have to pay the mortgage or the orthodontist or your mother's nursing home bill; your kids would still need a college fund; you would still want to create a retirement nest egg for yourself. The same lack of diversification would have been far less severe when you were 27. Then, your financial obligations were fewer and you had more years ahead to compensate for any income lost in lousy investments.

The importance of your three investment objectives—maximizing growth, tax savings, and diversification—is magnified if you are the recipient of a cash windfall such as an inheritance or a divorce settlement. Say you are about to get $100,000 but won't need the money or its earnings for ten years. Invest the cash in a low-growth money-market fund and in ten years you might have $180,000, before taxes. But invest the same $100,000 in a more aggressive growth-stock mutual fund and in ten years your windfall might be worth more than $300,000, before taxes. Invest the windfall in a way that will also let you defer paying income taxes on the earnings until a later date or that will eliminate a tax liability altogether, and you could prevent the IRS from taking 25 percent of the money between now and 1998. You will want to allocate the $100,000 among several different investments, to reduce the chance of betting all the money on a losing horse.

PRECISION IS EVERYTHING

The natural reaction to looking at a list of long-term goals can be summed up in one word: AAARGH! Coming up with enough money to pay for a college education seems impossible, let alone providing for retirement and your parents' well-being. Attempting to achieve the goals becomes a lot less frightening once you can answer three fundamental questions:

- Exactly how much money will I need to achieve my long-term goals?

- Exactly when will I need the money?

- How much investment risk am I willing to take with my money to achieve my goals?

Once you know the answers to those questions, you can begin intelligent planning to attain your long-term goals with the precision of a sharpshooter. Otherwise, you will be more of a crapshooter, throwing dice at your long-term targets.

The farther away your goals, the harder it is to determine the amount of money you will need to satisfy them. Take the goal of financing your child's college education. If your daughter is now 15 years old, you have a fairly good idea of the type of college she will want to attend and how much it will cost. But if you're the proud parent of a new baby, who knows? Even so, it is better to make guesstimates about the future and start saving now than to wait until a few months before you actually need the money and then scramble furiously to find the cash.

MEASURING YOUR RISK TOLERANCE

Before calculating the amount of money necessary to achieve your financial goals, you will need to establish the degree of investment risk you feel comfortable taking. If you can stomach risky investments, you will be able to set aside less money for your goals than if you like to play it safe. Reason: The greater the risk, the greater the potential return over the long run.

What is investment risk? Economists define it as the probability of losing, in the future, some or all of the money you put up today. But that's not quite the whole story.

All investments carry risk, even ones that appear to be 100 percent safe from the loss of principal or earnings. For example, take the federally insured bank passbook savings account. You probably put some cash in one of these accounts during the late 1970s when passbooks paid about $5^1/_4$ percent interest. Your money seemed safe. After all, the government guaranteed your principal and interest. In reality, the passbook account was pretty risky then. Inflation was barreling along at about 10 percent a year, yet your money was earning $5^1/_4$ percent interest. Every penny you earned was safe, it's just that inflation made each penny worth half a cent. So, sometimes the risk isn't that your investment dollars will vanish but that they will be worth *less* in the future.

You can reduce the risk that inflation will erode the value of your investments by putting some of your money in inflation hedges such as real estate, growth stocks, and gold. Each tends to produce returns higher than the inflation rate over the long term, especially when inflation is a major economic problem.

Another type of investment risk is financial or business risk—the chance that your investment will lose its value because of unfavorable business conditions. Anyone who owned stock in oil companies or in Houston real estate when the price of oil sank in 1985 and 1986 knows what financial risk means. Diversification among types of investments and types of industries reduces financial risk.

Interest-rate risk should be familiar to you, particularly if you tried to sell your house in the early 1980s when mortgage rates got so high that many would-be home buyers were priced out of the market. Interest-rate risk means that as interest rates rise, the value of some investments falls, and when rates fall, the value of some investments rises. Corporate bonds, municipal bonds, Treasury bonds, and bond mutual funds are investments other than real estate subject to interest-rate risk. Stocks of industries whose profits rise and fall depending partly on the direction of interest rates—such as banks, savings and loans, utility companies, and home builders—also carry a high degree of interest-rate risk.

Even the most respected economic forecasters have had rotten records when it comes to accurately predicting the direction of interest rates. So don't worry about being an ace prognosticator yourself. The best ways to reduce interest-rate risk are to diversify and to move your money out of interest-sensitive investments when business publications report that the consensus among economists is that rates are likely to rise. The consensus isn't always right, but it's about the best you can go on.

Yet another type of investment risk is market risk—the chance that your investment will outperform or underperform others like it. Market risk is most easily seen with stocks. The riskiest stocks are ones whose prices rise and fall more than the stock market as a whole. A common yardstick for measuring market risk is the Standard and Poor's 500 Stock Index, published daily in the business pages of most newspapers. You can compare the market risk or volatility of your stock versus this index by getting the *Value Line Investment Survey* in a public library or from your stockbroker. *Value Line*, a respected stock market publication, publishes key financial figures for most stocks traded on the major stock exchanges and over the counter and compares the figures with market averages.

As a rule, the smaller the company, the greater the market risk of its stock. This is only a rule of thumb. In the October 1987 stock market crash, virtually all stocks fell in value by 20 percent or so. You can cut down on market risk by diversifying among a variety of different stocks in different industries, by owning mutual funds that diversify for you, or by sticking with stocks whose volatility is historically average or below average.

Leverage is the last type of investment risk. By putting up only a fraction of the purchase price to acquire an investment and borrowing the rest, you are leveraging your money. The most common leveraging techniques are getting a mortgage on real estate and using a stock brokerage margin account, which allows you to buy shares by borrowing some of the money from your broker's firm. Leverage can dramatically increase the amount of money you can make on an investment. It can also be quite costly. The principal risks of leveraging are being unable to afford the debt payments in the future and having the investment depreciate in value.

Suppose you plan to sell your house and trade up to a bigger one costing $150,000. Assume, too, that the house will rise in value by about 10 percent a year and that you will sell it at the end of five years when it will be worth roughly $240,000. If you buy the house outright with no mortgage and sell it after five years, you will have made about 60 percent on your money, or an average of 12 percent a year. But if you leverage the purchase by putting down only 10 percent of the price ($15,000), you will get a gigantic return on your original investment.

So why doesn't everyone leverage to the hilt? Because leveraging is expensive. An 11 percent mortgage whose amount equals 90 percent of the purchase price of the house could require paying back $76,800 over five years, and most of that money will be interest on the loan, not equity build-up. Leveraging makes a lot of sense when inflation is high and you will be repaying your loan in dollars that will be worth less in the future. Leveraging also makes sense when you can easily handle the additional debt payments and you feel confident the investment will appreciate in value. You can reduce the risk of leveraging by minimizing your borrowing during periods of low inflation or when you have all the debt you can handle.

How much investment risk can you handle? In general, you should be taking as much manageable risk with your money as possible. You should probably look primarily for high-risk and medium-risk investments. (An elaboration of investment alternatives appears in Chapter 7.) For instance, put roughly 60 percent of your investable cash in stocks or stock mutual funds and 40 percent in bonds or bond funds.

A fairly aggressive risk-taking strategy is appropriate in your 30s and 40s for three reasons:

- You are young enough so that if your risky investments don't pan out in the short term, you can either switch to more promising investments or hold on in anticipation of better days ahead.

- You have already made most of the big purchases of your life and have an adequate cash reserve, so you can afford to take more risks.

- You have some discretionary income and don't need the certainty of small but reliable dividend or interest payments.

You can make your investment risks more manageable by diversifying among investments with varying degrees of risk. Your short-term and medium-term goals are best served by owning more reliable low-risk and medium-risk investments, while your long-term goals allow for more volatile high-risk investments that are likely to pay off over time. As you reach your 50s, 60s, and 70s, you will want to gradually move the tilt of your portfolio away from high- and medium-risk investments and toward ones carrying medium and low risks.

Remember that these rules of risk taking are not to be taken as gospel. Your family's present and future financial position and your temperament might call for radically different risk-taking investment strategies. For example, if both you and your spouse now work for pay but soon one of you will quit for a while, your ability to take big investment risks will be lessened. Preservation of capital—the household's remaining salary—will be critical. So your family will want to put its money primarily in safe places such as bank accounts or Treasury bills.

The same advice holds if you consider yourself conservative about money. One way to tell: If you own a stock or a stock mutual fund and you check its price in the newspaper daily, risky investments are too worrisome for you. Don't feel embarrassed; just be sure that your conservative bent doesn't prevent you from putting *any* money aside for the future.

THE TWO OTHER QUESTIONS ANSWERED

You can find answers to the two other key questions about long-term financial planning—how much money you will need to achieve your goals and when you will need it—by, you guessed it, filling out a short worksheet. (As you can tell, worksheets are a financial planner's best friend.) This one will tell you the total amount of money you will need to save over a given time period before taxes to achieve a given long-term goal and the amount you must set aside each month. Both will depend on the rate of return you expect to achieve, which is a function of the amount of risk you are willing to take with your money. But remember: These projected returns are not guaranteed, and the more risky the investment, the more likely the return will fluctuate wildly from year to year. Here is a list of the most common investments and their likely annual average returns:

Low-Risk Investments (4% to 10% annual return)	Medium-Risk Investments (8% to 15% annual return)	High-Risk Investments (12% to 20% annual return)
Treasury issues	High-yield bond funds	Options
High-grade bond funds	High-yield stocks	Emerging growth stocks
CDs	Growth and income	Aggressive growth
Money-market	funds	funds
investments	Growth stocks	Junk bonds
Annuities	Income-oriented limited	Growth-oriented
Savings deposits	partnerships	limited partnerships
	Real estate (direct	
	ownership)	

SOURCE: *Money* magazine.

The worksheet on pages 55 and 56 is helpful for nearly any long-term goal. But if your biggest long-term financial concern is providing for your retirement, use the special retirement worksheet in Chapter 12. Be sure to consult the key to the worksheet as you fill it out.

Plugging in some numbers will make the worksheet less daunting. Say your goal is funding your child's college education in ten years and you plan to provide $15,000 a year for each of the four college years. Assume that you feel comfortable taking moderate risks with your money and would put the cash earmarked for college in investments such as growth stocks, high-yield bond funds, and income-oriented limited partnerships, all of which are likely to produce an average annual return of 15 percent. Assume, too, that the current value of your savings and investments designated for the college fund is $5,000 and that this money is earning 15 percent a year, on average.

Managing Your Money Tip

Instead of using this worksheet, you can decide how much money to set aside for your long-term goals with Managing Your Money. If you select Goal Planning from the Analyze submenu, enter the data requested, and press F10, Managing Your Money will perform all these calculations automatically.

The amount of money you will need in ten years (Line 1) is $52,350 ($15,000 x 3.49). The amount you will need adjusted for an annual inflation rate of 5 percent is $85,330 ($52,350 x 1.63). Your $5,000 now designated for the college fund will be worth $20,250 when you need the cash in ten years ($5,000 x 4.05). So the total amount you need to raise within ten years to meet your target is $65,080 ($85,330 — $20,250). You thus need to put aside $260 a month ($65,080 x .004) to have the necessary cash for college in ten years.

HOW MUCH MONEY TO SET ASIDE FOR LONG-TERM GOALS

1. Amount of investment money needed for a single objective based on 1992 costs: $ _____

2. Total amount you will need, adjusted for inflation: $ _____

3. Current value of your savings and investments earmarked for this goal (do not include value of the house you live in): $ _____

4. What these savings and investments will be worth when you need them: $ _____

5. Amount you need to raise to meet your goal (subtract line 4 from line 2): $ _____

6. Amount you must put aside each month to reach the total: $ _____

Worksheet Key:

Line 1: If the amount of money you will need will require annual payments, such as a college tuition or a car loan, the figure on this line will be less than you might expect. Earnings on the money you set aside will help toward making the payments. For example, if you will be making payments of $15,000 a year for four years, the figure on line 1 will be slightly less than $60,000 ($15,000 x 4). For the total amount you will need, multiply the annual amount by the appropriate factor below:

4 years payout:	3.49	15 years payout:	8.37
5 years payout:	4.17	25 years payout:	9.98
10 years payout:	6.76	30 years payout:	10.37

Line 2. Multiply the figure on Line 1 by the factor below, which assumes an annual inflation rate of 5 percent:

5 years to goal:	1.28	20 years to goal:	2.65
10 years to goal:	1.63	25 years to goal:	3.39
15 years to goal:	2.08	30 years to goal:	4.32

Line 4: Multiply line 3 by the appropriate factor below. Pick a rate of return you think matches your risk tolerance:

	10% (low risk)	15% (medium risk)	20% (high risk)
5 years:	1.61	2.01	2.49
10 years:	2.60	4.05	6.19
15 years:	4.18	8.14	15.41
20 years:	6.73	16.37	38.34
25 years:	10.83	32.92	95.40
30 years:	17.45	66.21	237.38

Line 6: Multiply line 5 by the factor corresponding with your chosen rate of return:

	10%	15%	20%
5 years:	.013	.011	010
10 years:	.005	.004	003
15 years:	.002	.001	.0009
20 years:	.001	.0007	.0003
25 years:	.0008	.0003	.0001
30 years:	.0004	.0001	.00004

SOUICE: Money Magazine

Changing this example slightly, assume that every variable is the same except that you have no savings or investments now designated for the college fund. In that case, rather than needing to put aside $260 a month, you should be investing $341. But if you already have $20,000 set aside earning an average annual return of 15 percent, you only need to add another $17 to your $20,000 pot every month.

But what if you are more conservative about money, especially the money for your child's college education? In that case, assume all the variables are the same except that your college fund money will go in low-risk investments, earning an average annual return of 10 percent or so. These investments include money-market funds, savings deposits, bank certificates of deposit, high-grade bond funds, Treasury securities, and annuities. Again assuming that you already have $5,000 for the college fund stashed in low-risk investments, you will need to put $362 a month into the college fund kitty—about $100 more a month than if you took more risks with your money.

And if you have no money saved for college but want to start a low-risk college fund, you will need to set aside $427 a month. If you now have $20,000 of college fund money in low-risk investments, your monthly tithe works out to $167, quite a bit more than the $17-a-month outlay for the person whose $20,000 is in medium-risk investments.

When your financial goal is closer than ten years away, the numbers become a bit more numbing. Take the original hypothetical scenario but this time assume your daughter will be heading off to college in only five years. You will need a total of $67,008. Your $5,000 in college fund savings in medium-risk investments will be worth $10,050 then, so you must come up with another $56,958, or $626 a month. That's nearly two and a half times the monthly amount you must put away for a ten-year college fund. If you have no college fund savings yet but want to start a low-risk fund for a five-year goal, you need to scrape up—gulp—$871 a month.

Conversely, if your goal is 20 years away, you can breathe easier. In fact, if you already have $10,000 socked away earning about 15 percent a year, your 20-year college fund has already been paid for. By the year 2007, your $10,000 will have grown to $163,700, more than enough to cover the $138,727 you'll need for college.

WHERE TO GET THE MONEY

Now that you know how much money you will need to achieve your financial goals, the obvious question is: How will I ever get the money? The not-so-obvious answer is that you may already have the cash, but not in the appropriate investments.

For example, your family probably has cash parked in a money-market mutual fund or a bank money-market account. As a rule, it's a good idea to have such a cash reserve—equal to about three to six months of expenses. But if you're like many people in their 30s or 40s, that emergency fund has grown much larger than necessary and you're now sitting on a pile of cash that isn't working very hard. By redeploying some of your idle cash into more aggressive investments, you can reduce the trauma of having to amass a small fortune for the future.

You may also have money wasting away in other nonproductive assets. Perhaps you got in on the collectibles boom in the 1970s and bought some antiques that no longer excite you. Sell them and re-invest the profits. Trivial as it may sound, you could also get a start on the long-term fund by holding a garage sale, unloading some fur-niture, art, silver, and knickknacks, and putting the proceeds to work.

A thorough review and purging of your family's investment port-folio will also help you make every dollar count. You may have in-herited some stocks or bonds years ago or received some securities either as a gift or in a divorce settlement. This could be an opportune time to cash in the shares for a sizable profit. Perhaps you have bought your company's stock through a company savings plan but think the shares won't appreciate much more in value or pay sub-stantial dividends. You can probably withdraw some or all of your shares, sell them, and deposit the proceeds elsewhere in a more promising investment.

SORTING OUT YOUR CASH OPTIONS

Your problem might not be finding one financial spigot to tap but rather choosing among several. Perhaps a recent divorce settlement has given you the opportunity to buy out your ex-spouse's half-own-ership-of the house you are living in. You want to own the house but can't decide whether to get the money by selling some stock or mu-tual fund shares, withdrawing cash from a money-market account or your company savings plan, taking out a personal loan, or taking on some paid freelance assignments.

There is no right or wrong choice for everyone with such a predicament. The way to decide among these cash options is to determine which ones would serve you the least well. Get paper and pencil and list each option. Next to each investment and savings option, write the current average annual rate of return you receive and your projected annual return for the next five years. Next to each borrowing alternative, write the interest rate you would be charged and, as best as you can determine, your projected monthly payments. Next to your options for additional work pay, note the amount of time you will have to spend working and the amount of money you can expect to receive.

Consider cashing in present investment and savings havens—including company savings plans—that are likely to give you less than a 10 percent average annual return in the near future. Be careful about withdrawals from company plans, however. You will probably be restricted on the amount you can take out, on your ability to make another withdrawal soon, and maybe even the opportunity to reinvest in the plan shortly. You may also owe a tax penalty on theamount withdrawn. Try to avoid borrowing from a conventional lender, your life insurer, or your company unless the interest rate you will pay is less than 10 percent—the minimum rate you expect to earn on the loan proceeds.

Whether to take on extra work for pay is a personal decision. It depends largely on whether you are willing to give up some free time. Freelancing could be a suitable option if you don't mind taking on extra work; the pay will at least equal your hourly rate on the job, and—most important—you can discipline yourself to invest the money you earn.

The best-laid financial plans often go awry, due to circumstances beyond anyone's control: a burglary, a death in the family, a car accident, a disability, a house fire. To avert the possibility that your long-term goals won't be met, you need to be certain that your family is adequately protected against unforeseen events. That can be done by getting the right insurance coverage. Even if you think your family is currently properly insured, you are probably mistaken. You most likely have too much of certain kinds of insurance and not enough of others, as the next chapter explains.

CHAPTER

4

PROTECTING WHAT MATTERS MOST

*I bought a life insurance policy and made out
a will when I was 18. My friends asked me
if I was crazy or morbid. I told them, you
never know . . .*
Internationally syndicated columnist
Heloise, age 36

WHY INSURANCE IS CRITICAL

By the time you are in your 30s or 40s, your life is pretty much on course. You probably have a family, a comfortable home, a job history, and maybe some money in the bank. So you have a lot worth protecting. But without the proper insurance, this financial foundation you've built could crumble after an unforeseen emergency or disaster. There's no need to get morbid or delirious; there is a need to take precautions.

Insurance is one of those things—like the Strategic Defense Initiative or foreign debt problems—that you probably just can't bring yourself to think about. Besides, you figure, I'm already spending a bundle on insurance and my insurance agents will call if I need more coverage. Maintaining this attitude of benign neglect could be costly, though. Robert Hunter, president of the National Insurance Consumer Organization, a nonprofit public-interest group, and the former head of the Federal Insurance Administration, says most people have too much insurance and the wrong insurance for their needs. Too many people buy insurance out of fear and love, rather than reason, says Hunter.

So do yourself and your family a favor and take a serious look at your family's total insurance coverage. Then, review the insurance at least every few years as your family's needs and assets change. Major life events such as the birth or adoption of a child, a divorce, a marriage, the purchase of a house, a move, receiving an inheritance, the death of a dependent, a job change, and opening your own business also call for periodic insurance checkups.

Managing Your Money Tip

> As you read this chapter, keep in mind that Managing Your Money's Insure submenu can tell you
> - what your life expectancy is
> - how much life insurance you need
> - how to avoid paying too much for the life insurance you need
> - keep track of your coverage.

INSURANCE YOU PROBABLY DON'T NEED

The biggest insurance mistake people make is insuring the wrong types of risks. Crazy, but true. Have you ever stopped by the airport insurance counter and bought a flight insurance policy? Have you stopped to wonder why? If you really thought about the economics of buying flight insurance, you'd realize there are far better ways to spend your money and protect your family. Never mind the infinitesimal odds of your dying in a plane crash. The real questions you should be asking before buying flight insurance are: Why should my family receive more money if I die in the air than if I die some other way? And, why should I be paying for that additional coverage?

The cardinal rule for buying insurance is this: Get the broadest possible coverage you can, but don't pay to insure a loss you could afford to absorb yourself. The narrower the coverage, such as flight insurance (as opposed to plain old life insurance), the less economical it is. Flight insurance is just one example of a narrow insurance policy you probably don't need. Here are some others, also sold frequently on the basis of fear and love:

- *Credit life and disability insurance.* When you apply for a personal loan, a car loan, or a home improvement loan, you may be asked about signing up for insurance that will make any remaining payments on the loan if you die or become disabled. Although this insurance is voluntary, some lenders make such a hard sell that it seems mandatory. Credit insurance sounds inexpensive; it is usually described as costing only about 30 cents to $1 per $100 of coverage. Those pennies add up. Credit insurance can wind up adding between 1 and 3 percent to the interest rate on your loan.

  When you are in your 30s or 40s, you can usually get the same coverage for much less money by buying term life insurance or disability insurance from an insurance agent. Warning: Expect an even harder sell on credit insurance the next time you apply for a bank loan. In the past, banks had been severely restricted in the amount of credit insurance they could sell, but in 1986 the Federal Reserve Board removed some of these constraints, so more banks will probably be pushing credit insurance.

- *Waiver of premiums.* Some life insurance policies let you buy what is called a waiver-of-premium rider, which excuses you from making payments if you become disabled. The waiver typically costs between 2 and 5 percent of the cost of the life insurance policy. Like credit disability insurance, the waiver-of-premium is an expensive way of buying disability insurance and isn't necessary if you own a good disability policy.

- *Cancer insurance and other dread-disease policies usually sold by mail.* If ever an insurance policy was sold on fear, cancer insurance is it. Is there any reason you should buy health insurance that will pay only if you get cancer and not any other illness? Apparently, some insurance regulators don't think so: cancer insurance has been banned in a handful of states across the country. There often is less to a cancer insurance policy than meets the eye. Some insurers boast about paying hospital bills for their policyholders, but few cancer patients are hospitalized for long periods. Even if you do get cancer, a cancer policy won't cover many of your expenses.

- *Hospital insurance by the day.* If you watch a lot of television, you can't help seeing the commercials featuring elderly actors, with somber faces and cardigan sweaters, talking about the skyrocketing cost of health care. They then offer "help" in the form of health

insurance known as a hospital indemnity policy, which will pay
you a designated amount, say $50, for each day you are in the hos-
pital. You don't need this kind of "help." You would be much better off buying a broader health insurance policy that pays some of
your doctor's bills as well as a higher percentage of your hospital
bills- which typically run about $300 a day. Long hospital stays are
rare for people in their 30s or 40s.

- *Life insurance for a child.* Mark this insurance in the bought-out-
  of- love category. When an insurance agent calls to ask you to buy
  life insurance for your child, it might seem almost inhumane to
  refuse. It might, that is, until you stop for a second to think about
  the reason for buying life insurance: to supply the family with lost
  in-come as a result of the death. As harsh as this sounds, unless your
  child happens to be, say, an actor in a hit TV show or a teen rock 'n'
  roll star, your family won't lose much income should the child die.

- *Life insurance if you are single, have no dependents, and are not
  living with someone.* Here again, life insurance should be purchased to supply the deceased's family with lost income. Some
  agents will say that if you're single and in your 30s or 40s you
  should buy life insurance now because the policy will be more expensive in the future when you might have a greater need for the
  insurance. It's true that term life insurance costs more as you age.
  But that is still no excuse for spending money now on coverage that
  is inappropriate.

SUREFIRE INSURANCE SAVINGS

Before buying any insurance policy, be certain that you have fully *self-in-
sured* your family. This means having enough cash available to pay for
small financial losses and emergencies. Try to set aside an emergency cash
reserve equal to between three and six months of your family's typical expenses. The money should be kept someplace with easy and immediate
access, such as a bank money-market deposit account, a money-market
mutual fund, a short-term bank certificate of deposit, or Treasury bills.

The size of your cash reserve depends partly on the stability of your
family's income and the size of your family. If either you or your spouse
has a tenuous job or plans to quit work shortly, try to boost your family's
cash reserve to compensate. On the other hand, if your jobs are safe, you
can probably skimp on the reserve fund. The more small children you

have, the larger the emergency reserve fund you will want to maintain, as medical and other emergencies are more likely to crop up.

This savings fund will not only help bail you out to cover unexpected expenses, it will also lower your insurance premiums. The more you are willing to pay out of pocket in the event of a financial loss (your deductible), the less your insurance will cost. So when you shop for insurance—whether it is to cover your car, your house, or your health—be sure to ask for a premium scale that indicates rates for various sizes of deductibles.

While you are asking about deductibles, quiz your insurance agents about their policyholder discounts. You might be surprised at how much you can save on insurance just because you take good care of yourself, your family, and your possessions. For example, alarm systems in your home and car often qualify you for insurance discounts of 5 to 20 percent. Property insurance on a house built within the past two years usually qualifies for a 20 percent discount, too.

Nonsmokers usually pay less for life and health insurance than smokers. You can often save between 5 and 30 percent on your car insurance by proving to the agent that you have a good driving record. But be sure to tell the agent about all your precautions; otherwise he won't know that you deserve the discounts.

BUYING DISABILITY INSURANCE

Disability insurance may seem like a strange type to discuss first, but it is probably the insurance you need to beef up the most, whether you are self-employed or work for someone else. Disability insurance is essential for all workers, especially those who are young. Two statistics bear this out: At age 40, you are four times more likely to get disabled than to die. Between the ages of 35 and 60, you have a one out of three chance of becoming disabled for more than 90 days.

If you have no long-term disability insurance, you are hardly alone. Only 6 percent of the adult population own an individual long-term disability income policy, and only 15 percent of U.S. workers have disability insurance that covers them beyond six months.

Most people don't have enough disability coverage for a simple reason. It is said that insurance generally is sold, not bought, but disability insurance is rarely sold. The Life Insurance Marketing and Research Association recently conducted interviews with affluent women between the ages of 25 and 35 who had financial advisers. All the women had been asked about life insurance by their advisers, but none had been asked about their disability coverage.

Like many people, you might think that worker's compensation and Social Security disability insurance will cover you if you can't work for a period of time. But that coverage is paper-thin. If you cannot work because you get injured or become sick away from your job, worker's compensation won't pay a dime. The top Social Security disability insurance benefit, indexed for inflation, is merely $1,280 a month, or $15,360 a year. And you won't get any Social Security disability benefits at all unless you can prove that you will not be able to engage in substantial, gainful activity for more than a year or that your disability will result in death— and even then you must wait six months before the checks start to arrive.

Your family should have enough disability insurance coverage to replace between 60 and 70 percent of its after-tax income in the event of an illness or injury. Self-employed people should shoot for 70 percent of after-tax income so that the policy will help reimburse them for overhead costs of their business. A good disability policy costs about $1,000 a year per $12,000 of annual disability income coverage.

Check with your employer to see what, if any, disability coverage is provided. You might be eligible to receive only enough money to pay for a small number of sick days. A company with a cracker-jack disability plan provides its employees with full-scale disability income coverage (equal to 60 percent of the employee's salary until he or she reaches 65) through a group insurance policy.

Many employers fall somewhere in the middle and offer employees decent, but limited disability coverage for a fee. Like Social Security, many company disability plans kick in six months after a worker becomes disabled, and they limit monthly payments. The cap, which might be $3,000 a month, is generally more than enough for most workers but is inadequate for many middle managers and executives.

Some businesses offer disability insurance to all employees; others limit the coverage to people who have worked at the firm for a minimum of five years or so. Corporate disability policies often stop paying benefits when employees return to work, even if they can only manage to return part-time for a fraction of their previous salary.

Disability insurance coverage for pregnancy varies from company to company. When you are expecting a child, ask your employee benefits department whether women receive disability benefits if they can't return to work because of complications during or after delivery. If the answer is no, you might want to acquire a separate disability policy from an insurance agent.

Your company (or companies if you and your spouse both work for pay) may not offer you enough disability insurance to meet your needs. In that case, you will need to shop around for an individual policy or for two policies (if you belong to a two-income family). Roughly 200 companies sell individual disability insurance, most of them life insurers. But there are actually only a dozen companies that sell disability coverage in a big way. Of them, four insurers dominate: The Provident Companies in Chattanooga, Tennessee; Paul Revere Life in Worcester, Massachusetts; Northwestern Mutual Life in Milwaukee, Wisconsin; and Union Mutual in Portland, Maine. Most of the insurers selling disability policies have traditionally focused on affluent professionals such as doctors, lawyers, and corporate executives. Lately, however, the companies have made a serious effort to sell to the rest of the general public.

When buying a disability insurance policy, compare the amount of the premiums, the deductibles (the most you will have to pay before coverage starts), and the size of the benefits. Then ask yourself these four critical questions:

- *When do payments begin?* Disability policies, like other types of health insurance policies, have a waiting period—the time between when you first get sick or injured and when the payments start. The longer the waiting period, the lower your premiums will be. So if you have enough savings to tide you over for a few months and don't need immediate disability coverage, you can save hundreds of dollars on your premiums. Try to get a policy with a two-month or three-month waiting period.

- *When do payments stop?* Most policies continue coverage until you turn 65. But many insurers halt payments the day you return to work, whether you go back full-time or part-time. Lately, though, an increasing number of insurers have been selling a useful type of policy with what are called residual benefits for people who can work only part-time and will earn less than 80 percent of their regular pay. A residual disability policy continues to pay benefits in proportion to lost income while the person works part-time.

- *Which disabilities are covered and which ones are not?* The most restrictive policies pay out only if you are permanently disabled and unable to get any type of work. Some only cover disabilities resulting from accidents, not from illnesses. You should get more liberal coverage that will provide benefits once you cannot perform the duties of your former job for any reason.

  If you have a medical problem when you apply for a disability policy, the insurer might not cover that particular infirmity or coverage might be provided for an outrageously high price. You then have three choices: (1) pay the expensive premium; (2) ask to have your medical problem excluded from coverage so the premium cost will be back to normal; (3) get a policy with a limited exclusion rider so that you will be fully covered at a reasonable cost in exchange for either a lengthened waiting period or an earlier benefits cutoff date.

- *Can I renew the policy?* Not all policies are renewable or noncancellable. Find one that is. Ask your insurance agent for a policy that is noncancellable and guaranteed renewable until age 65 at the original premium price so you won't lose the coverage as long as you continue to make the premium payments.

Managing Your Money

> Managing Your Money doesn't help you shop for disability insurance, but if you do obtain coverage, enter it, and a brief summary of the terms of the policy in the Insurance Policy Organizer in the Insure submenu.

BUYING LIFE INSURANCE

Why is it that one of the most critical purchases you will ever make—life insurance—is the hands-down most complicated? Life truly is unfair. In a fair world, a family could figure out in a flash the exact amount of life insurance they need, compare similar policies from a few insurance companies, and then select one. Instead, getting the proper coverage requires extensive research, painstaking analysis, and hours spent listening to agents tossing around terms such as "participating policy" and "cash value." It's no wonder, then, that many people own the wrong type and wrong amount of life insurance. They either guess at their needs or let insurance agents or their employers make all the decisions for them.

Unfortunately, life insurance is not one of those purchases that can be made by following a simple rule of thumb, such as go to any agent and buy coverage equal to five times your salary. Some families need a good deal more life insurance because of health problems, a house full of small children, or little savings; others need to buy less. Unlike banks, where a certificate of deposit at one is pretty much the same as a CD at another, life insurers each serve up policies with a slight twist from those of their competition.

Before choosing among various companies and policies, you need to determine how much life insurance your family actually needs. Essentially, a family's life insurance should cover final expenses—funeral costs, unpaid bills, and so forth—and roughly 75 percent of the amount of the family's total current after-tax income until the youngest child starts college and the remaining spouse can support himself or herself.

Remember that Social Security sometimes pays monthly survivor's benefits. A surviving spouse younger than age 60 receives benefits if he or she does not earn very much and has at least one dependent child younger than 16. (If the surviving spouse cares for a child who became disabled before age 22, Social Security will continue paying survivor's benefits as long as the child is disabled.) Social Security provides a full benefit if the surviving spouse earns less than a designated amount, now roughly $6,000 a year. The benefit is reduced by $1 for every $2 of earnings above the figure. So don't count on any survivor's benefits from Social Security if you and your spouse each earn more than $20,000 annually. Social Security also pays benefits to surviving children until they turn 18 (19 if they are still in high school). Disabled children receive benefits as long as they are disabled and unmarried.

Figuring out the precise amount your family would receive in Social Security survivor's benefits is terribly complicated and best left to the Social Security employees. You can get an estimate by writing to the Social Security Administration, Office of Public Inquiries, Baltimore, Md. 21235.

Check your employee benefits handbook to see whether your company will provide your family with life insurance proceeds if you die. You may be able to buy optional life insurance coverage through your employer. The optional insurance could be a good deal, though not necessarily. That depends on how your employer prices it. If all employees are charged the same rate and you are under 40, you would, in effect, be subsidizing your older colleagues whose age makes them higher risks. Thus, you may be able to get life insurance less expensively elsewhere. Conversely, if your company charges lower premium rates for its younger employees, the optional insurance is probably a good buy.

The accompanying worksheet will help you estimate the amount of additional life insurance your family might need.

When you start shopping for life insurance, make sure you compare only policies sold by financially strong insurance companies that will be around as long as you will. You can rest comfortably if the insurers have a ten-year history of receiving A or A+ ratings from A. M. Best & Co., the independent rating service. (Best began giving A++ ratings in 1992.) Any decent insurance agent will have the current Best rating list, but you can also find one at most large public libraries. *Consumer Reports* also periodically publishes an exhaustive report on life insurance, with price comparisons for dozens of policies. The magazine's most recent series appeared in its June, July, and August 1986 issues.

Life insurance premium rates vary enormously among companies. In fact, they even vary enormously within the same company. An insurer might have a terrific deal for a 35-year-old nonsmoking woman seeking $200,000 of coverage but a ridiculously overpriced policy for a 45-year-old smoking man who needs $50,000 of life insurance. Nearly all insurers have three standard pricing rules: women pay less than men of the same age (because women live longer, on average); healthy people, especially nonsmokers, pay less than people with poorer health; and policies on annual premium billing cycles cost less than ones with semiannual, quarterly, or monthly premiums.

Life insurance comes in three basic flavors: term insurance (vanilla), whole-life (vanilla fudge), and universal- or variable-life (tuttifrutti). Term is plain insurance protection, whole-life is insurance protection with a built-in savings plan, and universal- or variable-life is insurance protection with a built-in savings plan that can be more flexible than that of whole-life.

Managing Your Money Tip

> You can use Managing Your Money to calculate how much life insurance your family needs. Select How Much Life Insurance You Need from the Insure submenu.

1. Managing Your Money handles what your family will need in the future in terms of what they will need until the children finish college, and what they will need after the children finish college So press Ctrl-F, type in the number of years until the youngest child finishes college that you wish to provide for your heirs, and press <enter>. Then type in the number of years after the youngest child finishes college that you wish to provide for your heirs, and press <enter>.

2. Next, press Ctrl-N.

   a. Multiply your current annual after-tax income by .75 For example, if your current annual after-tax income is $35,000, type "35000x.75", followed by <enter>. Then, type "a=r", followed by<enter>.

   b. Multiply the number of children you have by the number of years you intend to pay for their college by the amount you estimate their education to cost. (Again, that's about $5,000 a year at a public institution, and about $10,000 a year at a private institution.) For example, if you have two children, and you intend to provide for each of them to go to a private college for four years, type "2x4x10000", followed by <enter>. Next, type "b=r", followed by <enter>.

   c. Next, type "c=", then type in the number of years until the youngest child finishes college that you wish to provide for your heirs, and press <enter>. (That will be the number at the head of the column.) For example, if answered "8" as the number of years until the youngest child finishes college that you wish to provide for your heirs, type "c=8", followed by <enter>.

   d. Enter "d=", then the annual total of mortgage payments you want your insurance to pay for until the youngest child finishes college. For example, if your annual mortgage payments are $12,000 per year, and you want your insurance to pay for them, type "d=12000", followed by <enter>.

   e. Enter "e=", then enter the amount of any other financial goals you wish to provide for with life insurance before the youngest child finishes college, then"/c.". For example, if you want to pay off the family farm, and that costs $150,000, type "e=150000/c", followed by <enter>.

f. Now, type this formula: $((((c-4)xa)+b)/c)+d+e$, followed by <enter>. The result (r=) is the annual income need your heirs will have until the youngest child finishes college. Press <enter> again, and this sum will be entered into the space.

3. Next, press <enter>, and then press Ctrl-N.

a. Enter "d=", then the annual total of mortgage payments you want your insurance to pay for after the youngest child finishes college. For example, if your annual mortgage payments are $12,000 per year, and you want your insurance to pay for them, type "d=12000", followed by <enter>.

b. Next, type "c=", then type in the number of years after the youngest child finishes college that you wish to provide for your heirs, and press <enter>. (That will be the number at the head of the column.) For example, if answered "4" as the number of years after the youngest child finishes college that you wish to provide for your heirs, type "c=4", followed by <enter>.

c. Enter "e=", then enter the amount of any other financial goals you wish to provide for with life insurance after the youngest child finishes college, then"/c.". For example, if you want to pay off the family farm now that the youngest child has finished college, and that costs $150,000, type "e=150000/c", followed by <enter>.

d. Now, type this formula: c+d+e, followed by <enter>. The result (r=) is the annual income need your heirs will have after the young est child finishes college. Press <enter> again, and this sum will be entered into the space.

4. Press <enter>. Then enter the social security benefits you ex pect your heirs to receive annually until the youngest child finishes college. Press <enter>, and then enter the social security benefits you expect your heirs to receive annually after the youngest child finishes college.

5. Press <enter>, Then press Ctrl-N.

a. Type "a=", then type the interest rate you expect your assets to earn, followed by <enter>. For example, if you expect your assets to earn 15%, type "a=0.15", followed by <enter>.

b. Type "b=", then type the tax rate you expect that your heirs will have to pay on this interest, followed by <enter>. For example, if you expect that your heirs will have to pay 25% taxes on this interest, type "b=0.25", followed by <enter>.

c. Type "c=", then type the rate of inflation that you expect will prevail over the future, followed by <enter>. For example, if you expect that the prevailing rate of inflation in the future will be 7%, type "c=0.07", followed by <enter>.

d. Now, type this formula: 100x((ax(1-b))-c), followed by <enter>. The result (r=) is the interest rate that your heirs will earn on the assets that you leave to them. Press <enter> again, and this sum will be entered into the space.

6. Press <enter>, then press Ctrl-N. Add up what your family will need immediately (such as $5,000 for funeral expenses, current unpaid bills, estate taxes — usually zero if estate is smaller than $600,000, legal and probate fees, and from $1000 to $3000 in uninsured medical bills). For example, if funeral expenses will be $5,000, you estimate unpaid bills of $3,000, zero estate taxes, and estimate uninsured medical bills of $1,500, type "5000+3000+1500" and press <enter> twice. The sum will be entered in this space.

7. Press <enter>, then press Ctrl-N. Add up your current assets. These include your spouse's after tax income, bank accounts and money-market funds, stocks, bonds, and mutual funds, limited partnerships, equity in investment real estate, vested portions of company pension & savings plans, home equity, IRA & Keogh plans, and insurance proceeds. For example, suppose your spouse's after-tax income is $30,000, you have savings of $13,000, and have home equity of $30,000. Type "30000+13000+30000" and press <enter> twice. The sum will be entered into this space.

8. Press <enter> again, and then enter any other assets that your

heirs may have access to. For example, if your kids have wealthy grand parents who would see them through any emergency, you may want to adjust your life insurance needs downward. Then press <enter>.

When you're finished, just press F10. Managing Your Money will tell you how much life insurance you need.

Tax reform has increased the appeal of whole-life, variable life, and universal-life policies. Earnings on the savings portion of these policies are tax-deferred until the money is withdrawn. That was true before tax reform, too. But now that the tax law has eliminated many other types of tax shelters, life insurance is one of the few still standing.

When you were in your 20s, choosing the right type of insurance wasn't especially difficult. Universal-life hadn't been invented yet, variable-life was rare, and whole-life insurance was a pretty lousy buy, so term was the logical choice. But whole-life has been improved, term has become more expensive for you now that you are older, and both variable-life and universal-life are worth a look. Following is a closer analysis of each.

Term insurance is the simplest to explain. It is a basic policy, bought for a specified period of years, that will pay a certain amount of money to your beneficiary when you die. Term insurance is usually sold for a one-year or five-year term. The amount of the premium remains constant during the term of the policy but rises at the beginning of each new term as you get older. Most companies sell renewable term policies that guarantee you can renew at the end of the term without getting a medical exam. The renewable feature might stop when you reach age 60 or 70, however. Some companies also sell convertible term policies that let you transform the insurance into a whole-life or universal-life policy sometime in the future up until a specified age. The best term policy is one that is renewable and convertible.

You can buy either a participating term insurance policy or a nonparticipating policy. A participating policy is one in which the insurer pays its policyholders dividends that can be received as cash, can be put toward paying the next premium, or can be used to buy additional insurance coverage. Participating policies usually start out costing more than nonparticipating policies. But if the dividends are large enough, the money you get back will end up making the participating policy the less expensive type. Participating policies have been less expensive historically, although there is no guarantee that this trend will continue in the future.

The price of term insurance varies a good deal, but you should figure on paying roughly $300 a year for $200,000 of coverage at age 35 and $500 to $600 for the same coverage at age 45. Term insurance for those in their 30s or 40s is considerably less expensive than wholelife, variable-life, or universal-life. So if you plan to buy term insurance—and that's usually a good idea for people in their 30s and 40s—be certain that you can discipline yourself to invest the additional money you would have paid to buy other, more expensive types of insurance. If discipline is not your strong suit, forgo term in favor of whole-life, variable-life, or universal-life.

Term insurance is sold by insurance agents; through the mail via trade associations, credit card issuers, and alumni groups; and at banks in a few states. Banks and insurance agents usually have the best deals. Life insurance is available only from the banks known as savings banks in Connecticut, Massachusetts, and New York. You must work or live in one of those states to be eligible for savings bank life insurance. In Connecticut, you can buy only up to $30,000 in savings bank life insurance coverage. Massachusetts has a $60,000 ceiling. New York had limited coverage to $50,000 per individual, but a new legal loophole lets savings banks there sell unlimited coverage. The banks that have taken advantage of this loophole have chosen to restrict coverage to $250,000 per individual.

Insurance agents represent hundreds of companies selling term policies. Try to compare coverage of about six different insurers rated A or A+ by Best & Co for the past ten years. Tell the agent your age and the amount of renewable term insurance coverage you need. There is no single best company, and some of the better insurers don't sell policies in every state.

The *Consumer Reports* survey gave consistently high marks to term policies sold by savings banks and by these companies:

- First Colony Life in Lynchburg, Virginia
- Massachusetts Indemnity and Life in Santa Monica, California
- Northwestern Mutual Life in Milwaukee, Wisconsin
- Union Central Life in Cincinnati, Ohio

Whole-life insurance has received a lot of bad press over the years, and for good reason. Until recently, whole-life was not much of an insurance buy. It often cost ten times as much as term insurance for someone in his mid-30s, and the savings portion of the policy earned a measly 2 to 6 percent annual return, before inflation. A disciplined investor could have bought term for much less money and put the savings in an investment with a far better return.

But whole-life insurance has become more respectable of late. Many insurers now invest the savings portion of policies to earn between 7 and 12 percent a year. The insurance industry has a good reason for improving its whole-life policies: Agents generally make a lot more money selling whole-life than term.

While the investment feature of whole-life insurance has grown more attractive, the borrowing feature has lost a bit of its luster. Whole-life policyholders can borrow a portion of the cash value (the amount they would get if they cashed in the policy) at any time and repay the loan whenever they wish. If they die before paying back the money, however, the outstanding debt will be subtracted from the death benefits owed the beneficiary. Anyone who bought a whole-life policy in the early 1970s can borrow at a low interest rate of 5 or 6 percent. New policies have higher rates-typically 8 percent or so.

Like term insurance, whole-life is sold in participating policies and nonparticipating policies. A participating whole-life policy gives you the same options with its dividends as a participating term policy, except you can also reinvest the dividends with the insurer to earn interest in the savings portion of the policy.

Whole-life insurance costs much more than term when you are young, but whole-life premiums don't rise nearly as much as term premiums do. In your 30s or mid-40s, the first-year premium of a whole-life policy with $100,000 of coverage might be $1,000 to $2,000, versus $250 to $600 for the same amount of term insurance. At age 50, term and whole-life cost about the same. So if you have term insurance now or plan to buy some, start thinking about converting from term to whole-life.

Among the companies *Consumer Reports* noted as selling the best whole-life policies:

- Bankers Life in Des Moines, Iowa
- Federal Kemper Life in Long Grove, Illinois
- Mutual Life of New York in New York City
- New England Mutual Life in Boston, Massachusetts

- Northwestern Mutual Life in Milwaukee, Wisconsin
- Phoenix Mutual Life in Hartford, Connecticut

Variable-life insurance is whole-life with a slight twist. Whereas whole-life premiums are invested in conservative bonds or real estate to earn a guaranteed rate of return, variable-life premiums are put into investments that fluctuate more widely: stocks and money-market securities. Earnings, like those of any life insurance policy, are tax-deferred. So the variable-life policyholder is, in effect, buying a combination of life insurance and a mutual fund. In fact, some of the best-performing mutual funds in recent years have been those incorporated in variable-life policies. One of the shining stars is Zenith Fund-Capital Growth, sold by New England Mutual Life, which was up 53 percent in 1987.

Here's the catch: Unlike with whole-life, where cash value and death benefit are not only guaranteed but rise steadily, the cash value and death benefit of a variable-life policy can plummet as well as rise. Of course, the death benefit of a variable-life policy will never drop below the amount of insurance coverage you bought initially. You can limit your risk with variable-life by buying a policy that lets you exchange it for a traditional whole-life policy in the future.

Universal-life, and its cousins single-premium life and flexible-premium variable universal-life (a.k.a. universal-life II), are newer types of life insurance emphasizing flexibility and investment choice. Universal-life and universal-life II let policyholders choose each year the amount of money they want to pay in and the amount of their coverage, within limits. They can also withdraw a portion of their universal life cash value, something not possible with whole-life.

As with whole-life, a portion of universal-life premiums goes toward insurance coverage and a portion goes into a savings fund. Universal-life policies guarantee a minimum rate of return on their cash value, generally about 4 percent or so. But unlike whole-life, universal-life generally allows a policyholder to select and switch among a variety of savings options whose returns are not guaranteed. The investments are similar to money-market funds, stock mutual funds, and bond mutual funds. Single-premium life provides similar investment freedom, but, like the name says, you have to pay the entire premium charge at one time. The cost is typically $5,000 to $500,000.

A special benefit of universal-life is its clarity—at least relative to other types of insurance. When you buy a universal-life policy, you know exactly how much of your premium is paying the insurance company's expenses, how much is protecting you and your family, how much is being stashed in the policy's savings fund, and the rate of return on the savings portion of your policy. Whole-life, by contrast, is far more mysterious. It's practically impossible to know exactly where your whole-life premium dollars are going.

These fancy policies can be nifty tax shelters because of their tax-deferred earnings. The shelter can be especially large for a single-premium policy, enabling you to get tax-deferred earnings on an investment of $50,000 or so. Single-premium life insurance is a terrific way to borrow, too. You can usually borrow as much as 75 percent of the cash value during the policy's first year and up to 90 percent thereafter. The insurer charges you an interest rate of 8 percent or so, but your actual net cost of borrowing is usually zero. That's because a single-premium contract says the interest on its loans equals your return on the amount borrowed.

Universal life and its variations require a good deal of scrutiny, though. The insurers usually tack on high sales charges of between 5 and 9 percent, which can cut into your return enormously. You could actually lose money on some policies if you decided to cancel them within the first ten years of owning them. Beware, too, of high cancellation charges. Some policies require you to give up about 7 percent of your cash value if you cash in within a year after buying them. A few policies have surrender charges that are so severe you could lose the entire amount of your cash value by cashing in within a year or two.

The mouth-watering rates of return the insurers boast aren't always as impressive as they appear to be either, as fees and expenses sometimes haven't been deducted in the computations. Moreover, current rates of return are no guarantee of future returns. In fact, a company can push a policy with a tempting rate, then cut the yield sharply a few months later.

Comparing universal-life policies is extraordinarily difficult because the insurance industry has yet to adopt a good yardstick. But *Consumer Reports* came up with its own judging criteria and determined that the best buys for universal-life, if you are in your 30s or 40s, are sold by:

- Alexander Hamilton Life of Farmington Hills, Michigan
- Central Life Assurance of Des Moines, Iowa
- Security-Connecticut Life of Avon, Connecticut
- Woodmen of the World Life of Omaha, Nebraska

Money magazine also recommends policies sold by:

- Life Insurance Co. of Virginia in Richmond, Virginia
- Midland Mutual in Columbus, Ohio
- USAA of San Antonio, Texas

If you bought whole-life or term insurance back in the '60s or early '70s, it might be worth your while to switch to a new policy. A swap could be especially useful if you own a nonparticipating policy paying a low rate of return. Today's higher interest rates are reflected in the savings portion of new whole-life and universal-life policies. So swapping policies can let you keep the same coverage but boost your cash value over time. It might also cut the cost of your premiums. Switching from an old term policy to a new one could save you money, too. Reason: Insurers have dropped prices on term insurance because today's higher interest rates have let them invest their premiums and make more money.

Swapping life insurance policies shouldn't be done cavalierly, however. Don't let yourself get pressured into a switch by an insurance agent. Remember, agents make fat commissions when they sell new policies—and some agents now are pushing new "exchange policies." It is thus in their interest to get you to take out a new policy but not necessarily in your best interest.

Exchanging life insurance policies comes with a few strings attached. You may be required to take a new physical exam. A new policy might have fine print, not written into your old policy, restricting death benefits in certain cases such as suicide. If you cancel your new policy within a few years of getting it, you could also get socked with some stiff surrender charges and wind up walking away with a puny cash value.

Before making a switch, make a thorough comparison of the policy you own and the one you are thinking about getting in its place. See how much the annual premiums would be for each policy during the next 20 years. Ask, too, for projections of the annual growth in each policy's cash value. Find out about cancellation charges imposed if you drop the new policy. You might find that your best bet is to hold on to your old policy and buy a new policy (perhaps paying for the new one by borrowing against the old one).

If, after the head-to-head match-up, you are convinced a switch is advantageous, sign up for the new policy. Then cancel the old one. Never cancel the old policy first, or you could be caught without insurance before the new policy takes effect.

Managing Your Money Tip

> For other life insurance companies that offer good value, select How Much It Should Cost from the Insure submenu.

BUYING HEALTH INSURANCE

This might be an insurance policy you don't need to buy. Nine of ten working Americans get health insurance from their employers. Lately, though, as health-care costs have been rising between 7 and 10 percent a year, companies have been passing on a larger and larger percentage of their health insurance expenses to employees. You may be required to pay a higher deductible than in the past, to pay a higher percentage of each medical bill, or to get a second opinion before getting major surgery.

So now that your health insurance is probably costing you more than in the past, it is worth reviewing what you have and figuring out whether you need to supplement your health insurance policy. If you are self-employed or work for a small company and don't receive health insurance as a fringe benefit, it's especially important to buy appropriate coverage. Self-employed persons can now deduct 25 percent of the cost of health insurance for themselves and their families.

The best type of health insurance policy is a broad one that provides both basic protection and coverage for long-term illnesses through what is known as major medical. This type of policy pays a percentage of your doctor's bills, hospital stays, and other health costs, up to a specified amount. You pay annual deductibles before receiving any benefits.

For example, a policy might require a deductible of $50 to $200 for medical expenses other than hospital stays or emergency out-patient care, then pay 80 percent of your bills. A good major medical plan pays 100 percent of your stay in a semi-private hospital room up to a certain period of time (such as 120 days) and then pays 80 percent of hospital costs thereafter. It also provides each person covered with at least $250,000 in lifetime benefits. Some policies have a $1 million ceiling or even an unlimited lifetime benefit.

Comprehensive major medical policies, sold by Blue Cross/Blue Shield and private health insurance companies, usually require a deductible of $1,000 or $2,500 for hospital costs. Major medical policies generally cover you, your spouse, and children younger than 19 (up to age 23 if the child is in school).

Although company-provided health insurance policies are often comprehensive, they may not cover or may restrict payments for certain types of medical services. The full cost of such services as dental care, psychiatric care, home health care, and treatments for alcoholism or drug dependency might not be provided by your company's health policy.

When you start a new job, be sure to read up on the company's health insurance policy and in particular to find out whether new employees are covered immediately. Some firms delay coverage for a few months, leaving new hires to fend for themselves. This delay can be particularly troublesome if you are switching jobs while pregnant or while receiving medical care. To counter this problem you might be able to convert the group health insurance coverage from your former job to an individual policy, with a premium that costs about $100 per person per month.

A law passed in 1986 is some help for new hires, divorcees, widows, and widowers. From now on, if you lose your job, you are guaranteed continued health care coverage from your former employer for a year and a half or until you get a job with health insurance, whichever comes first. Similarly, if you get divorced or legally separated from your spouse or if your spouse dies, the spouse's employer is required to provide you with health insurance coverage for up to three years. The law doesn't apply to companies with twenty or fewer employees, firms that don't offer group health insurance, or the federal government. Companies also aren't required to supply health insurance coverage if you or your spouse were fired for gross misconduct.

If you don't have enough health insurance, get ready for a some-what irritating experience trying to secure coverage. Some health insurers don't sell individual policies, only group ones. Those that do sell individual health insurance policies charge quite a piece of change. Figure on paying $1,000 to $4,000 a year to cover a family of four, closer to $1,000 if you are single. Figure also on paying higher deductibles than those of most group insurance policies—say, $750 annually for medical expenses other than hospital bills. (By increasing your deductible above the one suggested by an agent, you can cut your premiums by 15 percent or so.)

You can probably also get a better price by buying some type of group health coverage. Your employer might permit you to purchase supplemental coverage. Or you might be able to buy health insurance through a professional association that qualifies for a group insurance discount.

Whether you buy a health insurance policy from an agent or through a group, get one that has a guaranteed renewable feature. That way, as long as you pay your premiums on time the insurer can't cancel your coverage or raise your premiums no matter how often you file for claims. Another tip: If the policy requires you to pay a certain percentage of medical bills, be sure there is an annual limit to your out-of-pocket expenses, such as $1,000 per person.

Should you be repeatedly turned down for coverage because of your health, contact your state insurance commissioner. Ask whether the Blue Cross/Blue Shield insurer in your area is required to open enrollment to all applicants at any time during the year. The insurance office can also tell you whether yours is a state that guarantees health coverage for high-risk people through what are called "assigned risk" pools. Premiums in these pools are often 15 to 50 percent higher than those for healthier people.

A divorce usually cuts off health insurance coverage to exspouses who don't work for pay. But most states now have laws allowing divorcees who lose health insurance to buy individual policies from their former carriers.

The alternative to traditional health insurance is the health maintenance organization (HMO). There are now more than 300 HMOs in 200 U.S. cities. At an HMO, you pay a flat fee each year (about $2,200 annually for a family of four plus $2 or $3 per office visit) and are assigned to a particular doctor or group of doctors. Patients normally can check into only those hospitals affiliated with their HMOs, although they can usually go to any hospital in an emergency. Unlike other insurance plans, HMOs typically have no deductibles or maximum lifetime benefits and pay a higher percentage of the cost of hospital stays and surgery.

The best way to check up on an HMO you're thinking about joining is to call the state agency that regulates the medical groups and ask about the reputation of the particular HMO. It's a good sign if the HMO belongs to the Group Health Association of America, the national trade group for HMOs. Find out which health-care costs are not covered or are restricted by the HMO. Some pay expenses for dental care, prescriptions, eye care, psychiatric care, and physical therapy, and some don't.

BUYING HOMEOWNER'S INSURANCE

There isn't a whole lot that needs saying about homeowner's insurance. The important thing to remember is that you always want to be sure your home and contents are insured for what it would cost to replace them. Sounds elementary, but plenty of homeowners insure their property for its actual cash value, not its replacement cost. Yet the actual cash value of property is its value minus depreciation, which can amount to a lot less than replacement cost—particularly for an older home.

Having the right amount of replacement-cost coverage is crucial. If you bought replacement-cost insurance years ago but haven't increased the coverage to equal at least 80 percent of the value of the property, you could be in for a shock. In the event of any loss, the insurance company will reimburse you only for the depreciable value of the damage. Insurance companies prefer you to buy coverage equal to 100 percent of the replacement cost of the property (excluding land and the foundation), but you can cut your premiums by about 20 percent by getting 80 percent replacement-cost coverage. Either way, make sure that the coverage you buy is indexed to inflation.

The good news for home buyers is that there is a new and improved type of homeowner's insurance policy called Homeowners Program. It provides better coverage than the traditional policy for about the same price, but with a higher deductible. The old home-owner's policy automatically insured up to $500 worth of jewelry and up to $1,000 worth of silver and provided personal liability protection of $25,000. Typical deductible: $100. The Homeowners Program policy insures up to $1,000 worth of jewelry and up to $2,500 worth of silver, with personal liability protection of $100,000. The policy also throws in insurance for $2,500 worth of business equipment, including personal computers. Typical deductible: $250.

You can get additional coverage for your personal property by buying policy endorsements from your insurance agent. The most important endorsement is one guaranteeing to insure the replacement cost of your contents. That could add another 10 percent or so to your annual premium, but it is money well spent. Most policies limit the amount of coverage on personal property to 50 percent of its value. You might want to buy an endorsement raising the limit to 70 percent for about $1 per $1,000 worth of coverage. For extra coverage on valuables, expect to pay between $2 and $3 per $100 worth of jewelry, $1 per $100 worth of furs, and 25 cents per $100 worth of art. It's a good idea to insure individually any valuable worth more than $2,500.

If you work at home, you will want to fully cover your business property. For about $20 a year, you can buy an endorsement that insures up to $10,000 worth of business equipment. That might not be enough, especially if your home is your primary place of business. In that case, get a special business owner's policy, which should cost about $250 for $20,000 of property coverage and $500,000 of liability insurance.

BUYING CAR INSURANCE

Shopping around for automobile insurance is just about as ghastly an experience as shopping for life insurance. Every time you think you have mastered the lingo and have enough information to compare policies, some wise guy agent asks you a question like "And how much medical payments coverage do you want?" To which you may be tempted to answer, "How the hell do I know?" But to which you actually answer, "How much do I need?" So here's a brief review of automobile insurance with some tips.

Car insurance is actually six (sometimes seven) policies grid-locked into one: bodily injury liability; property damage liability; collision; comprehensive; medical payments; uninsured and underinsured motorist; and (sometimes) personal insurance protection.

Bodily injury liability and property damage liability, sometimes lumped together as simply liability insurance, are the two most critical elements of a car insurance policy. The first applies when someone gets hurt in an accident when you are driving your car or someone else is driving with your permission. The second type covers damage to other people's property. The coverage pays any claims and attorney's fees as a result of an accident. Many states require a minimum amount of liability insurance, such as $25,000. You need more. Ask for liability coverage of $100,000 per individual and $300,000 per accident, sometimes called 10/30 coverage.

Collision coverage, which is self-explanatory, could be a waste of money if your car is at least five years old. Insurers reimburse you for the amount the car is worth at the time of the accident. If your car is old, the money you would receive might be less than the cost of the insurance. You must choose a deductible when you get collision coverage. The higher the deductible, the less the insurance will cost. A deductible of $250 to $1,000 makes sense today.

Comprehensive is essentially fire and theft coverage for your car. Like collision coverage, comprehensive might be something you can skip if your car is old. And like collision, comprehensive comes with a deductible. If you get comprehensive coverage, take out a deductible of $250 or more.

Medical payments coverage pays any medical bills for you or your family if you are injured in your own car, are hurt in someone else's car, or are hit by a car. This insurance also pays the medical bills for passengers hurt while in the car you are driving. Typically, medical payments coverage is limited to $1,000 or $5,000 per person. Some financial advisers suggest forgoing this coverage if you have a good health insurance policy. Don't. After all, your passengers might not have such fine health insurance coverage.

Uninsured motorist coverage protects you and your family if you are injured by an uninsured or hit-and-run driver. Underinsured motorist coverage kicks in when the other driver's coverage has run out. Aim for $100,000 of coverage per person and $300,000 per accident.

Personal insurance protection is offered only (and is sometimes required) in states where no-fault is the law. Coverage varies depending on where you live.

Your car insurance premiums may have gone out of sight recently, as insurance companies have increased premiums about 10 percent a year for the past two years. You can cut your car insurance costs by raising your deductibles and perhaps reducing your medical payments coverage. Increasing your collision deductible from $100 to $1,000 could cut your collision premiums by 60 percent or so. Don't skimp on liability coverage, though. In fact, if you bought your policy more than three years ago before people started suing for outrageous amounts of money, you probably have less liability insurance than you need.

When shopping for new auto insurance coverage, get a quote from an agent of a direct writer that sells insurance of only one company, such as State Farm or Allstate, and then compare this figure with ones from a few independent agents representing several different companies. If you are automobile-accident prone, ask the insurance agents whether their companies penalize customers by charging them a lot more after filing large claims, and stick with ones that don't. The car you buy might determine the cost of your insurance, too. Some insurance companies offer discounts on car models that are unlikely to be stolen and are inexpensive to repair, such as mid-size sedans. Conversely, some insurers charge more for cars that thieves can't keep their hands off, such as sports cars.

BUYING EXCESS LIABILITY INSURANCE

Sometimes, enough may not be enough. Case in point: your liability coverage in your homeowner's and automobile insurance policies. You may have enough liability coverage to pay actual damages and expenses for most accidents, but the coverage could be quite skimpy if your personal assets are worth more than the liability limits on your insurance. You could be sued for an amount equal to the value of your assets and be forced to come up with the cash if you lose the case.

Your liability coverage has other limitations, regardless of your assets. It doesn't protect you from being sued for libel, wrongful eviction, discrimination, or invasion of privacy. Your coverage also probably stops at the U.S. border, leaving you naked (figuratively speaking) if you owe money after causing an accident out of the country.

The answer: excess personal liability insurance, otherwise known as an umbrella policy. For $100 to $150 per $1 million of insurance, you can beef up your liability protection and close the gaps in your coverage. This insurance covers you and your family. Most insurance companies sell excess liability policies only to people who already have substantial automobile and homeowner's liability insurance coverage with limits of about $250,000 per person and $500,000 per accident on their auto policy and $100,000 on their homeowner's policy.

BUYING NURSING HOME INSURANCE

Your parents are approaching the age when they may soon be thinking about entering a nursing home. You can help make that move less painful for them, both psychologically and financially, by helping them buy nursing home insurance.

Until two or three years ago, nursing home insurance didn't exist. Consequently, thousands of elderly people struggled to pay their nursing home care costs, which average about $24,000 a year. Medicare pays only a small amount of the cost of care for the first 100 days spent in a Medicare-certified nursing home. After that, coverage stops. Most nursing homes are not Medicare-certified. Supplemental medical insurance known as Medigap insurance isn't much better. Medigap usually pays only for skilled care—performed by professionals—in a certified home, and only for 100 days. It's no wonder that two-thirds of all nursing home patients who start paying their own bills tend to run out of money within a year.

But now nearly seventy health insurers such as Aetna, AIG Life, CNA, Fireman's Fund, and Prudential have begun selling nursing home insurance. Many of these policies are not yet available nationwide, however. Some of the policies pay only a portion of costs of skilled nursing home care provided by a nurse or other medical professional. Others pay some of the cost of custodial care, which is help in everyday activities such as dressing, walking, bathing, and eating. Custodial care need not be provided by a medical professional. A few insurers pay some of the costs of care at home after a policyholder is released from a nursing home. Benefits vary enormously—from about $10 a day to $160 a day for a nursing home stay of two to six years.

The cost of nursing home insurance varies as much as the coverage. Annual premiums range from about $175 to $2,500. Generally, the younger and healthier a person is, the less expensive the policy. A 75-year-old can easily pay 50 percent more for the same nursing home insurance than a 65-year-old. Insurers usually don't like to provide coverage for people who have recently had serious illnesses. So if your parents wait too long to buy nursing home insurance, they could be too late to get any. Still, nursing home insurance is generally only worth buying once a person is in his or her mid-60s or older and is expecting to eventually move into a nursing home.

Look for a nursing home insurance policy that is guaranteed renewable and that covers both skilled care and custodial care. Find out the average daily cost of a nursing home near your parents and then get a nursing home policy that pays between one-half and two-thirds of that amount for custodial care. Some policies stop paying benefits after a few months; others pay for years. It's best to get the policy with the longest coverage available. A final cautionary note: Some policies exclude nursing home stays for mental or nervous disorders such as Alzheimer's disease or senility. Avoid them.

IF YOU'RE A BAD INSURANCE RISK

Maybe you're not quite the Boy Scout or Girl Scout type who qualifies for insurance discounts. Perhaps you are quite the opposite—what insurance companies would consider a bad risk. Perhaps your job requires dealing with hazardous materials or working in dangerous areas, increasing the chances that you will get hurt or sick at work. Or maybe your car somehow keeps hitting other cars, or your house seems to give come-hither looks to burglars. If so, many insurance agents will refuse to grant you coverage—at any cost. Some companies, however, insure risky people by selling what are called substandard policies. The coverage usually costs more or is less comprehensive than the norm. For example, someone with a dangerous job or a medical problem could pay three times as much for disability insurance as the typical policyholder.

Before agreeing to take a substandard policy for life, health, or disability insurance, be sure that you really are as risky as the insurance agent thinks. Many insurers and doctors supply the Medical Information Bureau, a record-keeping organization, with files on their policyholders and patients. Check the accuracy of your file for free by writing to the bureau at P.O. Box 105, Essex Station, Boston, Mass. 02112.

If you are indeed a high-risk insurance candidate, check with your employer to see whether you can get life, disability, or health insurance coverage at work. Should you need still more insurance, find an insurance agent who specializes in high-risk individuals.

Now that your family is protected against the elements, lawsuits, car accidents, illness, and thefts, you are ready to shield yourself from one of the greatest perils of all: The Tax Man. Shrewd tax planning has always been fundamental for people in their 30s and 40s whose incomes are on the rise. It is especially critical today after passage of the tax reform law, which calls for a variety of new tax-planning strategies and a junking of many old ones.

Managing Your Money Tip

You can keep records of all your insurance policies in the Insurance Policy Organizer. Other information that might be needed in an emergency — from your passport number to the number of your safe deposit box — should be entered in Vital Records & Estate Report in the Insure submenu.

CHAPTER

5

KEEPING YOUR TAX
BILL LOW

*You have to always adjust quickly, see where the tax
breaks are—maybe it's now historic buildings, maybe windmills,
maybe oil drills. All this changes fast, month to month.
Arnold Schwarzenegger in US magazine.*

HOW THE TAX RULES HAVE CHANGED

You can't argue with Arnold Schwarzenegger. Of course, who would
want to? As he indicates, the tax laws are ever changing. And they have
not changed more dramatically in the past 50 years than they did in
1986. The Tax Reform Act of 1986 required every American taxpayer to
reassess his or her strategies regarding investing, savings, and borrowing.
Much of what you have done in the past to shelter your income from
taxes no longer makes sense. It may even be illegal now.

Tax planning is especially important for you, now that you are approaching your peak earning years and your need for tax shelter is the
greatest. As a member of the highest-taxed generation in U.S. history, you
should welcome the tax reform law's lower tax rates. In 1986, the top tax
rate was 50 percent. In 1987, it fell to 38.5 percent, and in January 1988
the top rate dropped to 28 percent. It's now 31 percent (see the accompanying table).

Tax Brackets for 1992 and Beyond

Filing Status	Taxable Income	Marginal Tax Rate
Joint return	$0 to $34,000	15%
	$34,001 to $82,150	28%
	$82,151 and up	31%
Single return	$0 to $20,350	15%
	$20,351 to $49,300	28%
	$49,301 and up	31%
Head of household return	$0 to $27,300	15%
	$27,301 to $70,450	28%
	$70,451 and up	31%
Married, filing separate returns	$0 to $17,000	15%
	$17,001 to $41,075	28%
	$41,076 and up	31%

Managing Your Money Tip

> If the tax laws change, you can change the tax tables in Managing Your Money by selecting Tax Tables and Parameters from the Tax submenu. This option lets you change more than just rates; you can alter the threshold for medical deductions, the Social Security tax rates, and so on. (Just use PgDn and PgUp to see everything.)

Don't be too quick to jump for joy, though. Congress was able to dish out the lower rates only by taxing income such as unemployment compensation that had been tax-free before and by taking away or restricting some popular tax write-offs.

The law abolished these tax breaks:

- The interest deduction for credit cards, car loans, student loans and other personal loans
- The $3,000 deduction for dual-income married couples
- The state and local sales tax deduction
- The ability to exclude from taxes $100 in dividends ($200 for married couples filing jointly)

- The exclusion for long-term capital gains.

And tax-reform restricted the following tax breaks:

- **Individual Retirement Accounts.** If you or your spouse are covered by a company pension or savings plan, your IRA deduction was either limited or abolished. Congress in fall 1992 was discussing making the IRA more generous again.

- **Charitable contribution deductions.** You can now claim charity write-offs only if you itemize.

- **Medical expense deductions.** To deduct your unreimbursed medical costs, they must exceed 7 1/2 percent of your adjusted gross income; in 1986, they were deductible once they topped 5 percent.

- **Company savings plans.** You can contribute only up to roughly $8,475 a year in a 401(k) salary-reduction company savings plan, down from $30,000 before tax reform. Tax-favored techniques for withdrawals from company plans have been eliminated or cut back.

- **Deductions for unreimbursed employee business expenses and miscellaneous expenses.** Most of these write-offs are now deductible only if they exceed 2 percent of your adjusted gross income. The expenses include fees for tax and investment advice, safe deposit box rental fees, subscriptions to investment and trade periodicals, union and professional dues, and educational expenses that relate to your work.

- **Deductions for business meals and entertainment expenses.** Only 80 percent of these expenses are deductible now.

- **Deductible interest paid to finance investments.**

- **Moving expense deductions.** Now you can claim moving expenses only if you itemize.

- **Real estate depreciation.**

- **The real estate rehabilitation credit for investment property.**

- **Shifting income to your children.**

- **Deducting tax shelter losses.**

But the tax-reform law left intact the following tax breaks:

- **Deductibility of mortgage interest on your first and second homes.**

- **Deductibility of state and local income, real estate, and property taxes.**

- **Keogh deduction.**

- **Tax-deferred earnings on life insurance, annuities, company savings plans, IRAs and Keoghs.**

- **Child-care tax credit.**

- **Alimony.**

- **Casualty and theft losses.**

Since tax reform, however, Congress has found more ways to squeeze money out of taxpayers, mostly through two sneaky methods:

- The deduction for personal exemptions has been phased out by 2 percent for every $2,500 that your adjusted gross income exceeds certain thresholds—$150,000 if you're married and filing jointly, $125,000 for a head of household, $100,000 for single people and $75,000 for married people who file separately. If you are married and filing jointly with two dependent children, your personal exemptions are completely phased out once your taxable income reaches $192,930. The net effect is an increase in your marginal tax rate by about half a percentage point for each exemption you claim. So you could actually wind up in the 33% bracket, rather than the so-called top bracket of 31%.

- Itemized deductions have also been cut back for wealthy people. If you're single, married filing jointly or a head of household and your adjusted gross income is over $100,000 (or $50,000 if you're married filing separately), you must reduce your itemized deductions by 3 percent of the amount of your income over the threshold. (Medical expenses, casualty and theft losses and investment interest are not affected by this calculation.) Here again, the effect is an increase in your tax bracket—in this case, by roughly 1 point.

  Even if your federal income tax bill is lower now than before tax reform, you're probably being socked with higher taxes on a few other fronts. The Social Security employment tax has been increased seven times since 1980. It's now 7.65%; 15.3% if you're self employed. The tax ends once your income hits $53,400 (for 1991; the figure goes up with inflation).

Your state taxes are almost certainly higher now, too. In fact, although you probably got a federal tax cut from the tax reform law, you most likely pay more in total taxes (federal, state and local) than you did before. Most states have eliminated the same deductions for their residents as Congress has. What's more, state and local taxes are going up 2.6 points a year faster than federal income taxes, as a percentage of the average family's income. Some 36 states raised taxes by a record $16.2 billion for fiscal 1992. And three out of four cities increased their taxes in 1991. Over the next few years, several of the nine states that have no state income taxes are likely to enact them.

HELP, I NEED SOMEBODY

The tax reform law—jokingly dubbed the Accountants' Relief Act of 1986—might lead you to think that you now *must* get help with your taxes, even if you've always prepared your own tax return. In truth, you may be able to manage without a tax practitioner, as do an estimated 40 percent of those who itemize deductions, despite the tax changes.

You should be able to go it alone if:

- Your income is mostly salary.

- Your deductions are easy to compute.

- You do not own any limited-partnership units.

- You have not sold your home or any investments in the preceding tax year.

- You keep up with the latest tax-planning strategies.

If you want to handle your own taxes, spend $10 or so for a tax book that will help you. The best guides are the hardy annuals by J. K. Lasser, H&R Block, and the Ernst and Young accounting firm. You also should visit the nearest district office of the Internal Revenue Service and pick up a copy of the IRS's free booklet "Your Federal Income Tax."

Managing Your Money Tip

If you keep your finances in order with Managing Your Money, it's easy to prepare your taxes with Meca's TaxCut software. TaxCut prepares dozens of forms and worksheets, and it has an Interview that walks you through the whole process of doing your return. TaxCut's unique Expert System leads you through questions on any given topic. And TaxCut's Shoebox lets you take your year's receipts and tax records and, one by one, put each in its proper place.

The TaxCut Connection exports many of the numbers you need to prepare your taxes directly to TaxCut. In so doing, it prints a list of what it has imported (and where it has been put), along with a list of the things it couldn't import (because it didn't know enough about them) and where it should go.

Best of all, you can order the final version of TaxCut directly from MECA for about $50. (An early release version of TaxCut may appear in the fall, but you can't file a return with it. You're better off buying the final version directly from MECA, with which you can file a return, and saving yourself a few dollars.) You'll get a tax return guaranteed against mathematical answers, at a fraction of the cost of having your return prepared by an accountant (who may be using TaxCut anyway). Even if you have your return prepared professionally, you can use TaxCut to check your preparer's work.

KEEPING YOUR TAX BILL LOW

If you decide to use a tax pro or want to dump your current one, you essentially have four types of practitioners from which to choose.

The first, suitable for people with simple tax returns, is a tax preparer from a storefront chain such as H&R Block or Triple Check Income Tax Service. You will get reliable tax-return preparation but probably no tax-planning advice. The cost depends on the complexity of your return. The average fee at H&R Block for a federal and state tax return is $48. At Block's Executive Tax Service, where you work with a full-time preparer in a private office, the average fee is about $100.

Use a local storefront tax preparer only if he or she comes recommended from people you trust. Otherwise, you could wind up with a swifty who vanishes after April 15, leaving you without counsel if you are audited.

Options 2 and 3 are a certified public accountant and an enrolled agent. Such pros provide tax-planning advice in addition to preparing tax returns. They are best if you invest regularly or are self-employed. Be sure the CPA specializes in taxes—not all do. All enrolled agents have worked for the IRS as revenue agents for at least five years or have passed a demanding two-day IRS test. Both types of advisers charge hourly fees of $50 to $150, although enrolled agents sometimes undercut CPA's prices by as much as 25 percent.

The best way to find a CPA or an enrolled agent is through a referral from someone you trust who has family income and investments comparable to yours. The National Association of Enrolled Agents has a toll-free service (800-424-4339) that will provide names and phone numbers of members near you.

Talk with your CPA or enrolled agent at least three times every twelve months: in the fall to discuss your tax bill due in April, year-end planning ideas, and ways to reduce next year's taxes; in January or February to turn over your records for preparing your tax return; and after the return is completed to discuss the tax bill and ways to cut your next one. Also meet with your adviser before making investment decisions with tax implications, such as buying or selling real estate; before an important change in your life such as marriage, divorce, the birth of a child, or a job switch; and after passage of major tax legislation. (You can be sure another tax law is on its way.) These sessions usually cost about $100 an hour.

The last option—a tax lawyer—is necessary only when facing, say, a divorce or a will that requires both tax and legal advice. Such service will generally cost $75 to $250 an hour.

Deciding when to get rid of your tax practitioner is difficult, because performance results are hard to quantify. If your tax return is audited, don't fire your tax pro immediately—you will need him or her to help you through the ordeal. But should you wind up owing the IRS money on disallowed write-offs that your adviser has said were legitimate, find a new adviser. You might also ditch your adviser if he or she does not give much useful tax-planning advice all year round.

A QUICK REVIEW OF TAX TERMINOLOGY

Before dispensing any advice about how to cut your taxes in the post-tax-reform world, it might be useful to briefly review some important tax terms. You cannot make any intelligent tax moves until you understand the rules of the game. Some key tax terms and how they are affected by the tax-reform law include:

- *Tax filing status.* When you file your tax return, you must choose one of five types of filing status: single; married, filing jointly; married, filing separately; head of household; and qualifying widow or widower with dependent child. The taxes you owe will be determined, in part, by your filing status. Generally, a married person filing a joint return will owe less than a taxpayer with the same amount of income who uses another filing status. Widows and widowers file as single or married, filing jointly depending on when their spouse died. Taxpayers can claim head of household status if they are single and pay more than 50 percent of the cost of keeping a residence for the year for an unmarried child or grandchild; a married child or grandchild they can claim as their dependent; their mother or father whom they claim as a dependent; or a close relative whom they can claim as a dependent. Some married couples file separate returns because each wants to be responsible for only his or her own tax. But a couple will almost always pay more federal tax filing separately than filing jointly.

- *Gross income, adjusted gross income, and taxable income.* Your gross income comprises all income subject to taxes before you subtract any deductions, adjustments, or exemptions. Gross income includes wages, salaries, tips, interest, dividends, alimony, taxable pensions, rents, royalties, and most other money earned by working or investing. You can receive some money that is not considered part of your gross income; this includes interest you earn from most municipal bonds and other nontaxable investments, certain death benefits, money you receive for personal injuries, money paid by your health insurance company, and tax-free gifts.

  Your adjusted gross income is your gross income minus certain types of deductible expenses and investments. These deductions are adjustments you can claim without filing the Schedule A form for itemizing deductions. Your adjusted gross income will be important if you plan to deduct medical expenses, casualty losses, employee business expenses, or other miscellaneous itemized deductions. All must meet certain threshholds corresponding to your adjusted gross income before you can claim them as deductions.

  Your taxable income is the figure you get after subtracting your deductions and exemptions from your adjusted gross income.

- *Marginal tax rate or tax bracket.* The marginal tax rate is the amount of tax imposed on each extra dollar of income. As your income rises, your marginal tax rate goes up. Your deductions are based on your marginal tax rate. If you have a 28 percent marginal tax rate, you are in the 28 percent tax bracket and you will save $28 in taxes for every extra $100 of deductions you amass until the deductions bring your income level down to the 15 percent bracket. At that point, every $100 deduction will save you $15 in taxes.

It's important to know your marginal tax rate when making investment decisions. The closer you are to being in the next tax bracket with a higher marginal rate, the more attention you should give to tax-saving investments such as municipal bonds. The higher your tax bracket, the more valuable deductions become. Tax reform has probably made all your deductions worth less than before because you are most likely in a lower tax bracket now.

- *Tax withholding.* One basic rule in tax planning: It's not only how much you pay in taxes, it's when you pay it. If you are ecstatic when you receive a huge refund after filing your tax return in April, maybe you should be a little less cheerful. The refund really means you have given Uncle Sam an interest-free loan during the year. If you have the correct amount of taxes withheld from your paycheck during the year, you will probably get a small refund or perhaps no refund at all. You will, however, have the use of more of your money all year round rather than giving it to the government to hold for you.

- *Standard deduction.* The standard deduction had been called the zero bracket amount for a few years, but the tax reform law changed it back to its original name. Think of it as a freebie tax break. The standard deduction is that part of your income that is not subject to taxes. Once your deductions exceed the standard deduction, it pays to itemize. Otherwise, you will not be claiming deductions that are rightfully yours.

- *Exemptions.* Everyone who files a tax form can claim at least one personal exemption, worth about $2,050. The personal exemption amounts are phased out for high-income taxpayers.

You can also claim exemptions for your dependents: children, aged parents, and others you support. The IRS defines a dependent child as one who lives with his or her parents and is under age 19; one who is older than 19 with annual income of less than $1,000; or one who is a full-time student, regardless of age or income. Stepchildren, adopted children, and foster children who live with you all year can also qualify as dependents. You can claim an exemption for a child or parent who did not live with you during the year if you can prove you furnished more than half the person's total support.

In divorced families, the parent with whom the children live is automatically entitled to claim the dependency exemptions. One exception is that the custodial parent can give the exemption to an ex-spouse by signing a mutual agreement. An important tax reform change affecting the rules on exemptions: Children who are eligible to be claimed as dependents can no longer claim their own personal exemption on their tax returns.

- *Tax credits.* The most appealing type of write–offs—tax credits—are subtracted directly from your tax bill. Instead of saving, say, 28 cents on each $1 you write off, you slash $1 off your tax for each $1 of credits.

  The most commonly claimed credit is the one for child and dependent care expenses. To claim it, you must pay more than half the cost of running the house (property taxes, mortgage interest or rent, utility bills, repairs, homeowner's insurance, and food eaten at home) for a dependent or a child under age 15. You must also be working for pay, looking for a job, or attending school full-time when you incur the expenses. Married couples generally must file jointly to claim this write-off. The credit is figured as a percentage of the first $2,400 of expenses for one child or dependent and the first $4,800 for two or more chidren or dependents. The percentage works on a sliding scale, ranging from 30 percent if adjusted gross income is more than $28,000. The maximum child and dependent care credit allowed is $720 for one child and $1,440 for two or more.

- *Capital gains and losses.* The tax reform law changed the definition of capital gains radically. Before the law passed, if you had an investment that appreciated in value and sold it after holding it for at least six months, the profit was considered a long-term capital gain. Only 40 percent of the profit was taxed, making the top capital gains rate 20 percent (40 percent times the 50 percent tax bracket). If you sold the asset in less than six months, the profit was considered a short-term capital gain, and it was fully taxable at your tax rate, up to 50 percent. Now capital gains have pretty much lost their favored tax status because the partial exclusion is gone. The maximum tax rate on long-term capital gains is 28 percent.

The rules concerning investment losses also were shaken up by tax reform. Before the law, you could deduct capital losses first against any capital gains and then up to $3,000 of other income—but only half your long-term losses (from assets held more than six months) were deductible against other income. Now you can deduct all your long-term losses, up to $3,000. The upshot: You will probably pay more in taxes on your investment gains and be able to deduct more in taxes on your investment losses.

- *Alternative minimum tax and tax preferences.* Most people can compute their taxes using the standard tax tables. But if you have just realized a capital gain that rivals your salary or if you have relied heavily on limited-partnership tax shelters, you have to figure your tax both the normal way and under a special formula known as the alternative minimum tax. You pay whichever tax is higher. This tax was created by Congress as an attempt to ensure that everyone pays a fair share of taxes. The tax reform law made the tax stricter.

  Previously, the alternative minimum tax was a flat 20 percent. The income that was taxable included some items that were not normally taxed, known as preference items, such as the capital gains exclusion and some write-offs common to investment real estate and tax-sheltered limited partnerships. The tax also required you to give up all itemized deductions except mortgage interest and contributions to charity. To calculate your alternative minimum tax, you added the specified tax preferences to your taxable income and subtracted one large exemption equal to $30,000 if you filed as a single, $40,000 if you filed jointly.

  Now the alternative minimum tax rate is 24 percent. The exemptions are phased out once your alternative minimum taxable income exceeds $150,000 if you file jointly or $112,500 if you file singly. A few items have been added to the preference list, including untaxed appreciation of charitable contributions of property and interest on some municipal bonds issued after August 7, 1986.

Managing Your Money Tip

You can get an estimate of your alternative minimum tax liability with Managing Your Money. Just select Alternative Minimum Tax from the Tax submenu. Fill in any items that don't have an asterisk in front of then, then press F10 to see what your AMT liability stands to be.

- *Estimated taxes.* In addition to or instead of taxes you have with-held from your income, you may have to send the IRS quarterly estimated income tax payments along with Form 1040-ES. Most self-employed people file estimated taxes. The tax reform law requires more people to file quarterly. You may have to pay estimated taxes if, after subtracting withheld taxes and tax credits, your tax liability for the year is still over $500. If you receive less than $500 in unearned income such as interest and dividends, or if your gross income will be less than $20,000 ($10,000 if you are married and both you and your spouse receive wages; $5,000 if you are married but cannot file a joint return), you may not have to pay estimated taxes. Estimated tax payments are due in April, June, September, and January.

  Before the tax reform law, if you owed estimated taxes and had paid less than 80 percent of the amount by the due date of the last quarter's payment, the IRS could levy a nondeductible tax penalty equal to roughly 13 percent of the underpayment. But the new law says you must fork over at least 90 percent of the owed amount or you could be subject to the penalty. There are a few escape hatches from the underpayment penalty. You generally will be okay if your estimated tax payments equal your total tax liability for the preceding year. The IRS may also forgive the penalty if your underpayment is due to illness, disaster, or another unusual circumstance. You need to explain the reason for your underpayment when you file Form 2110, which is used to report underpayments of estimated tax.

TAX FORMS AND AMENDED RETURNS

You may be paying too much in taxes simply because you file the wrong tax forms. Some forms do not allow you to claim deductions and credits that others do. Some write-offs require you to complete special forms. The table on pages 102 and 103 provides a rundown of the most important tax forms, along with advice about which forms you should use.

Roughly 2 million people amend their tax returns each year, usually to get a refund of taxes overpaid in earlier years. But you can also file an amended return if you realize you used the wrong tax tables or forgot to report income. Filing an amended return is a snap. Just get Form 1040X and complete it within three years of the date the original tax return was filed or two years from the time the tax was paid, whichever is later. There is a seven-year grace period if you will be asking for a refund based on a deduction for bad debts or worthless securities. When you file an amended return, you must explain any changes to your previously reported income, deductions, and credits.

Tax Forms

Form	When to Use
1040EZ	For single filers with no dependents. Can't be used if you want to itemize deductions, if your taxable income exceeds $50,000, or if you have any dividend income or more than $400 in interest income.
1040A (short form)	For those whose income is only wages salaries, tips, interest, dividends, and unemployment compensation and whose taxable income is below $50,000. Can't be used if you want to itemize deductions or claim adjustments to income other than contributions to an IRA. Can't claim the child-care credit.
1040 (long form)	Must be used if your taxable income exceeds $50,000 or if you had interest, dividends, or other unearned income of at least $1,000. Must also be used if you are a widow or widower with a dependent child. This form lets you itemize deductions and claim Keogh and alimony payments.
1040-ES	Used for making quarterly estimated tax payments.
1040X	Used for filing an amended tax return.
2106	Used for claiming business expense deductions.
2119	Used when you sell or exchange your principal residence.
2210	Used if you underpaid your quarterly estimated taxes.

Tax Forms

Form	When to Use
2441	Used for claiming the tax credit for child-care or dependent-care expenses.
4562	Used for claiming depreciation.
4684	Used for claiming casualty or theft deductions.
4868	Used for receiving a four-month extension to file an income tax return.
5500-C	Used for claiming deductions for a Keogh plan.
6251	Used for paying the alternative minimum tax.
W-4	Filed with your employer to claim the proper number of withholding allowances so the right amount of income tax will be withheld from wages during the year.
Schedules A and B	Used for listing itemized deductions and interest or dividend income if either exceeded $400.
Schedule C	Used for reporting a profit or loss from your business.
Schedule D	Used for reporting sales of property such as stocks, bonds, or real estate that qualify as capital gains or losses.
Schedule E	Used for reporting income from rents, royalties, partnerships, estates, or trusts.
Schedule SE	Used for figuring Social Security taxes if you are self-employed.

TAX-CUTTING INVESTMENT AND SAVINGS STRATEGIES

There are really two ways to lower your tax bill: You can defer taxes and pay them in the future, ideally when your tax rate is lower, or you can avoid paying the taxes altogether. Usually, deferring taxes is about the best you can do. There are a few ways to avoid paying taxes, but many of the old methods have been legislated out of existence.

Before you start looking for ways to cut your tax bill by investing and saving shrewdly, ask yourself whether you are willing to risk a tax audit. The answer will determine how aggressive a tax cutter you want to be. The more aggressive you are, the more likely the IRS will want to have a word with you sometime.

Most tax-cutting investment and saving techniques are, thankfully, low audit risks. They are perfectly legal. As long as you have the proper paperwork and report your income and deductions honestly on your tax return, there is no need to fear the IRS.

Low-audit-risk investments include:

- *Your house.* Here's a shelter that's truly a shelter. Actually, after tax reform owning your home is one of the most reliable tax shelters around. Mortgage interest and property taxes are fully deductible, and it is unlikely that Congress will take away those popular write-offs. You can defer taxes on the gains on the sale of your home as long as you buy another home within two years costing as much as or more than the one you sold.

- *Individual retirement accounts.* The tax reform law has made IRAs less attractive tax shelters for many people by limiting their deductibility. Nevertheless, an IRA is still an easy way to defer taxes on your investment earnings. You won't owe taxes on your IRA earnings until you withdraw from your account. The tax rules governing IRAs, which are described more fully in Chapter 8, state that if neither you nor your spouse is covered by a corporate pension or profit-sharing plan, you can deduct $2,000 per worker for your IRA contributions ($2,250 for a one-income couple). But if you are single and are covered by a company plan, regardless of whether your benefits are vested yet, you can claim the full $2,000 deduction only if you earn $25,000 or less annually in adjusted gross income. If your income is higher, you lose $200 in deductions for every $1,000 in additional income. If your income is $35,000 or more, none of your IRA contributions are tax deductible. Married couples who file jointly and are covered by a company plan see their IRA deduction sliced when their adjusted gross income is between $40,000 and $50,000. Above $50,000, the deduction vanishes.

All IRAs require you to pay taxes on money withdrawn. If you take cash out before turning 59 1/2, you will also owe a tax penalty equal to 10 percent of the money withdrawn. There are two exceptions to the 10 percent penalty: You will not owe it if you are permanently disabled or if you take the money out in equal installments over the course of your lifetime.

- *Keogh plans for the self-employed.* If you run your own business, even if it is a part-time job, you can get a great tax shelter with a Keogh plan. A Keogh lets you put away up to 25 percent of your net self-employment income or $30,000, whichever is less. You can have a Keogh as well as an IRA. Investment earnings from a Keogh are free of taxes until you take the money out. There is a 10 percent penalty for withdrawals made before you turn age 59 1/2. One catch: Keoghs are paperwork monsters. At the very least, you will have to file a special form with the IRS each year, Form 5500-C. The deadline for filing the form for most self-employed persons is July 31.

There are a few types of Keoghs. The simplest are defined contribution plans whose maximum annual payment is fixed. Within this type of Keogh, there are two choices. The first is a money-purchase Keogh plan that lets you shelter from taxes as much as 25 percent of your income, up to $30,000 annually. You must contribute the same percentage every year, unless your business shows a loss. The alternative is the more flexible but less juicy profit-sharing Keogh plan. With this type of plan, you can contribute only 15 percent of your self-employment income, up to $30,000. You can alter your contributions each year.

The more complicated Keogh is called a defined-benefit plan. You can deduct the amount that will let you retire on the average of your highest earnings in three consecutive years, up to $90,000 if you will begin making withdrawals at 65 or $40,000 if you will retire at 55. The older you are, the more you can stash away each year to reach your goals. So a defined-benefit Keogh is really best for people 45 or older who can afford to put aside as much as the law allows. Defined-benefit Keoghs come with more paperwork than defined-contribution plans. You must file a special form every year with the IRS and get an actuary to certify that your calculations are valid. Expect to pay a lawyer about $1,000 to draw up the documents for a defined-benefit Keogh. The actuary may charge $500 or so every year for his or her work.

Managing Your Money Tip

> If you've budgeted for IRA or Keogh contributions in Budget Categories under the Money submenu (or accounted for contributions in Spend Money), your contributions will be included in the Form 1040 Worksheet in the Tax submenu. Just press F10. If you want to use a different amount, enter that amount in the Form 1040 Worksheet. Whatever amount included in the Form 1040 Worksheet will be included as an adjustment that reduces taxable income in the Form 1040 tax estate in the Tax submenu.

- *Simplified employee pensions.* Like a Keogh but without all the paperwork, a simplified employee pension (SEP) is another type of shelter for the self-employed. Your company must have twenty-five or fewer employees. With a SEP, you can contribute up to $7,000 a year of your pretax pay. You can open a SEP where you would open an IRA: a bank, brokerage house, insurance company, or mutual fund. SEP contributions can be made as late as April 15 and still allow you to take a deduction for the previous year. Like IRAs and Keoghs, SEPs come with a 10 percent penalty for early withdrawals.

- *Company savings plans.* One of the best and most painless ways to save taxes is by investing through a company savings plan. Earnings are tax-deferred until you withdraw them. Many companies match all or part of employee contributions, boosting tax-deferred returns. In some plans, known as 401(k) salary reduction plans, you invest with pretax dollars, giving you the effect of a tax deduction. The tax reform law limits annual 401(k) contributions to $8,728—the figure rises with inflation annually—but that's more than most people can afford anyway. (For more on these plans, see Chapter 8.) The tax reform law made company plans somewhat less attractive, largely by restricting withdrawals from the plans and requiring that taxes be paid sooner on withdrawals. Even so, company plans are still dandy tax shelters.

- *Tax-free money-market funds.* Like regular money-market funds, these are mutual funds that invest in short-term fixed-income securities. But your earnings from these funds are free of federal taxes and sometimes partially free of state and local taxes, too. You can withdraw cash from a tax-free money fund whenever you wish. Before tax reform, tax-free money funds were quite attractive for middle- and upper-income investors. But now that tax rates have fallen, these funds might not necessarily yield more, on an after-tax basis, than taxable money funds. Before investing in a tax-free money fund, compare it with a taxable fund and see which would give you the better return in your tax bracket.

- *Municipal bonds.* These bonds, issued by states and localities, pay interest that is generally free from federal taxes. (The tax reform law has also created a new type of muni bond known as a taxable municipal; its interest is not tax-free.) If you buy a bond whose issuer is in your state, the interest will be free from state and perhaps even local taxes, too. Some muni bonds, known as zero-coupon bonds, are bought at a huge discount and redeemed at a much higher face value in the future. You don't receive the tax-free income until you cash in the zero-coupon bond. The best way to invest in municipal bonds is through a municipal bond mutual fund or unit trust. Either will give you diversification that you probably could not afford otherwise.

- *Treasury bonds and U.S. Savings Bonds.* Interest from these bonds is taxed by the federal government but not by state or local governments. So if you live in a state with prohibitive income taxes, these government bonds could be a nifty tax shelter.

- *Whole-life insurance, universal-life insurance, variable-life insurance, and variable annuities.* As with an IRA, your earnings grow tax-deferred. You will owe a 10 percent tax penalty if you take money out of an annuity before turning 59 1/2. Now that your IRA might not be deductible, an annuity or a life insurance policy might be a worthy alternative. One advantage: There is no maximum annual contribution when buying an annuity or insurance policy as there is with an IRA. However, the annuities and policies are far less flexible than IRAs because their investment choices are limited to what the insurer offers. Fees are also often higher than those usually charged for IRAs or mutual funds.

- *Low-write-off limited partnerships.* The tax reform law has pretty much killed limited partnerships that let you deduct more than you invest. But low-write-off deals whose deductions are smaller are still around. Sold by stockbrokers, financial planners, and insurance agents, these programs tend to be real estate partnerships that do not borrow a lot to buy or develop properties. The real estate could be apartments, offices, stores, warehouses, hotels, even fast-food franchises. When the partnerships do not take out any mortgages, they are called all-cash deals. Your tax breaks in low-write-off partnerships come from depreciation of the properties, any mortgage interest or property taxes paid, and expenses the partnership incurs in managing the buildings. You receive a portion of the rents as income. Low-write-off partnerships are called public programs, and they are registered with the Securities and Exchange Commission. Minimum investment is typically $5,000 or so ($2,000 for IRAs).

The trouble with these partnerships is that they usually are illiquid. They usually last for 5 to 15 years, at which point the properties are sold off. If you want to sell your partnership units earlier, most buyers will pay you only 70 percent of what the units are worth. A fairly new type of program, called a master limited partnership, gives you potential liquidity because its units can be traded on major stock exchanges.

Medium-audit-risk investments include:

- *Income shifting.* Before tax reform, parents had a neat tax dodge. They could put money in a trust or custodial account for their children and cut the family tax bill dramatically. Earnings on the cash were taxed at the low tax rate of their kids—if the children had enough income to owe any taxes at all. In fact, until a few years ago, parents could even give their child an interest-free loan and get the same tax savings.

Income shifting is now down, but not out. Now, if you give your young child only a small amount of money, the income will still probably escape taxation because your child won't have enough to pay taxes. You can go to a bank or brokerage firm and set up a custodial account for your child under age 14. As long as he or she receives less than $1,000 in unearned income (interest, dividends, capital gains), the earnings either will be taxed at the child's rate or won't be taxed at all. So you could put $20,000 in a bank certificate of deposit earning 5 percent interest and still benefit from income shifting. Or you could invest the money in tax-free municipal bonds or stocks that do not pay dividends, at least until your child turns 14. At that point, all his or her unearned income above $1,000 would be taxed at his or her low or zero tax bracket. You might then move the money out of tax—free investments and into taxable ones. Of course, once your child reached the age of majority in your state—18 in most places—the principal and earnings would be the child's to do with as he or she pleases.

Although income shifting is perfectly legal, the IRS is suspicious of the technique. So don't be too surprised if an IRS auditor questions you about money you give to your child. If you have the proper documentation, however, there is nothing to worry about.

The tax reform law ended the income-shifting technique known as the Clifford trust, however. Previously, you could put money or property into a Clifford trust for your child, the earnings would be taxed at the child's tax rate, and you could get your principal back in ten years. But earnings from a Clifford trust set up after March 1, 1986 are taxed at the parent's tax rate, regardless of the child's age.

- *Vacation homes and rental properties.* You can still deduct all the mortgage interest and property taxes you pay on your second home, providing you use the home personally more than 14 days a year or 10 percent of the number of days you rent it out, whichever is more. But if the home or any other real estate you own is a rental property, your deductions could be limited under the tax reform law.

The size of your tax write-off for rental property will be determined by whether you actively manage the property and how large your income is. You will be allowed to deduct your mortgage interest, property taxes, depreciation, and expenses for the house as long as the total is no more than your rental income plus any passive partnership income you may have. If your expenses exceed the income, you can deduct up to $25,000 of the house's annual losses against your salary and any investment income as long as you meet three tests: (1) you own at least 10 percent of the property, (2) you are active in management decisions, and (3) your adjusted gross income is less than $100,000. You lose 50 cents of deductible losses for every dollar of your additional income between $100,000 and

$150,000. If you make $150,000 or more, you cannot deduct losses exceeding your passive income (the income from rental real estate and other partnerships). If you own less than 10 percent of the property or leave the management to someone else, you can write off losses only up to the amount of your income from the house and other passive investments.

You can write off losses up to the amount of your passive income. But you will be able to carry over unused tax losses as long as you own the property and use them in years when you have passive income as well as in the year you sell the building.

The same rules apply to other rental properties. Now that you can't necessarily deduct all your tax losses from owning real estate, it is more important than ever to invest only in buildings that will produce a positive cash flow—its rents must exceed your maintenance and financing costs—immediately or within a year. You can bet that the IRS will closely study tax returns of people with vacation homes and rental properties to be sure they are playing by the new rules.

The highest audit-risk investments are:

- *High-write-off limited partnerships.* The IRS says that any tax shelter that lets you deduct more than twice the amount you invest is an "abusive tax shelter" and one it is likely to audit. Such programs, which are called private partnerships and are not registered with the Securities and Exchange Commission, are not necessarily illegal. But their sponsors could be exaggerating the allowable deductions. These partnerships, like public programs, are illiquid. In fact, it is generally much harder to find a buyer for a private deal than a public deal because fewer people need the large deductions.

  The tax reform law makes high-write-off shelters far less attractive than in the past. Now you can deduct only an amount equal to your passive income from partnerships and rental properties (the limits are phased in for shelters bought before the law was signed). If the deal promises a lot of deductions but no income, the write-offs will be useless. So only consider investing in a high-write-off partner-ship if you and your tax adviser are convinced the promised deductions are legitimate and that you will have enough passive income to put the deductions to good use.

TAX-CUTTING BORROWING STRATEGIES

Until recently, borrowing money was a smart tax move. Interest on loans and credit cards was tax deductible, so Uncle Sam subsidized the cost of your borrowing. By incurring hundreds or thousands of dollars in interest, you increased your chance of being able to itemize deductions and claim additional write-offs. But now that tax reform has sharply restricted interest deductions and—through lower brackets—cut the value of any interest write-offs, you need to think seriously before taking out any new loans or running up your credit card tab. In 1986, all of your presonal interest was probably deductible. Now, none of it is—except for loans on your first or second home. The changes do not mean you should pay cash for every purchase. But they do mean you should be sure that when you borrow you are paying the lowest interest rate possible.

Deductions have been eliminated for payments on consumer interest: personal loans, credit cards, car loans, vacation loans, and the like. But the law carves out special exceptions for a home-equity loan on your first or second home, though Congress slightly restricted those exceptions in 1987 affecting loans taken out after January 1, 1988. So, if you need to borrow, you should strongly consider turning to your house for cash. Tax reform said you can fully deduct all interest on a home-equity loan up to the total of your purchase price of your house, purchasing expenses and the cost of improvements, medical expenses or your child's education. The change in 1987 said that, starting in 1988, all interest on new home-equity loans up to $100,000 is fully deductible, regardless of the house's purchase price, any improvements, or the way you use the borrowed money.

But the deductibility of new home-equity interest exceeding $100,000 does depend on how you use the money. If the excess is used for personal purposes, none of it will be deductible. If the excess is used in your trade or business, the interest is 100 percent deductible. If the excess is used to invest, the interest is deductible up to the amount of your investment income (money from dividends, interest, capital gains, and partnerships).

Don't borrow against your house casually, though. If you cannot make the loan payments, the lender could take away your home. You may also find that the fees charged for a home-equity loan could wind up making the loan more expensive than alternative, unsecured nondeductible loans.

Are you the kind of investor who likes to take out a margin loan from his or her broker to buy additional shares of stock or mutual funds? If so, watch out. Tax reform cut these interest deductions, too. Before the law passed, you could borrow on margin or use your broker's line of credit for any purpose and deduct interest up to the amount of your investment income plus $10,000. Now, your interest on a broker-age loan will be deductible only up to the amount it is offset by invest-ment income.

And you must also be able to prove that you used the money you bor-rowed from your broker for an investment other than tax-free municipal bonds in order to claim the write-off. Interest that cannot be deducted can be carried forward to later years to offset future investment income, though.

THE RULES ON ALIMONY AND TAXES

If you are divorced, the tax reform law just might get you and your ex talking again. Reason: The law has increased both the after-tax cost of paying alimony and the after-tax amount an alimony recipient can keep. Now that tax rates are lower, someone who deducts alimony payments is likely to get a far smaller deduction than previously. Conversely, the lower tax rates also mean that someone receiving alimony is likely to keep more of it, rather than turning the cash over to the IRS.

So if you are paying alimony, you may want to petition the judge who granted you the divorce and ask for a revised ruling. You may be able to convince the judge that the tax law has created a "substantial change in circumstances" and warrants a reduction in the amount of alimony you must pay to a figure equal to your original after-tax payment.

And if you are in the midst of a divorce proceeding, you might want to get an agreement that spells out a precise after-tax alimony payment fig-ure. That way, your payments will automatically be adjusted when tax rates drop or—heaven forbid—are raised again.

SHELTERING YOURSELF IN A BUSINESS

Having your own business has always been a great tax shelter. But tax re-form makes it an even better one when compared with other shelters, such as limited partnerships, that have been hurt badly by the new law. Most of the write-offs available to entrepreneurs before tax reform are still around: Keogh plans, depreciation of business purchases, deduction of commuting costs, and many other business expenses. The law even created and enlarged a few deductions for business owners. For the first time, you can write off 25 percent of the premiums you pay for health insurance for yourself, your spouse, and your dependents. The law also lets you deduct in one year up to $10,000 of the cost of any business equipment or supplies. Previously, you could write off only up to $5,000 immediately.

The law also made it tougher for employees to claim business write-offs that entrepreneurs get. To deduct employee business expenses such as the cost of travel or transportation for work, employees must now itemize, and the write-offs will be permitted only if the total plus other miscellaneous deductions adds up to at least 2 percent of adjusted gross income.

But the tax reform law also took away some of the tax benefits of having your own business. You can no longer claim an investment tax credit for buying business property. Only 80 percent of business meals and entertainment expenses are now deductible, down from 100 percent. You must depreciate over five years a car bought after January 1, 1987, that is used for business; before tax reform, you could write off a car over three years.

THE SNOOPY EYES OF THE IRS

The IRS, like Santa Claus, now has ways of telling whether you've been naughty or nice all year. Santa has a list, but the IRS uses a sophisticated computer matching program that shows whether you reported your proper income and write-offs on your tax return. The computer compares what you said on your tax return with statements the agency has received about you from banks, brokerage firms, and government agencies. Today, the IRS can corroborate without an audit: your interest income, dividends, salaries, wages, state and local tax refunds, proceeds from the sale of investments, IRA contributions, payouts from your IRA or pension, mortgage interest deductions, and alimony income. If the IRS determines you've been naughty and failed to report all your income or have claimed tax breaks you did not deserve, you will find a letter in your mailbox demanding that you explain yourself or pay the taxes, plus any interest and penalties. The letters—and there are about 5 1/2 million mailed out annually—go out no sooner than eighteen months after tax returns are filed.

But unlike Santa, the IRS is not perfect. Its computer system still has some bugs. So if you get a letter saying the computer matching program shows you to be in error, don't assume that the computer is right. Quite possibly, you were right. For example, the computer might determine that you claimed a bigger mortgage interest deduction than you were entitled to take. But in reality, you may have sent in a mortgage payment in late December that qualified for a deduction but was not logged into the IRS computers in time for the matching.

If you pay alimony, you may receive a letter from the IRS saying the computer could not verify your alimony payments. All you need to do is give the IRS the name and Social Security number of your ex-spouse. This will enable the computer to cross-check the amount of alimony you reported with the amount your ex-spouse reported.

THE DREADED TAX AUDIT

You may be one of the millions of Americans suffering from auditphobia: fear of an IRS audit. An audit is no picnic, to be sure. On the other hand, an audit does not have to be the equivalent of your going five rounds in the ring with Evander Holyfield. It's quite possible that you will come out of an audit owing no more in taxes than you did when you went in. That is the case for about one of every five taxpayers audited. Four percent of those audited even walk away with tax refunds. And thousands of others negotiate settlements with the IRS that leave them paying more taxes but less than the agency originally demanded.

What if you lose at your audit? Unless you have committed criminal fraud, it's unlikely that you will be sent to jail. But you could wind up owing not only the taxes that were due but additional money in interest and penalties. Interest is charged from the due date of your tax return. The rate fluctuates, but it has recently been 10 percent. If the IRS determines you were negligent, you could owe a penalty equal to 5 percent of the additional tax due and another 50 percent of the interest charged on any negligent items. Should the IRS nab you on civil fraud, you will then owe 50 percent of the additional taxes due plus 50 percent of the interest due on any items of negligence.

Unless you knowingly cheat on your taxes, you can be an audit champ and not a chump if your return is examined. And that's a big IF. Only about 1.3 percent of individual tax returns are audited each year. As a rule, if you have not heard from the IRS within a year and a half of the date you mailed in your forms, you won't. To protect yourself, you should keep your back tax returns indefinitely and supporting tax documents for five years or so.

Whether your tax return will be audited depends mostly on how closely your data conform to a set of IRS formulas known as the discriminate function system, or DIF. Roughly 70 percent of returns audited are picked out by the DIF computer, which then compares certain deductions, credits, and exemptions with the norms for taxpayers with your income. Only the top IRS officials know precisely what variables are considered by DIF or how much importance is assigned to each. And they're not telling. But the IRS openly admits that the higher your so-called total positive income—income before subtracting tax shelter losses and other adjustments—the more likely you are to be audited.

Managing Your Money Tip

Andrew Tobias' TaxCut features an audit function that not only checks your return for errors and overlooked deductions, but also tells you when your claimed deductions exceed average deductions for taxpayers with your income.

The other returns audited are chosen by IRS computers and personnel for a variety of reasons. A few tax forms are pulled because they have been filled out by people the IRS considers to be questionable preparers. That preparer list is also top secret. Other returns, called automatics, get singled out because they show deductions for unallowable items. Still other people get audited because revenge-seeking or bounty-hunting ex-spouses, relatives, and "friends" squeal on them. The IRS pays tipsters for leads to tax cheats. Some people get audited merely because the returns of their business associates are suspect.

You could also fall victim to a special IRS campaign, such as one against deductions from abusive tax shelters. Or you could be questioned because the IRS suspects you underreported your income. Waiters, taxi drivers, beauticians, and others who get paid mostly in cash are often potential audit targets.

If you get a letter saying your return will be audited, you generally have up to six weeks to get ready for a meeting. The IRS lets you respond by mail if the deductions can be easily documented. Either way, the place to start mounting your defense is in the office of your tax preparer, discussing how to prove to the IRS that your write-offs are legitimate. This strategy session might cost you $100 or so, but the investment should pay off. You may leave confident enough to meet with the auditor on your own and save yourself the cost of paying your preparer to accompany you. That fee can easily run into hundreds of dollars.

You don't have to go to the audit at all, though. The IRS will let you send your preparer in your stead. In fact, many IRS agents prefer working this way because they can get the audit done quickly by dealing directly with another tax professional. Only a CPA, a lawyer, or an enrolled agent may represent you in an audit, though.

The most important factor in deciding the outcome of your audit will be your evidence supporting your deductions, credits, and exemptions. Receipts, bills, and diaries do not guarantee that you will keep a write-off. The auditor can throw out your deductions if he or she does not believe you are entitled to take them. But the records are the most persuasive exhibits you can lay before an examiner. When you cannot find receipts, turn to secondary sources. For example, if you do not have proof of a business meal, get your dining companion to give you a written statement describing the details of your get-together.

Your attitude during the audit and the personal chemistry between you and the auditor will help seal your fate. Your immediate impulse might be to act defiantly. But belligerence will almost surely narrow your chances of victory. Joe Girard, author of several books on salesmanship and an IRS audit target for 12 consecutive years, has five audit don'ts: (1) don't speak loudly; (2) don't smoke; (3) don't wear tinted glasses, which make you look shifty; (4) don't show up with dirty nails or hair; and (5) don't wear jewelry that might cause the auditor to think your income is higher than you reported.

Many, though not all, audit issues are negotiable. Ask your tax preparer before the audit how much of each write-off under review he or she thinks you will be able to keep. Then you will know which battles to pitch and which to ditch.

If you are not satisfied with the outcome of your audit, you can appeal on the spot to the examiner's supervisor. The supervisor will review the case and come to his or her own conclusion. If you are still not pleased, you have 30 days to ask that your case be turned over to an appeals officer. You can call for an appointment, unless the IRS says you owe $2,500 or more. Then you must make your request in writing, briefly outlining your arguments. It can take several months to get an appointment with an appeals officer.

Once you do get an appeals officer, you might find him or her more willing to concede some or all of the issues than your auditor was. But an appeals officer can also reopen an issue closed by an auditor and even question deductions that weren't discussed in the first go-round. So appeal only if you are sure your case is as tight as a Tupperware lid.

Appealing an audit in court can be a slow and expensive process. The U.S. Tax Court lets you file a petition without first paying what the IRS insists you owe. But the odds of keeping all your write-offs after a tax court tangle are slim. Your odds improve if you appeal instead in the U.S. District Court or the U.S. Claims Court. But you must first pay the taxes the IRS says are due, then hope the court will overrule. Because you can get a jury in a district court case, you might well receive a favorable ruling if your story will elicit sympathy from your peers. The U.S. Claims Court is in Washington, D.C., so appealing there may be impractical for you.

When your audit is resolved, put together a folder containing all your IRS correspondence. Such a dossier could be especially helpful if you are an audit winner. You might have to meet with the IRS again sometime, and there is no better evidence that a deduction is legitimate than a letter from an auditor allowing the write-off on an earlier return.

CHAPTER
6

MAKE YOUR
SAVINGS GROW

*Is it wiser to save $200 in a savings account or
spend it on a dress that will make a millionaire
fall in love with me? This is why I never save
any money. If I could cash in my closet, my
financial worries would be over.*
Cathy Guisewite,
cartoonist of the syndicated comic strip Cathy

WHY SAVING PAYS

Chances are, if someone asked you to write down the things you do best,
saving money wouldn't be one of them. That's understandable. After all,
there isn't much immediate satisfaction gained by putting some dollars
away on a regular basis. In fact, saving deprives you of spending money,
and few people like to inflict self-deprivation. Not saving money actually
made good economic sense in the late 70s and early 80s, when inflation
was a raging beast. Borrowing was smarter than saving then. You could
repay a loan with cheaper dollars over time, whereas inflation sapped the
value of any money in savings.

Today, however, saving money pays off in both the short term and the
long term. When inflation is low, as is now the case, the money you earn
on your savings is money you keep. Over the long run, disciplined sav-

117

ings can pay to send your child to the college of his or her choice, provide a comfortable retirement for you, allow you to fix up your home and transform it into a small castle, or permit you to take the vacation you've dreamed about for years.

Those pennies you save can add up to a bundle over time, especially if the earnings compound. Put aside $100 a month earning 8 percent compounded monthly, and in 10 years you will have more than $18,000. In 15 years, that piddling $100 a month will be worth more than $34,000. A tip: When your goal is to double your money over time, use the rule of 72. Divide 72 by the interest rate you will earn on your savings and the result will be the number of years it will take for your money to double in value. When your savings earn 8 percent, your money will double in nine years. When you're paid 12 percent, the money doubles in 6 years.

Managing Your Money Tip

Managing Your Money will tell you precisely how long it will take to double your money. Select Compound Interest from the Analyze submenu. For present value, enter the amount you want to invest. On the addition line, enter zero. (If you were going to add to the initial amount of your investment, you would point to the addition window, type in the frequency that you intend to add to your investment (D for daily, W for weekly, etc.), and the amount of that addition.) For annual yield, enter the rate of return your investment will receive. For future value, enter the amount you want to have. Press F10, and Managing Your Money will give you the precise number of years it will take to double your money.

You probably have the wherewithal to save money today like never before in your life. Most of your big purchases may be out of the way. The family income is rising steadily, and you truly may not need to spend every penny you earn. By the time you are in your late 30s or early 40s, your family should be trying to save between 5 and 10 percent of its after-tax income and increasing the percentage saved each year.

Easier said than done.

But disciplining yourself to save—or forcing yourself, if saving just isn't in your blood—is not as painful as you might think. In fact, there are a variety of ways to save money routinely that are surprisingly painless. Company savings plans and many mutual funds will automatically withhold a portion of your paycheck and save it for you, if you ask. Asset management accounts sold by brokerage houses and some banks automatically pay interest on your spare cash. So do some credit cards, such as the Sears Discover card.

You should be saving money for two purposes, really. The first is for the proverbial rainy day. That's the emergency cash reserve you need to create before investing or saving any money for any other purpose. The cash reserve should be an amount equal to between three and six months of your family's living expenses. The second purpose for saving money is to have it at your disposal in the future when you need it for a reason other than an emergency. This saving fund doubles as your serious savings and your mad money.

ALL THOSE SAVING CHOICES!

You have more opportunities to save money today than ever before. Thank banking deregulation of the early '80s for this. Historically, banks, savings and loans, and credit unions were restricted by law on the interest rate they could pay savers and the types of accounts they could offer. Mandated penalties for early withdrawals were harsh, thus discouraging people from saving. Today, the wraps are off. Financial institutions can pay whatever rate they want on savings and set their own early-withdrawal penalties. They can also sell just about any type of account you can dream up. In fact, some banks let their customers design their own accounts. If you walk in and say you want to save money in a certificate of deposit that will mature in exactly one year and two months, that's the CD you will get.

All the saving choices can be a little bewildering and frustrating. You sometimes need to be as nimble as Michael Jordan just to navigate your way through a bank lobby, past all its posterboards that advertise current rates on CDs, NOW accounts, SuperNOWs, IRAs, and the like.

Keep in mind that when looking for a place for your savings, four criteria are paramount:

- *Safety.* This is, after all, money you probably cannot afford to lose. You should be 100 percent certain that your serious savings' principal—

the amount you put in initially—will never fall. So, stay away from stocks and stock mutual funds for your savings. You could lose money with those investments if you need to withdraw cash when the stock market has dropped. You also need to feel confident about the institution that will be holding your money. Avoid financial institutions that advertise rates of return far higher than the competition. The era of financial deregulation has opened the door to plenty of con artists who boast that they will pay you 30 percent or more on your money, only to vanish after they get your cash.

- *Convenience.* Saving money is hard enough. You don't need any other impediments. Find the most convenient ways to put money away and then stick with them.

- *Liquidity.* You may need to get at your savings at any moment, particularly the emergency reserve portion. So it is essential to be able to withdraw your cash easily at any time. Don't get too hung up on 100 percent liquidity, though. Too many people have passed up IRAs and bank CDs because they were bothered by the early-withdrawal penalties attached. Yet you can usually earn more by saving money, pulling it out, and paying an early-withdrawal penalty than by not saving the money at all. IRAs and bank CDs do have liquidity—you can get your money when you want it— but it might cost you. Real estate and collectibles, by contrast, are not usually liquid investments. It takes time to sell those properties, and time is generally something you don't have when you need to tap your savings.

- *Income.* The beauty of savings is that your nest egg keeps getting bigger and bigger. When your earnings are compounded or when they are tax-deferred, your chunk of cash may grow even larger than you had imagined. Income from savings is usually paid out regularly. But some bonds, such as zero-coupon bonds, withhold interest payments until the securities mature. Stocks of new small companies or mutual funds that buy such stocks are not the place for your family's savings, because they promise potentially large gains when you sell the shares but little or no dividend income while you hold on to them.

Following is an analysis of the most common savings alternatives: company savings plans, savings accounts, certificates of deposit, money-market mutual funds, U.S. Treasury securities, annuities, and zero-coupon bonds. You can put your IRA or Keogh cash in each one, except for company savings plans. Chapter 8 discusses managing IRAs and Keoghs in greater detail.

COMPANY SAVINGS PLANS

Probably the easiest way to save money is by having your employer do it for you. Most large companies, and a growing number of smaller ones, now offer savings plans to their employees. Sometimes the employer makes all the contributions. More commonly, an employee can voluntarily contribute to the plan through payroll deductions. In some instances, the employer will match part or all of the money the employee contributes to the plan.

A matching provision is a spectacular benefit and one you should take advantage of if it's offered. In a plan that matches 50 cents for every dollar you put in, you will get at least a 50 percent return on your money even if the plan itself doesn't earn much. Say you earn $35,000 a year and get annual raises of 7 percent. If you routinely put 6 percent of your pay into a company savings plan earning 10 percent a year and your employer has a 50-cent matching provision, in 15 years your savings will be worth more than $150,000.

Usually, you contribute money to plans with after-tax dollars, but the 401(k) plan [named for Section 401(k) of the tax code] lets you invest with pretax dollars. All employee and employer contributions are excluded from your taxable income and grow untaxed until you withdraw them. By law, you can only contribute up to $8,728 a year to a 401(k) plan, although the total of contributions from you and your employer can reach 25 percent of your pay or $30,000, whichever is less. Before tax reform, when you could personally invest up to $30,000 in a 401(k) plan, companies typically let employees set aside up to 10 percent of their paychecks in 401(k)s. Now that the amount an employee can contribute has been lowered, it's likely that businesses will also cut the percentage of pay their workers can put into the plans.

Company savings plans invest their money in various ways: in company stock; in a diversified group of stocks or bonds; in money-market securities; and in guaranteed investment contracts (GICs). A GIC, usually purchased through an insurance company, is similar to a bank certificate of deposit. It provides a guaranteed rate of return for a period of time such as one year or five years but might pay a higher rate if its investments score well. Your "serious savings" money should go into either the GIC or the money-market securities option rather than the more volatile stock fund.

Liquidity in these plans varies from company to company, but the tax reform law has made it more expensive to take your money out of a company plan. Now, if you withdraw cash from a plan while you are working for the company but before you turn 59 1/2, you will owe the IRS a penalty equal to 10 percent of the amount withdrawn. Exceptions: The penalty will be waived if you become permanently disabled or need the cash to pay medical bills or alimony. (This is similar to the penalty assessed on early withdrawals from IRAs.) Lately, a growing number of firms have also tightened their own withdrawal provisions, restricting withdrawals to people who can prove a financial hardship. Still, many plans permit withdrawals with no questions asked.

Some plans also let you borrow from your vested balance and charge you interest rates lower than those charged by traditional lenders. You can usually repay the money in 5 to 15 years. The tax reform law has also tightened up on these borrowing privileges, however. You cannot borrow more than $50,000 minus your highest outstanding loan balance during the past twelve months or the greater of $10,000 or half your accrued benefit under the plan, whichever is less. For most employees, interest on a 401(k) plan loan is no longer tax deductible. You now must defer deducting the interest you pay to borrow from a 401(k) plan or the interest on a loan from any company plan if you are considered a "key employee" of the firm. Instead of deducting the interest, you will be allowed to reduce the taxable amount of the sum you borrow by the interest you will owe. (And some call this tax simplification!)

If you and your spouse work for pay, compare your company savings plans before putting money into them. Size up each for its investment alternatives, withdrawal and borrowing privileges, pretax or after-tax feature, and company match. Then put as much as you can into the best plan.

SAVINGS ACCOUNTS AND CERTIFICATES OF DEPOSIT

Safety is the biggest draw of a savings account or CD at a bank, savings and loan, or credit union (where accounts are called share drafts and CDs are share certificates). Accounts of up to $100,000 are generally insured by the federal government; if a savings institution isn't federally insured, don't save there. You can get liquidity and attractive yields, too, although not necessarily together.

The most important rule about savings accounts and CDs is that the longer you agree to tie your money up, the higher the interest rate you will get. When money-market accounts—the shortest term available—are paying 3.5 percent, 6-month CDs pay about 4 percent, 1-year CDs pay about 4.2 percent and 5-year CDs pay about 6 percent. The corollary to this rule is that the longer you agree to tie your money up, the more you will be penalized for taking your money out early, generally speaking.

Other institutions that now sell savings accounts and CDs include brokerage houses, loan companies, and even some department stores. Each sets its own rates, maturities, and withdrawal penalties. Banking competition has become so fierce that the differences among the accounts and CDs, no matter what the institution, have become small. As soon as one bank in town comes out with a super-duper bonus interest rate, most of its competitors match it.

You can pretty much write off the passbook account, the NOW account, and the superNOW account as places for your savings. They don't reward you enough for saving. The passbook, when it can still be found, usually pays a paltry 3 percent to 4 percent. The NOW account pays the same rate as a passbook account but throws in checking, for a fee. The superNOW account is a souped-up NOW, paying a slightly higher interest rate for unlimited checking.

The money-market deposit account is truly the place to begin shopping for a home for your money. The interest rate fluctuates daily; money-market accounts tend to yield slightly less than six-month Treasury bills. You can withdraw money at will at a branch or automatic teller machine, without a penalty. The money-market account lets you write checks but limits you to three per month other than ones you write out to "cash." The minimum deposit varies, but $1,000 or $2,500 is common. Your interest rate might drop if your balance falls below the minimum deposit amount. Certificates of deposit are designed for savers who won't need their money right away. Maturities are all over the lot, but the most common ones are six months, 1 year, and 5 years. Typical minimum deposits are $500 or $1,000; some institutions take as little as $100. You generally cannot add to a certificate after you open it, although some places permit additional contributions at the initial interest rate.

Certificates of deposit require trading off liquidity for a higher return. Unlike money-market accounts, CDs have early-withdrawal penalties whose severity runs the gamut. Brokerage houses, which often sell CDs they buy from federally insured banks and S&Ls across the country, waive early-withdrawal penalties. But wait. If you want out of a brokered CD early, you must sell it like a bond and take whatever a buyer is willing to pay. If depositors can get a higher rate on new CDs, they won't want to pay the full face value for your old one, so you could suffer a loss by selling it early.

When you start shopping around for the best rate on a savings account or CD, don't drive yourself crazy. Unless you are looking for a place to put about $50,000 or more, the difference between an account paying 4 percent and one paying 4.2 percent is piddling. You can keep up with current interest rates on accounts and CDs by reading the "Scorecard" column published monthly in *Money* magazine. The column provides national interest rate averages and compares them with rates a month and a year ago.

A few additional pointers:

- Savings and loans and credit unions usually pay higher rates than the competition. Fees and required minimum balances are often lowest at credit unions, too.

- There are bargain days for CDs. Some banks raise their rates by a percentage point or so at Christmas. That's the time when banks are especially in need of cash because many of their customers are drawing on their accounts.

- Compare total returns on CDs, not just interest rates. Practically every institution calculates its interest differently. Some compound continuously, some daily, some weekly, some monthly, some quarterly, some semiannually, some annually. Some advertise simple interest, some compound interest.

  You will go nuts trying to compare rates that are compounded differently. Instead, determine when you want a CD to come due—in six months, a year, five years, whatever. Then, call a half-dozen or so financial institutions, tell them the amount of money you want to invest and the maturity date you have in mind, and ask how much money you will have when your CD comes due. This question might throw the banker temporarily. If he says he can't tell you, ask for someone else who can. If you still get no answer, search elsewhere.

- Ask whether your return will vary depending on the amout you deposit. Some places pay higher rates on deposits above certain amounts, such as $10,000. You might have to fork over slightly more than you had anticipated, but the added oomph could be worth it.

- Ask what the early-withdrawal penalty is on CDs. Walk away if the penalty is more than the loss of one month's interest for a CD of less than a year, or more than three months' interest for a CD with a longer term.

- You can usually get the best returns on savings accounts and CDs by casting your net across the country. Although banks are still legally prohibited from having branches outside their home states, savers can seek out banking bargains by phone and mail nationwide. You can probably find a bank somewhere else paying about 1/2 to 1 percentage point more than banks where you live. This means that for a 29-cent stamp you can earn an extra $100 a year on a $10,000 deposit.

Shopping for a savings account or CD outside your area takes a little doing. Just about every financial institution accepts out-of-state deposits, but most don't advertise nationally. The stockbrokers who sell CDs don't necessarily have the highest rates in the nation. The discount brokerage firm Charles Schwab has a toll-free hotline (800-543-8700), updated weekly, that provides names of about twelve institutions paying high rates. You can call Schwab to buy you a CD from one of those banks or S&Ls. But the rate may be as much as a quarter of a percent lower than what you would get by calling the institution yourself. If you want to sell the CD early, Schwab will charge you $25 to $100.

A weekly newsletter can help you find the best returns: *100 Highest Yields* (P.O. Box 088888, N. Palm Beach, Fla. 33408; $98 for one year). It publishes the names and addresses of the institutions around the country paying the most on money-market accounts and CDs, their minimum deposits, and rates and yields after interest is compounded.

Once you have selected a few banks or S&Ls consistently paying high rates, call and ask for the head of the savings department or the new accounts representative for more information. Some institutions accept collect calls. Don't send any money until the bank mails written confirmation of its rates, minimum deposits, CD maturities, and withdrawal penalties as well as an application form. When you open account, write a check made out to your account number and endorse it "for deposit only."

MONEY-MARKET MUTUAL FUNDS

Before there were money-market deposit accounts, there were money market mutual funds. A money-market fund is like any other type mutual fund in the way it pools money from thousands of shareholders and invests the cash. The minimum initial investment is usually $1,000 to $5,000. Money funds differ from traditional stock and bond mutual funds by investing solely in what are known as low-risk cash equivalents: Treasury bills, certificates of deposit, corporate IOU's, and the like. Tax-free money funds—a derivative—buy low-risk short-term municipal bonds whose interest is free from federal income taxes.

As with bank money-market accounts, the interest rate on money funds fluctuates daily. The rate paid by money funds in is usually a tad higher than that for federally insured bank money-market accounts. You can find the current rate of money-market funds in the business pages of most newspapers or by calling a fund's toll-free phone number. For a list of funds, including their phone numbers, addresses, and minimum deposits, write to the Investment Company Institute, 1600 M St. N.W., Washington, D.C. 20036.

Unlike bank CDs, money funds are not federally insured. But the securities the funds buy are so safe (they are often guaranteed backed by a federal agency) that the difference in risk is insignificant. Shareholders of only one of the 350+ money funds have ever been serious danger of losing their principal. In 1978, the First Multifund for Daily Income lowered the price of each of its shares from $1 to 93 cents, in effect reducing the principal of the fund's investors. After shareholders rushed to pull their money out, First Multifund merged with another money fund.

Money funds are more liquid than bank CDs and about as liquid as money-market deposit accounts. There is no penalty for withdrawing cash from a money fund. You can write checks against your money fund, typically an unlimited number, as long as each check is for $500 or more.

Money funds are slightly less convenient than accounts from local banks. You generally invest in a fund by sending a check in the mail. Stockbrokers also sell their own in-house money funds, and a few fund sponsors, such as Fidelity and Calvert, have walk-in offices in some cities. To get your money out, you can send your fund a written redemption request along with a guarantee of your signature by your bank or stockbroker. It might take a week or more for your redemption check to arrive.

A faster withdrawal method is to tell the fund, in writing, that you want to be able to call in the future and have your money wired to your bank account for a $5 fee. Be sure the fund has a file with your fund account number, your bank account number, the bank's name and address, and a signature guarantee from the bank. Then whenever you need money, your cash will be wired to your bank account that day or the day after you call.

Upper-income people can earn more with a tax-free money fund than with a taxable money fund or money-market account. The tax-free money funds usually yield about two-thirds as much as taxable funds or money-market accounts. When taxable funds yield 4.4 percent, tax-frees yield about 3.6 percent.

Traditionally, you have had to be in a tax bracket of about 38 percent or higher before you would earn more, after taxes, with a tax-free money fund than with a taxable fund. But now that tax reform has lowered tax brackets, tax-free yields have risen accordingly. So now, tax-free money funds are worth considering if you are in the 31 percent bracket.

If you live in a state with a high income tax such as New York, California, or Massachusetts, you can also invest in a tax-free money fund that buys only issues from your state. Your yield thus escapes state taxes as well as federal taxes. These funds are also likely to lose some of their luster once the tax brackets drop next year.

U.S. TREASURY BILLS, NOTES, AND BONDS

Slightly less convenient than bank accounts or money funds, but supersafe, are securities issued by the U.S. Treasury Department. All income from Treasury securities is exempt from state and local income taxes, but not federal taxes. This tax-sheltered feature usually pushes after-tax yields on Treasuries above those of bank CD with comparable maturities.

The Treasury sells bills that mature in three months, six months and a year; notes that mature in 1 to 10 years; and bonds that mature in 10 to 30 years. Treasury bills, priced at $10,000, are sold at discount and redeemed at face value on maturity. The interest you will earn is deducted from the purchase price. Treasury notes, with denominations of $1,000 and $5,000, pay interest twice a year. Treasury bonds can be bought for $1,000 and also pay interest twice year.

Your stockbroker, or sometimes your bank, can buy T-bills, T-notes, or T-bonds for you. Expect to pay $25 to $50 for this service. You can save the charge by buying the securities directly, either in person or by mail, from one of the Federal Reserve's thirty-seven banks and offices or at the U.S. Treasury Building (Bureau of the Public Debt, Washington, D.C. 20239). Here's how:

Ask for a "tender" form for the note or bond you want to buy at the next Treasury auction. Fill out the form and enclose your payment in the form of cash, a personal check, a cashier's check, Treasury security redemption check, or matured Treasury securities. Be sure to note that you want to make a noncompetitive bid. That will give you the average yield from the auction. (If you make a competitive bid and specify the yield you want, there is a goal chance the government will reject your bid because the actual yields are lower.)

Your noncompetitive bid must be postmarked at least a day before the auction. Competitive bids can be made until 1 P.M. of the auction day. Most daily newspapers publish announcements of upcoming auctions. You can get more detailed information by sending for the free booklet with the ever-so-catchy title "Buying Treasury Securities at Federal Reserve Banks." Write to the Federal Reserve Bank of Richmond, Public Services Dept., Box 27622, Richmond, Va. 23261.

The Treasury Department recently started a service, called Treasury Direct, that cuts down on your paperwork if you buy the government's bills, notes and bonds. Instead of receiving the actual certificates, your purchases are recorded electronically at the Treasury. Your interest, principal, and refund payments are deposited, also electronically, in your savings or checking account at your local bank. You can open a Treasury Direct account when you buy U.S. bills, notes and bonds by giving Treasury the routing number of your bank or S&L, which you can get from a bank officer.

Although there is a ready market for Treasury securities, liquidity is not a strong selling point for the notes and bonds. If you want to sell your note or bond after interest rates have gone up but before your security has matured, you could suffer a loss of principal just as you could with any other form of long-term debt. So don't buy T-notes or T-bonds for your emergency cash reserve. T-bills have less of a liquidity problem because their rates fluctuate less than securities with longer-term maturities.

U.S. savings bonds might be called the ugly ducklings of saving. For years, their yields were meager and savers shunned them. But the EE savings bond program was overhauled a few years ago; yields were increased dramatically and the ducklings have been transformed into swans. Today the bonds, which mature in 10 years (12 years for those issued after November 1, 1986), provide one of the best tax-sheltered savings alternatives for the little guy. That is especially true now that tax reform has knocked the stuffing out of so many other shelters. Interest, which is free of state and local income taxes, is paid when you redeem the bonds.

Savings bonds are especially useful if you don't have much money to put away just now. You can buy EE bonds for as little as $25 (worth $50 at maturity) through banks, stockbrokers, and company payroll plans. The bonds pay a variable rate equal to 85 percent of five-year Treasury securities—but only if you hang on to them for at least five years. The Treasury guarantees a minimum 6 percent return (down from 7.5 percent in October 1986) if you hold the bonds to maturity. Redeem the bonds early and you may get a yield as low as 4.16 percent. Redemption's are not allowed until you have owned the savings bonds for at least six months. Call 1-800-US-BONDS or ask your banker for the current rate and guarantee for EE bonds.

ANNUITIES

Life insurance agents, stockbrokers, and financial planners sell another convenient long-term savings account called an annuity. You can buy one with a single payment, typically $5,000 or more ($100 for IRAs or Keoghs), or through monthly contributions. As with an IRA or an insurance policy with a savings element, earnings from an annuity grow tax-deferred until they are withdrawn. You can take out your principal and the annuity's earnings in a lump sum or in fixed monthly payments for the rest of your life (receiving money monthly is called "annuitizing"). Then you will owe taxes on the earnings but not on the principal. You can defer the taxes ever longer by withdrawing money from the annuity and reinvesting it within 60 days in another tax-sheltered account, such as an IRA.

The tax-deferral feature gives an annuitant a big advantage over someone stuffing money in a taxable money-market fund or bank CD. A 35-year old who puts $10,000 in an annuity earning an average of 8 percent a year will have more than $100,000 in tax-deferred earnings by the time he or she is 65. At that point, the person could take out more than $1,000 a month for life.

The better annuities are safe and generate income well. Liquidity is a big drawback for all annuities, however. The company will hit you with hefty penalties if you take money out during the first five years or so that you own an annuity. So don't even think about buying an annuity for short-term savings.

The safety of your annuity depends on the company that sells it and the investments the company makes. All annuities guarantee your principal. But the guarantee is only as good as the company that makes it. Baldwin-United, one of the biggest annuity sponsors, went bankrupt a few years ago and couldn't make good on the guarantees it made to its annuitants. You can't be absolutely certain that any annuity sponsor will remain in business as long as you are alive. But you will be safest by dealing only with an insurer listed as A+ or A++ from A. M. Best & Co, an independent rating firm.

Annuities come in two types: fixed and variable. A fixed-rate annuity guarantees a rate of return for a specific period of time, such as one year or five years. The rate is about the same as what you would get from a bank CD of a comparable maturity, although the earnings are tax-deferred. When the time is up, the annuity gives you a new guaranteed return. The interest rate on a fixed annuity will never fall below a low minimum, such as 3 percent. A variable-rate annuity invests in stocks, bonds, or money-market securities. You choose the investment and you can generally switch among the portfolios as often as once a month.

Fixed annuities and variable annuities that invest in money-market securities are your best choices for long-term savings. Variable annuities invested in stocks and bonds are more suitable for the speculative portion of your investment portfolio.

When shopping for an annuity, ask your insurance agent, stock-broker, or financial planner to show you the annual rates of return, over the past ten years, for various annuities rated A+ or A++ by Best. Returns on variable annuities are tracked by Lipper Analytical Services, an investment advisory firm in Westfield, New Jersey. Don't jump at the fixed-rate annuity with the highest rate, however. Look instead for one with a good rate and an escape or bailout clause. This clause lets you take out all your money in the future at no charge if the interest rate has fallen 1 or 2 percentage points below your initial guaranteed rate. You can then switch tax-free to another annuity from another company.

Take a hard look at the fees of different annuities, too. Most insurers charge 1.5 to 9 percent of the amount you will put up. On top of that, annuities usually come with annual administration fees of 1.5 percent and back-end fees that you might owe when you take money out. The back-end fees, sometimes called surrender charges, deserve special scrutiny. Most annuities let you withdraw up to 10 percent of the amount you invested each year without a fee, although some require you to wait at least a year to receive this privilege. After you cross the 10 percent mark, though, most insurers will withhold between 5 and 7 percent for withdrawals made during the first year and then a declining percentage in successive years. The surrender charges generally disappear in 7 to 12 years. As you can see, buying an annuity is not a decision to make lightly.

ZERO-COUPON BONDS

Like annuities, zero-coupon bonds offer the long-term saver convenience, a good hunk of future income, and safety—but at the expense of liquidity. Zero-coupon bonds are a relatively new investment, created in 1982 by Merrill Lynch and now sold by most stockbrokers and many banks. Normally, bonds have two parts—interest coupons and principal—and interest is paid to a bondholder on a regular basis. But a zero-coupon bond strips the interest coupons from the principal portion and doesn't pay any interest until the bond matures, usually between six months to 30 years.

You buy zero bonds at a big discount—paying perhaps $150 for a bond that will pay you $1,000 in the year 2000. Some zero-coupon bonds sell for as little as $50. Your annual yield on a zero might be 7 to 9 percent or so—about a percentage point higher than buying non-zero Treasury bond of a comparable maturity. The longer than maturity of the zero-coupon bond, the higher your yield. As with a bank CD, you know exactly how much money you will receive when the zero matures. And safe? You can buy zero-coupon Treasury bonds or zero-coupon federally insured certificates of deposit.

Zero bonds have two problems, however. The first comes while you hold the bonds. The IRS makes you pay taxes each year on the interest you have earned from your zero, even though you won't actually receive the interest until the bond matures. You can avoid this annual tax bill by buying the bonds in your child's name. Your child is probably in the zero tax bracket, so he or she won't owe any taxes on the bond's accumulated interest, as long as his or her annual income is less than $1,000. Of course, the bonds will belong to your child when both the zeroes and he or she mature.

The other problem with a zero-coupon bond comes if you want to sell it before it matures. Like any bond, a zero falls in price when interest rates rise and vice versa. But zeroes can lose value more sharply than most bonds, so you are more likely to take a loss by selling a zero early than you are by selling another bond. That's why a zero-coupon bond is a fine way to save for the intermediate term or the long term but not desirable for your emergency savings fund. If you worry that you might need to cash the bonds in before they mature, limit your risk by sticking with zeroes that will come due in less than ten years.

Not all zeroes are alike. Some are ideal for your savings; others are not. The zeroes you will want to buy for your savings fund are federally insured zero certificates of deposit and the zero-coupon bonds issued by the U.S. Treasury Department, sometimes known as TIGRs (Treasury investment growth receipts), CATS (certificates of accrual on Treasury securities), or STRIPS (separate trading of registered interest and principal of securities).

TIGRs and CATS are issued by banks that hold the bonds that stockbrokers have stripped. STRIPS are stripped by the Treasury Department itself and then given to brokers and bankers, who sell them to the public. STRIPS yield slightly less than other Treasury zeroes, but they also usually cost a little less than the standard 2 to 5 percent commission paid on other zero bonds.

When you buy a Treasury zero-coupon bond, ask your broker or banker for the total amount of money you must invest (including all fees and commissions), the amount of money you will get when the bond matures, and the bond's effective yield to maturity.

The zeroes you don't want to buy as 100 percent safe savings purchases are ones issued by corporations, ones issued by municipalities, or those backed by mortgages. These are fine for the investor who can take the chance that the issuer won't be able to meet the payments on the bond, but they are not so fine for the saver who is counting on the income to achieve an important goal at a specific date.

Savers should also avoid zero-coupon unit trusts or bond funds, even ones with the words "U.S. Government" in their names. Funds and trusts usually have higher fees than individual zero-coupon bonds. Also, "U.S. Government" doesn't necessarily mean the U.S. Treasury. A government zero-bond trust or fund might also own bonds issued or backed by other government agencies that carry more risk. Sometimes the funds and trusts lump together zero coupon Treasuries with far riskier zero-coupon corporate "junk" bonds that have credit ratings of B or above.

For quick reference, the following table provides a report card on your best savings alternatives. Grades are from A+ to F.

A Savings Report Card

Alternatives	Liquidity	Safety	Convenience	Income
Company savings plans	B	B	A +	A
Bank accounts	A +	A +	A	A
Bank CDs	C	A +	A	A +
Money-market funds	A-	A	B	A
T-bills	B	A +	B	A
T-notes, T-bonds	C	A +	B	A
Annuities	C	B	B	A
Zero-coupon bonds	D	A +	B	A +

Now that you have taken care of your savings, you can finally get to the fun part: investing. If you thought the selection was good for savings, just wait! There are investments galore, no matter what your risk tolerance. You can usually get in for as little as $100, although some investments require quite a bit more scratch. But you can make big mistakes by choosing the wrong investments for your personal needs and risk-tolerance level. Knowing when to own various type of investments is essential, too. Hold on to a diamond of an investment for too long, and you could wind up with a handful of carbon. The next chapter takes you through the investment jungle and lets you walk out richer and wiser.

CHAPTER

7

MAKE YOUR INVESTMENTS GROW

Property. I want to put my money in property.
It's the best thing to make you money.
Jerry "Beaver Cleaver" Mathers,
1960, in The New York Times

In 1974 and 1975, I started buying single-family
houses like crazy and rented them out. It
worked out very well. Now I'm buying a lot
of international stocks and collectibles
like antiques.
Jerry Mathers, in 1986, at age 38

GETTING SMART ABOUT INVESTING

Investing is the most. It is the most exciting, most nerve wracking, most exhilarating, most depressing, most exalting, most humbling, most aggravating, and most lucrative thing you can do with your money. The crash of October 1987 notwithstanding, there is simply no better way to substantially increase your family's net worth over time than by investing your money. You will make mistakes. That is part of the game. But you can limit your errors and make bigger profits by arming yourself with as much knowledge as possible before parting with your cash.

A few words about the crash of 1987 are certainly in order. Anyone who dismisses the one-day 508-point decline in the Dow Jones Industrial Averages is a Pollyanna. But it is essential to keep the crash in perspective. Anyone investing for the long term—and that should be practically anyone who invests—must be prepared for down or bear markets. The bear markets could last months or years. But they will pass. They always have. If you cannot accept this type of volatility, forget about investing in the stock market and concentrate on saving money in safer ways. But accept, too, that you will most likely receive a smaller return on your money this way.

Finding sources of information about investing is no problem. Library shelves overflow with books and reference materials for budding investors. (A personal favorite is *The Money Masters* by John Train, a book that offers a glimpse into the strategies and backgrounds of some of the world's greatest investors.) The daily *Wall Street Journal* and *Barron's*, published each Saturday, are great resources for the serious stock market investor looking for tables, charts, graphs, and the latest market insights. *Business Week* and the biweekly *Forbes* and *Fortune* give you business news, analysis, and columns with specific investment picks. (*Forbes* is the most opinionated and contrary of the three.) *Money*, and *Kiplinger's Personal Finance Magazine*, published monthly, are aimed specifically at small investors. Hundreds of newsletters—often glorified tout sheets—dispense advice and musings on making money. A few are useful; most are useless. Public television's *Wall Street Week* (which airs Friday nights and is often repeated on weekends) and *Nightly Business Report*, as well as cable's CNBC, provide no-nonsense news and views about the investment scene, too.

GROWTH OR INCOME?

Once you familiarize yourself with the jargon of investing and acquire a little history about the stock, bond, and real estate markets, you should start getting serious about finding a portfolio of investments that are appropriate for you. By now, you know your investment temperament, so you can accurately gauge the amount of risk you feel comfortable taking with your money and the amount of investment diversification you want.

The next decision is to determine your prime objective. Do you want to concentrate on *growth* (receiving little or no current income but potentially cashing in big in the future) or *income* (earning immediate, steady returns)? You need not choose growth at the exclusion of income or the other way around. In fact, your portfolio should have a smattering of both growth and income investments, with a tilt in the direction you now favor. Some investments, such as real estate and dividend-paying stocks, provide a mix of growth and income.

When you are in your 30s or 40s, as a rule your portfolio should be weighted toward stocks and other growth investments that will perform well over a period of 10 to 30 years, rather than bonds and other income investments. In percentage terms, 60 percent of this model portfolio should be in growth investments and 40 percent in income investments and savings. You are young enough to be able to wait for the growth investments to grow and to ride out any depressed stock and real estate markets in coming years. As you near retirement, your portfolio should then favor investments paying regular, steady income in the form of interest, dividends, or rental income.

DO YOU WANT TO INVEST ACTIVELY OR PASSIVELY?

How much time and attention do you want to give to your investments? Put another way: Do you want to be an active investor, passive investor, or something in between? The beauty of investing is that you can tailor your portfolio to your level of commitment.

If you would never trust anyone (over 30 or under) to invest wisely on your behalf, you should be an active investor—selecting your own stocks, bonds, and rental real estate properties. Then when your investments pan out, you can brag about your prowess (use discretion, though, because a boastful investor quickly becomes boorish). Be prepared to make a serious commitment of time and energy picking and managing your investments. Understand, too that if your growth stocks wilt or your rental real estate doesn't rent, you will have no one to blame but yourself.

You might prefer to leave the driving of your investment portfolio to professionals who manage money for large groups of people. This type of passive investing—done through mutual funds, unit trusts, and limited partnerships—is especially useful when you have neither the time nor the interest to manage your money. (Some say mutual funds are the perfect investment for Baby Boomers: a quality product that requires virtually no work for its owner.) Passive investing also provides diversification by letting you own more stocks, bonds, or real estate properties than you could afford by buying them outright.

You might have no choice but to pool your money with a large group because you don't have enough cash to invest actively. This is often the case with real estate and with bonds, which frequently require minimum investments of $10,000 or more. You could still boast at cocktail parties about how well your mutual fund is doing, as if you were responsible for its success.

Passive investing is not entirely a hands-off proposition, though. You must still keep track of your portfolio and decide when it is time to switch from one investment to another. Passive investing can have a steep price, too, because you are hiring a professional to work for you. The sponsor of a real estate limited partnership might keep 30 percent of your investment for assorted fees—money that could otherwise have gone directly into the property if you had bought the real estate yourself.

There is also a middle road for investing. You can get together with a small group of friends or relatives and pool your money to buy stocks, bonds, or real estate. Sometimes these pools take the form of investment clubs and require monthly contributions of about $10 to $25 per member; other times they are partnerships. You can designate one member of your group as the bookkeeper, perhaps paying him or her a small fee. Such mini-money pools let you make investment decisions by sharing advice and information with others, while leaving most of the dirty work of record keeping to someone else. A word to the wise: Don't invest this way unless you are absolutely certain everyone in the group has the same objectives and risk tolerance.

For a list of investment clubs near you, write to The National Association of Investment Clubs (P.O. Box 220, Royal Oak, Mich. 48068). The NAIC can provide advice about setting up and running a club. It also publishes a monthly magazine for members, called *Better Investing*, that contains stock tips. Annual membership in NAIC costs $30 per club and $7 per member.

WHY "ETHICAL INVESTING" IS NOT AN OXYMORON

A final question before taking the investment plunge: Will your ethical standards prevent you from making certain types of investments? That's okay. You need not compromise your principles to make money. In fact, studies have shown that so-called "ethical investment" stock portfolios—which shun investments in nuclear plants, for example—typically perform as well as or better than the market averages. Ethical investment portfolios were among ones that held up best during the October 1987 crash.

You can get a free list of stockbrokers who use social criteria in picking stocks by writing The Social Investment Forum (711 Atlantic Ave., Boston, Mass. 02111). A handful of mutual funds are known as social-investing funds and buy only securities that meet their ethics tests. They are:

- Calvert Social Investment Fund-Managed Growth Portfolio and Money Market Portfolio (800-368-2748)
- Dreyfus Third Century Fund (800-645-6561)
- New Alternatives Fund (516-466-0808)
- Parnassus Fund (415-664-6812)
- Pax World Fund (800-343-0529)
- Pioneer Fund, Pioneer Three, and Pioneer Bond Fund (800-225-6292)
- Working Assets Money Fund (800-543-8800)

The remainder of this chapter is devoted to an analysis of your various investment alternatives: stocks, stock mutual funds, bonds, bond mutual funds, unit trusts, rental properties, real estate partnerships, real estate investment trusts, universal-life and variable-life insurance, annuities, stock options, oil and gas partnerships, commodities, gems, metals, gold mutual funds, and collectibles. The Investment Risk Triangle below, devised by Financial Strategies, a Washington, D.C. financial-planning firm, will help you remember how the various investments differ in their degree of risk.

Managing Your Money Tip

> Managing Your Money's Portfolio submenu is a full-fledged portfolio management system. For more information on this menu selection, see the Portfolio submenu section in the abridged manual in the appendix.
>
> You also can use Managing Your Money to design the most-risk free portfolio possible to reach a given rate of return with Asset Allocation (in the Net Worth submenu.) For more information on this menu selection, see the section on asset allocation in the abridged manual in the appendix.

Gems
Commodities   VERY RISKY
Exploratory
oil deals
Precious metals
Options

Oil income deals
Corporate and municipal   RISKY
bonds and bond funds
International funds • Gold funds
Aggressive stocks

Real estate • Zero bonds   MODERATE
Other stocks • Stock funds   RISK

Tax-exempt bond trusts   MINIMAL
Government funds • Tax-exempt money funds   RISK
Treasury bills • Certificates of deposit (CDs)

Money-market accounts • Money funds
Checking accounts • Savings accounts   SECURE
Share draft accounts

BUYING STOCKS AND STOCK MUTUAL FUNDS

When you think of investing, you probably think of the stock market. You should. A respected study by the Chicago investment research firm Ibbotson Associates showed that stocks (as measured by the Standard & Poor's 500 index, a broad market average) have consistently outperformed corporate bonds and Treasury bills for investors. During the past 40 years, the annual average total return for stocks was 11.2 percent, versus 4.6 percent for T-bills and 3.8 percent for bonds. Stocks also beat bonds and T-bills over the last 30 years, the last 20 years, the last 10 years, and the last 5 years. That's an impressive record.

You will note that the comparisons don't include performance records for the last year or the last three months. That is intentional. Stocks should not be like disposable razors that you buy today and discard in a week or two. You should buy stocks with every intention of holding on to them for a while, selling quickly only in three in stances: (1) if the stock price has tumbled and you can't foresee it rising in value, (2) if the stock has gone up as much as you believe it will, or (3) if you must sell the stock because you need the cash.

It is possible to make money as a trader of stocks, buying and selling constantly. If that's your style, consider yourself a speculator rather than an investor. And be prepared to pay a heap of money in brokerage commissions and taxes on any profits you take. Also, buckle your seat belt for a bumpy ride: plenty of your stock picks will be losers.

If you have enough money to buy shares of at least eight to ten different stocks in different industries, you can invest in the stock market by yourself with enough diversification. But if you can't afford such diversification yourself, stick to stock mutual funds. Otherwise, you won't have enough variety in your stock portfolio and could be badly hurt financially if the few stocks you own go sour.

How do you pick winning stocks? Truth is, no one knows how find winners unfailingly. Despite what some Wall Street wizards claim, stock picking is an art, not a science. But you can stack the odds in your favor by knowing a little about fundamental analysis and technical analysis—the techniques Wall Street professionals use to select stocks.

Fundamental analysis is the method of looking for undervalued stock. This school of thought was founded by Benjamin Graham, Columbia

University finance professor of the 1930s who is considered the father of serious stock market analysis. Graham disciples called "value investors," buy dividend-paying stocks of strong companies without debt problems.

Fundamental analysts focus on a company's earnings as represented by its price/earnings ratio, or P/E (the share price divided by the company's earnings per share). They prefer stocks with low P/E ratios. When a P/E ratio (also called a P/E multiple) is calculated using reported earnings from the company's last four quarters, it is called a "trailing P/E." This figure is listed along with a stock's price in a newspaper's stock tables. When the ratio is calculated using a brokerage analyst's estimates for future earnings, it is called a "forward P/E."

The trailing P/E multiple of stocks of the Standard & Poor's 500 index has averaged about 13 during the past 40 years. A stock with a P/E much higher than the current market average is usually a growth stock of a high-flying company, often a young one. High P/E stocks generally don't pay dividends. Low P/E stocks are typically those of older companies—mature businesses or out-of-favor firms. They usually do pay dividends.

Fundamental analysts also hunt for promising companies with shares that are selling for less than the company is worth on paper. You can find such undervalued stocks by comparing a stock's price with its book value—a figure calculated by taking the value of the company's assets, subtracting its liabilities, and dividing the figure by the number of outstanding shares. Stocks of industrial companies have recently been trading at roughly 200 percent of book value. Stocks selling for less are considered undervalued.

The other important yardstick for a fundamental analyst is a company's return on equity (ROE), which measures the profitability of a business. It is derived by dividing the company's earnings per share by its book value. Fundamental analysts prefer stocks whose ROE is higher than current long-term interest rates. Earnings of such stocks are likely to continue growing because it will be in the company's best interest to reinvest profits in the business rather than to invest them in bonds.

You can get most of the information you need for fundamental analysis at a large public library. Ask for either the *Value Line Investment Survey* or the *Standard & Poor's Stock Guide*. Both reference publications are chock full of statistics and research about most stocks.

Technical analysts are partly number crunchers, partly historians, and partly amateur psychologists. Devoted *Wall Street Week* fans know technicians as "the elves" who measure the show's Technical Market Index. Some skeptics of technical analysis, and there are plenty, think technicians are little more than glorified tarot card readers. Indeed, a few technical analysts correctly forecast that stocks would fall just before they collapsed in October 1987. But not many of them expected stocks to fall 26 percent in two days. And many technical analysts missed calling the crash altogether.

Technicians, or chartists, like to plot charts and graphs of market trends that show the way particular stocks trade over time. They look for changes in the number of a company's shares sold on a given day—the stock's volume—and whether the stock's price is fluctuating more than usual. When technicians spot fast increases in stock prices and a surge in the number of shares changing hands, a stock market rally is often underway. Technical analysts also track what is known as market breadth, looking at the behavior of the various stock market indexes. When most stock groups are moving in the same direction, up or down, technicians say the market has breadth.

Technical analysts also often study previous bull (up) and bear (down) markets and look for ways that history might repeat itself for investors. The analysts subscribe to the Dow Theory, which says that the stock market is in a long-term bull market when the Dow Jones industrial average continues to break its previous record highs. Such had generally been the case from 1982 to the fall of 1987. Technicians also employ a perverse psychology about the stock market. When technicians believe that small investors are exceedingly bullish on stocks, the analysts turn bearish, and vice versa.

Just about the only thing technicians like to do more than analyze charts is to write about them. You can take your pick of dozens of technical market newsletters. Among the best: Stan Weinstein's *Professional Tape Reader* (P.O. Box 2407, Hollywood, Fla. 33022; $250 a year) and Bob Nurock's *The Astute Investor* (P.O. Box 988, Paoli, Pa. 19301; $197 a year).

Once you are ready to begin searching for growth stocks, look for companies whose annual earnings are likely to increase by 15 percent or more regardless of the economy. Earnings should also be expected to grow about one and a half times as fast as those of stocks as a whole. A good growth company will also have a strong competitive position. The less long-term debt the firm has, the more financially secure it is.

Concentrate on stocks of small and medium-size growth companies—those with annual revenues of $500 million or less. They are more likely to be overlooked by the big institutional investors such as pension funds and mutual funds and therefore represent better undervalued bargains. The *Standard & Poor's Stock Guide* notes how many shares of a company are owned by institutional investors. The smaller the percentage of all outstanding shares, the better for you.

You can get investment help by subscribing to an advisory service that specializes in turning up growth stocks such as: Charles Allmon's *Growth Stock Outlook* (P.O. Box 15381, Chevy Chase, Md. 20815; $125 a year). Allmon not only knows when growth stocks look appealing, he is not ashamed to say when he thinks they do not. He discouraged growth stock investing for several months before stocks crashed in late 1987. Ask your broker or financial planner whether he or she already gets this newsletter. You might be able to share it and save the subscription price.

You just might be the type of investor who believes that the conventional wisdom is usually wrong. This contrariness doesn't win many friends, but it can be quite lucrative if you really do turn out to be right and everyone else was indeed wrong. One way to invest as a contrarian is to buy shares with a low P/E—about 80 percent or less of the average multiple for the S&P 500. Such contrarian investing is frequently profitable; stocks with low P/E ratios outperformed the S&P 500 each year from 1981 through 1984.

Some stocks are particularly good buys at certain points in an economic cycle and are therefore called *cyclical stocks.* These are generally stocks of companies whose sales and profits take off when an economic expansion begins and plummet when the economy turns down. Examples: manufacturers of cars, appliances, building materials, paper, steel, and chemicals. Because a cyclical stock's fortunes typically are tied to the nation's economy, they should usually be bought in the middle of a recession before the economy starts improving and should be sold within two or three years.

Some stocks, such as those of utilities, are terrific for income but not so hot for growth. Their companies don't reinvest much of their earnings but instead pay them out to shareholders as steady dividends. Income stocks usually yield less than bonds initially. As earnings grow, however, dividends of an income stock rise, too. Within about five years, the income stock's yield is usually higher than that of a comparable bond. The key to turning up a good income stock is finding a healthy company.

One indicator is its ranking in the S&P *Stock Guide.* A rating of B + or higher signifies a strong firm.

With luck, your stocks will go up and you will be a happy investor.

Stocks can also go down, of course. You should limit your risk of losing a bundle by placing a stop-loss order with your broker when you buy the stock initially. A stop-loss order requires your broker to sell your shares if their price falls below an amount you have designated. For example, you might buy 100 shares of a stock at $50 a share and place a 10 percent stop-loss order of $45. That way, the most you can lose is $500, or 10 percent of your investment.

Managing Your Money Tip

> See the Portfolio submenu section in the abridged manual in the appendix for information on how to handle purchases, sales, and price updates of stocks.

If you lack the money, time, or interest to select your own stocks, invest in a stock mutual fund. These funds, which buy and sell stocks with money they receive from thousands of small investors have become so numerous that you can now find one for practically every conceivable investment objective. For instance, you can buy a fund that invests only in stocks of small, growing companies or one that buys only shares of health-care companies. Some funds buy stocks of companies from all over the world, while others invest in firms located in one region such as the southeastern U.S. There are mutual funds that shoot for growth but not income and others that invest for income and not growth.

Make no mistake, stock mutual funds will rise and fall as stock do. During bear markets, so-called growth funds will not grow much if at all. In October 1987, when the Standard & Poor's 500 stock index fell 21.5 percent, stock funds fell 21.6 percent on average and growth stock funds dropped in value by 23 percent.

You can buy shares of most mutual funds for as little as $1,000 and sometimes less. Once you are a fund shareholder, you can buy more shares as often as you like, usually with a minimum of $100 for subsequent investments. In fact, buying mutual fund shares regularly is a great way to become a disciplined investor. You should try to invest a certain, fixed amount every month in a stock fund, using a strategy called dollar-cost averaging. You might even be able to transfer a specified amount of money automatically each month from your checking account into a mutual fund. By buying fund shares regardless of whether the stock market is going up or down, you will prosper with the fund's success without worrying whether you picked the single best time to buy.

Stock funds generally feature easy liquidity. Like their money-market fund cousins, stock funds let you withdraw money by calling the funds and having the cash wired to your bank account or by writing and having the money sent to you. So, why the word "generally"? Liquidity froze during the crash of 1987 and could do so again during the next market collapse. Some funds temporarily delayed payouts to investors for five business days because so many people wanted to get their money.

Most stock funds are now part of fund families that include other stock funds, bond funds, and money-market funds. Some of the most well known fund families are Dreyfus, Federated, Fidelity, Keystone, Putnam, Scudder, SteinRoe, T. Rowe Price, Value Line, and Vanguard. In a fund family, you can call the fund and transfer money from the fund you are in to another one in the family. This transfer feature comes in handy when your objective switches from, say, growth to income, or when you think another type of investment will provide a better return. Most fund families charge about $5 or $10 per switch.

Some mutual funds, called no-load funds, are sold through the mail. Other funds, called load funds, are sold by stockbrokers and financial planners. The no-loads have no up-front sales charge, while the load funds typically charge between 4 and 8.5 percent of your initial investment. A growing number of funds that appear to be no-loads have hidden charges, however. Called 12B-l funds (named for a section of a federal securities law), they use a percentage of their assets to pay for marketing and distribution costs. Both no-loads and loads levy an annual management fee, generally about one-half of 1 percent a year of the fund's assets. A few funds charge you when you take money out, similar to the surrender charges for annuities. They are to be avoided. Mutual funds, after all, are not supposed to be liquidity traps.

Is it worth it to pay a fee for a load fund when you can get a no-load without a big up-front sales charge? Generally, no; sometimes, yes. Historically, no-load funds and load funds have had similar performance records. That evidence makes it difficult to justify paying a sales charge when you can make just as much money without paying one. But some load funds have been outstanding performers, earning far more for their investors, even after deducting the sales charges, than most no-loads. One example: a few of the load funds in the Templeton fund family, known for scouring the world in search of the best investment opportunities. So, the question shouldn't be whether to buy a load fund. It should be: Which is the fund that will make me the most money for my investment objectives?

You may, however, prefer investing in a load fund for its personal touch. Investing in a load fund means you can call the stockbroker or financial planner who sold it and discuss whether to sell your fund shares, buy more, or diversify. Comforting words from your adviser could keep you from engaging in panic selling during a market rout. Many advisers offered precisely such help during the 1987 crash. No-load fund investors have no such counselors.

Managing Your Money Tip

> The Portfolio submenu section in the abridged manual in the appendix contains a special section on handling mutual funds.

The best way to shop for a stock mutual fund is by determining what your investment objectives are and then getting prospectuses for the funds that meet those objectives. Most no-loads have toll-free numbers for ordering prospectuses, and your broker or financial planner can get you prospectuses for the load funds he or she sells. You can get a free list of most funds and their phone numbers from the mutual fund trade group, The Investment Company Institute (1600 M St. N.W., Washington, D.C. 20036). Twice a year, *Money* magazine publishes a list of funds that also includes the objective, performance, and sales charges of each. *Forbes* and *Business Week* magazines publish similar lists once a year.

The fund you want might not be available. Some of the best-performing mutual funds become so popular that their fund managers stop accepting money from new, would-be investors. These fund managers fear that if they let their funds grow any larger, they won't be able to manage them as well. In some instances, managers of the closed funds open so-called clone funds. These are new mutual funds with the same investment objectives as the old, closed ones. But the clone funds often are not managed by the same people who were responsible for the success of the closed funds. Clone funds also have no track record. So, unless you feel confident that the clone will be run as well as the original, don't invest in it. Sooner or later, the original fund will likely reopen to new investors.

When you leaf through the prospectus or look at the *Money, Forbes,* or *Business Week* lists, note your prospective fund's five-year and ten-year performance records. See how the fund stacked up against other funds with the same objective over the same time period. If you are looking for a diversified stock fund that will consistently outperform the stock market as a whole, compare the fund's record with the S&P 500 index or other broad stock market averages. Such comparative figures usually appear in fund prospectuses.

The accompanying table lists the ten diversified stock mutual funds still open to investors that had the highest total return (appreciation in value plus dividends) during the five years ending April 1, 1992, according to Lipper Analytical Services.

Although one of the biggest advantages of a mutual fund is its ability to diversify, many investors have become enamored lately with the 100-odd *sector funds* that specialize in particular industries. Fidelity Investments, an enormous mutual fund family, has the widest assortment of sector funds. At last count, Fidelity had thirty-one such funds specializing in everything from leisure stocks to electric utility stocks to regional bank stocks.

Sector funds can pay off handsomely if you are smart enough to pick the right sector at the right time and are equally deft at knowing when to sell your sector fund shares. Trouble is, few people can time the market that well, and most of the funds are too new to have long-term performance records. If you invest in a sector fund and the stock market takes a beating, your shares are likely to drop more in value than those of a more diversified fund. That is because sector funds must stay pretty much fully invested in their industries even when the stock market is weak. Managers of bigger, diversified funds can, by contrast, ease out of a bad market and buy money-market securities (in effect, cash) until they are ready to start buying stocks again.

You shouldn't put all your mutual fund dollars into any one sector fund. But you might consider investing up to 20 percent of your fund money in one or two sector funds. Then follow the news of your sectors so you can be ready to switch out of the funds at the right time.

After you invest in a diversified stock mutual fund and perhaps a few sector funds, try to round out your portfolio. You can do that by putting

Ten Terrific Mutual Funds

Fund	5-year Total Return	Sales Charge
Founders Frontier (800-525-2440)	139.9%	None
Berger One Hundred (800-333-1001)	139.7%	None
Alger Small Capitalization (800-992-3863)	130.1%	None
Fidelity Contrafund (800-544-8888)	129.0%	3.0%
IDEX II (800-443-9975)	129.0%	5.5%
Twentieth Century Ultra (800-345-2021)	123.2%	None
Kaufmann Fund (800-237-0132)	120.1%	None
Dreyfus Strategic Aggressive (800-782-6620)	119.2%	3.0%
Monetta Fund (800-666-3882)	118.5%	None
Janus Twenty (800-525-8983)	117.7%	None

10 percent of your assets into an international stock fund that invests in companies around the world. After all, 35 percent of stocks are in foreign countries. Why limit yourself to making money with U.S. firms? Finally, put 5 percent of your investment money in a fund that buys stocks of companies that mine gold. This will be primarily an inflation hedge, since the price of gold tends to shoot up when inflation climbs.

Another type of mutual fund getting increased attention is the closed-end fund. Unlike most mutual funds, which continue to sell shares as long as there are buyers for them, closed-end funds have a fixed number of shares that are sold by stockbrokers on various stock exchanges. Closed-end fund share prices are therefore set by the supply and demand of the marketplace. There has been a flood of new closed-end funds in the past few years. Most specialize in stocks of a particular country, such as Australia, Korea, or Italy. Frequently, shares in closed-end funds actually sell at a discount from their net asset value. That's a bargain! When you invest $1,000 in a closed-end fund selling at a 10 percent discount, you are actually getting $1,100 of value for your money. But shares sell at premiums soon after a closed-end fund is initially offered to the public. The premium helps pay the fees for launching the fund. Closed-end funds sometimes sell at premiums long after they go public. You shouldn't buy into a closed-end fund while it is still selling for a premium. Wait until the premium becomes a discount. You will get more bang for your bucks that way.

Once you have selected a mutual fund and mailed in your money or handed it over to your broker or financial planner, put the prospectus and your confirmation statement in a drawer and forget about the fund for a month or two. Then you can turn to the mutual fund pages of your daily newspaper and check to see how the fund is doing.

When you look at the mutual fund tables in the business pages of your paper, the first figure you'll see next to your fund's name is its net asset value, or NAV. That is the current price per share of your fund. The next figure, called the buy figure, is the latest price per share plus any sales charge. The last figure, called change, will tell you how much a share of your fund rose or fell in value the day before (+.02 means each share is now worth 2 cents more; -.31 means a share lost 31 cents in value).

Share values of stock funds, unlike those of money funds, fluctuate every day. Don't let yourself go crazy over each day's gyrations. Try not to look at the mutual fund pages more than once a month. After all, the fund should be a long-term investment. Your fund will send you quarterly statements, noting its recent performance and often the current investment outlook of the fund's manager.

Figuring your own fund's performance is more than a bit tricky. Your fund statements list your transactions and the fund's most recent performance but don't report your own actual annualized gain or loss, based on when you bought in. Don't get too riled about this omission. If your fund provided individualized performance figures for each shareholder, it would spend a lot more money for bookkeeping and the expense would come out of your return.

The following calculation will help you figure out your rate of return on your mutual fund over the past two years or less. You will need your most recent fund statement and last year's annual fund statement to fill in the blanks.

Managing Your Money Tip

Here's how to use the Managing Your Money calculator to calculate this result:

1. Type Ctrl-N.

2. Enter "a=", then the number of months of performance that you are measuring (line 1 of the worksheet). For example, if you're measuring 15 months, type "a=15", followed by <enter>.

3. Enter "b=", then the share price at the start of the period, then "x", then the total number of shares owned then (line 2 of the worksheet). For example, if you owned 50 shares at $30 per share, type "b=50x30", followed by <enter>.

4. Enter "c=", then the current share price, then "x", then the total number of shares owned now (line 3 of the worksheet). For example, if you now owned 150 shares at $45 per share, type "c=150x45", followed by <enter>.

5. Enter "d=", then the amount of any unreinvested income, such as total dividends of capital gains received in cash during the period (line 4 of the worksheet). For example, if you received $100 in dividends, type "d=100", followed by <enter>.

6. Enter "e=", then the amount of net redemptions or investments during the period, which will be a minus figure if redemptions exceeded investments (line 5 of the worksheet). For example, if you had $200 of redemptions, type "e=200", followed by <enter>.

7. Now, type this formula: $(((c+d-(e/2))/(b+(e/2)))-1) \times 100 \times (12/a)$, followed by <enter>. The result (r=) is your annualized return.

BUYING BONDS, BOND FUNDS AND BOND UNIT TRUSTS

When your investment objective is income rather than growth, bonds are the place to turn. A bond, which is really just an IOU from a company or a government agency, will pay you a specified rate of interest if you hold it until maturity. The longer the maturity, the higher the bond's yield, generally speaking. Usually, interest checks are paid out every six months. When your bond matures, you get back your original principal. Bonds, like stocks, trade freely. So you can buy either newly issued bonds or ones issued years ago that are now for sale by their bondholders.

Your first, and perhaps only, experience with bonds was one you undoubtedly have forgotten. When you were born, some friend of the family or relative probably bought U.S. savings bonds in your name and gave them to your parents. If you were bar mitzvahed, confirmed, or married, you probably got a few savings bonds then, too. The bonds most likely have been kept in a safe deposit box, unless you already cashed them in at the bank. The savings bonds were truly a worry-free investment.

During the 1950s, 1960s, and early 1970s, when interest rates barely moved, all types of bonds were virtually no-risk propositions and were considered extremely safe. Since then, of course, interest rates have had more ups and downs than NBC's prime-time ratings. So bonds have become both more risky and potentially more profitable than in the past.

If you ask your stockbroker or banker to sell a bond early, you must accept whatever price a buyer is willing to pay. When interest rates are stagnant, there's little risk involved. Say you bought a 30-year bond with a face value of $1,000 when long-term interest rates were at 10 percent. You receive $100 in interest a year, with what is called a coupon rate of 10 percent. If interest rates haven't moved and you want to sell your bond early, a buyer will pay you the same price you originally paid. You wanted to earn the going rate on long-term bonds, which was 10 percent, and now he wants to earn the going rate on long-term bonds, also 10 percent.

But say you bought that 30-year bond yielding 10 percent and now interest rates on new 30-year bonds are up to 15 percent. If you want to sell your bond prematurely, nobody will want to give you the $1,000 you paid for your 10 percent bond, since they can pay the same price and get a bond yielding 15 percent. People will, however, pay you about $600 for your 10 percent bond. That way, they will get the same yield as if they had bought a 15 percent bond for $1,000. So, if you want to sell your bond early and rates have risen, you may have to take a loss on your investment.

Now, imagine that rates have dropped to 5 percent since you bought your 10 percent bond. You're sitting pretty. Plenty of investors would be thrilled to own your bond. In fact, they might pay you $2,000 for your $1,000 bond, so the $100 annual interest will give them a 5 percent yield. Thus, if you sell bonds early after interest rates have fallen, you can make a profit on your investment—in addition to the interest income you have earned. Plenty of bond investors have scored big gains in recent years because they bought their securities before interest rates fell.

You can see why the time to buy bonds is when interest rates are stable or falling and the time to avoid bonds is when rates are rising.

The longer the maturity of a bond, the more interest-rate risk it has, because there is more time for rates to rise. Long-term bond investors are rewarded for taking this extra risk by getting higher yields than investors with short-term bonds. Interest rates are never predictable, but they are increasingly unpredictable as you stretch out the time period. So you need not be too concerned about interest-rate risk if you are buying a one-year or five-year bond (or a note or bill maturing in less than a year). Interest-rate risk should be a consideration if you want to buy a bond that will mature in ten years or longer, though. Of course, if you can be confident that you won't cash in your bond before it matures, interest-rate risk is not an issue. At maturity, you will have received the principal and interest as originally promised, regardless of interest rate fluctuations while you have held the bond.

Aside from this interest-rate risk, bonds also have payout risk. That is, there is a chance that your bond won't pay the interest you were promised for as long as it promised. Payout risk can be a real problem when interest rates fall dramatically. Many bonds have provisions stating that their issuers can call in the bonds at some point in the future, paying back the bondholders earlier than anticipated. Bond issuers often exercise this call feature when rates fall, because they no longer want to keep paying rates of interest exceeding current market rates.

A bond call is one call you probably won't be thrilled to receive. When your bond is called, you are stuck trying to find a place to reinvest the money. This can be maddening when you must receive the cash at an interest rate far below the one you had on the bond before it was called in. When buying a bond, check to see whether or when it can be called. No investor likes to be unpleasantly surprised.

Credit risk is the other danger with bonds. If a bond issuer defaults on its interest or principal, you take the loss. You can eliminate credit risk altogether by buying only bonds guaranteed by the federal government. That may be overdoing it, though. If you buy bonds with the highest ratings from the independent rating firms Standard & Poor's and Moody's, you will be well insulated from credit risk and will get higher returns than on government bonds. Understand, however, that the higher the bond rating, the lower the bond's yield compared with similar bonds with lower ratings. Standard & Poor's ratings range from AAA to D and Moody's ratings range from AAA to C.

Bond shoppers have a choice of corporate bonds, U.S. government bonds, or municipal bonds:

- *Corporate bonds* yield the most because they are riskier than U.S. bonds, and, unlike most municipal bonds, their interest is taxable. Tax reform has added to the luster of corporates; with lower tax rates, less of your corporate bond's interest will be taxed. Newly issued corporate bonds generally sell for $1,000. The $1,000 is called the bond's face value. Corporate bonds normally yield about between .25 and 2 percentage points more than Treasuries of similar maturities. If safety is as important as income, stick with corporate bonds rated AA or AAA by Standard & Poor's or Moody's. Lately, many corporations have seen their bond ratings fall because the companies have taken on extra debt either to take over other firms or to protect themselves from being taken over. Bonds of utility companies are usually safer than those of industrial firms.

- *U.S. Treasury bonds,* which yield about .25 to .75 percentage points less than corporate bonds, pay interest that is exempt from state and most local income taxes but not from federal income taxes. They are usually issued with face values of $1,000. There's no need to worry whether these bonds will default. Another advantage of Treasuries: They generally can't be called in early. The exception is the 30-year Treasury bond, which can be called after 25 years. U. S. savings bonds, which are a special breed of Treasury bonds, sell for as little as $25. Their interest rate fluctuates, but you will not earn less than 6 percent if you buy a savings bond and hold it at least five years.

- *Municipal bonds,* which usually sell in $5,000 denominations, yield less than corporates or Treasuries because they are generally exempt from U.S. income taxes. (All muni bond interest was free of federal taxes before the tax reform law. But the new law created a hybrid bond, called a taxable municipal, whose interest is not tax exempt. Such bonds should be shunned until they have been around long enough to develop a track record.) Municipal bonds issued by your state or local government usually pay interest free of state and local taxes, too. Typically, high-quality municipal bonds yield about 65 to 75 percent as much as Treasury bonds of similar maturities. But muni yields have been especially high lately; particularly when compared with comparable taxable bonds.

How municipal bond yields will compare with corporate and Treasury yields in the future is anyone's guess. But it seems a good bet that the lower tax brackets created by the new tax reform law will mean that fewer people will want to buy municipal bonds in the future.

Most municipal bonds can't be called in by their issuers for at least ten years. But the bond issuers can default on their securities. You can protect yourself from the possibility that the muni bond issuer will default by buying an insured municipal bond. This is a muni that would normally be rated A or higher but gets a AAA rating because it has insurance that guarantees continued timely payments of interest and the return of your principal in a default. Municipal bond insurance nicks you, however. You must usually accept a yield that is between .25 and .50 percentage points less than that of an uninsured muni bond.

The bond market breaks down even further. There are:

- *Deep-discount bonds.* These are corporate, Treasury, or municipal bonds issued 10 or 15 years ago, when interest rates were much lower than they are today. Consequently, they sell for much less than their original prices—say $700 for a bond that originally sold for $1,000. A deep-discount bond will pay you a measly 4 percent or so while you own it, but when the bond matures you will receive an amount equal to its original price. That can turn into a sizable profit.

- *Junk bonds.* These are low-quality corporate bonds, rated BBB or less, and they had been extremely popular in recent years. Reason: Junk bonds reward investors for taking the extra credit risk by paying them higher yields than bonds with better ratings. You can sometimes earn as much as 5 percentage points more on a junk bond than on a Treasury bond. Junk bonds might be especially appealing if you are an interest-rate chaser fuming that the cash you sunk into a money fund is now earning only 3 percent or so. Some junk bonds yield as much as 12 percent. A junk bond can deliver capital gains, too, if the financial health of its issuer improves and the bond's price increases.

Always keep in mind, however, that there is an excellent reason why junk bonds yield so much—namely, their issuers may be so wobbly or debt-laden they might not be able to continue making their payments. Unless you are willing to accept the possibility of a default, keep out of the junk pile. Junk buyers should especially avoid bonds issued in connection with takeovers and leveraged buy-outs, because the future of their issuers is too difficult to predict. The safest junk bonds are ones rated B or BB issued by companies whose financial condition is healthier than their ratings suggest.

- *Zero-coupon bonds.* As described in the preceding chapter, zeroes are bonds that accumulate interest and pay it out when the bonds mature. There are corporate zeroes, Treasury zeroes, and municipal zeroes. Although you will not receive your zero's interest for a while, the IRS requires you to pay taxes on the accumulated interest annually (except with a tax-exempt muni bond). Don't even think of investing in a zero-coupon bond that isn't issued by the Treasury or rated A or better. Otherwise, you will be taking a big gamble that the issuer will be able to pay all the promised interest at some point in the future.

- *Convertible bonds.* These might be called the mermaids of the bond family: half bond/half stock. A convertible is used as a corporate bond but gives the investor the opportunity to swap the security in the future for a predetermined number of shares of the issuer's stock. The bond's price moves in lockstep with the company's stock, though generally the price rises and falls a bit less, on a percentage basis, than the stock price. You must usually wait two years to swap the bond for stock, and you can convert the bond only if the stock has risen to a preordained level. So you can get a decent yield from your convertible bond and ideally get in on the action of a roaring stock market, too, with future capital gains. Of course, if the market falls, one of the major advantages of your convertible vanishes. Because of their equity kickers, convertibles usually yield 3 or 4 percentage points less than comparable bonds that can't be exchanged for stock. (Preferred stock, like a convertible bond, can also be exchanged for regular shares of stock.)

Unless you can afford to buy at least five to ten different corporate or municipal bonds, you ought to buy bonds through bond mutual funds or bond unit trusts. Such pools not only provide greater diversification than you can afford, they reduce the risks of bond investing. The pros who run the funds and trusts can also probably do a better job of timing the purchases and sales of bonds than you can.

Bond funds, like stock funds, let you buy or sell shares at any time, usually for a minimum investment of $1,000. Bond fund managers constantly change their portfolio mix of 100 or so bonds to keep up with trends in the bond market. Some bond funds are no-loads; others are loads with sales charges as high as 8 1/2 percent.

The variety of bond funds, sometimes called income funds, is remarkable. There are funds for every degree of risk, from Treasury funds to junk bond funds (often called "high-yield" or "high-income bond funds). High-grade funds, by contrast, are ones that invest primarily in the highest quality bonds. Some funds buy only short-term bonds, others buy only intermediate-term bonds, and still others buy only long-term bonds. A few bond funds invest in zero coupons, and few have just convertibles.

The best way to compare bond funds is to look at their total returns, not their yields. Total return includes the past year's dividends as well as the change in the fund's share value. Look for consistently impressive bond funds the way you would select stock funds. Analyze annual returns of comparable bond funds for the past five or ten years.

Unit trusts also buy bonds with money pooled from investors: ($1,000 minimum, typically). But unlike the funds that constantly trade their bonds, the trusts buy a group of roughly twenty bonds and hold them until maturity. So, like a bank CD, a unit trust comes due in a specified period of time. You can get unit trusts ranging in maturity from three months to 30 years, although it's safest to stay with ones maturing in 10 years or sooner.

Unit trusts provide more certainty than bond funds, whose share values change daily. But you give up quite a lot for the ability to lock in a yield. Unit trusts typically charge a sales commission of 4 percent and price their shares, called units, above what they paid for the bonds. Trusts are not as liquid as bond funds, either. Units can be sold prematurely, but you will be paid 3 to 6 percent less than the currently offered price of the bonds. And you will never get back the 4 percent load. Unit trusts also can't buy any more bonds after they have collected money from investors. So, if your unit trust sponsor has to sell a bond because its issuer is in trouble, the trust will lose some of its diversification.

Be wary of unit trusts advertised to yield far more than bonds of similar maturities. A higher yield usually masks higher risk. The yield could be inflated because the trust holds bonds with rating lower than A. Or the trust might mature in 30 years. Or the trust could be hyping its yield by promoting a "current return" instead of a standard yardstick such as "yield to maturity." A current return doesn't take into account the probability that some of the trust's bonds will be called in early.

Unless you feel certain that you can hold on to a unit trust until maturity, diversify with bonds through mutual funds. A handy rule of thumb is that unit trust sales charges and administrative fees make the trusts more expensive than no-load bond funds unless you will hold on to the trusts for at least eight years.

Managing Your Money Tip

> The Portfolio submenu section in the abridged manual in the appendix contains a special section on handling bonds.

BUYING GINNIE MAES

If it looks like a bond but isn't one, it's probably a Ginnie Mae. A Ginnie Mae is actually a security issued by the Government National Mortgage Association and backed by the home mortgages that the association holds. GNMA is not truly part of the U.S. government. It was created by Congress, however, and is now generally considered to be a quasi-government agency. In fact, interest and principal payments are federally guaranteed. A Ginnie Mae mortgage-backed certificate is sold by a stockbroker for a minimum investment of $25,000 (or $10,000 for older Ginnie Maes). Its yield is typically about a percentage point higher than that of comparable Treasury bonds. Interest and principal are sent to investors as the mortgages are paid off, usually in monthly installments.

Ginnie Mae mutual funds and unit trusts, which buy dozens of the certificates, have become extremely popular in the past few years because of their high yields, diversification, and low minimum investments. You generally need as little as $1,000 or $3,000 to get into a Ginnie Mae fund or trust. Some of the pools are no-load, while others charge loads ranging from 1 to 5 percent. Some funds and trusts let you automatically reinvest your monthly interest and principal payments.

Ginnie Maes have a special type of payout risk, however. You can't predict with absolute certainty when the principal on the Ginnie Mae mortgages will be repaid, so your monthly income fluctuates. Some homeowners prepay their principal early; others are late with their payments. When mortgage rates fall, as they did in 1985 and 1986, many homeowners refinance their high-interest loans. That, in turn, means that the Ginnie Maes are often repaid early, forcing investors to seek alternate places for their cash. Investors in Ginnie Mae mutual funds who bought shares when mortgage rates were high have seen their yields fall as their fund managers have had to reinvest money at lower rates.

BUYING INVESTMENT REAL ESTATE

Investment real estate is a lot like the girl with the curl on her forehead. When it is good, it is very, very good. But when it is bad, it is horrid. The best real estate investments provide steady rental income and tax breaks while you own the properties, followed by big profits when you sell them. They deliver positive cash flow—your money going out in the form of mortgage payments, property insurance, property taxes, and maintenance expenses adds up to less than the amount of your rental income coming in. You can probably imagine the worst real estate investments: Rental income is meager if there is any at all, saddling you with negative cash flow; your tax breaks are minimal; and when you decide to sell the property, it is worth less than the original purchase price.

Tax reform has taken much of the attractiveness out of real estate investing. Your deductions for mortgage interest and property taxes will probably be worth less to you than in the past, because you most likely will have dropped into a lower tax bracket. The law now requires investors to depreciate residential real estate bought after 1986 over 27.5 years. Before the law, you could write off the property over 19 years. The recent tax rules also eliminate the favorable capital gains tax treatment when you sell the property.

In addition, Congress has limited the amount of tax losses you can claim on rental property. The size of your deductions will be related to how actively you manage the property and how large your income is. You can deduct up to $25,000 of the property's annual losses against your salary and any investment income as long as you meet three tests: you own at least 10 percent of the property, you are active in management decisions, and your adjusted gross income is less than $100,000. Active management requires that you write the maintenance checks and have some say in choosing your tenants. You can deduct only 50 cents in losses from your taxable income for every dollar your adjusted gross income exceeds $100,000. If your earnings top $150,000, you can write off losses only up to the amount of your passive income—that's the money you receive from partnerships, rental properties, and the like.

The types of properties hurt most by tax reform have been huge downtown office buildings and apartment complexes. They have often been built primarily as tax shelters for very wealthy investors.

As long as you exercise discretion when investing in real estate, tax reform should not pose a major problem. In fact, tax reform has already had some beneficial effects for real estate investors. Some sponsors of real estate partnerships have cut the fees they charge investors and have increased their expected rates of return. Some property owners have also lowered the prices of their buildings to attract buyers spooked by tax reform.

Real estate still has three advantages over other investments:

- You can have a lot more control over the return on your investment in a building than you can with a stock or bond. There isn't much you can do to raise the price of your stock, but you can do a variety of things to make your real estate more appealing and increase its return. For example, you can fix up the building, lower its rent, advertise it, or hire a manager to care for it.

- Real estate historically has been an excellent inflation hedge, something that can't be said for, say, bonds. When inflation heats up, real estate appreciates in value, too—as you can probably proudly report if you bought a house in the 1970s. Bonds are victimized by inflation because their yields don't necessarily rise as consumer prices do.

- You can buy a property for a fraction of its value, through leverage. What other investment lets you put down 10 percent of its purchase price (or even less!) and walk away an owner?

But real estate lacks one important feature common to most other investments: liquidity. You can't sell a duplex or a small office building with a simple call to your broker, the way you can unload a stock or a bond. It can take months, sometimes years, to sell your property for the price you believe it deserves. If you've ever sold your home, you know too well that finding a buyer is only half the story. Closing the deal can take several extra months, not to mention a chunk of cash.

So, you should invest in real estate to balance out your investment portfolio as long as you expect to hold on to the property for at least three to five years. Otherwise, stick with more liquid investments and other inflation hedges such as gold coins.

Investing in real estate, to many people, begins and ends with buying their own home. Such a purchase is nothing to sneeze at: your house, condominium, or cooperative apartment may well be the biggest investment you will ever make. But there are a variety of other ways to invest in real estate, some for as little as $1,000. You can buy and rent out a home, pool your money with others in a real estate limited partnership, or buy real estate stocks. Now that mortgage rates are relatively low, the cost of getting into real estate has come down.

How to invest in real estate depends on the time and effort you are willing to commit. People who find, buy, and manage their own properties—landlords—have the most control and pay the lowest fees. Passive investors who are limited partners in real estate partnerships or who own real estate stocks can get more diversification with fewer headaches, but they must pay fees or commissions.

Most real estate analysts suggest that a novice investor begin by buying and renting out the largest number of residential rental units he or she can afford, whether that is a single-family home, a duplex, a fourplex, or something larger. The more tenants, the lower the operating cost per unit and the less of a risk that one vacancy will sap the entire rental income. Residential properties are easier to purchase and manage than commercial buildings, and they almost always cost less.

Your best bet is to find a building within 50 miles of your home. That way, you can easily get to the property and check up on its condition. You will also be more familiar with the nearby housing markets, increasing your odds of getting a good investment. Try, also, to invest in a tight rental market where the vacancy rate is below 5 percent.

The most lucrative properties are usually the ones that are most popular among renters. So, look for homes in well-maintained neighborhoods close to shopping centers and offices. House styles most in demand are typically colonials, Cape Cods, and ranches. If you are handy, a shrewd investment might be a building that needs improvement but is situated in an appealing neighborhood. Just don't buy a property that will require you to spend more than 15 percent of its purchase price on repairs. The investment is unlikely to pay off.

There isn't much difference between buying a house and buying a condominium as an investment. But purchasing a co-op as an investment property is something altogether different. Co-ops are shares of stock in corporations that let owners lease apartments in their buildings. A prospective buyer must be approved by a co-op's board of directors. If you are lucky enough to pass that stage and then want to rent out your co-op, you will again need board approval. That can be extremely difficult, because many co-op residents frown on renters.

Buying residential rental property is no guarantee of a positive cash flow. Far from it. The combination of lofty purchase prices, mortgage rates, and high property taxes (often the equivalent of about 15 percent of gross rental income) makes negative cash flows quite common. Expect to pay between 0.5 and 1.0 percentage point more in interest for a mortgage on an investment property than on a primary residence. Negative cash flows were tolerable before tax reform, when you were allowed to fully deduct your losses. But now that the rules have changed and deductible losses are limited, there is no reason to buy a property that won't be profitable.

The key to successful real estate investing is finding good tenants who will pay you reasonable rents on time. Have prospective tenants fill out a detailed application with the name of their employer and supervisor, their bank, and at least two previous landlords. Check with the employer to see that the applicant has enough income and job security to pay the rent. Tenants whose gross income is at least four times your rent are generally dependable. Call a local retail credit bureau to see whether the applicant has been a prompt bill payer, and also ask the applicant's previous landlord whether the tenant was desirable.

If you can't or won't screen tenants yourself, hire a professional management firm to do the work. This could cost the equivalent of one month's rent per tenant and the loss of deductibility of any real estate losses. Once you have approved an applicant, have him or her sign a one-year lease and pay you the first month's rent in advance, as well as a security deposit equal to at least another month's rent.

Being a landlord with one or two dwellings to rent out will probably take three to six hours of work a month. You can hire a management company to reduce that time commitment and take care of your bookkeeping and routine maintenance. This is likely to cost roughly 10 percent of a year's rent. If you want nothing to do with managing the property, figure on paying between 8 and 20 percent of the gross annual rental income to a professional management company. You can find competent managers by getting a directory of accredited management organizations from the Institute of Real Estate Management (430 N. Michigan Ave., Chicago, Ill. 60611).

Vacation homes are not usually great investment properties. They often are the first type of real estate to get hurt in a recession, because when people are short on cash they tend to cancel their pleasure trips. If you want to buy a second house in the country, near the beach, or in the mountains, enjoy! Just don't figure on making money on it.

Tax reform has changed the way write-offs are figured on vacation homes, too. The amount you can now deduct on such a property depends largely on whether the IRS views the place as your second home or as a rental property. The house will certainly be deemed a second home as long as you don't rent it out to anyone. You can then keep deducting your mortgage interest and property taxes, albeit at a lower tax rate. You may be allowed to claim additional deductions, such as depreciation and expenses, if the house meets the tests for investment property: you own at least 10 percent of it and actively manage it.

There are two types of real estate limited partnerships sold by stockbrokers and financial planners: private and public. Both types buy and develop apartments, offices, hotels, shopping centers, business parks, and mini-warehouses, or they hold mortgages on such properties. Their yields vary, but many of the best provide annual average returns of 7 percent or so.

Partnerships give you professional expertise and management, though you pay a high price for the assistance. Roughly 10 to 15 percent of the money you invest in a private deal and 20 to 25 percent in a public one is used to pay fees to the sponsor and its associates. It is also difficult to sell your partnership shares for what they are worth before the program expires, usually in five to ten years. A few companies, some partnership sponsors, some stockbrokers, and some financial planners will buy back your units. But they usually will pay only about 70 percent of what your shares are actually worth. An exception to the liquidity trap: master limited partnerships whose shares are traded on the New York and American stock exchanges.

A *private partnership* generally pools between $20,000 and $150,000 from each of up to thirty investors (the limited partners) and buys or develops a single building. Investors are often able to make their payments in annual installments, over five years or so. A program's sponsor, usually the general partner, doesn't have to file detailed information with the federal Securities and Exchange Commission. In the past, private deals frequently let investors deduct twice the amount they had invested. But tax reform has put an end to such enormous tax breaks. Now, about the most that can be deducted on a private partnership is the amount invested.

Public partnerships are for the masses. They are especially useful for generating steady interest or rental income for individual retirement accounts or Keogh plans, or to be sheltered by losses from other real estate investments. You can usually invest as little as $5,000 in a public program; $2,000 for an IRA. These deals usually involve hundreds of investors, who often pool more than $50 million for diversification in several projects or mortgages around the country. Public partnerships rarely permit an investor to deduct as much as he or she invests. Some partnerships are not tax-deductible at all.

Choosing a real estate partnership is a lot like selecting a mutual fund. You want one with a good long-term track record in both up and down markets. Public partnerships are rated in *The Stanger Register* and *The Partnership Record,* two monthly publications available in many brokerage or financial planning offices. Private partnerships aren't rated this way. You will have to consult your accountant and investment adviser for advice on investing in a private deal.

The biggest drawback to real estate investing—liquidity—disappears when you buy shares of a real estate investment trust (REIT). A REIT pools money raised from shareholders and invests it in properties as a partnership would. But you can sell your shares with a call to your broker, just as with any other stock. Equity REITs buy income-producing properties, mortgage REITs lend the money to developers, and hybrid REITs do both. If you invested in REITs in the mid-1970s, you undoubtedly are skittish about them today. Then, REITs mostly loaned money, and many lost much of their value in a collapse of the REIT market. Today's REITs are safer, because most buy real estate rather than lend and the lenders are more prudent than their predecessors.

REITs must pay to shareholders 95 percent of the rental and interest income they receive. Many REITs have been yielding between 5 and 9 percent, although there is no guarantee that those returns will last. Mortgage REITs usually have the highest yields but are the riskiest. Equity REITs have the lowest yields and are the safest.

Because REITs are traded like stocks, their share prices tend to rise and fall with the market. But REITs have not been especially volatile in the past few years. Plan on holding on to your REIT shares at least three to five years, though, so you will own the stock when the company is likely to sell some of its buildings and pay its investors capital gains. But don't be in a rush to buy shares of a new REIT offering. The stocks often drop in price soon after their initial offering and then hover or rise in value.

A superb monthly newsletter that specializes in real estate is *John T. Reed's Real Estate Investor's Monthly* (Reed Publishing, 342 Bryan Dr., Danville, Calif. 94526; $96 a year).

BUYING LIFE INSURANCE AND ANNUITIES

Universal-life and variable-life insurance let you invest a portion of your premiums in stock and bond pools that are managed by the insurers. Taxes are deferred on any interest and dividends earned until you withdraw the money from your insurance policy. If your insurance cash value falls because your investments have not fared well, you will have to pay additional premiums or give up some of your insurance protection.

Traditionalists argue that insurance is insurance and investments are investments and the two should never be mixed. There is some merit to this argument. Insurance, after all, is too important to take a chance on. Still, some of the insurance companies' stock and bond portfolios have performed as well as or even better than the best mutual funds. Also, life insurance is a long-term proposition. If you believe, as most investment analysts do, that the stock and bond markets have tremendous long-term potential, using your insurance policy partly as an investment is not such a bad idea as long as you understand the implications.

Variable annuities are another investment alternative from insurance companies and are essentially tax-deferred mutual funds. They can be superb long-term investments but miserable short-term investments. Variable annuities are sold by insurance agents, stockbrokers, and financial planners, usually for $5,000 ($100 for IRAs or Keoghs) or through smaller monthly contributions. A variable annuity lets you invest in a stock fund, bond fund, or money-market fund and switch among the portfolios as often as once a month. Your earnings grow tax-deferred until they are withdrawn.

Most variable annuities have sales charges ranging from 1.5 to 9 percent of the amount you put up and annual administration fees of 1.5 percent or so. Annuities also come with back-end fees, called surrender charges, which will withhold a portion of your money if you take it out during the first ten or so years. In addition, the tax-reform law requires anyone younger than 59 1/2 to pay a 10 percent penalty to the IRS when withdrawing money from an annuity. That's why a variable annuity is only worth a look if you view it as a long-term investment.

Pick a variable annuity the way you would a mutual fund: Examine its ten-year performance record. Returns on variable annuities are tracked by Lipper Analytical Services, an investment advisory firm in Westfield, N.J. A good life insurance agent or financial planner will be able to show you the most recent Lipper annuity rankings.

BUYING EXOTICA

Here are a few slightly exotic investments and investment techniques that might be worth your while:

- *Stock options known as calls and puts.* Calls and puts allow you to invest in the stock market without risking a lot of money and to protect your current holdings against sharp market declines. When you buy a call from your stockbroker, you have the right to purchase 100 shares of a certain stock at a certain price for up to nine months. The price is called the exercise or strike price. You buy a call because you are betting that the price of a particular stock will rise. If you bet correctly, you can exercise your option. That, in effect, requires the seller of the call to give you the 100 shares at your price, which will be lower than the market price, and lets you resell the stock at the higher market price for a nice profit.

In reality, the process is a bit more streamlined and chancier. When your option is up, you just sell it and take any profits or losses that come your way. To buy a call option, you must pay a fee (called a premium) costing perhaps $2 to $10 per share. You will lose this premium if you have bet wrong and the price of your stock hasn't moved or has fallen. (Many, if not most, call buyers lose money.)

A put is the opposite of a call. When you buy a put, you have the right to sell 100 shares of a particular stock at a certain price for up to nine months. Here, you are betting that the price of the stock will go down. If you bet correctly with a put and the stock drops, you can sell your contract for a profit. If you bet wrong, you lose the premium you paid for the put. But you will never lose more than that amount.

Put and call options are traded on only about 500 stocks, roughly 6 percent of all listed stocks and generally ones of the biggest companies. Options are generally traded on the Chicago Board Options Exchange, the American Stock Exchange, the Philadelphia Stock Exchange, and the Pacific Stock Exchange.

If you like to shoot craps, you will love index options, which let you bet on the entire stock market. An index option is a put or call traded on the Standard & Poor's index of 100 stocks or fourteen other market indexes. Index options are far more volatile than individual stock options and thus even harder to use profitably.

Stock options are listed in tables on the financial pages of daily newspapers. Each option appears with a few expiration dates, usually three months apart, and each expiration date has several strike prices. Premiums for options with high strike prices and short expiration periods are the least expensive. Reason: It is unlikely that your stock will shoot up dramatically in a short period of time and make you richer. Long-term options, the most expensive type, are best for patient, conservative investors. Stockbrokers who specialize in options can tell you which options they believe are priced well and which should be avoided.

Stock options can also be used as an insurance policy against your stock holdings. If you own a stock but can't decide whether to sell, you can sell your shares and buy calls on an equivalent number. If the stock keeps rising, you will make money from the calls. If the stock drops, you will lose the premium.

Managing Your Money Tip

> The Portfolio submenu section in the abridged manual in the appendix contains a special section on handling puts and calls.

- *Buying stocks or stock funds on margin.* Another way to control more stocks than you actually own is to use money you borrow from your stockbroker. Buying on margin requires putting up your cash or securities as collateral in an amount equal to half the price of the stock or mutual fund shares you want. The money you borrow from your broker will make up the difference. The interest rate charged on the amount you borrow is usually 1 or 2 percentage points lower than what you would pay for a consumer loan at the bank.

  Such leverage enables you to double your gains. But if the stock or mutual fund shares lose even half their value, your original investment will be entirely wiped out. Once the value of the shares you bought with borrowed funds and the shares you used as collateral fall by 30 percent, your broker will order you to come up with more cash or marginable securities. If you don't, your broker will sell your stock and demand that you immediately repay your loan plus interest.

  Use margin accounts sparingly, if at all, and only when you believe your shares will rise in value by more than the amount you will pay in interest. Give your stockbroker a stop order for your margined shares, to limit the amount you could lose.

- *Selling short.* The stock market is a perverse place: You can make money on stocks that go down. The way to do so is by what's known as selling stock short. Here's how: First, you find a stock you believe is overpriced. Next, you borrow shares of the stock from your broker. Then, you sell the borrowed shares. With luck, the stock price falls and you then pay the broker for the borrowed shares and pocket the difference between the original price and the current price.

  You can easily wind up on the short end of a short sale. Here's why: You must put up at least half the value of the stock in cash or securities to borrow the stock you want to sell short. Then you will owe interest on the other half—the margined half—until you replace the shares. What's more, if the stock pays dividends while you have borrowed it, you must come up with the money out of your own pocket and pay it to the stock's original owner. If you have bet wrong and the stock rises in value, you must buy the replacement shares at the higher price and take a loss. That loss can wind up being much higher than your original investment; indeed, it can be unlimited. Few people have the stomach for selling short. If you do, be sure to place a stop order with your broker to limit the amount of money you can lose should the stock fail to take a hit as you expect.

Managing Your Money Tip

> The Portfolio submenu section in the abridged manual in the appendix contains a special section on handling short sales.

- *Oil and gas limited partnerships.* Once the rage, but scorned lately as the price of oil has dropped, oil and gas partnerships let you invest with hundreds or thousands of other investors and share in profits from drilling and exploration. The partnerships usually dissolve in 5 to 15 years, so they are most definitely long-term investments. (Exception: master limited partnerships whose units are traded daily on major stock exchanges.) Like real estate partnerships, oil partnerships (also called oil funds) are sold by stockbrokers and financial planners. The minimum investment is usually $5,000 for public partnerships and $50,000 or more for private deals. Fees usually equal about 12 percent of the amount you invest.

  The risk, returns, and tax write-offs vary dramatically among oil and gas funds. A public partnership that drills oil wells can let you deduct as much as 90 percent of your investment in the first year—but your annual write-offs are limited to the amount of passive income you receive during the year (the tax breaks can be carried over into future years). Unless you are investing in rental real estate or other partnerships, it's unlikely that you will have much passive income. So, the oil and gas write-offs will be useless.

  The only way to claim all the write-offs available for investing in oil and gas is by becoming a principal in an oil company, owning what is called a "working interest" in the business. But that means you will accept unlimited liability and conceivably will be forced to come up with far more money than you originally invested. That's probably more risk than you should take, tax breaks or no.

The return from a drilling fund is nearly impossible to predict because no one knows how much oil will be found or the price the oil will eventually sell for. You should steer clear of the riskiest drilling funds, which invest more than 50 percent of their money in exploratory drilling projects.

The safest oil and gas partnerships provide income with little or no write-offs. These are called oil income funds and typically yield about 6 percent a year.

Analyzing oil and gas partnerships is far more difficult than comparing mutual funds, because oil deals are more complicated. Past performance is not especially useful, either, now that lower oil prices and reduced consumption have turned the world of oil on its head. Many oil and gas partnership sponsors are in shaky financial health. So, if you really want to invest in an oil fund, look for sponsors that have been around for at least ten years and have enough cash in reserve to indicate they will be around for a while more. Such information is listed in an oil fund's prospectus. The two monthly partnership publications, *The Stanger Register* and *The Partnership Record*, rate oil and gas deals and provide information about the financial strength and history of the sponsors.

INVESTMENTS YOU DON'T NEED

Most other investments are ones you will probably be wise to ignore. Many are sucker deals that promise mouth-watering returns that never materialize. Many, like collectibles and gems, require specialized knowledge. Some, such as commodities, turn into sucker deals if you don't have specialized knowledge. (Most commodity investors lose money most of the time—and that includes the professionals.)

A few investments are little more than marketing gimmicks and ought to be avoided. They include:

- *Insured bond funds and insured unit trusts.* Insurance is fine when you own only a few bonds and want to protect them. But the sheer number of bonds in funds and trusts provides the necessary diversification to protect you in the event that one or two of the bonds

default. Buying a fund or trust with insurance is like wearing a belt
and suspenders. In addition, the cost of insurance will cut the yield
of your bond fund or trust by between .25 and .50 percentage
points a year.

- *Zero-coupon hybrids.* Marketing types at financial institutions
have been looking for ways to dress up zero-coupon bonds ever
since Merrill Lynch invented them. Limited-partnership sponsors,
for example, have put together zero-coupon partnerships that are
half zero bonds and half real estate or oil and gas investments. Brokerage houses have been hawking "total growth trusts" that are
unit trusts made up of zero bonds and growth stocks. The problem
with the zero-coupon hybrids is that the whole invariably costs
more than the sum of its parts. That is, you pay more for the package than if you had bought the zero-coupon bonds and the other
investment separately. If you want zero bonds and you want
growth stocks, buy them. Just buy them separately.

- *Market-driven mutual funds.* Some mutual funds have no innate
investment value but are purely marketing products. For example,
a few years ago a stock mutual fund came out called the Libra
Fund. It was promoted as a mutual fund for women. But when
you think about it, are there any stocks that only women should
buy? If your stockbroker pitches a new mutual fund whose purpose
he or she can't defend, take a pass on the fund.

- *Exotic limited partnerships.* Stockbrokers and financial planners
like to sell limited partnerships because they make very good
money on them from high sales charges. But that doesn't mean
you should buy the deals. Research and development programs
and equipment leasing deals are two types of exotic partnerships
you should probably shun. The R&D partnerships generally are
quite risky, offering little chance that you will ever make money on
them. The leasing deals often lease equipment, such as computers,
that quickly becomes obsolete and difficult to lease. The newest
type of exotic partnership: one that buys parking lots.

It may take a while before your portfolio of investments becomes large and diverse enough to require a lot of management.
But you might be surprised at how quickly your IRA, Keogh, and
other pension fund investments add up, requiring astute manage-

ment. If you have been investing $2,000 or $4,000 a year in the plans since, say, 1981, you now have a sizable amount of money stashed away. Even if you have not yet been contributing regularly to an IRA, Keogh, or other pension fund, sooner or later you probably will. It's time to give some serious thought to this money. You need to know whether your investments are working hard enough for you, how to move your IRA and Keogh money around expeditiously, and how and when to withdraw cash from the plans.

CHAPTER
8

MANAGING YOUR
IRA, KEOGH, AND
PENSION FUNDS

*Basically, I'd like to be like Scrooge McDuck
and put all of my money in Shop 'N Save bags
and keep it in a vault to play around with.
Novelist Stephen King,
in* Newsweek

YOU'RE THE PORTFOLIO MANAGER

When Congress passed the law a decade ago that let every working American have an Individual Retirement Account (IRA), the politicians probably never dreamed they were creating a nation of portfolio managers. But that's exactly what happened. Today, 40 million Americans—28 percent of the public between the ages of 25 and 44—have invested in IRAs. Add to the number of IRA investors all the people who have been stuffing up to $30,000 a year in Keogh retirement plans for the self-employed and the many employees who have invested in their company savings plans, and the result is millions of people who have found themselves in the unexpected role of portfolio manager.

If you are an IRA addict, you know this role especially well. You qualify as an IRA addict if:

- Every year that you have been allowed to have an IRA, you have squirreled away the maximum amount into an account.

- You have a basketful of IRA accounts and the paperwork to match.

  The first year you could have an IRA, you may have opened one in a safe, convenient bank. The next year, you might have taken a flier with a mutual fund IRA or bought some stocks for a self-directed IRA account at a brokerage firm. A year later, you may have diversified with a real estate partnership IRA. What's more, your spouse may have put his or her annual $2,000 contribution in altogether different investments. By now, your combined IRA accounts could total more than $30,000—not yet large enough to qualify you for the millionaire status the original IRA ads promised, but still a substantial chunk of money.

- Every February, March, and early April, you have found yourself entranced by all the IRA advertisements, whose sponsors beckon you to turn over your cash. The mutual funds dazzle you with phrases such as "up 150 percent" (the total return to investors over the past ten years), and the banks nuzzle you with the security they offer through federal insurance.

  When you started contributing to your IRA, Keogh, or company savings plan, there wasn't much to think or worry about. You invested the cash and forgot about it. But now that the money has grown and your drawers are bursting with quarterly statements from the plan sponsors, it is time to step back, take a look at what you have, and ask yourself three important questions:

- Do I really need all those separate accounts?
- Is my money diversified enough?
- Have I earned as much as I expected?

If the answer to any of those questions is no—and that's quite likely—you need to manage your portfolio better.

There are two other reasons to review your IRA, Keogh, and company plan portfolio. The first is tax reform. The 1986 tax law dramatically changed some of the rules for retirement accounts. The second reason you need to review your IRA, Keogh, and savings plans is to be certain they fit your current investment needs and preferences. For example, most company savings plans give employees a choice of investment alternatives, such as a stock fund, a bond fund, a money-market fund, an insurance-backed certificate, or company stock. You might have selected your investment upon joining the company years ago. Today, however, that choice may be totally inappropriate. Similarly, the IRA that looked great in 1982 could be a dog today. Some of the best-performing IRA investments in 1982 were gold stocks; since then, they have had mediocre to abysmal records.

THE OLD AND THE NEW RULES

There's no question that the tax reform law has changed the rules about IRAs, Keoghs, and company savings plans. But to paraphrase Mark Twain, the reports of the death of IRAs are greatly exaggerated. So by all means, don't let tax reform provoke you into withdrawing all the money you have funneled into your IRA accounts over the years. In fact, chances are that you may still want to contribute to IRAs as long-term investments.

Before tax reform, the IRA rules were fairly simple. Anyone who worked for pay could invest up to $2,000 a year in an IRA and could fund the account as late as April 15 for the previous year's tax return. A married couple with two incomes could put away $4,000, while a married couple with one working spouse could invest up to $2,250. All contributions were tax-deductible. All earnings were tax-deferred until you took the money out. Upon withdrawal, you would owe taxes on the money at your current tax rate. If you took out any cash before turning 59 1/2 (or becoming permanently disabled), you owed an additional tax penalty equal to 10 percent of the amount you withdrew. You could invest your IRA with a bank, stockbroker, financial planner, insurance agent, or mutual fund and put the money in just about anything, with a few exceptions: gold, other collectibles, and life insurance.

Today most of these rules still hold. For example, IRA earnings are still tax-deferred, and early withdrawals are still generally assessed a 10 percent tax penalty. But an important change concerns the deductibility of IRA contributions. Whether you or your spouse can now deduct IRA investments depends on your company's benefits and your family's income. Here's how the new rules work:

- If neither you nor your spouse is covered by a corporate pension, tax-deferred savings plan, employer-sponsored annuity, or Keogh plan, you can both still deduct your IRA contributions. The key word is "covered." You do not have to be vested in your company's pension to be covered by it. Congress says you're covered as soon as your company starts putting money away for you in a plan or lets you contribute to a plan. Generally, the only employees of companies with pension and savings plans who are not covered are new hires or part-time workers. If you have any doubt about whether you are covered by a company plan, ask your employee benefits department.

- You can continue deducting contributions to an IRA even if you or your spouse is covered by a company plan provided that your family's adjusted gross income falls below certain proscribed dollar amounts. You can still claim the entire deduction if you are married and your family's adjusted gross income is under $40,000. The same holds if you are single and your annual income is less than $25,000.

- Neither you nor your spouse can deduct contributions to an IRA if either of you are covered by a company plan and your family's income exceeds certain limits. Sadly, you have spun the Wheel of Misfortune and lost your IRA write-offs if you are married and your family's adjusted gross income is at least $50,000 or if you are single with income of $35,000 or more. Your IRA earnings will still grow tax-deferred, though. If you invest in an IRA thinking you will be able to deduct it and later in the year you realize the IRA will be nondeductible, you can pull your money out without owing an IRS penalty.

- If you or your spouse is covered by a company plan and your income falls between $40,000 and $50,000, or you are single with income between $25,000 and $35,000, you can claim a partial write-off for your IRA. You will lose $200 in write-offs for every $1,000 in income above the base amounts of $40,000 or $25,000, depending on your marital status.

- Anyone prohibited from claiming an IRA deduction will not owe income taxes on nondeductible contributions upon withdrawing the cash. Only deductible contributions and earnings will be taxed. Say that 20 percent of your total IRA holdings represent nondeductible contributions. When you take money out of your IRA, 20 percent of that cash will not be taxed, but 80 percent of it will be.

The tax reform law changes the IRA rules in two other ways: (1) You can now invest your IRA in gold and silver coins issued by the United

States government, and (2) you won't be assessed the 10 percent early-withdrawal penalty for taking money out of your IRA before age 59 1/2 if you will receive the money as an annuity, paid out in equal installments.

The specific rules about Keogh plans haven't changed, but there are some new rules about company plans in general, and Keoghs are considered a type of company plan. Even so, any person with self-employment income can still fund a Keogh with up to 25 percent of that income or $30,000, whichever is less. A self-employed person can still contribute to a Keogh and an IRA in the same year, though the IRA might no longer be tax-deductible. (For a fuller explanation of Keoghs, see Chapter 5.)

The rules concerning company savings plans including Keoghs have changed slightly, penalizing you for withdrawing cash from them. Any money you and your employer contribute to profit-sharing, stock ownership, 401(k), or other savings plans will still grow tax-free until it is withdrawn. The 401(k) contributions, unlike those of the other plans, are still made with pretax earnings. You and your employer still cannot contribute annually more than 25 percent of your pay or $30,000, whichever is less. One switch: You can't put more than $8,728 a year into a 401(k) plan. But then, how many people could afford to save that much anyway?

The biggest wrinkles in the rules about company plans affect withdrawals from 401(k) plans. Before the law passed, you could take out all your contributions and earnings and sometimes your employer's contributions, if you were retiring, became disabled, or could prove financial hardship. Companies defined the word "hardship" differently; they usually limited hardship withdrawals to money needed for medical reasons, tuition payments, or financial emergencies. Some firms, however, were far more liberal and let employers take money out of their 401(k)s in order to buy cars or remodel their homes.

Now even if you can prove hardship, you generally will owe a 10 percent penalty as well as ordinary income taxes on the amount withdrawn. And you can now withdraw only your contributions to a 401(k) — not your employer's contributions or your earnings. You won't owe the penalty if the money will be used to pay medical expenses exceeding 7 1/2 percent of your adjusted gross income — for example, $3,750 on a $50,000 income. The tax reform law also slapped on the 10 percent penalty if you take any money out of a company profit-sharing plan or other plan, unless the cash will be used to pay medical bills. This penalty affects only withdrawals of contributions you made after 1986.

You will also pay taxes sooner than in the past if you withdraw money from an after-tax company savings plan. From now on, all such withdrawals will be considered a combination of your contributions, your company's taxable contributions, and the plan's taxable earnings. Before the law passed, you could take out only your own contributions, which would not be taxed.

The law also makes it tougher and more expensive to borrow from a company plan. Previously, if your company let you borrow from its plan, you could get a loan for as much as $50,000. Now the most you can borrow is $50,000 minus your highest outstanding loan balance from the plan during the past twelve months-even if you have already paid back the loan. If you took out a $20,000 loan in January, you can borrow only another $30,000 between now and next January. Interest on loans from most company plans is no longer tax deductible.

TO IRA OR NOT TO IRA?

Now that you may not be allowed to deduct your IRA contributions, the obvious question is: Should I keep investing in an IRA? At first glance, you might believe that an IRA without a tax deduction is not worth having at all. But think of an IRA as being like a free Dairy Queen hot fudge sundae. Would you turn down the free sundae if your DQ ran out of hot fudge sauce? Probably not. With an IRA, the tax-deferred earnings are like the ice cream and the deduction is like the fudge. Sure, the deduction is sweet. But tax-deferred earnings are still tasty. Say you have $2,000 to invest and could earn 8 percent on it. If you put the money in a tax-deferred IRA, you would have about $9,000 after 20 years. But if you invested the same $2,000, earning 8 percent, and paid taxes on the earnings each year at a 28 percent tax rate, you would wind up with only about $6,000 after 20 years—roughly a third less. But now, more than ever before, you need to think of an IRA as a L-O-N-G term involvement. In the past, you could pull money out of an IRA after five years or so, pay the 10 percent penalty, and still come out better than if you had not opened the IRA. That's because without the IRA, the money would have been taxed, up to 50 percent, and there would be no deduction. After tax reform, though, it will now take about eight years before you will come out ahead with an early withdrawal. And that assumes you can still deduct your IRA. If you can't, the break-even point will come in fourteen years or so!

If you work for a company with a 401(k) plan, put as much as you can into that plan before contributing to an IRA. You will still be allowed to invest in your 401(k) with pretax dollars, which is tantamount to a deduction, but there's no guarantee that you'll be able to deduct your IRA.

And you will probably be allowed to contribute more to the 401(k) than to an IRA. Your company also might match all or a portion of your 401(k) contributions, a feature no IRA can deliver. You may also be able to borrow against the 401(k) or withdraw some money without penalty, two other advantages over IRAs.

The 401(k) has one major drawback when compared with an IRA: Your investment choices are limited to those offered by your employer. So after you've socked away as much as possible into the 401(k), if you can still afford to fund an IRA, do.

The table below provides a head-to-head matchup between the IRA and the 401(k).

IRA vs. 401(k): How They Stack Up

	IRA	401(k)
Advantages	Tax deductible (sometimes)	Pretax contributions; like a deduction
	Earnings are tax-deferred	Earnings are tax-deferred
	Variety of investment choices	Employer may match your contributions
	Ability to move money around	Sometimes able to borrow against funds
	Can contribute until April 15 for previous year's deduction	Sometimes able to withdraw money without a penalty
		Can contribute up to $8,728 a year
Disadvantages	Maximum contribution is $2,000 a year	Limited investment choices
	Sometimes not deductible	Limits on moving money around
	Penalty for early withdrawals	Early withdrawals not usually permitted
	Generally can't borrow against it	
	No employer matching of contributions	

An IRA will also continue to act as a kind of insurance policy against the possible loss of pension income from future job switches. If you leave your current company or one in the future before vesting in its pension plan, you could wind up in retirement without any pension. But if you continue to fund your IRA every year, no, they can't take that away from you.

The IRA will come in especially handy if you leave your job and are fortunate enough to be able to take along a lump-sum payment from the pension or profit-sharing plan. Before the tax reform law passed, you could take advantage of a tax break known as ten-year forward averaging that let you compute the taxes owed on the payout as though you received the cash over ten years. But the tax reform law ended ten-year averaging for anyone younger than age 50 on January 1, 1986. From now on, if you get a lump-sum payment, your best bet will be to take advantage of the IRA rollover law. You can roll over the entire lump sum into an IRA, even if it's more than $2,000. You get no deduction when putting the money in a rollover IRA, but all earnings grow tax-deferred until you withdraw the money in the future.

YOUR BEST IRA INVESTMENT STRATEGY

The tax reform law indirectly changed the way you should invest in your IRA. Before the law passed, many astute investment advisers recommended that you fill up your IRA with income-producing bonds, bond funds, money-market funds or money-market accounts, certificates of deposit, annuities, and dividend-paying stocks. They suggested keeping the growth portion of your portfolio out of your IRA—stocks, stock mutual funds, and other investments that didn't pay interest or dividends but might appreciate in value. Why? Interest and dividends were taxed at ordinary income rates, up to 50 percent, outside an IRA. But capital gains from the sale of stocks or other property held outside an IRA longer than six months were taxed at lower capital gains rates, a maximum of 20 percent. So, you would get the biggest bang for your tax-deferred bucks by loading your IRA with investments that would otherwise have been the most heavily taxed. Furthermore, losses cannot be deducted in an IRA. So by putting stocks in an IRA, you would give up the opportunity to deduct losses in case you had to sell shares for less than you paid for them.

Tax reform has practically turned this investment strategy and practically turned it on its head, because it essentially eliminates any distinction between capital gains and ordinary income. *All* income, whether from stocks, bonds, bank certificates, or whatever, is now taxed as ordinary income, up to 33 percent.

So, if you want to invest in growth stocks or growth mutual funds with your IRA money, go right ahead. In fact, tilting your IRA toward growth has become a pretty smart strategy. An IRA, after all, is designed for the long term, and so are growth stocks. You might even want to consider shifting your previous IRA contributions and earnings out of fixed-income investments and into growth investments.

A few other tips about investing in IRAs:

- Generally, the best time to invest in an IRA is in early January. That way, you can have your earnings growing tax-deferred all year long. But if you plan to invest your IRA money at a bank, savings and loan, or credit union, wait until the heavy IRA-buying season in March and early April. That is when the financial institutions usually have their best deals and highest rates on IRA accounts.

- The highest rates from banks are on their long-term certificates of deposit—the ones that mature in five years or so. But don't be greedy. Stick with CDs with shorter terms of about one years. Tying up your money for five years is too big a risk these days when interest rates fluctuate so much. Today's 5 percent rate on a five-year CD could look miserable in 1997 if other interest rates shoot up in the interim.

- Mutual funds provide the most flexibility for IRAs. If you invest in a family of mutual funds, you can switch at will from, say, a growth stock fund to a corporate bond fund and back again. The transfer will be easy and inexpensive. Most fund families charge about $10 per switch.

- Brokerage house self-directed accounts give you the greatest freedom of choice. You can invest your brokerage IRA in stocks, bonds, mutual funds, unit trusts, limited partnerships, governmental securities, U.S. coins, annuities, stock options, certificates of deposit, and real estate investment trusts. But the wide selection usually pays only if you have at least $10,000 or so. Otherwise, you generally won't have enough cash to take advantage of the available diversification and afford the fees charged. If you plan to invest your IRA money in a certificate of deposit every year, avoid paying the steep brokerage house fees for IRA CDs and go directly to the bank.

- Banks, savings and loans, and credit unions typically have the lowest IRA fees. Most do not charge for opening or maintaining an IRA account. Brokerage houses charge the highest up-front fees.

Most stockbrokers charge about $25 to open a self-directed IRA, $25 a year thereafter, and $50 to close the account. Brokerage commissions are extra. (Some discount brokers now offer no-fee IRAs.) Insurance companies are the most sly about their fees. Most charge nothing to open an annuity but have high surrender charges: They will keep as much as 7 percent of your money if you want to pull it all out within a year. Mutual funds come out in the middle; most charge between $5 and $15 in annual maintenance expenses in addition to any fee for buying the funds initially.

IRA ROLLOVERS, TRANSFERS, AND WITHDRAWALS

Many people think that opening an IRA is like putting money into a box with a big sign that reads "Do Not Open Until Age 59 1/2." The common misconception is that once you choose an IRA investment, you are locked into it until retirement. Truth is, IRAs are yours to manage as you please. You can move cash around among IRA accounts as often as you like and continue deferring taxes on the earnings.

Moving your IRA money around is not only legal, it's sensible. Economic conditions change, and you need to adjust your investments to suit the times. As you age, your financial needs and preferences change, too. Your IRA should change along with you. Every now and then, new investments also come along that may be suitable for your IRA. Case in point: the relatively new zero-coupon bonds that cost much less than other bonds and don't pay interest until the bonds mature.

You have two choices when considering moving money from one IRA to another: an IRA rollover or an IRA transfer. Each has advantages and disadvantages. You will probably want to use both options during the course of your IRA investing years, so it is a good idea to understand the rules about both rollovers and transfers.

- *Rollover.* This technique is best suited to those who know they want to take money out of their current IRA investment but don't yet know what investment they would rather have. A rollover gives them two months to make up their mind.

    To roll over your IRA from one investment to another, you write to the custodian of your current IRA and indicate how much you want to withdraw as a rollover. The custodian sends you the cash and you then have 60 days to decide what to do with the money. If you put the cash in a taxable investment before reinvesting it in another IRA, you will owe taxes on any earnings you accrue during the 60 days.

And what if 60 days pass before you get around to reinvesting the money? You lose. The IRS will treat the transaction as a withdrawal, requiring you to pay taxes on the full amount, as well as the 10 percent penalty if you are younger than 59 1/2.

Incidentally, the IRS will assess the penalty even if the missed deadline wasn't your fault. That can happen. Some custodians are notoriously slow about moving IRAs for their customers. So if you plan to roll over your IRA, be sure to ride the custodian until the money is actually deposited in the new IRA account.

Don't make an IRA rollover decision lightly, however. The IRS lets you roll over funds from the same IRA only once every twelve months. If you try to roll over the cash more often than that, the IRS will consider the second rollover a taxable withdrawal and might hit you with the dastardly 10 percent penalty.

- *Transfer.* If you are the kind of person who changes his or her mind frequently when investing, get to know the IRA transfer. This technique lets you move money around among IRAs as often as you like. The catch: You can't personally touch the money. When transferring money from one IRA to another, get the proper forms from the new sponsor you plan to use. Fill them out, and then send a letter to the present custodian of your IRA, explaining that you want money transferred to the new account. Tell both sponsors exactly how much money will be transferred. Find out from your current custodian whether you will owe any fees and how much they will run. Ask, too, whether you must get a signature guarantee verifying your handwriting from a bank or broker to set the transfer in motion. Your present custodian will then move your money directly to the new account.

  If transfers are so nifty, why would anyone use a rollover? Simple: A transfer requires you to depend on the kindness and diligence of not one but two financial institutions. If you are a bit leery about leaving the money changing to others, you have good reason. Some banks and brokerage firms are painfully slow about transferring IRA money for their customers, especially when the cash will wind up in the hands of their competitors.

  Banks are generally speedy when handling transfers, usually completing the transactions in a week or two. But brokerage houses sometimes take as long as six months to carry out transfer orders. There truly is no reason why a transfer should take two months at the absolute longest. If your transfer drags on beyond that point, demand action from the branch manager or the institution's head of IRA accounts. Should that tactic fail to bring relief, contact the appropriate state regulator—usually the department of banking, securities, or corporations.

Brokerage houses sell a few IRA investments that cannot be transferred or that are extremely difficult to transfer. So before opening a self-directed IRA brokerage account, ask about the firm's policy of transferring money out at a later date. If the broker starts stammering, stay away from that particular investment. Currently, brokerage firms are prohibited by law from transferring zero-coupon certificates of deposit and generally will not transfer mutual funds they sponsor because of bookkeeping problems. Other slow-to-move investments include limited partnerships, insurance company annuities, and zero-coupon bonds.

IRAS AND DIVORCE

When a marriage breaks up, financial turmoil can break out. Fortunately, splitting and funding IRAs is pretty easy after a divorce. IRAs of divorcing couples will usually be lumped together with other assets and then apportioned by a judge.

Typically, judges let each spouse keep his or her own separate IRA. When one spouse has an IRA that is significantly larger than the other's, the judge will usually compensate by giving the spouse with the smaller IRA a disproportionate share of other assets. TheIRS waives the 10 percent early-withdrawal penalty for a spouse who is ordered to give some or all of his or her IRA to the ex.

Incidentally, you can fully fund an IRA even if your only income is from alimony, not earned income. Or course, the rules regarding the deductibility of IRA contributions apply to investments made with alimony money, too.

Besides being their own portfolio managers, parents need to be something of portfolio managers for their children, too. About the only way you will come up with enough cash to pay for your child's future college tuition is to start saving and investing today. The next chapter shows you how.

CHAPTER

9

PAYING FOR YOUR CHILD'S COLLEGE EDUCATION

I'm thinking in terms of making as much money
as I can and providing a large pension fund
and an education for my children ... I used
to think much less of the future than I do now.
Chevy Chase,
at age 40, in Rolling Stone

BREATHE DEEP AND START SAVING

Teachers have a pet maxim they like to use when parents complain about how expensive college has become: "If you think education is expensive, try ignorance." True enough. But the fact is, college is more costly than ever and the prognosis for future bills for tuition, room, and board is not good. Today, the total tab for one year at a public university is about $5,500; private universities run about $15,000 a year. Education analysts expect college costs to increase at an average annual rate of about 7 percent for the next 15 years or so. If you have a four-year-old, his or her college education could wind up costing roughly $50,000 at a public college and $90,000 at a private one. (Just raising a child can drain you financially. The Urban Institute, a Washington, D.C., think tank, estimates that it now costs more than $95,000 for a working suburban couple to raise a child to age 18—college not included).

While annual increases in college bills have been running way ahead of inflation, the tactics for paying for college have changed dramatically. The federal government has sharply cut back funds for its student loan programs, made it more difficult for many students to qualify for the loans, and increased the cost of many loans. The 1986 tax reform legislation put an end to some of the most popular ways to save for college. At the same time, more than 700 colleges and many states have brought out novel creative financing programs for parents and students.

So today, more than ever before, you and your children need to get intimately familiar with the various ways to pay for college, saving for tomorrow as well as applying for the $16 billion now available in loans, grants, and scholarships. Your family must also determine precisely where all your child's college money will come from and what must be done between now and the first semester to amass the necessary cash. The sooner you decide how the bills will be paid, the easier it will be to fund the education expenses. For example, if you expect your son or daughter to pay some of the bills from his or her own savings but the child has never worked, help the kid get a job as soon as possible. If you own a business, you may even want to hire your son or daughter.

Everyone knows college is expensive, so you might think that parents your age are busy socking away money for the day when Junior goes to State U. Wrong. Even though most families today expect that their children will go to college, many are not saving to pay for the education costs, according to a recent survey by Market Facts, a Chicago market research firm. Its poll found that 86 percent of parents want their children to have a college education but only 54 percent have actually put money away to help them. Unless you are absolutely certain that your child's college bills will be covered entirely by other sources—financial aid, your present investments, an expected windfall—don't let yourself fall into the save-not group. Like retirement, a college education for your child is a major expense that requires a serious financial commitment from you.

Tax reform has made it even more critical that you save regularly for those college bills. In effect, the tax changes have raised the cost of paying for college. Before the new tax law, you could set up a trust or a separate account for your child, whose earnings would be taxed at your child's low tax rate. But the law now says that, except for certain circumstances, any earnings on money you give your children under age 14 now will be taxed at *your* tax rate. So, now that the IRS will be taking a bigger cut out of your college savings funds, you will need to save even more than before just to come out even. For example, if you put aside $10,000 for your child in 1986, the money might have been taxed at a 16 percent rate. Today, such a fund might be taxed at a 31 percent rate. The new tax changes will also prevent you and your child from deducting interest on college loans. Scholarship money will be taxed, too.

HOW MUCH WILL YOU NEED?

One of the hardest questions for parents of young children is: Exactly how much money will I need to save for my child to go to college? This question is a tough one because it requires being able to answer a host of other difficult questions. How much will colleges cost in the future? No one really knows. What college will your child attend? Will it be an exclusive four-year private university such as Harvard or Stanford? Will it be a state-supported public university such as the University of Texas or the University of Michigan? Will it be a junior college? A community college? Will your child continue on to graduate school? For how many years? Add to those questions ones about the type and amount of financial aid that will be available when your child is ready for college, and the issue becomes even more complex.

With all these unknowables, you may be tempted to throw up your hands and decide to deal with college costs when the time comes. That will be too late. Imagine what would happen if you either oversaved or undersaved for college. In the first instance, you would have more money set aside for college than is actually necessary. You could then use the surplus for other purposes—maybe a vacation or a new car or your retirement. But in the second instance, you wouldn't have enough money for college. Your child would have to either attend a less-expensive college or go to no college at all, or you would have to borrow money at whatever the current interest rate is to make up the shortfall. Then you would have to find a way to come up with the cash to make the loan payments.

There are three good ways to figure the amount of money you will need to save for college. The first way is to let someone else do the figuring for you. Merrill Lynch, for instance, has a free service called The CollegeBuilder program. You tell a Merrill Lynch broker how old your child is and where the child might go to college someday, and the CollegeBuilder computer program will spit out how much Merrill Lynch thinks the college will cost. Of course, the broker will more than likely try to sell you stocks, bonds, or annuities designed to help pay those future college costs.

The second method of calculating future college costs is to do it yourself. First, pick several colleges you think your child might attend and find out the current four-year costs there. Consult *The College Cost Book* (published by The College Board) for current fees. Then assume that costs will rise 7 percent a year. Increase the current prices by the appropriate amount for the number of years until your child will be in college. Once you have those figures, determine how much money you would need to save each year, assuming that the cash earned a reasonable return of, say, 7 percent a year before taxes. Remember that a portion of your savings will be taxed each year. No one knows what tax brackets will be in the future, so, for argument's sake, assume that you will be in the 31 percent tax bracket between now and when college will start. In other words, add 31 percent to the amount you would otherwise have to save.

Managing Your Money

The third way to calculate future college costs is to use Managing Your Money. Managing Your Money will tell you precisely how much you can expect your child's education to cost, and how much you'll need to save annually. Select Tuition Planning from the Analyze submenu. Fill in all of the fields. Press F10, and Managing Your Money will give you the amount you'll have to save under four approaches:

1) if you want to have enough to cover tuition by the time college starts;

2) if you continue paying after college starts;

3) if you want to increase your annual tuition savings as your income and ability to save rises;

4) if you just want to set aside a lump sum today, and not make any additions to that amount.

Here's the upshot: If you now have a baby, you will have to put away between about $1,500 and $4,000 a year to pay for all the future college costs. If you have a third-grader and haven't begun saving yet, figure on putting aside $3,000 to $7,000 a year. Of course, those frightening figures assume that your savings will fully fund tuition, room, and board. Many parents will rely on loans, grants, scholarships, and their children's savings to help foot the bills.

HOW TO SAVE AND INVEST FOR THE FUTURE

Saving for college is just like saving for any future expense. You want your money to grow as much as possible, with a minimum of risk. Current, steady income is not essential, because this is money that you won't need for some time. But keeping the money out of the hands of the tax man is critical. The less the savings are taxed, the less you will have to save. So, the bulk of your college fund should go into tax-deferred or lightly taxed growth investments.

Before you look for specific investments, you must understand how the tax laws now treat your money versus your child's money. The tax reform law has wiped the blackboard clean of the old rules, and new rules have replaced them.

Under the old law, you could save for college and save on taxes in two ways: with Clifford trusts and with custodial accounts. Both have been battered by tax reform—Cliffords virtually mortally. A Clifford trust lets you put money into an account under your child's name. In ten years, the money and any earnings return to you. During the life of the trust, however, you do not have access to the money. In a custodial account established under the Uniform Gifts to Minors Act (UGMA), money is also put aside under your child's name and Social Security number. You can open a custodial account through a bank, stockbroker, or mutual fund, and either you or another adult of your choosing acts as the custodian. One problem with custodial accounts is that once your child comes of age—18 in most states—the money is his or hers for good, to do with as he or she pleases. You can give away as much as $10,000 a year ($20,000 if you and your spouse make the gift together) without owing federal gift taxes.

In the past, earnings on money in Clifford trusts and custodial accounts were taxed at your child's tax rate, not yours. So, more money would accrue after taxes than if you had put the money in an account of your own, taxed at your higher rate. This has all changed under the 1986 tax reform law.

Cliffords are all but obsolete now. All income from Clifford trusts set up after March 1, 1986 is taxable to whoever sets up the trust. Income from a trust set up before that date will be taxed at your rate until your child turns 14. So, there's really no point in creating a Clifford anymore. You get no tax advantage for setting one up, and you still give up access to your money for ten years.

If your child already has a Clifford trust, don't go through the trouble of dissolving it. Instead, make future contributions with tax-deferred or tax-free investments. U.S. savings bonds are a particularly sound investment. The bonds are safe, they pay a decent return (6 percent guaranteed if held at least five years), and federal taxes on the interest can be deferred until the bonds mature. By that time, your child will most likely be older than 14 and the bonds will then be taxed at his or her rate. Municipal bonds whose interest is free of federal taxes are also worthwhile for a pre-tax reform Clifford trust. Another alternative: growth stocks, which won't be taxed until the shares are sold—ideally, after your child is 14.

Now that Cliffords are virtually dead, custodial accounts are the only tax-saving college financing arrangements left, and they should be funded to the hilt. But even custodial accounts have been watered down. The new rules say that if your child is younger than 14, his or her first $500 of income will be tax-free and the next $500 will be taxed at his or her rate. Additional income will be taxed at your rate. Once your child turns 14, however, all of the account's earnings above $500 will be taxed at his or her rate. The law on custodial accounts applies regardless of when an account was set up.

If you plan to put as much as $10,000 into a custodial account for a child younger than 14, and thereby avoid owing gift taxes, stick with investments that don't pay out a lot of current income. Otherwise, the interest or dividends could exceed $1,000 and be taxed at your rate. Stay away from, say, bank certificates of deposit and invest instead in savings bonds (whose income is deferred until the bonds are cashed) and growth stocks and municipal bonds—either directly or through mutual funds. Once your child turns 14, you can switch strategies and invest for current taxable income, if that's your preference. At that point, the earnings will be taxed at your child's rate. Look then for the safest high-yielding investment around. That might be a high-quality corporate bond mutual fund or a Ginnie Mae mutual fund. Don't stretch for higher returns by taking extra risks. College will be approaching too soon to gamble with your money.

A zero-coupon municipal bond is a particularly ideal investment for a college savings fund, whether or not you set up a custodial account. You can select a bond that will mature shortly before your child will start college. The bond doesn't pay interest; you buy it at a deep discount from face value and get back the full amount when the bond comes due. Because zeros sell at such big discounts, they are inexpensive compared with other bonds. You might be able to buy a ten-year $1,000 zero municipal bond, yielding 7 percent, for only $400. Before buying a zero bond, make sure that the issuer cannot redeem it prior to the bond's maturity date. You are buying the bond for a particular purpose with a particular date in mind and can't afford to have your plans derailed.

Don't put all your college savings into zeros, however. Interest rates are too volatile to tie so much money up at a rate that could look pitifully low in five or ten years when the bond matures. Create a balanced portfolio, tilted toward zeros but with a mixture of other, more liquid investments just in case interest rates shoot up.

TUITION FUTURES: THEY RARELY ADD UP

Want to beat the high—and getting higher—cost of college? How about this deal: Even though your child hasn't reached puberty, you pay the tuition bills *now* for the college he or she will attend after graduating from high school. Talk about bargains. You might pay $7,000 today instead of the $20,000 or more that college will cost when your son or daughter actually enrolls. The younger your child, the bigger your discount.

This pay-now, enroll-later idea is catching on. More than twenty-five colleges—including Canisius College in Buffalo, Duquesne University in Pittsburgh, and the University of Detroit—now have such programs, which are called endowed tuition plans or tuition futures. Several states, such as Michigan, New Hampshire, and New Jersey, are looking at setting up state-wide tuition futures programs for their public universities and community colleges.

Sure, you will have saved money by signing up for a tuition futures program. But at what price? Can you really predict with absolute certainty that your child will want to go to a particular college ten years in advance, let alone qualify for admission? Will today's top-flight school with a tuition futures program retain its academic excellence in the future? Maybe, maybe not. Most, but not all, of the colleges offering tuition futures will refund your money if your child does not enroll. But don't expect to get back the interest your money will earn over the years—interest you could have been earning yourself.

The long-range tuition futures deals are really too risky. But a number of colleges have short-term variations of these financing programs that do warrant consideration. Their financing arrangements let parents of incoming freshmen lock in the current tuition rate for four years by prepaying the full tuition bill up front. Some colleges will lend parents money for these lump-sum deals at interest rates around 9 percent. Among the schools offering the lock-in programs are Case Western Reserve in Cleveland; Grinnell College in Grinnell, Iowa; the University of Chicago; the University of Florida; the University of Pennsylvania; the University of Southern California; and Washington University in St. Louis.

Your savings on such programs depend on three factors: how much the college's tuition will actually rise over the next four years, what you would do with the money otherwise, and whether you have the cash. If, for instance, the tuition will rise 7 percent a year but you are disciplined enough to invest the money and believe you can earn more than 7 percent annually on it, don't sign up. If, however, you have the cash now but think you might fritter it away, the lock-in plan will be a useful forced savings plan that will save you money, no matter how much the college raises its tuition. Borrowing to lock in today's tuition fee makes sense only if you plan to take out college loans in the future anyway. If you borrow now and interest rates fall over the next four years, however, you will be paying a higher interest rate than necessary.

HIRING YOUR CHILD NOW

Entrepreneurs have an advantage over employees when it comes to saving money for college. They can hire their children in the family business. If you run a company and put your child on the payroll, his income will be taxed at his low tax rate and you will be allowed to deduct the salary as a business expense.

Social Security also gives parents a break for hiring their kids. If your business is either a proprietorship or a partnership with your spouse, you won't have to pay the employer's share of Social Security taxes on your child's earnings. Nor will your child owe the employee's share of Social Security taxes. Together, the two add up to 15.3 percent of wages paid.

THE FUTURE IS NOW: GRANTS, SCHOLARSHIPS, AND OTHER WAYS TO GET FREE COLLEGE CASH

Your child is a high school senior and you're short on cash to pay for college. Before looking into borrowing money to make up the shortfall, be sure you have exhausted the variety of no-cost alternative financing arrangements. There are more than you think. For example:

- *Grants and scholarships.* Most colleges and state governments as well as the federal government hand out grants and scholarships to families of moderate incomes. These programs don't require students to pay back the money or work to earn it, although most require families to prove they have a financial need. Scholarships often demand that students meet other criteria.

   The federal government has two grant programs. The Pell Grant program gives needy undergraduates between $200 and $2,400 to attend college. The amount students can get depends on their family's finances, the cost of their college, and whether they will be full-time or part-time students. The Supplemental Educational Opportunity Grant program awards students between $200 and $4,000 (though Congress may not allocate enough money to provide grants exceeding $2,000). Although the federal government supplies the cash, the colleges parcel it out to needy students. A student must be a U.S. citizen enrolled as an undergraduate in an accredited college or university to qualify.

   Practically every state has a scholarship or grant program for its own residents. Most of these programs require that families prove financial need and that the students attend in-state schools. The size of the grants and scholarships varies from state to state. A few states, including Alabama, Florida, Georgia, Michigan, North Carolina, Ohio, and Virginia, have what are called tuition-equalization grant programs. In many cases, any of their residents who attend in-state private colleges full-time can apply for grants, regardless of financial need. Your child's high school guidance counselor should be able to provide you with details on your state's programs.

   Many colleges also offer their own grants and scholarships, and they don't necessarily require students or families to prove financial need. Nearly nine out of ten colleges now offer merit scholarships for qualifying students, regardless of financial need. The merit programs generally require that applicants have better-than-average high school records and Scholastic Aptitude Test scores. The merit scholarships range in size from $100 to as much as full tuition plus living expenses.

Private scholarship programs abound, too. In fact, there is now a cottage industry of companies that will try to find scholarships for your child. Some scholarships, such as those of the National Merit Scholarship Program, are awarded to students who demonstrate academic excellence. Others are given to students of particular religions or ethnic backgrounds; to athletes, to artists; to children of union or fraternal organization members; to children of employees of certain corporations; and to students who plan to embark on given careers.

You and your child should explore every possible source of scholarship aid. Ask your company, church or temple, and any organization you belong to whether they offer any college assistance. Contact the local Chamber of Commerce to see whether any businesses in your area give money to graduating high school seniors. Your local public library is a valuable resource. Spend a few hours with your son or daughter skimming through the library's books listing scholarships. The library may also have a bulletin board or brochures that provide details about financial aid programs.

- *The College Work-Study Program.* Many colleges participate in this federally financed program, which finds paying jobs for undergraduates and graduate students who demonstrate financial need. Most of the jobs are on campus in places such as school cafeterias, libraries, and offices, though some are in private businesses. The pay is usually the minimum wage or higher and work hours vary; 10 to 15 hours a week is typical.

- *Cooperative education.* Nearly 900 colleges and universities now let students alternate semesters of schooling and full-time employment. The federal government employs about 15,000 students a year in co-op programs, and more than 30,000 other employers also participate in co-op plans. Not only can a co-op job cover college costs, it might launch your child in a career.

- *Service academies and ROTC.* Send your child to a U.S. service academy such as West Point or Annapolis and the federal government will pay all expenses plus provide a monthly stipend. Your senator or congressman must nominate your child for admission to any service academy other than the Coast Guard's. Students must apply in their junior year of high school.

More than 600 colleges and universities have Reserve Officer Training Corps (ROTC) programs for full-time undergrads between ages 17 and 25. ROTC scholarships pay tuition, fees, and books and also provide a $100-a-month stipend. Recipients must meet certain academic and physical requirements and must agree to serve in the military after graduation for a minimum of four years' active duty and two years' reserve duty.

THE FUTURE IS NOW: WAYS TO BORROW

Scholarships and grants are great, as far as they go. Trouble is, they don't go very far for middle-income and upper-income people. Odds are that you or your child will have to take out a loan to help pay for college. The federal government, most state governments, and many colleges offer reasonable financing terms. In many cases, however, your child will be required to show financial need in order to qualify. You may get the best college financing deal by borrowing against your life insurance policy, your house, or your company's savings plan. Here are the borrowing options:

- *Perkins Loans.* These loans, financed by the federal government but administered by colleges and universities, are generally reserved for families with incomes of $30,000 or less. They are the least expensive way to borrow, if your child is eligible. The government charges 5 percent interest and allows undergraduate and graduate students to repay the loans over ten years, beginning nine months after graduation. Maximum loan amount: $4,500 in the first two years, up to a total of $9,000 for undergrads and $18,000 for grad students.

- *Stafford Student Loans* (SSL). The big daddy of the federal college loan programs, the SSL plan is handled by banks, savings and loans, credit unions, and state lending authorities. It's often the next best borrowing deal after Perkins loans. Stafford loans are available to students who can prove financial need, regardless of their parents' income. A student will qualify only if the family will be making federally mandated contributions toward college costs and will still need additional cash. For example, a two-parent, one-child family whose adjusted gross income is $70,000 must come up with about $13,000 in cash for college before the student will be allowed to get a SSL. Students will usually qualify for the loans if their family's income is less than $65,000-especially if the family has more than one child in college or the school is expensive.

The recent interest rate on SSLs was 6.94%. The rate changes annually. Undergraduate and graduate students can repay loans over ten years; some students with large college loans can repay SSLs over 25 years. Maximum loan amount: $2,625 a year for the first two years of undergraduate study and $4,000 a year for each of the two subsequent years. Grad students can borrow up to $7,500 a year. There is an up-front origination fee of 5 percent of the loan amount. Starting July 1, 1993, the maximum SSL for undergrads will be $5,500.

Congress also recently created a spin off called unsubsidized Stafford loans. The rates and sizes of these loans are the same as SSLs, but unsubsidized Staffords are available to all families, regardless of financial need. But borrowers must begin paying interest on these loans immediately, not upon graduation.

- *Parent Loans for Undergraduate Students* (PLUS). These federally subsidized loans, sometimes called Auxiliary Loans to Assist Students (ALAS), are also handled by some local lenders. PLUS loans are available to all parents of undergraduates and graduate students themselves. The government was recently charging 4.26%. PLUS loans have variable interest rates pegged at 3.1 points above the one-year Treasury bill rate, with a maximum rate of 10 percent. These loans demand that borrowers start making principal and interest payments with 60 days after they receive the money. Maximum loan amount: $4,000 per year, up to $20,000 for dependent undergraduates and grad students. Starting July 1, 1993, the maximum will be the full cost of education minus any other financial aid.

- *State loan programs.* Most states have their own college loan programs for residents. Some state loans are also available to out-of-state students. The loans rarely require students to prove financial need, but interest rates, repayment terms, and loan amounts vary from state to state. Typically, states charge a little less than PLUS loans but a little more than SSLs-currently about 9.5 to 11 percent.

Many states provide larger loans than the federal government; loans of up to $5,000 or $10,000 are common. Most of the state loan programs let students repay the money over ten to fifteen years. Students apply for state-sponsored loans either through their colleges or through state education agencies.

- *College-sponsored loan programs.* Many colleges and universities have set up their own loan programs, geared to students whose families cannot qualify for SSLs. In some instances, parents take out the loans. In others, students do. And some colleges have students and parents apply together.

  Here, too, the interest rates, terms, and loan sizes vary. But schools typically charge between 7 and 9 percent for loans of up to $10,000 a year and let borrowers repay the money in six to ten years. Many loans come with variable rates; the interest rate fluctuates annually but generally remains lower than what banks charge on consumer loans. The Consortium on Financing Higher Education, a group of thirty Ivy League and other expensive private colleges, has its own program that doles out annual loans of $2,000 to $15,000. Families can repay the loans over fifteen years.

- *Commercial loans.* A handful of companies around the country specialize in making loans to parents of undergraduate and graduate students. The loans usually come with reasonable interest rates and repayment plans. For instance, the Knight Insurance Agency Tuition Repayment Plan (800-225-6783) lets parents borrow up to the full amount of college costs and charges an interest rate that is 4 1/2 percentage points above the three-month Treasury bill rate. The rate, which is generally lower than what most banks charge on consumer loans, is adjusted quarterly. Parents can repay the loan over 15 years. There is a $55 nonrefundable loan origination fee.

- *Company-sponsored loans.* If you work for a major corporation, or perhaps even a smaller firm, your employer might make below-market-rate college loans. You might also be allowed to borrow from your account in the company's savings plan.

- *Banks, savings and loans, and credit unions.* These local lenders will also let you take out a personal loan to pay for your child's college education. The interest rate will probably be several percentage points higher than the rate of SSLs, and you will most likely be expected to repay the loan over four years or so.

- *Life insurance.* If you own a whole-life insurance policy, you may be able to borrow against it at an interest rate lower than what the banks are charging. Some policies charge an interest rate as low as 5 percent a year. You repay the money at the schedule you choose.

- *A line of credit against your savings.* Many lenders will let you borrow at below market rates by pledging your savings as collateral. You have to tie up your money for the life of the loan, which could be six years or longer. But a credit line is worth pursuing if you lack the discipline required to leave your present savings alone and to build up future savings to repay an unsecured loan. Two companies provide such a credit line nationwide: Collegeaire (P.O. Box 723355, Atlanta, Ga. 30339) and the U.S. Trust Co. (P.O. Box 373, Boston, Mass. 02101). You can borrow up to two and a half times more than the amount you put up as collateral. U.S. Trust charges an interest rate equal to the amount of interest your deposit earns. Collegeaire costs about 1 percent a year.

- *Borrowing against your house.* More and more parents are dipping into the equity of their houses to pay for their children's college costs. These loans are likely to get even more popular because of tax reform. The new tax law, which eliminates deductions on most forms of consumer interest, included a special loophole permitting write-offs for interest on a second mortgage if the money was used to fund college. When Congress changed this rule again in 1987, it eliminated the special break for parents but instead allowed full deductibility, starting in 1988, for interest on these loans of up to $100,000, regardless of the use of the proceeds. So, as long as the college costs you pay do not exceed $100,000, any interest you borrow against your house will be fully deductible. You can borrow on the house by applying to a lender for either a fixed-rate second mortgage or a variable-rate line of credit otherwise known as a home-equity loan. You can usually borrow 70 to 85 percent of your equity (the house's market value minus the unpaid balance on your first mortgage). Danger: If you can't make the loan payments, you could lose your house.

A home-equity line is a more convenient college financing tool than a second mortgage. When you apply for a second mortgage, the lender gives you a big lump of cash and you must start paying interest on the full amount right away. A home equity credit line lets you write checks or use a credit card to borrow only the amount you need, when you need it. You then pay interest only on the amount you borrow. Banks, savings and loans, credit unions, and stockbrokers offer home-equity lines and usually charge rates of 1 3/4 percentage points above the prime rate. You can repay the loan over five to twenty years. The credit lines come with a truckload of other closing costs, which can end up costing 3 1/2 percent of the loan amount.

HOW TO APPLY FOR FINANCIAL AID

It's never a pleasure to apply for a loan. But applying for college aid is especially difficult and frustrating, probably Number 2 in aggravation (with filling out income tax forms being Number 1). You and your child will have to deal with myriad confusing forms and ribbons of red tape. If that isn't bad enough, you will have to bare your most personal financial data to total strangers at colleges and banks. Foul up on the applications, and you could have real problems paying for your child's college.

If you understand the aid process and play by the rules, however, the application procedure will be tolerable. The best time to start the financial aid process is a year before your child will enroll in college. Here, in a nutshell, is the ideal sequence of events:

- In September of your son or daughter's senior year, he or she should start the hunt for aid in earnest by meeting with the high school guidance counselor. That's also the time you and your child should visit the library and bookstores to read up on sources of aid.

- In November, your child should write to the financial aid offices of the colleges he or she might attend and ask for financial aid applications.

- December is the time to pull together the financial records necessary for completing the application forms. You will need to tell the schools your family's income, assets, home equity, and household expenses, among other things. So get copies of your most recent federal and state tax returns, your bank, mortgage, and brokerage statements, recent medical bills, and paycheck stubs.

- In January, all the aid applications should be sent to the colleges—even before your child gets his or her acceptance or rejection letters. You will need to send each college a copy of your current tax return. If there is any reason why your family's financial circumstances are unusual and your child will require more than the normal amount of financial aid for your family's income, say so in a letter accompanying the aid applications.

You will make the process less trying by getting to know the financial aid officer at the college your child hopes to attend. The better acquainted you two and the financial aid officer are, the easier it will be to get any questions answered. You will also increase the likelihood that the college will make special exceptions for your student who might otherwise not qualify for aid or for as much aid as you would like.

- The colleges will send your child a letter in February or March saying whether he or she will qualify for aid and how much aid will be provided. If your son or daughter will need more financial aid, he or she should make an appointment with the college aid office and go to a local bank to apply for a Stafford Student Loan.

- The college will give your child his or her financial aid check in September, upon enrolling.

- Three months later, your child will need to begin applying for aid for the sophomore year.

RECOMMENDED READING

A number of books are especially useful tools to help you and your child pay for college. Some are excellent sources of college aid; others will walk you through the financial aid application process. Among the best:

Don't Miss Out: The Ambitious Student's Guide to Scholarships and Loans (Octameron Press)

Need a Lift? (The American Legion) Sources of scholarship and loan information

The College Blue Book: Scholarships, Fellowships, Grants and Loans (Macmillan)

The College Cost Book (The College Board)

The A's and B's: Your Guide to Academic Scholarships (Octameron Press)

Winning Money for College (Peterson's Guides)

CHAPTER

10

YOUR HOME AND
YOUR MONEY

*We got a ride on the inflation train that you
would not believe! In 1978, we bought this
house for $150,000. If we sell our house and
don't put it back into a behemoth, we
have $140,000 of profit!*
Albert Brooks, to his on-screen wife,
Julie Hagerty, in the 1985 movie
Lost in America

THAT GREAT INFLATION TRAIN RIDE

The quote from *Lost in America* probably makes you smile with recognition. Like Albert Brooks's character, you may well have bought a house in the 1970s that has risen in value more than you could have imagined. Now, though, there are more than a few questions facing you and fellow passengers on the inflation train:

- Should you sell your house and rent?

- Should you sell your house, cash in on your profits, and trade up?

- Should you keep the house but begin some serious remodeling to make the home fit your family better?

- Should you stay in the house but cash in on some of its appreciation by taking out a second mortgage or a home-equity loan?

- Should you start paying off the mortgage faster?

- Should you refinance your mortgage for one at a lower interest-rate?

- If you buy another house, should you get an adjustable-rate mortgage or a fixed-rate mortgage?

- Should you get a 30-year loan or a 15-year loan?

- Should you take a mortgage with a higher interest rate but fewer points or a lower rate but more points?

- How big a down payment should you offer?

Such problems. Actually, consider yourself fortunate. You got in on the housing boom at the right time. Younger members of the Baby Boom generation who didn't buy their first houses until the 1980s have been faced with much higher mortgage rates and home prices than you were. The median price for an existing single-family house is now roughly $90,000, more than twice the price in 1977. In fact, many experts say that people who bought homes before prices and interest rates took off will be better off financially their entire lives than those who bought later.

HOUSE PRICES AND MORTGAGE RATES: WHERE THEY'VE BEEN, WHERE THEY'RE GOING

The housing market has changed considerably from the 1970s. If you are contemplating buying or selling a house and haven't done so in years, prepare yourself for a whole new experience.

Ten years ago, if you needed a mortgage, you called any savings and loan, asked for its current rate and points on a 30-year fixed-rate loan, and applied. Today, the competition among mortgage lenders has become fierce. Alongside the S&Ls are banks, credit unions, mortgage bankers, K Mart, Sears, and a host of others. Their mortgage terms vary enormously, requiring you to ask a lot of questions about the rates, points, and maturities of the loans. Shrewd mortgage shopping can save you thousands of dollars over the life of your mortgage.

House price appreciation is a lot less predictable now than it was in the 1970s, too. Then, you could count on your home growing in value by about 10 percent a year. House prices appreciated a percentage point or two more than the inflation rate, on average, as had been the case historically. From 1980 through 1984, though, things changed. Inflation plummeted and so did the growth in the appreciation of house prices. Houses continued to rise in value, but by only a few percentage points a year in most places. More startlingly, many house prices rose less than inflation. Then in 1985 and 1986, mortgage rates dropped to their lowest levels since 1978—as low as 7 percent on a 30-year adjustable-rate loan—and house prices started streaking skyward again in many places, far more than the nation's annual 2 percent to 4 percent inflation rate.

In the past few years, however, house prices have barely kept up with inflation in many places. In New England, the New York City metropolitan area and parts of California, house prices even fell. Now that mortgage rates have dropped again—to roughly 8.5% for a 30-year, fixed-rate loan—home prices in most places have been rising at or slightly above the inflation rate.

What will happen to mortgage rates and home prices in the next few years is truly anybody's guess. Most economists have been off-target in their previous prognostications. William Melton, senior economist for IDS Financial Services, studied the forecasts of fifty top economists to check the accuracy of their predictions for the direction of interest rates. He found that 64 percent of the economists were wrong in 1983, 67 percent in 1984, and 63 percent in 1985.

That said, many housing economists forecast that 30-year fixed-rate mortgages will average between 8 percent and 11 percent for the next few years. If they are right, home prices in many areas are likely to continue rising in excess of the inflation rate. Average annual housing appreciation of 4 percent to 10 percent is a distinct possibility if mortgage rates do not rise.

As for today, you can make the best of your housing dollars by following the pointers given in the remainder of this chapter.

TO MOVE OR NOT TO MOVE

Maybe your home sweet home is becoming a little cramped. Or perhaps the neighborhood just isn't what it was when you moved in. The school system in your area might leave room for improvement. Whatever the reason, by now you have undoubtedly considered whether to remodel your house or trade up. Which to choose depends on why your present house has outgrown its usefulness.

Sometimes the choice is simple. If you're restless for reasons having nothing to do with the house itself, move out. You will want to trade up for such niceties as better schools, better recreation areas, a better neighborhood, more acreage, less traffic, or an easier commute to work. Perhaps every room of your house is now too small for your family. You are also a perfect candidate for a move. A recent survey of move-up buyers in *Builder* magazine showed that most traded up to houses 19 percent larger than their former homes and no smaller than 2,000 square feet. But if you've grown accustomed to your place and it has become a little too cozy, remodeling will let you stay where you are and gain some elbow room.

The choice is not always so simple, however. Frequently, homeowners can't decide between remodeling or moving, because both have advantages and drawbacks. Both options entail hassles, lead to family squabbles, and are costly.

Take moving. First there are the closing costs. They could run 6 percent of the selling—and purchase—prices of your houses. Hiring a mover could run another $1,000 or so. Then there are all the expenses after you move. New home buyers spend more on their houses during the first year they move in than at any other time, according to a 1986 survey by the Simmons Market Research Bureau of New York for *New Home* magazine. The survey, which queried 1,259 people who had just bought homes costing more than $70,000, found that homeowners spent up to $3,600 on new furnishings within the first six months and planned to spend another $2,900 within the six subsequent months. Remodeling within a year after moving was planned by 80 percent of the owners surveyed. The cost of interior and exterior painting averaged $1,300.

Take the typical costs of remodeling your present house: A room addition could cost $12,000 and up, a new kitchen could run $10,000 or more, a finished attic or fancy bathroom could be $6,000, a finished basement or standard bathroom could total $4,000. Installing a swimming pool? Figure on about $12,000. You will recoup some, but not all, of those expenses when you eventually sell the house.

Remodeling is certainly easier than moving because you will be dealing with fewer unknowables-the neighbors, the area, structural problems with the house. So, if you like where you live and you can solve your present housing problems by making better use of your existing house, do so. Don't let high heating or air-conditioning bills force you out of your home. Most roaring home energy bills can be tamed by some fairly painless energy-efficiency moves, such as installing insulation, replacing a furnace's burner, or buying better window coverings.

Just be sure before doing any remodeling that your local zoning laws permit the work you plan to do. Sometimes zoning ordinances and deeds prohibit homeowners from expanding their houses as much as they would like. Employees at your local municipal building department will tell you what can and can't be done on your house.

Moving usually will make more sense than remodeling if the combination of the cost of the work needed on your present home and the house's current market value would be more than 20 percent higher than the price of comparable homes in your neighborhood. Otherwise, you probably would never recover your renovation costs. Don't remodel if the improvements would make your house too different from those of your neighbors or you will also have trouble selling your home. The time is right to move if property values in your neighborhood have not been rising. And if your house is too big for your present family or you want a newer home with fewer maintenance problems, moving is the answer.

WHEN REMODELING PAYS

In the current era when house prices generally are not appreciating in value the way they did in the 1970s, it has become increasingly important to build value into your home. Some remodeling efforts will more than make up for their expense, while others will never come close. You shouldn't deny yourself the pleasure of installing a hot tub or a swimming pool simply because they will probably be poor financial investments. Just be sure you understand beforehand what a project will cost and whether you will be paid back for the effort.

The first rule of remodeling is that the more you customize a renovation project, the less likely it will appeal to future buyers and thus the smaller the probable return on your investment. The second rule of remodeling is that you should avoid a major overhaul of your home unless you expect to live there at least another five years. Otherwise you won't have enough time to enjoy the restyled house and you probably won't get your money back from the work.

The more you can do yourself, the more likely you will recoup your cash outlay. Labor usually represents between half and two-thirds of the expense of most remodeling jobs. Even if you haven't the time, patience, or expertise to sand the floors or knock down the walls, you can cut your remodeling costs by doing as much as possible to make your house ready for the professionals before they begin their work. For example, move the furniture and appliances out of the rooms that will be improved and you won't have to pay the contractor's work crew to do it.

Improving your master bedroom, adding on a bathroom, and renovating the kitchen are generally the best remodeling jobs for the money. You can expect to recoup roughly the cost of these projects and sometimes even a bit more. Master bedrooms often are the rooms home buyers zero in on first. If you have one bathroom and plan to build either another full bath or a half-bath (just a toilet and sink), it's quite likely that the work will pay for itself. Adding a bathroom onto a bedroom for privacy is usually a surefire investment, too. New kitchens are often high on the must-have lists of home buyers. So if yours is out of date or poorly laid out, remodeling will pay off. Just refrain from going overboard and spending more than 10 percent of the market value of your house, unless you are confident that you will recoup your investment when you sell the home.

Home buyers almost always warm up to fireplaces. In fact, some buyers won't even look at houses without them. So if you build a fireplace, you can probably expect to get back its cost or more. Figure on paying somewhere between $3,000 and $8,000.

By contrast, expect to lose some money on a room addition. The next person who lives in your house might well have preferred the room to have been left alone. If you need an extra bedroom or an office, design the room so it can suit a variety of needs for prospective buyers. Outdoor porches, decks, and patios—which typically cost between $750 and $8,000—also usually return only about half the amount you will pay for them. The same is true for converting an attic, garage, or basement. Swimming pools, hot tubs, and tennis courts usually return only 20 to 50 percent of your investment because most buyers don't want them. Exception: neighborhoods where such leisure amenities are de rigueur.

FINDING PROFESSIONAL REMODELING HELP

Unless you are extraordinarily handy and have loads of time on your hands, you will need to hire one or more professionals for your remodeling job. Don't be stingy. Invest in your house by hiring the best skilled craftsmen you can afford, rather than simply the least-expensive ones. You'll derive more pleasure from living in the house in the future, and the workmanship will appeal to buyers when it's time to sell the house.

Major remodeling projects—those costing about $20,000 or more—call for the talents of an architect or building designer. Either will help you crystallize your renovation ideas and, if you wish, provide you with plans and the building materials you will need. The architect or designer will also coordinate your project if you so desire. Building designers have less training than architects and generally cost a little less.

Some architects and building designers charge an hourly rate of between $35 and $100. That's fine if you are hiring one for advice and some plans. The total cost of such help can come to between $2,500 and $10,000. Others charge a flat fee of 10 to 20 percent of the total building cost.

A general contractor typically is the field general of a remodeling project. He or she supervises all the work, hires and monitors subcontractors such as electricians or plumbers, and takes care of other related chores. Contractors make bids that usually include profit margins of 10 to 25 percent of the cost of construction. The contractor pays the subcontractors for you.

It's a good idea to get competing bids from several local contractors. Once you choose one, get a written contract and have your lawyer look it over. Pay the contractor in installments: 10 percent at the beginning of the remodeling and then in 30 percent increments as the work gets done.

You may also want to hire an interior designer to help redecorate your home. Designers can usually save you money if the project will cost more than $2,000. If you have a smaller task in mind but still want some assistance, buy some of the newest home-decorating books and magazines. Independent decorators typically charge an hourly fee of $35 to $100 or a flat fee of 25 percent of the cost of the redesign. Some require you to buy furniture and materials from them through what is known as a purchase agreement. Pay an hourly or percentage fee for a small project, but ask for a purchase agreement when you are redecorating your house from attic to basement.

PULLING MONEY OUT OF YOUR HOUSE

Sometimes the appreciation in the value of your house must make you feel as though you're sitting on a pile of cash or, more precisely, living in one. There are three ways to tap this home equity: getting a second mortgage, refinancing your original mortgage, and taking out a home-equity line of credit. Each can help you pay for a remodeling job. You might also be able to reinvest the cash elsewhere or use the money to pay some big expenses, such as the college tuition of your children.

Tax reform has increased the appeal of these forms of borrowing. Now that the deduction for interest on consumer loans is gone, the only loans that remain fully deductible are those on your first or second home. The law said that you cannot deduct more than the amount you paid for your house plus home improvements and any family medical expenses or education costs. That was true for loans taken out in the past. Now, however, all interest on a home-equity loan for a first or second house is deductible, up to $100,000. The deductibility of the interest exceeding that amount depends on how the money is used.

You will need a good employment and credit record to qualify for any of the mortgage loans. But if you think you will qualify, be sure you fully understand the advantages and disadvantages of each. Understand, too, that second mortgages, refinanced mortgages, and home-equity lines share one feature: Each can get you into serious financial trouble if you don't manage the debt carefully. Unlike with other loans, if you can't make the payments on these, your lender can take your home away. So before pulling out any money from your house, be certain you can afford to do so.

Most homeowners prefer using second mortgages, especially when they need a lot of money and a lot of time to repay the loan. Banks, mortgage bankers, and savings and loans make second mortgages, which let you borrow up to 80 percent of the market value of your house minus any unpaid balance on your first mortgage. The maximum size of a second mortgage is usually $100,000 to $200,000, but there is rarely a minimum. Lenders typically charge a percentage point or two more in interest for second mortgages than for first mortgages and offer fixed-rate loans as well as adjustable-rate loans, whose interest rates fluctuate. Seconds can often be repaid over 30 years, although 12 to 15 years is typical.

High closing costs make seconds too expensive if you want to borrow $5,000 or less. Expect to pay between $250 and $700 in assorted fees and up to 3 points for a second mortgage. (Each point equals 1 percent of the amount of the loan.)

Refinancing your original mortgage will let you borrow at a lower interest rate and for a longer period of time than you could on a second mortgage. The savings can be impressive. You would save more than $300 a month by refinancing a 30-year $75,000 mortgage at 15 percent and trading it for a 9 percent loan. You will be able to borrow at the same rate charged a new home buyer and can refinance the loan for as long as 30 years. Lenders also let borrowers refinance up to $500,000, considerably more than the limit on seconds. But the lenders will sock it to you with closing costs that are higher than those for second mortgages. For example, you might have to pay as many as 4 points. That amounts to $3,200 on an $80,000 mortgage. Figure on paying 3 to 6 percent of the amount of your mortgage in refinancing closing costs.

You need not refinance with the lender who originally granted you the first mortgage. Any S&L, bank, or mortgage banker will be delighted to handle the refinancing. Be sure to ask your original lender about refinancing terms, though. Many mortgage lenders cut closing costs for their borrowers who want to refinance.

Mortgage lenders like to say that refinancing pays when the interest rate you will get is at least 1 1/2 to 3 points below the one you already have. But that's not necessarily right, because the equation doesn't take closing costs fully into consideration. A better way to determine whether refinancing will pay is by dividing the total cost of refinancing (the lender's fees, your attorney's fees, a title search, a termite inspection, and any taxes due) by the monthly savings in your mortgage payments. The result will tell you the number of months it will take before the costs of refinancing are recouped. The smaller the figure, the more sense it makes to refinance. Don't refinance if you will have to wait more than twenty-four months to recoup your costs.

The homeowners who will save the most money by refinancing are those who bought their houses between 1979 and 1982, or in 1986, when mortgage rates were going through the roof. Refinancing can make your financial life more predictable, regardless of when you bought your house, if you exchange an adjustable-rate loan for one with a fixed rate. Those who will save the least by refinancing are homeowners who plan to move within two years or who got their mortgages less than a year ago and could be required to pay a prepayment penalty of up to six months' interest. Many lenders waive such penalties.

The Internal Revenue Service has made refinancing costlier in the short run. The IRS in May 1986 began enforcing a rule that prohibits taxpayers from deducting points for refinancing a mortgage the year they take out the loan. The cost of the points must be prorated over the remaining life of the mortgage. In other words, refinancers will be able to deduct the same amount of money, just over a longer period of time. Points paid to buy or improve a house can still be deducted all at once. So, if you use the appreciation in your home to refinance your mortgage for more than the loan's current balance and put the excess cash toward remodeling, you will get something of a reprieve. You will be able to deduct, in the year you refinance, the portion of your points that match up with the percentage of the loan used for the remodeling.

Home-equity credit lines, those tantalizing deals constantly pitched by brokerage firms, banks, S&Ls, finance companies, and credit unions, offer the most flexible way to get money out of your house. But they also have the greatest potential to blow up in your face. If you are not a disciplined saver, you shouldn't get a home-equity credit line.

A home-equity loan lets you borrow up to 70 to 80 percent of the market value of your house minus the unpaid balance of your loan, like a second mortgage. The loans resemble department store revolving credit and let you borrow the amount you want when you want. You borrow simply by writing a check for the amount of cash you want to extract from your house. The interest rate on a home-equity line fluctuates and is adjusted monthly, but it winds up being about the same as what you would pay for a second mortgage. Rates often are pegged to the prime rate and are 1 to 3 percentage points above prime. Most lenders let you repay the money you borrow on your home-equity credit line in 5 to 10 years.

Home-equity lines are roomy. You can borrow up to $2 million—far more than second mortgages. The minimum borrowing requirement ranges from $2,500 to $10,000. The home-equity lines are also often less expensive than second mortgages because of lower closing costs. For example, you need not hire a lawyer for a home-equity line, as you would in a normal mortgage closing. But unlike second mortgages, home-equity lines require borrowers to pay annual fees of about $20. Initially, you will pay about $1,500 in loan-origination fees.

Home-equity lines are riskier than they first appear. Some lenders require you to repay the interest borrowed in monthly installments and let you repay the principal at your own schedule. That makes the monthly payments considerably smaller than those of a second mortgage. Sooner or later, though, the principal will be due—typically in ten years or so. If you can't come up with the cash at the appointed time, the lender can foreclose and take possession of your house. That's why disciplined saving is so essential for people with home-equity credit lines.

PREPAYING YOUR MORTGAGE

Now that you have lived in your house a while and your monthly payments are more manageable than they were when you first got your mortgage, look into paying off the mortgage ahead of schedule. Prepaying the principal on your loan can save you thousands of dollars in interest. (Don't forget: Your interest deductions are worth less to you now that you are in a lower tax bracket than in the past.) You will also build equity faster and own your house free and clear sooner than anticipated. You can turn a 30-year mortgage into a 20-year or shorter-term loan. The effect: Your debt load will be cut enormously, and you will have more money to spend, save, and invest.

What's the catch? There are actually three things to consider before applying to your lender to prepay your mortgage. First, a prepayment plan will increase your monthly payments until the loan is paid off. So this technique won't work if you can't afford to make higher monthly payments. Second, you must have a mortgage without a prepayment penalty or a lender who will waive the penalty. Third, prepaying your loan will mean losing the tax deduction for the mortgage interest you won't have to pay.

Here's how a mortgage prepayment plan might work: Once a year, when you send your lender one month's payment of principal and interest, add in the principal due for the following month. This will cut the length of your mortgage by a month, so you won't have to pay that month's interest. Don't skip the mortgage payment for the month in which you prepaid the principal, though. That payment will just be credited toward the next one due.

You can begin prepaying a mortgage at any time during the life of the loan. But the sooner you start prepaying, the easier it will be. The principal portion of your monthly payment is smallest in the early years of your mortgage. Say you have a $75,000, 30-year, 10 percent mortgage whose monthly payments are $658.18. In the first year of the loan, $33.18 each month goes toward repaying your principal and $625 is interest. Only 5 percent of your monthly payment represents your principal. By the end of the fifth year, $59.31 a month is principal (9 percent of the payment) and only $598.87 is interest. After ten years, $97.59 a month is principal (15 percent of the payment) and $560.59 is interest. After fifteen years, $160.57 is principal (about 25 percent of the payment) and $497.61 is interest.

Ask your mortgage lender how to arrange to prepay your loan. Some lenders require borrowers to send the payments to a particular person's attention. Have the lender send you what's called an amortization schedule, which will show you how quickly you are paying off your principal. If yours is an adjustable-rate mortgage, your lender will be able to give you an amortization schedule for only as long as your interest rate is locked in. You will have to get a new schedule annually for an adjustable-rate loan whose rate changes once a year.

It's a good idea to write separate checks for the prepayment amounts for record-keeping purposes. Once your mortgage is paid off, have your lender write you a letter saying so. In many states, the notification must be written on your loan documents. Bring the letter to your city recorder's office to be recorded.

SELLING YOUR HOUSE

Perhaps you have decided to move and want to sell your house. If so, find out how much comparable homes are selling for and how quickly they are moving. A good local real estate agent should be able to provide the information. Hire a professional appraiser to tell you the actual value of your home. Meanwhile, gradually begin the search for your new house. Read the real estate ads in the newspaper serving the community where you hope to live. Drop in on open houses at homes that are for sale. This will give you an idea of the types of houses available and their prices.

But before agreeing to buy another house and shopping for a mortgage, it's usually wise to sell your present house. If you purchase another home without lining up a buyer for your current residence, you could find yourself in the sticky and expensive predicament of owing two monthly mortgage payments. That could wipe out your entire savings and propel you into debt.

The danger of selling first and buying second, of course, is that you could wind up having to move out of your present home without having another place to live. Do whatever you can to negotiate with a buyer to prevent such a calamity. For instance, try putting off the closing date for a few months to give you time to find a new house. If that won't fly, see whether the buyers will let you stay in the house for a few months, paying them rent all the while, until you secure a new residence.

Not all buyers will be agreeable to such arrangements, however. Should you get stuck with an implacable buyer demanding a quick closing followed immediately by your eviction, don't panic. Find a place you can rent temporarily, a storage company that will hold your belongings, and—as quickly as possible—a new home.

You might be faced with the reverse problem. The person selling the house you plan to buy could insist on a closing that will be sooner than the one on your present home. Then your problem will be coming up with the cash for the down payment while your equity is still tied up in your first house. If you don't have the scratch in savings, apply to a bank for what is called a bridge loan. This is a one- to four-month quickie personal loan designed to tide you over in just such a situation. Your collateral will be your equity in the house you are leaving and sometimes also the equity in the new house. Expect to pay an interest rate roughly 2 percentage points higher than the prime rate.

What if you fall in love with a house before you have sold your current one? The hard-hearted financial adviser would tell you to forget about this new house because purchasing it without a buyer for your present home could pose real money problems. Phooey.

To paraphrase Lee Iacocca, if you can find a better house, buy it. Just be sure to insert a clause into the sales contract stating that the purchase will be contingent upon the sale of your present house within a specified period of time. The deal will be off should you be unable to sell your house in time. Your seller may well flinch at such a clause, but you may be able to persuade him or her to go along by paying a little more for the house. Be prepared for the seller to put an additional clause in the contract letting him or her keep the house on the market during the contingency period. If the seller gets a higher offer than yours while you are looking for a buyer for your present house, you will probably have three days to make a counter offer or lose the house.

Some real estate brokers can come to your rescue. They pledge to buy your house if it doesn't sell within a certain period of time, such as seven months. Don't expect to get the full market value for your house with such a guaranteed sales plan, though. After the broker subtracts his or her commission and profit, you could wind up receiving a price that is 25 percent less than the appraised value of your home.

Your employer might also help bail you out if you are moving because of a job transfer. Most large companies now work with professional relocation companies that help sell the homes of transferred employees. Typically, the relocation company gives you a check for the equity in your home and your company pays the cost of carrying the house until it sells.

The only other ways to sell your house in a hurry are less pleasant: Lower the price, or offer buyers mortgage financing with an interest rate about 2 percentage points lower than what traditional lenders are charging. Seller financing is tricky and generally to be avoided. But if you have no choice, be certain to get at least a 10 percent cash down payment and solid credit references from the buyer. Hire a knowledgeable real estate lawyer to write a mortgage contract or deed of trust as well as the financing note.

HIRING A REAL ESTATE BROKER TO SELL YOUR HOUSE

When mortgage rates are low and going lower, selling your house without a real estate broker is not a bad idea if you live in a hot housing market. There are generally plenty of buyers around. Many of them are young and unable to afford a home whose price has been artificially raised by a seller to cover the cost of the real estate broker's 6 or 7 percent sales commission. So, after spending some money on local newspaper ads, you shouldn't have much difficulty finding a buyer who will pay a fair price for your house. Just be certain that a buyer who makes an offer will be able to qualify for mortgage financing.

Generally, however, it's worth paying to hire a good real estate broker. He or she will be more familiar than you with the local housing market, mortgages, and the desires of buyers. A broker can also suggest a realistic selling price. The competence of real estate agents varies as much as houses do, though. You will do best to hire a full-time broker who has been in the real estate business for at least a year.

A broker will want you to list your house with him or her for as long as possible, preferably six months. Instead, sign a contract that limits the listing period to three months. When the three months are up, you will have the option to relist or find another broker. Real estate brokers have four types of arrangements for listing houses: an exclusive right to sell, an exclusive agency listing, an open listing, and a net listing. The first two are worth considering, but the second two are not.

An exclusive right to sell requires you to pay the broker a commission if your house is sold to anyone during the period it is listed with the broker. This is the method brokers prefer because they get paid even if you wind up finding a buyer on your own. An exclusive right to sell does, however, put your home in the multiple-listing service of all the local real estate brokers and thereby increases the chance that a broker will bring you a buyer.

An exclusive agency listing is similar, but you won't have to pay the commission if you find a buyer yourself. Some brokers won't put houses listed this way on the multiple-listing rolls, however. So you could be cutting down the number of prospective buyers who will know about your home.

An open listing sounds appealing but is actually worth avoiding. It allows you to hire other real estate brokers or sell the house yourself without owing a commission. Open listings have two problems: They are never multiple-listed, and brokers usually don't work very hard on them because they are unlikely to get paid.

Never sign up for a net listing. This arrangement requires you to pay a broker the difference between the price your house lists for and the price it sells for. Say you list the house for $85,000 but it sells for $100,000. The commission you will pay will be $15,000, or 15 percent of the sales price—more than double the standard commission rate.

You should also probably stay away from discount real estate brokers with sales commissions as low as 2 percent or brokers who charge flat fees to sell homes. Discounters often have a hard time bringing in many potential buyers. The full-priced brokers, who must share commissions with the discounters if they find buyers, frequently prefer to concentrate on sales that will be more lucrative. The brokers who charge flat fees of about $700 to $1,000 do little more than find potential buyers. Thus you, the seller, have to spend the time showing the house.

HIRING A BROKER TO HELP YOU BUY A HOUSE

Should you hire a real estate broker to help you buy a house? That depends. If you plan to move locally and there are a good number of real estate ads for houses like the kind you want, there is little reason to use one. You will be well enough acquainted with the area to know the type of house you can afford. The only drawback is that you will miss out on seeing the unadvertised, exclusive listings of local real estate brokers.

But if you plan to move to an area you don't know very well or one with few advertised listings, a real estate broker is essential. Look for a broker who has been in the business for at least a year and who specializes in both the area and type of home you have in mind. Be certain that the broker subscribes to the local multiple-listing service. One way to locate a good broker: Stop by a few advertised open houses and chat with the brokers selling the homes.

Never forget that real estate brokers work on behalf of home sellers and are paid by the sellers. The higher the sales price a broker can squeeze out of a buyer, the more money he or she will make. So, be prepared to dig in your heels about purchase prices when you hire a real estate broker. Otherwise, you could end up paying more than necessary for a house.

A relatively new breed of real estate broker, called the buyer's broker, works a little differently. As the name suggests, a buyer's broker works for the home buyer. He or she sells homes from the multiple-listing books as well as those for sale by owners. Ideally, a buyer's broker will show you only the types of houses you want. A traditional broker might instead push houses he or she is trying to unload for sellers—ones that aren't right for you. Most buyer's brokers charge an hourly rate of $70 or so. Others take a percentage of the purchase price of a house or a flat fee equal to about half the standard 6 or 7 percent commission of other brokers. The hourly rate is best because it is more likely to keep the broker honest. Finding a buyer's broker could be difficult; there are only about 6,000 in the country. Ask your local Board of Realtors for names.

PICKING A HOUSE

After selecting a mate or having a child, picking a house is about the biggest personal decision you can make. Only you and your family know the age, style, and size of house that's right. There is no guarantee that the home you choose will appreciate in value. But there are ways to increase the likelihood that you will make a profit on the house when you eventually sell it.

- *Look for a good local school system.* Even if you don't have children, many other home buyers do, and schools are a big drawing card. If you do have children, researching school systems is critical. Get the local PTA officers to tell you the pluses and minuses of the local schools. Find out how the students perform in standardized tests compared with the national averages (recent Scholastic Aptitude Test averages for high school seniors were 431 for verbal and 475 for math). Ask for the percentage of high school seniors who go on to college—50 percent is the national average.

- *Look for reliable municipal services.* You can probably gauge this yourself just by driving around and eyeing the condition of the streets, sidewalks, and sewers.

- *Look for strong residential and commercial growth.* A community that attracts home buyers and new businesses is one that is on the move. Home prices are almost sure to rise here.

- *Look for an area where houses are selling briskly and at close to their asking prices.* This suggests that the area is in demand and that prices will keep on rising. Your best bet is an area where houses get swooped up within three months and sell for at least 95 percent of their asking price. The local Board of Realtors can give you information about such things.

- *Look for beauty and convenience.* The closer the house is to trees, parks, recreation facilities, shopping, restaurants, and businesses, the more likely it will appreciate in value. Neat landscaping also indicates that the homeowners care about their properties.

Managing Your Money Tip:

> Another factor to consider is how much home you can afford. Managing Your Money will tell you how much you can afford to pay for a home, based on the amount of a down payment you can afford, and how much you can afford to pay in mortgage payments. Just select Home Affordability from the Analyze submenu. Fill in all of the fields. Press F6 and Managing Your Money will calculate your optimal downpayment (the amount that allows you to buy the most house). Press F10, and Managing Your Money will give you the amount you can afford to pay for a home.
>
> You also can use Managing Your Money to compare the total cost of buying vs. renting. Just select Buy/Lease/Rent from the Analyze submenu. Fill in the information, press F10, and Managing Your Money will give you the total net cost of buying and renting.

MORTGAGE SHOPPING

These days, whether you are buying a house or refinancing your current mortgage, choosing the right mortgage for you is a monumental financial decision. It isn't easy. You need to compare (among other things) interest rates, mortgage maturities, points, closing costs, and required down payments. Some local newspapers help out by periodically publishing tables that list nearby lenders and their mortgage terms. In many places, such as the New York City area, the Washington, D.C., area, Baltimore, and parts of Texas, California, and Florida, you can buy a similar list for $10 to $25 from a company that tracks mortgages. A call to a real estate broker, mortgage banker or the mortgage department of a savings and loan will tell you whether such a list is published for the town where you have agreed to buy a house and how to get the list.

Mortgage shopping also requires some good old-fashioned leg-work. You will have to keep your eyes peeled for mortgage ads and call around to a dozen or so lenders to compare their offerings. Before making any calls, get a fix on the amount of the mortgage you will need and the type of loan you would like. That way you can save yourself from paying non-refundable mortgage application fees of $150 to $350 to lenders who don't have the loan you want.

It will also help to know exactly what your monthly mortgage payments would be at different interest rates so you can determine the type of mortgage you can afford. The accompanying table lists some mortgage payment examples, based on a 30-year fixed-rate loan.

Monthly Payments on a 30-Year Mortgage

Mortgage	Interest Rate					
	9%	10%	11%	12%	13%	14%
S 50,000	$ 402	$ 439	$ 476	$ 514	$ 553	$ 592
70,000	563	614	667	720	774	829
100,000	805	878	952	1,029	1,106	1,185
120,000	966	1,053	1,143	1,234	1,327	1,422
150,000	1,207	1,316	1,429	1,543	1,659	1,777
180,000	1,448	1,580	1,714	1,852	1,991	2,133
200,000	1,609	1,755	1,905	2,057	2,212	2,370
220,000	1,770	1,931	2,095	2,263	2,434	2,607
250,000	2,012	2,194	2,381	2,572	2,766	2,962
300,000	2,412	2,634	2,861	3,082	3,316	3,552

Managing Your Money Tip:

> Managing Your Money will tell you what your mortgage payment (or any other loan payment) will be. Just select Loans & Annuities from the Analyze submenu. Fill in the amount of the loan, the interest rate, and the number of monthly payments. Press F10, and Managing Your Money will calculate your monthly payment. Want to know how much you can borrow? Leave the amount of the loan blank, and fill in the desired monthly payment instead. Press F10, and Managing Your Money will tell you what amount of loan your monthly payment will support.

Your first decision when selecting a mortgage will be whether to go with a fixed-rate or an adjustable-rate mortgage (ARM). Both types usually have 15- or 30-year maturities. The interest rate on a fixed-rate mortgage never changes, whereas the rate on an ARM fluctuates: When other interest rates go up, so will the rate on your mortgage; when other rates fall, so should yours. Warning: A new type of ARM does not lower its rate when other rates fall. Avoid such an ARM-twister at all costs.

You pay a premium for the certainty of a fixed-rate loan. The rate is usually between 1 and 3 percentage points higher than that of an ARM. The difference can be dramatic. The monthly payment on a 30-year, $150,000 fixed-rate loan at 11 1/2 percent is $1,485, but the payment on an adjustable-rate loan at 9 percent is $1,207.

Go for a fixed-rate loan if:

- You are the conservative type who craves predictability in your life.

- You can afford the monthly payments.

- You expect the trend of interest rates to be upward while you hold the mortgage.

Go for an adjustable-rate loan if:

- You can handle the uncertainty of not knowing how much your monthly payments will be from year to year.

- You will be able to afford the monthly payments if the interest rate on your loan rises by 5 percentage points within three years.

- You believe your family's income will continue rising.

- The rate starts at least 1 1/2 percentage points below that on comparable fixed-rate mortgages.

- You expect the trend of interest rates to be stable or to move downward while you hold the mortgage.

- You plan to move out of the house within three to five years. (It's doubtful that interest rates will shoot up so much during that short a time that you would pay a higher average annual rate than you would by taking today's fixed-rate loan.)

Should you decide to get an adjustable-rate mortgage, be prepared to ask a whole lot of questions. ARMs have become more standardized over the years, but they still vary greatly from lender to lender. The typical ARM—and one you should try to get—looks something like this:

- The interest rate is indexed to the one-year Treasury securities' yield and can rise or fall.

- Interest and monthly payments are adjusted annually.

- The rate cannot go up by more than 2 percentage points a year and a total of 5 points over the life of the loan.

- There is a built-in profit margin that lets the lender automatically raise the rate by about 2 points in the second year above its indexed rate, even if other rates have not risen. (While this is not a pleasant provision, it is typical. There are loans with even larger built-in profit margins.)

- There is no prepayment penalty for repaying the loan ahead of schedule .

There are three types of ARMS you should refuse, in addition to the type that does not allow its rate to fall. The first is what's called a teaser loan. This is an adjustable-rate mortgage whose rate is laughingly low compared to that of the competition. When the rate on fixed-rate loans is 9 percent and most ARMs charge 7 1/2 percent, teasers have 6 to 6 1/2 percent rates. Invariably, the fine print of a teaser loan allows the lender to either jack up the rate in the future or force you to come up with a lot of cash at some point. The cash represents the difference between what you have paid for the teaser rate and what you would have paid with another ARM.

The second ARM to pass up is one that allows you to convert the loan to a fixed-rate mortgage during the first three to five years you have it. You will pay as much as a percentage point more in interest for this conversion feature plus other points and fees at the time of conversion. Result: You probably would have been better off taking a fixed-rate loan originally.

The third ARM to skip is one that puts a cap on your monthly payments without capping the interest rate. If your adjustable-rate loan's monthly payment is $1,000, it will remain $1,000 even if interest rates rise. This feature looks swell at first glance. But closer scrutiny shows that such a limitation can be dangerous to your wealth. When interest rates rise but your payments cannot, the lender will just tack on the extra money you owe because of the higher rates in additional monthly payments at the end of your loan, increasing the length of the mortgage.

Once you decide between a fixed-rate loan and an ARM, the next choice is a 30-year mortgage versus a 15-year mortgage. It's a toss-up. The 30-year loan, which is the conventional type, has lower monthly payments than a 15-year mortgage. But the 15-year loan usually has a lower interest rate—between a quarter and a full percentage point less than that of a 30-year mortgage. By taking the short mortgage, you could save yourself more than $100,000 in interest and build up equity in your house more quickly. You would, of course, give up the tax deductions on the forgone interest. But your mortgage deduction could very well be worth less than in the past if tax reform has dropped your family into a lower tax bracket.

Next you will want to compare the closing costs charged by lenders, such as the loan application fee, the loan processing fee, and points. Other miscellaneous settlement charges include those for the title search, the survey, homeowners' insurance, your lawyer, prorated utility bills and taxes, prospective property tax bills, and perhaps mortgage insurance.

Many lenders charge different mortgage rates depending on the number of points a borrower is willing to pay. The lower the rate, the more points charged. For example, a lender might let you choose between a 9 percent loan with 2 points and a 9 3/4 percent loan with 3 points. Which to accept depends on how long you plan to own the house. The shorter your intended stay, the fewer points you should pay. To figure out the trade-off in your case, you will need to calculate the real cost of various mortgage alternatives. Here's how:

(1) Multiply the mortgage interest rate by the number of years you plan to own the house. (2) Add to that figure the number of points being charged. (3) Divide that figure by the number of years you plan to own the house and you will get the effective annual interest rate.

Assume you can choose between a 9 percent loan with 1 1/2 points and an 8 1/2 percent loan with 3 points. Assume also that you expect to stay in the house for ten years. Mortgage number 1 has an effective annual interest rate of 9.15 percent (9% x 10 years = 90 + 1.5 points = 91.5 ÷10 = 9.15). Mortgage number 2 has an effective annual interest rate of 8.8 percent (8 1/2% x 10 years = 85 + 3 points = 88÷10 = 8.8). You would be better off paying the additional points with mortgage number 2.

Watch your step before agreeing to take a no-points mortgage. A number of lenders are pushing these loans, which have much lower closing costs than most other mortgages. Of course, you wind up paying the missing points somehow. The no-points mortgage usually spreads the money you would have paid in points over the life of the loan, thereby increasing the size of the mortgage and your monthly payments. In other instances, the lender just makes you pay a higher mortgage rate. Unless you have a real problem coming up with the cash to pay points, there is no point to a no-point mortgage.

After selling your present house, you will probably have enough cash to make a sizable down payment on the next one. That could be a smart move. A big down payment will cut your monthly payments dramatically and make it easier to afford a 15-year mortgage, should you want one. The large down payment might also lower your mortgage's interest rate. Lenders charge higher rates on so-called jumbo loans: mortgages exceeding $133,250. By scraping up a down payment that brings your mortgage below the jumbo level, you could qualify for a mortgage rate as much as a percentage point lower.

Ask lenders about their policies regarding locking in interest rates on their mortgages. A few will permit you to get a guaranteed rate when you are approved for their loans. Others won't determine your rate until the day you close on the house. In some instances, you will be allowed to lock in a rate up to 15 days or a month before your closing date. Should interest rates fall after you have secured a date, you will be out of luck. But if rates go up, you will be in clover.

Once you have completed the great mortgage hunt and have come up with three or four lenders with suitable mortgages, have them send you application forms. Then choose the best deal in the lot and fill out its application form at home. Make an appointment with the loan officer to hand over the completed application form and to answer any questions.

Don't quit now. Stay on top of your mortgage to the point of annoyance. If you don't, it's quite likely that the lender will be missing important paperwork that could stall or derail your mortgage. A watchful eye is especially necessary if you are refinancing your mortgage. Refinancings get lower priority than first mortgages. Ask the person processing the application constantly whether he or she has all the documents and information needed from you. Ride your boss, too, so he or she will quickly send along your employment and salary verification to the lender.

Your smothering attention may irritate your mortgage lender, but that's the lender's problem. Once your loan is approved (and if it is rejected, find out why and reapply), apologize to the lender for your behavior. Then, don't forget to celebrate with your family.

CHAPTER

II

PLOTTING YOUR
WORK FUTURE

I will go where my sensibility leads me, and I
expect I'll be wandering for some time until I
just get interested in things. That's how I got
started working on Lotus.
Mitch Kapor,
founder of Lotus Development Corp., one of
the most successful computer software
companies in history, upon resigning as
Lotus's chairman in July 1986, quoted in
The New York Times

A TIME TO RETHINK YOUR WORK LIFE

Turning 40 is a milestone that almost automatically throws a person into a state of reflection about his or her life. Self-analysis revolves around such questions as: How did I get to this point? Is this where I want to be? Where am I heading?

The sharpest growing pains associated with this phase are career related. You probably have another 25 years of working life ahead, a prospect that could be thrilling or conceivably unbearable.

Job and career concerns weigh especially heavy for members of your generation. You could well have ended up in your current job more by accident than by design. (The scene from *The Graduate* where "plastics" is whispered into Dustin Hoffman's ear may strike home.) Very few people now in their late 30s or early 40s plotted career paths upon graduating from college. Not very many sought lucrative jobs in business, as today's college grads do. Some of today's 40-year-old men went to college and stayed on for graduate degrees to avoid the Vietnam draft, not giving much thought to the jobs they would take afterward. *In Great Expectations: America and the Baby Boom Generation,* Landon Jones wrote that from 1969 to 1976, 27 percent of Baby Boomers were forced to take jobs they had not been trained for or were unable to find work at all. Today, many of these same people and others of the Baby Boom generation are disillusioned or bored with work. Maybe you're one of them.

You may also be reevaluating your career for personal, not business, reasons. Your current job might not give you enough time to spend with your children. Or perhaps your children are now old enough that you can either return to work or take on a more demanding job. On the other hand, after years of working for pay you may be able to afford to cut back or stop altogether.

Recent dramatic changes in the economy and in American business are further reason to give you pause about your work life. Your generation has had an enviable history of steady promotions and big raises. Until recently, that is. In the past few years, lavish corporate personnel policies have been junked in favor of thrifty ones. Raises have been smaller and less frequent. The promotion escalator has slowed down or stopped at some companies.

In the past, middle managers could look forward to frequent raises, promotions, and safe jobs until retirement. Not anymore. Restructuring—the new corporate buzzword—has led to massive lay-offs, particularly among middle management. Since 1985, more than 300 large businesses have announced cutbacks, including Apple Computer, Chevron, Exxon, Ford, General Motors, Greyhound, and Kodak.

If you are a middle manager, you probably know the score all too well, as a recent Business Week/Harris Executive Poll of middle managers at 600 companies showed. When asked, "Do you think that as long as you do a good job, you can stay with your current employer for as long as you like?" 44 percent said they thought they could stay, but another 44 percent said they may not be able to. The future doesn't look much more promising for middle managers. Noted career counselor Richard Bolles, author of *What Color Is Your Parachute?*, says that middle managers and farmers are the two most endangered species today.

There is nothing wrong with taking inventory of your work life at or near age 40. In fact, it's desirable, traditional, and perhaps critical. A U.S. Department of Labor study shows that more people switch jobs at age 40 than at any other age between 35 and 54. You are at an age when you can still afford, financially and psychologically, to take calculated risks in your work life. That could mean asking for a promotion or transfer at work, leaving your company for another, starting your own business, or taking some time off just to reflect.

You can also seriously consider switching careers entirely—and not necessarily for the last time in your life, either. Now that people are living longer, the average work span has increased. You might end up working for nearly 60 years, long enough to have three or four different careers. Giving up, say, medicine for business might once have been thought of as crazy. Not today. In fact, a recent poll by the Ethan Allen Company found that 31 percent of people ages 35 to 49 said they would like to start a different occupation in the next five years for the betterment of their family lives.

HOW IS YOUR JOB?

Career consultants can put you through a battery of tests to determine whether you are in the right job, but a quicker way is to answer a simple question: How do you feel about going to work most mornings? No one can honestly say he leaps out of bed every weekday, burning with desire to get to work. Neither can anyone honestly say he loves everything about his job. If you look forward to going to work most days, you are one of the lucky ones. But if you hear the word "work" and immediately associate it with words like "dull," "frustrating," "mundane," "detestable," or "stifling," you should stop groaning and start taking steps toward a better job and career.

You may, like many people in their 30s and 40s, have mixed emotions about your job. Work may not be horrible, but perhaps it's not enjoyable, either. Like the homeowner who has outgrown his or her house, you wonder whether to make the best of where you are or to move elsewhere.

It's fairly common for people to plateau in their jobs at age 40 or so. You might be plateauing if you have had the same job without a promotion for at least the past five years. Even if you have climbed the work ladder and received a promotion within the past few years, you may now feel stagnant because the jump to the next job level seems unlikely or uninteresting.

There are a variety of ways to get out of a rut at work, short of leaving. Develop more specialized skills, both technical and personal. This will make work more interesting. Moreover, it will make you a more valuable employee and more likely to get future raises and promotions. Take courses at a community college or technical school, if necessary. Your company might subsidize the tuition. Employers admire self-starters, so if you can take on a new project without being asked, that should also help you and your company.

Explore other opportunities at your firm. Check the employment office at work for openings. You might be able to switch to another job in another division with more chances for promotions. A job transfer might be just the ticket.

All you may need is a little time away from the job. A growing number of companies are granting sabbaticals to employees who have been with them for at least three or four years. Some of the firms require that employees taking a leave use the time to perform community service. Among the big businesses that offer senior employees sabbaticals ranging from four weeks to a year are Apple, IBM, McDonald's, Wells Fargo, and Xerox. The longer you have toiled for your firm, the more leverage you will have when asking for a short leave of absence. Don't be surprised if your company has no official policy on sabbaticals; few do. That doesn't mean you can't instigate one or take an informal leave, though.

NEGOTIATING A RAISE

Some additional pay may be all the incentive you need to stick with your job. But extracing an enormous raise is difficult these days. Most employers are giving their workers 5 or 6 percent raises, on average, and rarely more than that. Many companies have cut their standard merit raises to 3 or 4 percent. Some hard-hit firms have been abstaining from giving out raises altogether. Another common tactic: Rather than rewarding employees with an annual raise, many companies are doling out the money every 15 months or so. That way, a 5 percent raise appears to be honorable, even though it actually works out to be a 4 percent annual raise.

Going to your boss to ask for additional money a la Dagwood Bumstead has never been a pleasant task. But it is even more difficult these days when raises are smaller and less frequent. The secret is to clearly state your case for a raise of a specific percentage or dollar amount and if your employer flinches, to negotiate in a businesslike manner.

The more evidence you can bring in supporting your argument, the more likely you are to get the raise. Try to find out what others are paid at your job level at your company and at the competition. You may be able to get such information through casual conversations at the water cooler. The public library also has shelves of books and magazine articles that list current salaries for various occupations.

Be prepared to enumerate for your boss your achievements on the job during the past year. Provide examples of work you performed that was above and beyond the call of duty—extra hours, beating deadlines, coming up with good ideas. Show him or her how you made the company more profitable and increased its productivity. Whatever you do, don't plead poverty or unload your personal financial problems on your boss.

TO QUIT OR NOT TO QUIT

Leaving a good job at age 40 is a gamble. On the one hand, 40-year-olds seeking new jobs are often highly valued by employers because they usually offer experience and self-confidence. Job recruiters say the tide has turned away from hiring young MBAs, which was the trend of the '70s, and toward hiring older, more mature employees who need less training.

But tacit (though illegal) age discrimination against job applicants typically begins at 40, particularly for women. Switching jobs at 40 also cuts the likelihood of receiving a substantial pension. You might quit before vesting in the pension plan and then not stay at the next firm long enough to qualify for a company retirement check. Also, if you are vested in a pension plan and you leave before reaching the outfit's retirement age, your pension benefits will generally be frozen and won't grow with inflation.

The Federal Reserve Bank of Boston has compared the pensions of two hypothetical people after 40 years in the work force: a job hopper who switches jobs every 10 years (vesting each time) and a long-time employee who works for the same company for 40 years. The example assumes that both workers start at $20,000 salaries and receive annual 6 percent raises. The result is not unlike what happened with the tortoise and the hare: The job hopper would receive an annual pension totaling about $42,000, while the steady, loyal employee would get nearly double that amount, about $82,000. The job hopper's pension would be even smaller if he or she left the companies before vesting in his or her pension plans.

Job hoppers will be penalized less in the future for moving around. The tax reform law speeded up vesting, making it more likely that mobile workers will receive pensions. Companies must now vest their employees in seven years or less.

Before deciding to chuck your job for another one or for a new career, give the notion a lot of thought. Career switches are riskier and more prone to disappoint than job switches. You should not start a new career or business until you have done a thoughtful, objective analysis of your skills and personality. Harry Levinson, a business psychologist who runs the Levinson Institute in Belmont, Massachusetts, says such a change is especially risky for people who tend to be dependent and lean on organizational structure at work. If you are someone who has either consciously or unconsciously sought long-term job security, leaving your present place of employment is probably not advisable. But if you are easily adaptable or feel burned out in your present career, a well-thought-out switch to a new field cauld be the best work move you will ever make. The U.S. Department of Labor's *Occupational Outlook Handbook,* found in most public libraries, can tip you off to growing fields and their salaries.

IF YOU ARE LAID OFF OR FIRED

The maxim "Make the best of a bad situation" is particularly apt when you lose your job. The more you can handle the termination in a businesslike manner, the better your chances of getting back on your feet fairly quickly. Negotiate the best possible severance package you can obtain, and ask your personnel office about outplacement services offered by the company. The firm may be willing to help you put together a resume, let you make calls to set up job interviews, and even train you for the interviewing process. Before you leave your job, get written references if possible.

Check with your personnel office to see whether you can convert your group health insurance policy to individual coverage. That way you won't be without comprehensive health insurance between jobs. If the company won't let you convert its health insurance, try to buy a six-month health insurance policy from an insurance agent. At the very least, get a hospital indemnity policy that will pay a specified amount for each day you are in the hospital.

While you are unemployed, you will need to tap your emergency reserve savings fund and cut back on spending and borrowing. This may be the time to take out a quickie loan against your life insurance policy or against the equity in your house. If you will have trouble meeting your monthly payments on your mortgage, personal loans, or credit cards, explain your plight to your lenders. Most decent lenders will try to work out temporary repayment plans lasting until you get a new job. Call your local unemployment office to learn whether you will be eligible for unemployment compensation.

The average job search today takes five months, so be prepared to invest some time looking for work. A good rule of thumb is to figure on one month of job hunting for every $10,000 of your former salary. Get into the habit of working six hours a day trying to find a new job. Your full-time job after losing a job is securing a new one.

Keep your sights as wide open as possible. Consider whether and where you would be willing to relocate. Think about making a dramatic career switch or going back to school. Just weigh your options as rationally as possible, putting anger aside.

When you interview for a new job, don't be afraid to admit you were laid off or fired, especially if your company is undergoing massive job cutbacks. Firing has lost much of its stigma by now. Don't bring up the subject, but if it comes up during the interview, explain matter-of-factly why you left your job. You may not have much leverage when negotiating for salary. Try asking for 10 percent more than you earned on your last job.

One nationwide group, called 40 Plus, can be especially helpful if you are older than 40 when you lose a managerial or professional job. The group has twelve local chapters across the country whose purpose is to help its members get rehired. The 40 Plus chapters are typically run by men and women who know the local job market well and have excellent networking contacts. You can get the location of your nearest chapter by writing to 40 Plus Club of New York, 15 Park Row, New York, N.Y. 10038.

HIRING A CAREER COUNSELOR

If you don't trust yourself to perform an honest self-appraisal or would just like some useful employment advice, hire a career counselor. This kind of professional assistance can also be useful if you decide to launch a serious job search. But career counselors, like financial planners, vary enormously in competence. More than half the states don't require counselors to be licensed, so anyone who wants to hang out a career counseling shingle can do so.

When looking for a career counselor, set up interviews with several and ask the following questions:

- *How much will it cost?* Most counselors charge an hourly rate or provide a package with workshops. Either way, the cost will probably run between $300 and $1,000. Many colleges have career courses costing $200 or less. Other counselors require you to sign a contract and to pay between $2,000 and $5,000. This contract gives you access to the counselor for five years and often allows you to attend future workshops.

- *What will you do for me?* You can get a spectrum of services, ranging from a single conversation with the counselor, to tests that measure your aptitude and interest in different fields, to regular counseling sessions and workshops with books and cassette tapes. One of the better testing organizations is the Johnson O'Connor Research Foundation (11 E. 62nd Street, New York, N.Y. 10021). It charges about $400 for 1 1/2 hours of tests at fifteen locations around the country. Most reputable counselors won't guarantee you a job, and you should be suspicious of any who do.

- *What is your background?* Because it is easy to call oneself a career counselor in many states, the depth of experience of counselors varies. Find a counselor who has been in the business at least five years, preferably one who is licensed. Get information about the history of the counselor's company, too. It won't hurt to call the local Better Business Bureau to see whether there have been any complaints against the counselors you have interviewed.

- *Whom can I call as references?* Any reputable counselor will not hesitate to give you names of at least two or three people who have been satisfied with his or her work. Get a short list and call the people, asking them about their experiences.

WHEN JOB HUNTING

You've had it with your present job and are ready to move on. Three don'ts and a do:

- Don't quit your job before having another one lined up.
- Don't slough off at work or start complaining excessively about your job; either could make it difficult to get a good reference for your next job.
- Don't jump at the first job offer that comes your way.
- Do proceed cautiously before making a change.

When considering a similar job elsewhere, look for one paying at least 20 percent more than you now earn. The raise will compensate you for any unreimbursed relocation costs or loss of fringe benefits, plus the emotional upheaval involved. Be ready to negotiate for your pay. Ask about the company's policy on raises, too. How often are raises awarded, and what is the company's current average raise, in percentage terms?

It is essential to find out about a potential employer's fringe benefit package. At large companies, fringes such as company-paid health, disability, and life insurance, pensions, and corporate savings plans often add up to 30 percent of the salary of a 40-year-old worker.

Be particularly rigorous in your research before leaving an established company for a new, small one with an uncertain future. If you switch to a tiny business and the company goes under, your family could wind up having serious financial problems. There may not be enough money to pay for medical expenses, college tuition for your children, a new car, or your eventual retirement.

Before going to any job interview, learn as much as you can about the company and its business. Spend time in the public library reading articles about the firm and its field. Talk to people who work at the company or its competition, if you can. See whether someone at the company can send you materials about the business, too. The more informed you are going into an interview, the better impression you will make. Such knowledge will also help you determine whether the company is one you would want to work for.

Ask every question that is on your mind. The last thing you need when accepting a new job is an unpleasant surprise. Some key questions to ask:

- *What happened to the person who had this job previously?* The answer you want to hear is that the person was promoted or left for a better job at another firm. The answer you don't want to hear is that the person was fired because he or she couldn't do the job required or couldn't get along well with the boss.

- *Is the company's business growing?* You hope the answer will be affirmative, of course. But find out where the corporate growth is and the likely prospects for annual growth in the next few years. Ideally, your job will be in one of the growing divisions. If not, the company might soon shut down the division, and you could be out of a job.

- *What are the opportunities for advancement?* You could conceivably end up working for the company for another 25 years, so it is important to find out early what the future might be like for you there.

- *Am I likely to be relocated?* At this stage of your life, you may not be willing to make another move geographically. If so, make sure your interviewer understands. Conversely, if you are looking forward to working for the company in another location in the future, it's good to spell that out early and learn your chances of eventual relocation. Should the job call for relocating immediately, find out precisely what the company will do to cover your costs. Many large firms routinely spend $50,000 or more to move an employee and his or her family and subsidize their relocation costs.

    If it is at all possible, try to talk with other people at the company who hold jobs similar to the one you are applying for. That will provide a more candid appraisal of the firm, its corporate culture, and opportunities for advancement for men and women. You also can get a good idea about the type of boss you would have.

    Once you get a serious job offer, take a few days to think it over. In the meantime, get a copy of the company's employee benefits handbook and read through it. Find out how quickly new hires receive medical and life insurance coverage. Check to see whether the health plan has any restrictions that your old plan did not. If any of the restrictions seem unduly harsh, discuss them with the person who interviewed you and see whether the rules can be bent at all.

STARTING YOUR OWN BUSINESS

If you are tempted to strike out on your own, as increasing numbers of Americans seem to be, the good news is that this is the best time in years to be an entrepreneur. Low inflation, falling interest rates, and lowered taxes make the costs of starting and running a business far more affordable than it was in the 1970s. Borrowing costs are now manageable, and prices of supplies are stable. Seed money is abundant because investors are willing to give entrepreneurs cash in exchange for the opportunity to share future profits. Bankers also have more money to lend to small-business owners. Multimillionaire venture capitalists have been joined by venture-capital clubs and networks in many cities made up of small investors with as little as $10,000 to spare. There were six such clubs in 1984; now there are more than seventy. The groups match entrepreneurs who need cash with small investors who have some. Venture networks are generally housed at colleges, such as the University of New Hampshire, Case Western Reserve, and St. Louis University.

In your 40's, you have some advantages as a would-be entrepreneur that you didn't have when you were, say, 25: a storehouse of self-confidence; a longer credit history, which makes it easier to get bank loans; and a better idea of your prospects at your current company. Starting your own business can be fun, thrilling, and financially rewarding, and it can fill you with a strong sense of achievement. That's the glamorous side. Entrepreneurship can also be lonely, scary, and uncertain. In order to make it as a successful entrepreneur, you need to be a patient self-starter who can accept a lot of rejection. It often takes between two and five years for a new company to turn a profit and then several more years to get the firm on strong financial footing. Statistics show that more than two-thirds of new businesses are likely to fail within five years.

Leaving your job to open a business requires taking a variety of risks. There is the risk of giving up the security of a large company for the precariousness of a small one. There is the risk of not having an artillery of experts around you at work. When you work for a large organization, a lot of things are done for you; you become spoiled. There is the financial risk of getting enough money to get the business off the ground and keep it running. There is the psychological risk involved in a small but tight business partnership. There is the risk of failure. Once you're out of the corporate world, it's difficult to get back in, and it becomes increasingly difficult as you get older unless you have a highly developed specialty. Your skills may become obsolete, and you may lose your corporate contacts.

The one risk that has been greatly exaggerated, however, is the risk that starting your own business will pull your family apart. Truth is, most successful entrepreneurs are still married to their original spouses. While there are no reliable figures on the divorce rate among entrepreneurs, academics believe this rate to be no higher than the national average. Sure, entrepreneurs work hard and for many hours. But so do enterprising corporate employees. Some business owners say that their ability to set their own work hours actually gives them more time to spend with their families than they had when they worked for their former employers.

You will lessen your venture risks by easing into a business launch through taking calculated risks. Rather than quitting your present job today in hope of starting your own firm next month, do some research. Spend time in the library reading everything you possibly can on the type of business you want to own. Look into taking an entrepreneurship course at a local college; more than 300 colleges offer such courses for undergrads and MBA students.

Then, expand your research to primary sources. Talk to other entrepreneurs and their employees in businesses similar to the one you want to start. This way, you can learn what your life could really be like as a boss. See what the competition charges, how much they advertise, how successful they are, and whether they have repeat customers. Talk to the local Chamber of Commerce and ask whether the population is growing or shrinking in the area where you want to start your company. Call on potential suppliers and compare prices. Find out how much it will cost to insure your business.

Try moonlighting in a business like the one you have in mind while you still have your present job. That will give you the best first-hand experience you can get, without sacrificing your family's finances doing so.

Once the research and spadework is done, begin laying the foundation for a stable company. By all means, prepare a solid business plan. Work with an accountant and a lawyer. You may also need the assistance of a small-business consultant, who is likely to charge a minimum of $1,000. These professionals can help you with the technical aspects of getting a company off the ground and are likely to spot any pitfalls in your idea. Sit down with a financial planner and review your family's finances to see how much money you can afford to put into the business. Line up as many business contacts as possible.

Put together a good management team composed of people who excel in the business talents that you lack. If your expertise is in sales and marketing, find a finance whiz and vice versa. A savvy partnership will help attract investors and lenders looking to profit from companies with growth potential.

To finance your venture, start with your family savings. You might want to borrow against your life insurance policy or the equity in your house, but only if your family can afford it. Then hit up relatives and friends. Try to get money from them in the form of long-term loans rather than give up part ownership of your company.

Once these accessible sources have been exhausted, you can make appointments with lenders or try to find small investors. Your lawyer, accountant, financial planner, stockbroker, and banker may be able to supply you with names of potential investors. Ask the local Chamber of Commerce for leads, too. Banks, savings and loans, finance companies, the Small Business Administration, and business development companies are worth contacting if you want a loan of $100,000 or less.

When your venture will require more cash than $100,000, seek out professional venture capitalists. Sometimes these investors will lend money, but usually they want to give you cash in exchange for a piece of your business. Professional venture capitalists tend to fund fledgling companies near their own offices, which are mostly located in California, Massachusetts, New York, and Texas.

If you need really big bucks—$500,000 or more—your best bet will be to put together a limited partnership with local wealthy investors. Talk to your accountant, lawyer, or stockbroker. These professionals may have experience setting up such partnerships.

STARTING A BUSINESS FROM HOME

Starting a business from your home can be a terrific way to open a company on the cheap while working within a few yards of your children. A home business can be a dandy tax shelter, too, allowing you to write off some expenses that would otherwise have been personal and nondeductible. If you have a personal computer and a discount long-distance telephone company, you've got a head start.

But in some ways working out of your house is a bit trickier than setting up shop elsewhere. And it isn't for everyone. Most people like to get out of the house weekdays and literally go to work. They like the change of scene and the opportunity to get away from their home and family for eight hours a day. For these people, working at home would undoubtedly lead to a bad case of cabin fever. If this sounds like you, don't even consider starting a home-based business.

If you are seriously thinking about working at home, either full-time or part-time, check with your local government officials and a lawyer to be certain that your community permits home-based businesses. Many localities have zoning laws that restrict them. Some apartment buildings, co-ops, and condos also frown on firms located within their confines. Some state and federal laws also regulate the types of commercial products you can make at home.

The homeowner's insurance policy you have will probably not be sufficient to cover your business. You most likely will need a separate policy for the company or at least a rider on your home-owner's policy. The additional insurance will provide the business with liability protection and coverage against damage to your business equipment.

There is an association for practically every business group, and home-based businesses are no exception. The International Association for Home Business offers counsel as well as a bimonthly newsletter called *Mind Your Own Business A Home.* You can join the group and get the newsletter by sending $75 to the association at P.O. Box 14850, Chicago, Ill. 60614. Another helpful group is the National Alliance of Homebased Businesswomen (P.O. Box 306, Midland Park, N.J. 07432). Membership fee: $30. This group also has a bimonthly newsletter called *Alliance.*

THE FACTS ABOUT FRANCHISING

You can reduce some of the risks of starting a business by buying a franchise. Well-run franchise companies in dozens of industries from restaurants to car repair shops have already proven they can succeed. Still, there is no guarantee that your particular franchise will be a hit. A big advantage of going with a franchise is the advice and training you will get from the franchisor. You can get help in picking a location, and the franchisor is likely to buy equipment and inventory for you. The company will also help you hire your first employees and answer questions if calamities arise.

Franchising has two big drawbacks: its cost and your lack of total independence. Getting in on an established franchise, the safest type, can be quite expensive. Down payments often start at $30,000 to $100,000. Once you buy the franchise, you will share your profits with headquarters. Franchisors often require franchisees to give them up to 12 percent of their annual gross sales. In exchange, you can use the company's trademark and its services for a specified period, typically 10 to 20 years. Franchisors also usually have rules to guarantee standardization, but these rules can also inhibit your business creativity.

Some of the hottest franchises today are maid services, printing and copying companies, and office temporaries. You can get information about more than 1,300 franchisors by obtaining the U.S. Commerce Department's *Franchise Opportunities Handbook* (Superintendent of Documents, U.S. Government Printing Office, Washington, D.C. 20402). The book describes the types and locations of various franchises and notes how much it costs to buy them.

A franchise is generally only as good as the parent company behind it. So find out as much as you can about a particular franchisor before you buy in. Talk to franchise operators recommended by the company as well as ones who aren't recommended but who will be more objective. Quiz them about their relations with the company and any problems they may have had with the business. Stay away from new, faddish franchises that are hot today but are likely to cool down tomorrow. (Think for a moment about all the local computer retailers, video game outlets, tanning parlors, and video-cassette rental stores that have closed in the past few years.)

Have your lawyer look over a franchising agreement before you sign it. Be sure you will have the option to renew the contract with-out major changes and the ability to sell the franchise at its market value when you're ready. Also, ask your accountant to take a look at the franchisor's books, so you can feel confident that the company is financially healthy and likely to stay that way.

GOING BACK TO WORK

You may be thinking about getting a job for pay after being out of the work force for years. The children might now be old enough to allow you to leave the house during the day. Your family may need the additional income. Your spouse may be disabled, or you could be recently divorced, separated, or widowed. Whatever the reason, getting a paying job after years without one can be a difficult experience. That is especially true if your work skills are outdated or have been made obsolete by technology. There are ways to make the transition practically painless, however, and to get hired fairly quickly.

Your biggest obstacles are probably a lack of self-confidence and a lack of knowledge about applying for jobs. Try to find a support group that will help build your confidence and prepare you for the employment process. Many cities now have groups specifically for women reentering the labor force who need to sharpen their skills of resume writing and interviewing. You might find such groups at colleges, counseling centers, or the YWCA or through your state's Department of Labor.

Two nationwide organizations can help, too. They are Displaced Homemakers Network (1010 Vermont Ave. N.W., Suite 817, Washington, D.C. 20005) and Catalyst (250 Park Ave. South, New York, N.Y. 10003). Both are information clearinghouses, but Catalyst specializes in women in the work force. Catalyst also has 200 resource centers across the country and a useful career library at its headquarters.

The more distinct your skills, the easier time you will have getting a good job. For example, someone who knows how to operate a word processor will be a more desirable candidate than someone who tells a prospective employer that he or she works well with people. Once you have decided on the type of job you want, find out what skills and experience are required for it. You may need to take some courses at a college or technical school to be adequately trained. Instructors at the school may be able to put you in touch with companies that are hiring.

A gradual return to working for pay could be less stressful than immediately taking a full-time job. Consider applying for part-time or temporary jobs. They will give you an inkling about different types of companies and fields without requiring you to make a total commitment to any one firm right away. You will also be able to build up a network of job contacts.

You may end up taking a full-time job but detesting it. Don't panic. But don't wallow in misery either. If the job doesn't fit, start looking for another one while you are still employed. Once you find a job that seems a better match for you, resign on good terms with your employer and start looking forward to the new adventure in your life.

CHAPTER

12

RETIREMENT AND ESTATE PLANNING

I'm tired . . . my tennis game has gone to the
dogs . . . I'm ready to lie on the beach.
John Poelker,
explaining why he quit his job as
BankAmerica Corp.'s chief financial officer
in 1986; quoted in The Wall Street Journal

TIME TO THINK ABOUT THE LONG, LONG TERM

Living well is the best revenge. But living well during your entire life-time takes some serious retirement planning. And letting your children and other heirs live well calls for some estate planning on your part, too.

Retirement and estate planning have always been important, although probably never as important as they are today. Modern medicine is let-ting people live longer these days. That means that once you retire, in 2010 or thereabouts, you are likely to have more years of retirement ahead of you than your parents and grandparents had. So, you will need more money set aside for those extra years. A longer life will also give you more time to build up a sizable estate to pass on to your heirs—not to the IRS.

Tax reform and, to a lesser extent, the stock market crash of 1987, have altered and complicated the rules for retirement and estate planning. In

241

fact, if you have done either type of planning to date, now is a good time to reexamine your strategies. Some may no longer make sense. An error in this post-tax reform era could be costly.

The most important tax reform changes affecting retirement and estate planning have both negative and positive effects. For example, the new law might make you less inclined to save for retirement because it restricts the deductibility of Individual Retirement Accounts and because the lower tax rates make any deductions for IRAs and Keoghs worth less than before. The new law also takes some of the pizzazz out of company savings plans by further limiting the amount you can invest in a 401(k) company savings plan, adding new penalties to withdrawals from company plans, and requiring you to pay taxes sooner on payouts from company plans. But the law makes it more likely that you will receive company pensions because it requires employers to vest employee benefits much more quickly than before.

The law puts the kibosh on some of the most popular trusts used in estate planning. And by not lowering tax rates for estates at the time they cut income rates, Congress increased the importance of finding ways to cut your future estate tax bill.

Long-term planning for your retirement and your estate is neither easy nor especially reliable. Tax laws and other legislation affecting retirement and estates will surely change over the coming decades. No one really knows what Social Security will look like after the turn of the century, if indeed there will be a Social Security program. (If you're a Social Security skeptic, join the crowd. More than 70 percent of people ages 25 to 39 with household incomes of at least $30,000 say they have little or no confidence in the future of Social Security.) Who knows exactly when you will retire? Who knows whether you will want to leave your estate to your present spouse or children?

The natural temptation, then, is to shrug off retirement and estate planning. A recent survey of people in their 30s by the polling firm Yankelovich, Skelly & White bears this out. Some findings of the poll, which appeared in *The Wall Street Journal:*

- 74 percent say they are in fair or poor shape financially for retirement.

- 73 percent say they have difficulty saving for retirement.

- 61 percent worry that they won't have enough money to retire comfortably.

But you will be making a serious financial mistake if you continue to ignore retirement and estate planning. No one can predict the future, though one thing is certain: By not doing any retirement or estate planning, you will guarantee yourself and your family a financial future that is less comfortable than it could be.

CASH FLOW IS KING IN RETIREMENT

Your retirement is probably about 25 years off. Fortunately, that gives you plenty of time to start saving for those years and to build up a substantial pension at work. But remember that your retirement could easily last for 15 years or longer. So a retirement fund of, say, $200,000 might look large but could easily be used up in a few years.

The secret of financing retirement is controlling cash flow. Once you have mastered cash flow—balancing income with outgo—you will be able to live as well in retirement as you did while working. Coming up with cash flow projections for your 60s and 70s will be an imprecise exercise at best. But even rough estimates will give you a notion of the savings you will need. By the time you reach your mid-50s, the figures will become firmer and you can adjust your savings targets accordingly. Then you will have a better idea of the size of the three ingredients in your retirement pie: your pension, Social Security benefits, and savings.

To begin guesstimating your cash flow in retirement, decide how much you will want to live on after you stop working. Aiming for income equal to the last year before your retirement may be unrealistic. Few people have the financial resources to replace their salaries completely. Few people need to, anyway. Reasons: Your tax bill will almost certainly drop in retirement, and some expenses will dwindle or disappear when you quit work. You will not have any work-related expenses, your housing costs are likely to fall as your mortgage is paid off, and you can cut back on life insurance coverage once your children are grown.

But inflation is sure to hurt you during retirement. Pensions are rarely indexed to inflation. Nor are conservative fixed-income investments such as Treasury bonds and bank certificates of deposit.

You can expect to maintain your preretirement standard of living during retirement with an income that is between 60 and 80 percent of your former pretax earnings. The higher your preretirement income, the smaller the percentage you will use in your calculations, mostly because of lower taxes in retirement.

After arriving at a suitable annual retirement income, next comes the truly morbid but absolutely crucial estimate of your life expectancy. That is to ensure you don't outlive your retirement savings. At a minimum, use the national mortality tables that your insurance agent has. To be safer still, double the number of additional years the tables say someone your age can expect to live. If today's 40-year-old couple reach age 65, they can expect to live on to ages 81 (for the man) and 86 (for the woman), according to U.S. Census Bureau projections.

Managing Your Money Tip:

> Managing Your Money will tell you precisely what your life expectancy is. Select Your Life Expectancy from the Insure submenu. Fill in all of the fields. Press F10, and Managing Your Money will tell you precisely what your life expectancy is, taking into account such factors as your health, exercise level, family longevity, and the effect of your job and neighborhood.

Multiplying your target income by double your anticipated years in retirement will give you a workable idea of the amount of money you will need on hand to retire without a financial care in the world. That seven-digit figure will give you the willies. Fortunately, you won't have to come up with all the cash yourself: Social Security benefits and a company pension or Keogh can easily make up two-thirds of your ideal retirement income, leaving one-third of the funding to you. If you retire after working 30 years or longer with one of the more generous U.S. corporations, you may even have enough without doing much saving at all.

Managing Your Money Tip:

> Managing Your Money will tell you what you'll have to retire on. Just select Retirement Planning from the Analyze submenu. Fill in the information, press F10, and Managing Your Money will estimate the assets that will be available when you retire.

YOUR SOCIAL SECURITY BENEFIT

Will you get a Social Security benefit? Probably.

Will the money be enough to live on during retirement? Definitely not.

Will you get back from Social Security as much money as you will have paid in as payroll taxes? Probably not.

Barring another depression, the Social Security system will be on firm financial footing until 2049, long after you are likely to retire. At least that's what the legislators said in 1983 when they stitched together a Social Security bailout plan. The Social Security Administration sticks by that projection. It seems unlikely that Congress will let Social Security die off, because the politicians will continue to need the votes of the people who have been paying into the system for years.

But it is equally unlikely that the system won't be tinkered with before you retire. After all, by then nearly twice as many people are expected to be collecting Social Security checks as today. But at that time, there should be only about 2.5 workers paying Social Security taxes for each retiree. Today, the ratio is 3.3 to 1; in 1945, it was 42 to 1. Doctoring Social Security will help shore up its financial health and help pay your retirement benefits.

In fact, the bailout plan of 1983 has already changed some of the rules, although not all the revisions have taken effect yet. Among the most important scheduled changes:

- You will have to retire later to receive full benefits from Social Security. Starting in the year 2000, the minimum age for getting full benefits will be raised by two months a year. In 2005, the minimum age will reach 66 and it will stay there through 2016. Then the age will be hiked again annually, reaching 67 in 2027.

- You will be rewarded for retiring later. Today, Social Security enlarges your retirement check by 3 percent for each year you delay taking full benefits between age 65 and 70. That's in addition to the annual cost-of-living increase. The delayed retirement credit will inch up a bit for anyone now 62 or younger. The credit will increase by .5 percent every other year until it reaches 8 percent in 2008, when you will be about 60.

- You will get less money by retiring early. Today, you can quit at 62 and get 80 percent of your Social Security benefit. But starting in the year 2000 and lasting through 2022, that percentage will get whittled away—to 70 percent in the year 2022.

- You will see more of your Social Security income taxed. The law says retirees have to pay taxes on up to half of their benefits if their other income plus half their Social Security benefits exceeds $32,000 for married couples filing joint tax returns and $25,000 for single people. You must add in any tax-exempt interest from municipal bonds when calculating whether your Social Security benefits will be taxable. But here's the catch: The $32,000 and $25,000 threshholds are not indexed to inflation. Only about 15 percent of today's retirees are taxed on their benefits, but by the time you retire, there is about a 50-50 chance your Social Security will be taxed.

Other changes are nearly inevitable. Don't be surprised to see:

- A delay in the retirement age. Don't rule out a retirement age of 68 or even 69 by the time you call it quits.

- A cutback in the percentage of pay that Social Security will replace. Today, someone consistently earning an amount equal to the pay at which Social Security taxes stop will get 24 percent of his or her preretirement pay from Social Security. The benefit is usually tax-free. But you might retire with a taxable benefit equal to only 20 percent of your preretirement pay.

- Higher Social Security payroll taxes. Today, the Social Security tax rate is 7.65 percent for employees and 15.3 percent for the self-employed. Self-employed workers can deduct from their gross income half their Social Security taxes. Some Social Security analysts predict that the payroll tax rate for employees will jump to between 12 and 20 percent within 40 years.

How much you will actually receive in Social Security benefits depends on the number of years you have worked, your annual earnings, and the age at which you begin collecting the benefits. You will not be able to get a reliable figure for your future benefits until you are at least 60. At that time you can write to the nearest Social Security office for a free estimate of your future benefits.

In the meantime, try to get a rough idea of your benefits by determining the percentage of your pretax, preretirement income that will be replaced—what's known as the Social Security replacement rate. The higher your income, the lower your rate. It's about 24 percent for someone retiring today at 65 who previously earned the salary at which employers stop withholding for Social Security taxes (roughly $45,000). The replacement rate is about 8.5 percent for a person retiring from a $100,000 salary. Figure on receiving a Social Security benefit equal to roughly 10 to 20 percent of your preretirement pay. If you are married and your spouse won't have earned enough to get his or her own Social Security benefit, count on one check for the two of you equal to one and a half times your benefit.

Managing Your Money Tip:

> Managing Your Money can estimate what your monthly Social Security benefits will be. Just select Retirement Planning from the Analyze submenu.
>
> 1. Fill in the six fields at the bottom — age, tax bracket, age at withdrawal (when you plan to retire), assumed rate of inflation, and the age after which no penalty for retirement plan withdrawals will be assessed (currently 59.5).
>
> 2. Then press F6, and using the arrow keys and the "x", create a graph that shows your earnings from the first year you worked through 1992.
>
> 3. Now press F10. Managing Your Money will estimate your monthly Social Security benefit.

YOUR PENSION BENEFIT

The size of the pension you will receive in retirement depends on a variety of factors but chiefly on your length of service with your employer. If you stay with the same company for 10 years, your pension will probably equal 10 to 15 percent of your final salary. After 20 years it will amount to 20 to 25 percent of pay, and after 30 years, about 35 percent. It's conceivable that by the time you retire, your pension could well make up half your retirement income. But if you hopscotch jobs throughout your career, you might end up in retirement with only a tiny pension fund or no vested pension at all.

The precise makeup of your pension plan is something you should get to know well now. That includes understanding how your company calculates its pensions, what benefits you can expect and at what age, the type of survivor's pension benefit your spouse might receive, how much you can or must contribute to the plan, and when your employer's contributions will belong to you.

Company retirement plans differ as much as their balance sheets. Some firms merely provide plain vanilla pensions that pay a flat monthly amount from the day you retire until the day you die. Others pile on additional savings elements: profit-sharing plans, thrift plans, 401(k) salary reduction plans, and stock ownership plans.

The defined-benefit pension plan is the oldest and most common employer-provided program. Your company determines how large a pension you will get based on your earnings and length of service and then pays out the money in monthly installments after retirement. Usually, the employer funds the plan without contributions from workers.

Defined-benefit plans don't pay pensions until you are vested. Before tax reform, that typically meant ten years after starting work at the company. But the new law requires that plans vest employees fully after either five or seven years of service. A plan with seven-year vesting must vest 20 percent of your benefits after three years plus 20 percent in each of the following four years. Years you have worked for the company count toward the new formulas, so if you started working for your company in January 1986 and the pension plan switched to five-year vesting in 1990, you became fully vested in January 1991.

In the past, the more often you changed jobs, the less likely you were to get much of a pension. But the tax reform law's faster vesting rules will increase the chances that you will retire with decent company retirement benefits. Even so, you will get a much larger pension if you stay at one company for most of your working life rather than switching from job to job. That's because once you leave a company, the size of your pension benefit will be frozen. It will be eroded by inflation by the time you retire.

After vesting, you can feel confident about getting some, if not all, of your pension money at retirement. The Pension Benefit Guaranty Corporation, a federal agency, uses employer-paid premiums to guarantee pensioners and vested employees annual benefits. The maximum annual pension guaranteed in 1991 was $27,000. That figure increases each year with the cost of living.

It is possible, though unlikely, that your employer will scrap its pension plan someday. Companies are not required to provide pensions and have great freedom to terminate their plans. When companies can their pension plans, they usually replace them with new pensions or with savings plans. When a company terminates its pension plan, retirees continue to receive their benefits—assuming the company has enough cash to pay them.

Most companies will give a worker's spouse some of the pension after the worker dies, provided he or she was vested. If the worker made any pension contributions, the spouse will get that money automatically. Otherwise the survivor's pension benefit is typically half what the worker would have received. The cash is usually paid out monthly beginning the year the worker could have retired.

Lately, businesses have been supplementing their pension plans with savings and stock purchase arrangements known as defined-contribution plans. You or your employer or both put a specified amount of money into the plan each year—generally a percentage of your pay. Investment earnings grow tax-deferred. Contributions to your savings plans from you and your employer cannot exceed 25 percent of your pay or $30,000 a year, whichever is less.

There is no knowing what you will get from these plans when you retire; payouts are based on how well your investments perform. This fact was brought home especially harshly during the stock market crash of 1987. Many company savings plans were fully or partially invested in stocks before the crash. According to the Employee Benefit Research Institute, savings plans fell about 15 percent in value from the August 1987 market peak to early November. But the losses in company savings plan accounts that were fully invested averaged 26 percent.

Even so, you will probably prefer defined-contribution plans to defined-benefit plans. Your benefits under a defined-contribution plan usually vest fully within five years, and you can take the money with you when you quit at any age, not just when you retire. You also have more say regarding where your money is invested.

It is a good idea to take a hard look at your company's pension and savings plans. By understanding how they work, you will have a clearer picture of the retirement income you will receive from them.

Start by asking your employee benefits department for what is called the "summary plan description" of the pension. This description notes how soon you will be vested and at what age you can get a full pension. It also outlines eligibility requirements for participating in the pension plan, how to calculate your benefit, and how time off is counted for vesting.

Be sure also to comb through the personalized employee benefit statement you most likely receive once a year. This document will show not only your accrued pension benefit but an estimate of what you will receive at retirement.

If you feel confident you will get a pension, the next step is to figure out how large it will be. Companies typically determine pension benefits by multiplying the number of years you have participated in the plan by 1.4 to 1.7 percent of your average salary during your last years at work. Ideally, you would like a pension that equals your years on the job up to, say, 20 years, times 2 percent of your final salary at retirement. Your company's employee benefits counselor can tell you the size of your future pension, but the figure will be very rough. It is based on the assumption that you will stay at the firm until retirement and on a hypothetical salary you will get more than 20 years hence.

Most companies base their pensions on a salary that's the average of your last five years at work or longer; the best ones average your last three years. Some plans use your career-average salary; benefits from these plans could be meager because the formula includes your early, low-earning years. A career-average pension can often be less than half the size of one based on final pay. Some plans, particularly those subject to collective bargaining, use another formula: They pay a flat dollars-per-month figure for each year an employee works. Today, that figure often averages about $20. That is less than cushy, and heavily unionized companies have been known to cut pension benefits in tough times.

Your pension could be chopped by 10 percent or more if you are married. Companies must give a retired married person the option of taking a pension in the form of a joint-and-survivor annuity: a guarantee of monthly income to the worker and, upon death, the worker's spouse. The employer pays an insurer more for a joint annuity than for a single one, and the employee usually shares the extra cost by accepting a reduced retirement benefit. The younger the spouse, the more the pension is likely to be trimmed.

RETIREMENT AND ESTATE PLANNING   251

If you are considering working past age 65, find out whether those extra years on the job will count in the company's pension calculations. Today most plans stop accruing benefits for their employees who work past the company's normal retirement age, usually 65.

Your pension almost certainly will be reduced if you retire early, too. About half of large U.S. companies scale back pensions for workers who quit at 62 after 30 years of service, and 89 percent do so for employees retiring at 55, according to a study by Hewitt Associates, a benefits consulting firm. Typically, a company cuts pensions by a third for employees who retire at age 60 and halves them for workers who leave at age 55, no matter how long they have worked for the company.

Assuming you will get a pension, how will you actually receive the money? At most companies, you have no choice: a pension check will appear in your mailbox once a month during retirement. But about 20 percent of employers let their retirees take their pensions in one lump sum. A new 1992 law requires the IRS to withhold for taxes 20% of such lump sum distributions, unless the money is rolled into an IRA.

It's much easier to size up a company savings plan than a pension. All the information you will need appears in either the summary plan description or the quarterly and annual statements of investment performance given to plan participants. Look for six pieces of data: how soon you can participate, when you will vest, how much you can and must put in, how much the company will contribute, which of your contributions are pretax, and how the plan has done compared with similar investments.

Typically, you can enroll after having worked for the company for a year, regardless of your age. The better vesting schedules let you claim the employer's contributions after three years. The more you can invest pretax, the more attractive the plan. You should be able to withdraw at least some of your own contributions while still working at the company, but you may have to wait as long as a year after a withdrawal before you can start contributing again.

When determining whether the plan is a good place to put your savings, compare the return on its investments with that of similar investments. Don't forget that if your company matches your contributions, you have an automatic profit. If the fund is a diversified stock portfolio, track its previous six-month and five-year performance against the Standard & Poor's 500 Stock Index. A bond fund should measure up to the top corporate bond funds tracked monthly in *Money* magazine's Fund Watch column. Plans that guarantee a fixed return for a year ought to yield a bit better than current rates on one-year bank certificates. And if the plan buys only company stock, check the annual report for a chart of the stock's historical performance. Keep your money out of a plan whose holdings fluctuate dramatically. Otherwise you will be taking a risk with your retirement that is easily avoidable.

YOUR SAVINGS

Your employer and the federal government will do their share to help pay for your retirement. The rest is up to you. Exactly how much you will need to set aside is hard to say. An admirable goal: Each year, try to save for retirement an amount equal to 10 percent of your family's pretax income. The more generous your pension and the better your investments perform, the less you will have to save. If you expect to retire without much of a pension or if your investments have been losers so far, you will need to compensate by stashing away a greater chunk of cash for your later years. There's always the wild card—a windfall. If you receive a pile of money from a rich relative, your retirement worries could be over.

When saving for retirement, as with other long-term savings, shoot for growth and tax savings. Invest for growth by purchasing stocks of reliable companies, mutual funds that buy such stocks, and real estate. Look for tax savings from IRAs, company savings plans, and Keogh plans. Once you have put as much as you can into tax-favored accounts, load up your retirement accounts with taxable investments and savings alternatives. As you near retirement, rejigger your investment portfolio so it delivers income, rather than growth. At that time, you will want to be in bank certificates of deposit, bonds and bond mutual funds, Treasury bills, bank money-market accounts, and money-market mutual funds.

It's best to err on the side of caution and set aside more for retirement than you expect you will need. When calculating the amount of money to save for retirement, remember that you will not need all the money at once. You will want the money to provide a steady stream of income for the rest of your life. Remember, too, that if you want the income to last 20 years after you retire, you will only have to save about 17 years' worth of living expenses. That's because most of the money in your retirement accounts will keep earning interest or dividends.

For exact projections of your anticipated Social Security retirement benefits, call the Social Security Administration (800-772-1213). To estimate the size of your company pension, ask your employee-benefits counselor

Managing Your Money Tip:

Want to see if you'll have enough to support yourself after you retire? Here's how to use the Managing Your Money calculator to calculate this result:

1. Type Ctrl-N.

2. Multiply your current annual income by the percentage of current income you expect to need after you retire. This percentage should be between 60 and 80 percent. For example, if your current annual income is $35,000 and you think you'll need 70% of your current income to live on after you retire, type "35000x.70", followed by <enter>.

3. Next, type "a=r", followed by <enter>.

4. Add your estimated income from Social Security to your annual pension at retirement. For example, if you estimate income from Social Security to be $6,000, and you estimate that your annual pension at retirement will be $18,000, type "6000+18000", followed by <enter>.

5. Next, type "b=r", followed by <enter>.

6. Enter "c=", then the amount that you've already saved for retirement. For example, if you've already saved $5,000 for retirement, type "c=5000", followed by <enter>.

7. Enter "d=", then the multiplier indicated in column A that corresponds to the number of years before you expect to retire. For example, if you expect to retire in 10 years, type "d=1.219", followed by <enter>.

Number of Years Before	Multipliers	
You Expect to Retire	A	B
5	1.104	.192
10	1.219	.091
15	1.346	.058
20	1.486	.041
25	1.641	.031
30	1.811	.025
35	2.0	.02

8. Enter "e=", then the multiplier indicated in column B that corresponds to the number of years before you expect to retire. For example, if you expect to retire in 10 years, type "d=0.91", followed by <enter>.

9. Now, type this formula: ((a-b)x17)-(cxd), followed by <enter>. The result (r=) is the amount you need to save.

10. Then type this formula: rxe, followed by <enter>. The result (r=) is the amount you need to save each year.

Managing Your Money's Asset Allocation program will tell you whether your savings will cover your retirement income needs or not.

1. Select Asset Allocation from the Analyze submenu.

2. Select Estimate Future Return. Then enter the period you wish to base your prediction of future performance. For example, if you want to use the period 1971-1991, enter "1971" as the starting year and "1991" as the ending year. Then press <esc>.

3. Select Asset Mixes. Press F6 to extract your asset mix from your Portfolio (or simply enter a mix that you want). Then press <esc>.

4. Select Analyze Required Wealth from the Analyze submenu. Fill in the information listed to reflect your current financial situation. (Press F6 to extract current information from your Portfolio.)

5. Now press F10, F6, and fill in the information listed on the screen to calculate how much you'll need for retirement expenses (your retirement wealth goal). This the same kind of information that the worksheet calls for. Press F6 again, to extract the information you listed in Retirement Planning in the Analyze submenu. After you've filled in all the fields to your satisfaction, press F10.

6. In the lefthandmost column, Managing Your Money will tell you what your portfolio will be when you retire (expected wealth), and compare it to the wealth that you'll need for retirement (required wealth). The other six columns give you alternative, increasingly risky portfolio mixes, and compare their expected wealths with your required wealth. The key is to have the least risky portfolio mix possible that shows a surplus (the expected wealth exceeds your required wealth). When you're finished, press F10 again.

If none of the portfolios show a surplus, you'll need to save more for retirement. Select Retirement Planning from the Analyze submenu. Play around with the fields until the assets that will be available when you retire meet the wealth you required for retirement.

EVALUATING AN EARLY-RETIREMENT OFFER

Retirement might not be so far off. Thousands of employees are finding that they can retire a lot earlier than they had expected because their companies are offering early-retirement incentive packages. More than 300 companies, including Chevron, DuPont, IBM, and Union Carbide, have given their workers such enticements in the past few years. Some offers are restricted to people in their 50s, but many are open to all employees. Trouble is, you are usually given less than three months to make up your mind.

Most such offers are take-it-or-leave-it propositions. But should you decide that the package isn't lucrative enough, you can sometimes negotiate with your employer for a better deal. If the package is offered to only select employees and you are not one of them, you can ask to be included.

You may even be able to initiate your own package. Such bargaining is usually done on the QT.

Should you accept an offer if one comes along? Maybe. Here are some key factors to consider:

- *Assess your prospects at work.* What is likely to happen to you if you turn down the package? If your job is shaky, the offer may be one you cannot afford to refuse. The most telling clue about your job security is the scope of the package itself. You have not been singled out if the same package of incentives is being made available to all employees. But if the offer applies to a select group of employees—only middle managers or only employees of targeted divisions—the company is probably sending you a signal: If you do not take the package, you may not be a survivor at the company in the future.

- *Determine how rich the package is.* Will you be able to afford to quit? Call in your accountant and any other financial advisers for assistance. The juiciest offers usually come from companies that already have the most lucrative employee benefits packages (a savings plan with matching employer contributions, a pension plan, and comprehensive medical insurance).

- *See how people your age will fare.* Many offers are geared toward people in their 50s and beef up pensions. But your best offer would be one made to younger employees as well as older ones. Such plans typically pay a one-time cash bonus whose size varies with the employee's tenure at the company. Tops among these packages are ones that let you walk away with up to a year's salary in cash.

- *Look for a lump-sum option.* The better packages let you take your pension as a lump sum if you wish, rather than as an annuity with lifetime monthly income. Invested reasonably, the cash could produce more income than the pension. Taking your pension and savings plan money at once can also prevent the tax man from turning your lump sum into a dim sum. You can roll over the money into an Individual Retirement Account and defer the taxes until you start withdrawing the cash, although there is a 10 percent penalty on withdrawals made before you turn 59 1/2. The penalty will be waived if you receive the IRA rollover money in monthly installments over your lifetime. You will owe a 15 percent excise tax in any year you receive more than $112,500 from either your pension, savings plan, or IRA rollover, however.

- *See which benefits you will keep.* By the time you are 40, roughly one-third of your pay could be in the form of fringe benefits. Giving up health and life insurance, a company car, and even the company cafeteria could get costly. When you leave your company, you can definitely say good-bye to any future contributions or employer matches to your company savings plan. But an incentive package may let you continue getting other perks, such as medical and life insurance—if you are old enough and have worked at the company long enough to be considered an early retiree. Your life insurance coverage might be reduced to an amount equal to 25 percent of your final salary, however. You could also be asked to make larger co-payments for your medical insurance. Chances are, if you are in your 30s or 40s you will not meet your company's early-retirement test and you will lose company-paid life and dental insurance. But a new law requires companies with more than twenty employees to continue providing you with health insurance coverage for up to 18 months after you quit.

- *Remember the intangible factor.* Determine how much it will be worth to you just to slam your office door for the last time. Some people would gladly sacrifice $25,000 in pay and benefits in exchange for their chance to leave with money in their pockets.

- *Try negotiating a better deal.* You may be able to sweeten your company's offer by getting your employer to hire you as a consultant. Such jobs often pay $400 a day or more, though few consultants are fortunate enough to work for such pay daily.

- *Create your own package.* The ultimate negotiated early-retirement offer is the one you draw up yourself. You might initiate a deal letting you leave to become a consultant, taking on your ex-employer as a client. Few employees have the leverage to wangle this type of arrangement. Generally, managers are more likely to consider such offers in more creative fields, such as computer programming, advertising, and communications.

    You will be in the best position to write your own ticket if you are one of two types of people: a highly valued employee whose company wants to retain him or her as a consultant, or a problem employee whose boss wants to remove him or her. You won't have any bargaining power if you are just someone who does a good job.

Under most circumstances, though, asking your boss for a special early-retirement package is dicey. If the boss goes along, you can make out well. But if he or she refuses and you decide not to quit, your boss might hold the request against you. Future raises might be meager, and you might even lose your job.

So before approaching your supervisor, snoop around to see whether anyone else has ever snared such a package. Talk to that person and get the details about the deal. Then tell your boss precisely how much money per year you want in salary and benefits. If you might want to return full-time some day, try to retain part-time status. By staying on the payroll, you will continue accruing pension benefits.

Within a few weeks, you ought to get an answer from your boss. Should the offer be approved, have your company's legal department draw up an agreement. That way, even if your boss eventually gets the boot, you will still have a contract and—more important—your financial independence.

YES, YOU NEED TO DO SOME ESTATE PLANNING

When the subject of estate planning comes up, you may subscribe to the philosophy of *Mad* magazine's Alfred E. Neuman: "What, me worry?" Truth is, everyone should do some estate planning, even if that only means drawing up a will. Otherwise, when you die your assets could be divvied up in ways you never expected. Those you care about most could wind up getting the least.

You may be surprised to learn how quickly an estate adds up. Think your estate amounts to less than $600,000, the size at which estates can be subject to federal estate taxes? Think again. Add together the market value of your home, the value of your family's life insurance policies, your investments and savings, any real estate holdings, your furniture, your cars, any art, your pension and company savings plan benefits, your IRA, and your Keogh. Presto! Chances are, the total exceeds $600,000, and possibly by quite a bit. Of course, a married couple can have, in effect, a tax-free estate of $1.2 million—$600,000 times two.

Estate planning means more than just figuring out who will get your possessions when you go. It also means deciding how to own the property you and your spouse have: jointly, separately, or some variation thereof. In addition, shrewd estate planning will let you give your heirs the most you can while giving the Internal Revenue Service and your state tax collector the least they deserve. And, of course, proper estate planning will avoid the nuisance and expense of probate—the legal term for proving in court that your will is valid and transferring the ownership of your property to the new owners. Probate can sometimes take years and eat up as much as 10 percent of the value of an estate.

An often overlooked, but crucial, part of estate planning is knowing, as best as you can determine, what you will get from your family and relatives when they die. Frequently, people in their 30s and 40s get blindsided upon their parents' death because they often are ignorant of their parents' finances. The surprise can become an unpleasant one if you suddenly have to manage properties or pay a big tax bill on your parents' estate. To prevent such a situation, you need to have a serious talk with your parents and in-laws about their inheritance plans.

Needless to say, such a discussion will be a delicate one. The hardest part may be just getting your parents and in-laws to talk about their wills. One way to get the ball rolling: Tell your parents you want to discuss any inheritance they might leave for your children. Grandparents are usually suckers when it comes to their grandchildren. Consequently, they often find it easier to discuss finances concerning their grandkids than their own children. Once you begin talking about any cash your children will get, talking about your own inheritance will come naturally. Another tactic: Ask your parents whether they will let their lawyer talk with your lawyer about their wills. You may find them more receptive to working through these disinterested, professional third parties.

WHERE THERE'S A WILL . . .

Estate planning begins with your will. You don't have one? Don't be too embarrassed. Only a third of adults have wills. Dying without a will is not very smart, though. In most cases, when there is no will your property will automatically be split between your spouse and your children. Probably one-half to two-thirds of your inheritance will automatically go to the kids. If you have no children and die without a will, your assets might be split between your spouse and your in-laws—not your relatives. If, heaven forbid, you and your spouse die together without wills, the state will decide who will wind up raising your children.

Then there are the additional costs imposed when you die without a will. The court must appoint an administrator to supervise the distribution of your assets. This administrator will usually be paid an amount equal to 3 to 5 percent of your estate. The administrator will also have to post a bond, which usually costs $200 or more. That fee is taken out of your estate as well. The tax man might also keep a large portion of your estate if you have no will.

Managing Your Money Tip:

> MECA's Home Lawyer software will prepare a legally enforceable last will and testament, as well as a living will and a form to revoke that living will. It also features an estate planning worksheet that will tell you what your total net worth is for estate planning purposes. Home Lawyer also can prepare powers of attorney, various employment agreements, and other legal documents. Best of all, the software costs a fraction of what an attorney would charge for just one hour of his or her time.

By hiring a lawyer to draw up a will, you can name a relative or friend to be your executor. That will avoid the court having to appoint an administrator. Your executor need not be bonded and, if the executor is truly a good person, will perform the duties gratis. You may want two executors: one to carry out your overall directives and another to manage your financial assets when you're gone.

A will also guarantees that your estate will be divided the way you prefer. You will be able to order that some of your property be given to, say, a live-in lover or a charity. A will allows you to name a guardian for your minor children, too. Such a provision can assure you that your children's money will be managed professionally.

Drawing up a will requires serious consideration. The more skillfully written the document, the less likely it will be contested in court by a seething relative or friend. Don't write a will by following one of those do-it-yourself books with formula documents; your property is too important to toss off casually. Hire a lawyer. At the very least, the lawyer will make sure that the will complies with your state's laws. Expect to pay between $100 and $300 for a simple will, more if your will is complex. Keep the will at your lawyer's office, but keep a copy at home where you can review it.

You can change your will at any time. In fact, you ought to update your will whenever there is a major change in your life—a marriage, a divorce, a baby, a death in the family, a move—or if your finances change markedly. It's a good idea to take a fresh look at your will at least once every five years. Have your lawyer also look over your will whenever federal or state tax laws change dramatically. If you had a will written before the Tax Reform Act of 1986 passed, ask your lawyer to review it. Chances are, the will needs freshening up.

Minor changes in your will can be taken care of with amendments called codicils. Whatever you do, don't cross out words in your will or tear out pages. That could invalidate the will altogether. Be sure that your codicils are signed and witnessed. When your will needs a major rewrite, however, start from scratch and be sure to revoke the old will.

If you know your will seems a little unusual—you plan to leave all your worldly possessions to the Cub Scouts, for example—give your lawyer a handwritten letter explaining your reasons. You might do this if the will calls for leaving most of your estate to your children or to another relative rather than to your husband or wife.

Wills have limitations. You cannot use one to transfer property that is jointly owned. When you die, any jointly owned property will automatically be passed along to your partner. Neither will the will cover property with a named beneficiary, such as your life insurance policy, IRA, Keogh, pension, or profit-sharing benefits.

Perhaps the most important use of a will is taking care of your children. If your kids are minors—age 18 or younger in most states—you should name a guardian for them in your will. The guardian will be responsible for raising your children. If your spouse will not be the guardian, it's wise to write a letter explaining how you would like your children raised.

You can also appoint the guardian to manage your children's inheritances until the kids are no longer minors. But you would do better instead to include in your will a trust to hold your children's inherited money and property. That will cut down on a guardian's paperwork and guarantee that your children will not get control of the money until the date you have selected. Expect to pay a lawyer between $250 and $5,000 to draw up such a trust, depending on the size of your estate and the complexity of the trust.

THE IRS AND YOUR ESTATE

You can't talk about estate planning for very long before the subject of estate taxes comes up. To many people, the whole point of estate planning is keeping the tax man's hands out of their pockets. That may be overdoing it a tad, but unquestionably tax planning and estate planning go hand in hand.

When Congress passed its mammoth tax reform law in 1986 and lowered income tax rates, it didn't touch the tax rates for gift and estate taxes. Those tax rates start at 18 percent and hit the dizzying height of 55 percent. The top rate for estate taxes was scheduled to drop to 50 percent in 1988. But Congress, looking for extra revenue in 1987, passed a law freezing estate tax rates, thereby keeping the 55 percent rate on the books.

An earlier tax law passed in 1981 has helped greatly in reducing the chance the IRS will mess with your estate. The law lumped together federal gift and estate taxes and provided a single $600,000 exemption from the taxes that applies to the size of your estate when you die and any gifts you make while you are alive. So, married couples can bequeath estates of up to $1.2 million to their heirs and the IRS won't take a nickel. And you can leave your spouse an estate of any size free of federal taxation through what's known as the unlimited marital deduction.

The unlimited marital deduction can be a trap, however. Sure, you can give your spouse all your property tax-free. But when he or she dies, your heirs could be faced with enormous tax bills on the survivor's estate. So the key to shrewd estate planning is arranging your assets in such a way that the spouse who dies first will not leave the survivor with a taxable estate exceeding $600,000.

One way to cut the chance of your estate being taxed is by making gifts to your children, friends, and relatives during your life-time. You can bestow tax-free gifts of up to $10,000 a year each to as many people as you wish. A married couple can give away as much as $20,000 a year per person without incurring gift taxes. Once you exceed those limits, your gifts can be taxed, but only if the total exceeds the $600,000 lifetime exclusion for federal gift and estate taxes. When you give away more than the $10,000-a-year limit, be sure to file Form 709, the gift tax return.

Another way to trim your taxable estate is by giving assets to charities while you are alive. Charitable donations are not subject to gift or estate taxes. Of course, the donations will also be tax-deductible if you itemize.

TRUST IN TRUSTS

Another way to cut your estate tax bill is by setting up trusts that keep some of your assets out of your estate. A trust is essentially a contract between you (the grantor) and someone else (the trustee). The property in the trust will be managed by the trustee for the benefit of another person, the beneficiary. The trustee can be anyone, but it is best to appoint either a reliable friend or relative with a good mind for finances or a professional such as a lawyer, accountant, bank trust officer, or trust company officer. Professionals typically charge fees equal to between .75 and 1 percent of the assets in the trust.

Your trustee will keep the original trust agreement, but you should keep a copy for yourself and one for your attorney. It will be up to you to be sure the trust remains up-to-date. If you set up a trust before last year's tax reform law passed, ask your lawyer to reread it. Quite possibly, the trust will need updating. Like a will, a trust should also be reviewed when your financial situation changes or when there is a birth, death, marriage, or divorce in your family.

Trusts are either testamentary or living. *A testamentary* trust is one that you include in your will and takes effect when you die. This is probably the type of trust you will want if you have young children who will be receiving money. But a testamentary trust will go through probate, and its assets could be taxed when you die.

A testamentary trust could, however, be just the ticket for a married couple who want to avoid taxes on their estate. Say you have an $800,000 estate. Rather than leaving everything to your spouse and potentially thrusting a large estate tax bill on your heirs, you could write into your will a *bypass testamentary trust* for up to $600,000 of your assets. (This trust does not qualify for the marital deduction.) You would give the remainder of your estate to your spouse. Your spouse would receive some, all, or none of the income from the bypass trust while he or she is alive, depending on how you write the will. Your spouse can also get as much as

5 percent of the trust's principal or $5,000, whichever is greater, each year. The remainder of the trust will pass to your heirs without showing up in your surviving spouse's estate.

Alternatively, you could set up a *marital deduction trust* in your will, particularly if your spouse will need income. Unlike a bypass trust, this type requires that the spouse receive all the income the trust produces. The surviving spouse does not control the money in a marital deduction trust, but the estate is likely to escape taxation because of the marital deduction. An advantage of such a trust is that a professional trustee might be able to manage the trust money better than your spouse.

An increasingly popular type of marital deduction trust has an unlikely name: the *Q-TIP trust.* (The full name is Qualified Terminal Interest Property trust, and that's an earful.) A Q-TIP lets you give your spouse the trust's income for life but give the principal to someone else, such as your children. The trust's assets will be taxable in your spouse's estate. These trusts are especially inviting to people with stepfamilies. By setting up a Q-TIP trust, you will be able to guarantee that any children from your first marriage will get part of your inheritance.

Another variation of this theme is a *general power of appointment trust.* Unlike a Q-TIP, you let your spouse decide who will receive the trust's assets when he or she dies. In every other way, however, a general power of appointment trust is like a Q-TIP: Both qualify for the marital deduction, both are part of the surviving spouse's estate, and both provide income that must go to the surviving spouse.

As a rule, you should put assets you expect to appreciate greatly—stocks, real estate—in a bypass trust and leave other investments in marital deduction trusts. That way, if the assets in the bypass trust are worth $600,000 or less when the trust begins, they will be tax-free no matter how much they grow.

Living trusts, sometimes called inter vivos trusts, are used—surprise!—while you are alive. The assets in a living trust do not pass through probate when you die. The trouble with living trusts is the nuisance factor. You must change the title for all of your assets to the trustee's name. That means revising the titling documents of stocks, bank accounts, and real estate. If you fail to change the title on these documents, the property in your name when you die will go through the dreaded probate.

A living trust can be either revocable or irrevocable. In a *revocable trust*, you can control the property and change or end the trust at any time. This flexibility has a price: The assets are part of your estate and could be taxed when you die.

As a precautionary measure against the change that you become incapacitated, you might set up a type of revocable living trust known as a *standby or convertible trust.* Your lawyer prepares a legal document giving a close friend or relative of yours so-called durable power of attorney over your assets. This way, if you become incapacitated the person you choose will be able to transfer your assets at that time to the standby trust. Some states do not permit giving someone durable power of attorney, so be absolutely sure yours does before setting up a standby trust.

An irrevocable trust is a common tool for keeping an estate exceeding $600,000 free of taxes. The trust requires you to give up control of the assets, and you cannot change the trust once it is written. But an irrevocable trust will not be included in your taxable estate. This type of trust also lets you pass your entire estate on to your kids, even if the estate exceeds the $600,000 estate and gift tax exemption.

You can also use trusts to give money to charities and lower your estate taxes. Charitable trusts are particularly valuable for single parents who cannot use the marital deduction but want to give their children the biggest inheritance possible. A *charitable remainder trust* lets you give away an asset but keep receiving its earnings until the trust dissolves. The termination date of a charitable remainder trust can be as long as 20 years away or the date of either your death or the death of another beneficiary. Then the charity will take control of the assets.

If you start such a trust while you are alive, you can claim a tax write-off for your contribution in the year you make it, as long as you itemize your deductions. The size of your deduction will depend on the size of the gift, you rate of return on the money, and your age. The smaller the return and the older you are, the bigger your tax break. If you write this trust into your will as a testamentary trust, the property you give away will be considered part of your estate, but some of its value will be deductible before estate taxes are owed.

Another type of charitable trust, the *charitable lead trust,* can give you bigger income tax deductions than a charitable remainder trust, but your heirs won't get any income from such a trust for a while. This trust could be especially useful if you have income-producing property that you don't need. A charitable lead trust is usually testamentary and works the opposite way of a charitable remainder trust. When you die, the property passes to an irrevocable trust paying income to your designated charity for usually more than ten years. The assets of the trust then go to your heirs when the trust terminates. Your estate will be able to claim a charitable deduction, perhaps even one large enough to offset the value of the property your heirs will receive.

The tax reform law put a stake through the heart of two types of popular trusts. The first is the *Clifford trust*. This trust let you give money to your children for ten years, at which point you could get the principal again. The income was taxed at your child's tax rate, which presumably was lower than yours. But the new tax law says that if you set up a Clifford trust after March 1,1986, income will be taxed at your tax rate, not your child's. So there is no point in starting a Clifford anymore. Income from a Clifford trust created before March 1,1986, will be taxed at your tax rate until your child turns 14. Then the income will be taxed at his or her rate.

The second type of trust clobbered by the tax reform law is the *spousal remainder trust*. It's like a Clifford trust for married couples. The spousal remainder trust let you give money to your husband or wife for ten years and then get the principal when the trust terminated. But like Cliffords, spousal remainder trusts will now be taxed at the tax rate of the donor.

Successful estate planning demands keeping your estate liquid enough to pay any taxes due upon your death as well as any debts and miscellaneous expenses. One way to do so is by purchasing life insurance, whose proceeds will not be subject to probate. The danger of loading up on life insurance is that the proceeds could boost the size of your estate over the federal estate tax exemption. The way to avoid this trap is by transferring the ownership of your insurance policy to an *irrevocable life insurance trust*. Your spouse will receive income from the trust while he or she is alive. When your spouse dies, the proceeds will go to your heirs. There is a catch, however. If you die within three years of setting up a life insurance trust, the insurance proceeds will be included in your estate. So, have your attorney include in the trust a clause saying that if you die within three years, the insurance will pass directly to your spouse or go into a marital deduction trust. This technique will let you avoid estate taxes on the money or at least defer them until after your spouse dies.

DON'T FORGET STATE TAXES

Federal estate taxes are bad enough. But your state will probably want to get its paws on your estate when you go, too. So, to do estate planning properly, it is important to understand how states treat estates and inheritances. Some thirty states and the District of Columbia collect death taxes. A few are nasty enough to tax estates as small as $100. To find out the rules where you live, ask your lawyer or call your state's department of taxation.

Your state may levy either estate taxes or inheritance taxes, but not both. An estate tax is imposed on the value of the estate. Inheritance taxes are assessed on each heir's share of your assets. The taxes are usually collected by the state in which you were a legal resident before you died. But real estate is taxed by the state where the property sits. The same goes for cars, boats, and household goods.

Fortunately, you will slash your state tax bill when you employ the techniques advised for reducing your federal estate tax tab: Taking advantage of deductions and exemptions, giving money away, and setting up trusts.

THE PROS AND MOSTLY CONS OF JOINT OWNERSHIP

Couples often hold most of their property jointly. That generally includes their homes, bank accounts, brokerage accounts, art, cars, furniture, and real estate. Joint ownership makes life easy and death, too. But joint ownership is not necessarily the best way to own all your property.

There are actually three ways to hold property jointly:

- *Joint tenancy with the right of survivorship.* Any two or more persons can own property this way. Each owner is a joint tenant with an equal share of the property. You can sell or give away your interest without getting approval from co-owners. When you die, your share is divided equally among the other owners.

- *Tenancy in common.* When you die, your share of the property goes to the heirs named in your will. If you die without a will, your interest goes to your relatives.

- *Tenancy by the entirety.* Only married couples can use this setup. You and your spouse own equal shares of your property, and when you die, your interest is automatically transferred to your spouse. But unlike with joint tenancy, you cannot sell or give away your interest without getting an okay from your spouse.

People who live in community-property states (Arizona, California, Idaho, Louisiana, Nevada, New Mexico, Texas, Washington, and Wisconsin) play by slightly different rules. In these states, any income a couple earns during their marriage and all the assets the couple acquire are owned in equal portions by both. The exceptions are individual inheritances and gifts. When the first spouse dies, half of his or her share of community property passes to the survivor and the other half goes to the inheritor named in the decedent's will.

Joint tenancy can be dangerous. For example, take a couple who own all their property jointly and have no will. If the husband dies first, his interests pass to his wife. But when she dies, the entire estate will go to her relatives. Her husband's family won't get a penny. Or imagine that you and your co-tenant are not married. In most states, judges do not assume the surviving partner is entitled to claim any money in a joint bank account.

Owning property jointly can also produce tax headaches, particularly if you have assets that have appreciated greatly in value or if your estate is sizable. You could end up saddling your heirs with massive estate tax bills. Say you're married, own all your property jointly with your husband, and he dies. No estate taxes will be due when he dies. But when you die, the portion of your estate exceeding the $600,000 will be taxable. Had you and your husband held some of your property separately, you might each have been able to take advantage of the $600,000 exclusion.

Owning property jointly sometimes makes sense. For example, if your only asset of any value is your home and it is worth less than $200,000 or so, you probably can own it jointly without a worry. But in many other instances, you would be better off either owning property separately or setting up trusts to avoid the problems that sometimes come with joint ownership. Consult with your lawyer for advice about the way you and your spouse should own your assets.

That does it. Now you know how to put your financial house in order and even keep it standing after you go. Knowing all this information is great. But it won't do you any good unless you put the advice into practice. Get started today, and you will undoubtedly avoid a personal financial crisis.

APPENDIX A

MANAGING YOUR MONEY ABRIDGED MANUAL

CHAPTER 1: GETTING STARTED

QUICK START

Welcome! To get going fast, just follow the steps below. But then be sure to read, or at least skim, the rest of this chapter.

You've paid a lot of money for Managing Your Money and will be using it extensively, we hope, for years. It's important to get off to a good start. Please don't dive in until you can find a couple of uninterrupted hours to lay a good foundation. In that time, you should be able to master the basics, get the program running on your system, and take an informal tour of its myriad capabilities.

One more thing. Before you even start, send in your registration card. With toasters, it's silly to send in a warranty card. With software, it's silly not to. Please—do it before you forget.

HARD DISK ONLY

Managing Your Money requires a hard disk.

QUICK START INSTRUCTIONS

1. Insert Disk 1 in Drive A (or B).

2. Type a:install (or b:install).

3. Follow the prompts to install, and then run Managing Your Money.

   If you have any trouble with this, come back to the manual and read the more leisurely getting-started instructions later in this chapter. Initially, you'll need about 3MB of free space on your hard disk for the program and your data.

4. Your first time into Managing Your Money, we offer to take you straight to Hello, New User, our tutorial. We hope you'll accept. But you can also select the Quick Start option (F6) and visit the tutorial later.

   We next show you some of our program settings and let you change them if you want (F6). This is where you can specify what printer you have and whether F10 or Enter is your Action Key. You can change any of this later using Program Setup on the FILE menu. When you're through, be sure to save your changes.

5. Choose New Data Set on the FILE menu to create a data set called "Herb92" (if you're Herb and it's 1992). Use it for your data; keep the set of data Managing Your Money comes with—which you'll see goes by the name "Original"—as a blank slate. Doing this is not required. But it takes just a minute (and about 260K on your hard disk), and will save you a little trouble should you later want to set up new sets of data for your spouse or your business.

Please ... once the program is up on the screen and you've had a chance to look around, come back here and read the rest of this chapter.

A BRIEF TOUR

There's an awful lot here, which is why it's important to have an overview and to decide which sections of the program you'll want to start using first. Any one of our sections is a simple, powerful program all by itself, easily mastered and put to use in an afternoon. But don't expect to start using them all the same afternoon! Take your time! Here's what each does:

FILE is a catchall for housekeeping chores: customizing the program to your system, choosing screen colors, turning off our beeps if they annoy you, switching date formats if you're Canadian, setting up passwords if you want them, setting up separate sets of data for your business or a family member—and much more. Some of this is important, and it's all described here, in this chapter of the manual.

DESK contains ten pop-ups you can summon from anywhere in the program. Three of them are just small conveniences—a five-memory Calculator (Ctrl-N, as in "Number cruncher" — hold down the Ctrl key and press the N key), a graphic Date Display (Ctrl-D), and a Quick Key List of our shortcuts (Ctrl-K). But the other seven are complete programs:

- Five of them—a Time Summary and the four tributaries that flow into it—help you organize your time and work. With them, you'll never forget a birthday or CD maturity again. You can keep your daily schedule here—with notes attached to each appointment—

or even keep lists of ongoing projects, prioritized by importance and sorted by which employee or family member is responsible for each. The Time Summary (Ctrl-T) pulls together information from Phone Calls (Ctrl-P), Appointments (Ctrl-A), Reminders (Ctrl-R) and To-Do's (Ctrl-O). The Time Summary also lets you know when your insurance policies, driver's license and passport are about to expire (it gets this information from INSURE, described below).

- With the Card File (Ctrl-C), you can store vital statistics on friends, clients, patients, associates, fellow alumni—whomever. It prints phone lists and address labels, in case it's your job to get those fellow alumni to show up for the reunion. And it retrieves selectively, in case you want a list of only those alumni you've coded "Big Givers." It dials phone numbers, addresses letters —in concert with our built-in word processor, it even generates your very own personalized form letters.

- A Word Processor (Ctrl-W), popularly known as MYM-Write, that lets you write letters or speeches or anything else without having to leave the program, and lets you edit the reports we print for you, in case there's some touching up you'd like to do. (MYM-Write's "iceberg mode," accessible in many places with the F2-View/Edit key, lets you attach notes of almost any length to specific data entries.)

For details on how these seven features work, please see Chapter 2 of this manual: DESK.

MONEY is, for most of us, the heart of the program. If you write a check to the doctor here, your checkbook balance automatically knows, your budget automatically knows, your cash flow projection automatically knows, Schedule A of your taxes automatically knows, and so does your Net Worth. MONEY helps you budget, forecasts your available cash, and generates reports. It tracks loans and credit cards and, if you want it to, accounts payable and receivable. It prints checks and invoices and can even send electronic payment instructions.

TAX is an estimator that handles Schedules A, B, C, D, E, F, SE, Form 1040, a variety of worksheets, and the Alternative Minimum Tax. All you have to do to see a schedule is press its letter. A second later, it's there. We've made it easy to accommodate changes in the tax code—and to switch between tax years and regulations at the touch of a key. And we've provided a W-4 calculator to help you figure out how many income tax withholding allowances to claim.

Tax doesn't print your actual return; our companion program, TaxCut, does that. But it's a powerful tool for planning.

INSURE tells you how long you are likely to live, given your background and habits (we claim no special accuracy here), helps you calculate how much life insurance you need, and tells you what it might cost. It also helps you record and organize all your insurance policies—not just life—in one place. And it provides a Vital Records section that prompts you for virtually everything you and your spouse may wish to keep track of—from your blood types to the location of your safety deposit box key.

It even prints a comprehensive report, complete with a letter of instructions to your spouse or executor.

ANALYZE is more than a dozen programs in one. Though you won't use it the most, in some ways this is the most important part of Managing Your Money. It will help you decide—in English—whether to refinance your mortgage, how to save for your kids' education and other goals, and how to plan for retirement. It has a powerful rental property module, another to help you decide whether to buy or lease your next home (or car), and one to help you figure out how much home you can afford. *ANALYZE* has all the features of an ordinary business calculator (sections on present and future value, annuities, bond maturities and such)—but with everything in English (and HELP), so you're sure it's answering the question you meant to ask. There's even a screen for deciding whether to make a new contribution to your retirement plan and another to help you estimate what your Social Security benefits will be when you do retire.

Over a period of years, the decisions this chapter helps you with affect huge amounts of money. Our hope is to help you make these decisions just a little bit smarter—and feel more confident about them.

PORTFOLIO knows the difference between taxable, tax-deferred (IRA/Keogh/401K) and hypothetical portfolios, and can handle many of each, as well as brokerage accounts with check-writing privileges (CMA's). You may use it for your stocks, bonds, mutual funds and options; someone else may use it to catalog and code stamps, coins and antiques. It's powerful and flexible. It can even compare the performance of your assets with that of the market as a whole, both individually or in the aggregate. Our optional communications package, Managing the Market, will call Dow Jones and update your prices automatically.

NET WORTH takes what it knows about you from the other parts of the program, lets you add as much or as little detail as you want (a complete household inventory, for example), and prints your balance sheet. It also keeps a historical record of your progress and tracks your "debt/equity" ratio.

Its Asset Allocator can help you decide how best to deploy your assets among various classes — stocks, bonds, real estate and gold, for example — to achieve your investment objectives with the least possible risk. Designed by one of the leaders in the field of asset allocation, we believe our asset allocation model is at least as sophisticated as its leading stand-alone competition. And it's built right into MYM.

THE COMMUNICATIONS OPTION

An optional sister program, Managing the Market, allows you to "call Dow Jones" direct from within Managing Your Money and update your portfolio prices automatically over the phone (and to access all the other Dow Jones/News Retrieval Services).

THE TAX OPTION

A second sister, TaxCut, imports much of your data from Managing Your Money and prints an IRS-acceptable tax return.

THE ELECTRONIC PAYMENT OPTION

Managing Your Money includes a built-in link to CheckFree, a service that allows you to pay your bills electronically with your existing checking account.

STEP #1: INSTALLING THE PROGRAM

Okay, let's get going. The disks in your package contain all the Managing Your Money files in compressed form. We call them the "master disks." To install them on your hard disk, simply insert Disk 1 in Drive A and type A:INSTALL <Enter>. (It's OK, but unnecessary, to switch to the A> prompt first. And it's OK to use Drive B, instead, and type B:INSTALL.)

Once you do, we will guide you through a brief series of questions, with help for each at the bottom of the screen, and prompt you to insert the other disks as needed.

When you're all done, put the master disks someplace safe.

To run the program, just type MYM. The first time you do, we'll offer to take you straight to Hello, New User, our tutorial. Even if you're a computer pro, I urge you to take the few minutes required to breeze through it. You're bound to discover at least a few things about the program, and a few navigational shortcuts, you might miss otherwise.

IF YOU GOT MYM FOR CHRISTMAS—LIE

If it's right near the end of the year and you don't plan to record transactions with Managing Your Money for real until the new year begins, you may want to lie to us about the date when you first start the program. Tell us it's January 1992, even if it's December 1991. That will spare your having to run through our Close Out Past Year procedure a few days from now.

WHAT INSTALL DOES; WHERE WE PUT THINGS

What we're doing is decompressing the files on our master disks and copying them onto a directory of your hard disk.

We put all the program files in the main \mym8 directory (or whatever you tell us to call it). These are files that any set of data can share. We put all the data files (except for those that can be shared) into a subdirectory of the \mym8 directory called \mym8\original. These are the original data files we start you off with. If you use our "New Data Set" command on the FILE menu to make up new sets of data files—for your spouse, say, or your business—we will put them into new subdirectories we create called \mym8\spouse and \mym8\business (or whatever name you give). To switch between separate sets of data, you just use FILE's "Open Data Set" command and choose the one you want.

CAN'T SEE THE SCREEN?

On certain monochrome monitors—laptop and notebook computers, for the most part—you may not be able to make out the screen. If so, try installing by typing A:INSTALL -M instead.

NOTHING HAPPENS WHEN YOU TYPE "MYM"?

We've put MYM in its own directory—called \mym8, unless you instructed us to call it something else. To run the program, you must first change into that directory. Type CD \MYM8 first and then type MYM.

ONE OF OUR FLOPPIES DEFECTIVE?

It's highly unlikely you will have a problem. But if your computer should give you an error message that it can't "read" one of the disks that came with the program, try removing it from the disk drive and tapping its edge gently against your desk, as if trying to slice the desk with the disk. Now insert the disk and try again. If your computer still can't read it—but is reading other disks OK—you'll need to send it to us for replacement.

NOT ENOUGH ROOM ON YOUR HARD DISK?

Initially, you will need about 3MB for Managing Your Money's program and data files—more as your data grows.

FILES YOU CAN DELETE TO SAVE SPACE ON YOUR HARD DISK

This is not a good idea. There are really only two files you can get away with deleting from the \mym8 directory of your hard disk if space is tight: INSTALL.EXE and, if you do not plan to use CheckFree, CFMYM.EXE. You can later install new copies by running Install with the floppies that came in your package. But what if those disks aren't handy when you decide you need them? Or what if you forget you can do this? Theoretically, you could delete even more, such as our large HELP.HLP file, and copy it to a separate floppy. But if you ever pressed F1 for help—and we hope you'll press it often!—the program would hang until you inserted the floppy with HELP.HLP. Not recommended!

SEPARATE SETS OF DATA

Pre-Version 7 customized-setup hard disk users: As part of the install-upgrade routine, we will put one of your sets of data in the \mym8\data subdirectory and create separate subdirectories for the rest. If you upgrade from Version 7, we'll create a Version 8 data subdirectory with the same name as your Version 7 subdirectory.

When we install Managing Your Money on a hard disk, we put its program files in a main Managing Your Money directory called c:\mym8 (unless you direct us to call it something else) and its data files in a subdirectory called \mym8\original. All you have to do to set up a new set of data is select New Data Set from the FILE menu and follow our instructions. We'll create a subdirectory for that data—c:\ mym 8\ grandma—and other subdirectories for as many more sets of data as you care to create.

Once created, you can switch from one to another simply by choosing Open Data Set from the FILE menu and selecting the one you want. Do some work there, then choose Open Data Set again, if you like, and switch back. Eventually, you'll have several subdirectories, including one for each prior year. But Open Data Set gives you easy access to them all.

You may assign separate passwords to each set of data, just in case you'd rather not have him looking at hers or them looking at yours. But note: MYM normally starts with the set of data you were last using. If you and your daughter, Felicia, each have separate passwords, and you were the last one to use the program, when your daughter starts it up, it won't budge if she can't supply your password. The solution is to have her type mym felicia to start the program and load her data (assuming her data set is called "felicia").

> WARNING! Just be careful, when you're leaving the program and we offer to backup your data to floppies, to insert the correct backup disk. You don't want to backup grandma's data files over your own.

COLOR YOUR DATA

I suggest you use a different color scheme for each active data set so you don't inadvertently pay your mother's bills from your personal data set. I use black and white—like an old movie—for all prior years' data sets.

HOW NEW DATA SET WORKS

When you select New Data Set from the FILE menu, we ask you for the name you want to give your new set of data. We then create a subdirectory of \mym8 by that name and copy the current set of data files to it. (So before you create a new set, if you have more than one, be sure to load the one you want to copy.) Typically, you'll want us to copy the almost-empty "ORIGINAL" data set MYM came with, so you or a family member can start fresh.

When we're done, you'll be at the title screen of your new set of data. If it wasn't copied from a virgin ORIGINAL set, the first thing you'll probably want to do is go through and delete all the Money Accounts, and so on, that don't apply—clean the slate, as it were.

This can be a bit of a chore if you've got loads of data throughout the program, which is why in Getting Started we suggested you leave our ORIGINAL set of data files empty. If you followed that suggestion, just open your ORIGINAL data set before you create a new one. (Or else use your original, master disks to load a fresh set of database files onto this new subdirectory—being very careful not to copy them over your own, real database files by mistake. Just insert Disk 1 in Drive A and, from DOS, type a:install and follow our prompts to install only the data files, copying these empty ones into the new subdirectory where you want empty ones.)

Hint: When you start up the program, we load whichever data set you were using last. To start it with another data set, type the name of the data set after the name of the program: mym dataset.

TO SWITCH BETWEEN SETS OF DATA

Just select Open Data Set from the FILE menu. The name of the currently loaded data set appears at the bottom center of the Menu Bar screen.

TO DELETE A SET OF DATA

You normally wouldn't want to do this, of course. But if, say, you had used New Data Set to create a new data set called GRANNY and then decided, nah, you didn't want to do this after all, here's what you'd do. Just go into DOS and change into the \mym8 subdirectory. Type del granny and, when DOS asks if you're sure, say Yes. The contents of the GRANNY subdirectory will be gone. Now type rd granny to remove the granny subdirectory itself. That's it. Just be careful not to delete the wrong subdirectory by mistake!

FANCY SETUPS

You actually have three choices when you use New Data Set to create a new data set:

1. By far the best choice (if you ask me) is to give us a simple name, like JACK92, and leave it at that. We'll create a \jack92 sub directory under your \mym8 directory and put your new set of data there.

2. You can type a drive letter before the name if you have more than one hard disk in your system. If you enter D:JACK (no slashes or spaces), we will create a \mym8\jack directory\subdirectory on your Drive D (assuming you have a Drive D), and put the data there. (If you used a different directory name when you originally installed the program—say you had us install it on a directory called "\mym8v8"—we'd automatically use that name instead— \mym8v8\jack.) But why make life complicated unless you have a really good reason? And if you do have us stick your data on Drive D, note that you will have to type "D:JACK" each time you want Open Data Set to load it. Only the data subdirectories directly under your c:\mym8 directory (or wherever you installed the program) are displayed by Open Data Set; any other you want to use must be entered manually.

3. You can enter just "A:" or "B:" as the name—nothing more. In that case, we'll copy the data set onto the floppy in Drive A or B (and onto a second, if it won't all fit). Whenever you select this data set with Open Data Set we'll look to Drive A for your data. (And look there, also, the next time you use Managing Your Money, if that's the data set you were using last, because we always start with the same data set you were using last.)

STARTING A NEW YEAR, CLOSING OUT AN OLD ONE

Every time you enter Managing Your Money, we make you tell us the date. The first time you enter a 1992 date (if you began using the program in 1991), a screen will appear asking you whether you really mean 1992. If so, a new selection appears on the FILE menu: Close Out Past Year—"COPY." Under COPY is another menu. The last item there is also called Close Out Past Year, and here we really mean it.

Don't choose it! At least not for a while. As we'll advise you, Managing Your Money is able to keep track of two years at once, so at least for the first month or two, until you're sure all your prior year's data has been entered and reconciled, it will be easier just to live with both sets of data. Some of you, in fact, may wish to wait until the end of the current year before closing out the prior one, to make it really easy to look up old transactions. ("Honey, how much did we pay the plumber when the pipes burst last year?")

Eventually, you may find your budget.dbs file growing too large to fit on a floppy backup disk. Otherwise, you can pretty well wait as late into the year as you want to choose Close Out Past Year. (But you must choose it eventually: we can't start recording next year's transactions until you've dispatched last year's. We can't keep three years in mind at once.)

Whenever you do choose to run through COPY, just follow the instructions that will appear. What we'll do, simply, is copy all the past year's stuff into a new subdirectory of your hard disk. (You should then copy it onto a floppy, so you have a backup someplace safe.) At the same time, we'll delete all those prior year transactions from your current set of data.

Of course, we only delete past transactions. We don't delete any of the other work you've done.

USING A PREVIOUS YEAR'S DATA

After you've gone through Close Out Previous Year, it's very easy to look at or print reports from—or even change—a previous year's data. Just use Open Data Set on the FILE menu to select that data set when you start the program.

Of course, once we've closed out a year, changes you make to its data naturally won't affect your current balances. They're no longer connected.

Say you visited your old 1991 data and recorded an extra $1,000 in income you had forgotten. Fine. But the bank balance in your current,

1992, data set naturally won't reflect the extra $1,000. So if your bank balance really is off by $1,000, go into your current data and record a receipt of $1,000 from a payor named "To Balance," or else go to the account balance directly, by selecting this Money Account, and adjust it.

But this is not likely to be a problem if you reconciled your bank statement before you went ahead with Close Out Past Year. A $1,000 discrepancy is kind of hard to miss.

PRINTING
SETTING UP YOUR PRINTER

Select Program Setup from the FILE menu, then Printer, and read the instructions on the screen (and F1 for HELP). Mainly, press F6 to select your printer from our list.

Note that "GENERIC" is not an obscure printer brand but, rather, the "lowest common denominator" that should accommodate just about any parallel printer. (If you don't know whether your printer is serial or parallel, rest assured it's almost certainly parallel—so be sure to leave the "baud rate" and "parity" fields blank, also.) GENERIC won't do underlined printing or bold face or any of that, but at least it will print something until you have time to consult your printer manual for the proper setup strings it needs.

We don't support Postscript printers directly, but most Postscript printers can be set to emulate something else on our list—usually a LaserJet.

While you're on the Printer Setup screen, you can also press F7 to enter custom printer setup strings from your printer manual, or F8 to test your printer.

If you've made changes to the printer setup, turn off your printer and then turn it back on, so it can reset itself before you attempt to test the changes.

F4—THE UNIVERSAL PRINT KEY

On screens from which a report or document may be printed, F4 will normally be displayed. Typically, you will press it two or three times on the way to producing your report—first to summon one or more screens on which you can define the kind of report you want, then to start the actual printing. (Some of those screens may say to press the Action Key, but F4 will usually work, too.)

PRINTING SCREENS AND GRAPHS

Whenever you'd like to print out the contents of a screen where F4 is not offered, just press your computer's Print Screen key. (On some keyboards, you need to hold down the Shift key when pressing PrtSc; on the Tandy 1000, it's Alt-P.)

Microsoft Windows takes over the Print Screen key. If you're running Managing Your Money full-screen in Windows, the Print Screen key will save the screen to the clipboard. You'll need to load text screens into another program, such as Windows' Notepad, to print them (retrieve them from the clipboard file, which is probably DEFAULT.CLP in your Windows directory). You'll have to load graph screens into Windows' Paintbrush to print them.

PRINTING REPORTS

Managing Your Money prints scores of them, including many you can customize to suit your own needs. Reports may also be printed to disk (see below) and then edited with any standard word processing program—or with our own. Until you've amassed a few months' data, they're not much to look at. It may even be hard to picture how they'll look or how useful they will be. But as your data builds, I think you'll be impressed by their power and flexibility.

At the end of the year, you'll be able to print in minutes a complete report of the year's transactions. In fact, print four:

- A report organized and subtotaled alphabetically by payee

- Another organized chronologically

- A third organized by check number

- And, best of all, a fourth organized and sub-totaled by budget and tax category, ready to hand your accountant—or for your own tax preparation.

I make a set of reports like this three or four times a year with the Report Generator (on the MONEY menu). The last set, printed at year's end, I keep permanently. With these four reports, it should never take you more than a few seconds to find anything. (As for those who say there's no place in the computer age for paper—well, I disagree. Sometimes, as in this case, a printed report can be very handy.)

PRINTING CHECKS

See page 324: "Step #10: Printing Checks."

PRINTER PROBLEMS

Don't panic! Before you call Tech Support or your printer manufacturer, please see the "Neat Printer Trick" on the next page.

PRINTING TO DISK

We give you a choice. You can print reports to your printer—which is to say, on paper. You can print them to the screen. Or you can print them to a disk.

If you choose "disk," we ask for a filename, preceded by the letter of the disk drive you want us to aim for. For example, "b:budget.doc" would send whatever you're printing to the floppy disk in Drive B and stick it into a file called "budget.doc." Careful: If such a file already existed, it would stick it there anyway, overwriting the previous contents.

Once the report is in its own file, you can manipulate it with your word processor or by pressing Ctrl-W and loading it into ours. Include it in a proposal; insert a little poem in the middle; improve our format; add, delete or rearrange things. But note: This is a one-way street. You can send copies of Managing Your Money reports to files all day long; but there's no way to take your newly word-processed version (with the poem in the middle) and stick it back into Managing Your Money. We don't do poems.

THE ".DOC" EXTENSION IS HANDY

You may want to give your reports a ".doc" extension. Because when you ask our word processor to show you a list of the files in your data directory, its first instinct, as you'll see, is to display all your ".doc" files.

NOTE: Avoid Invalid Filenames

If you're new to DOS, you may not realize that filenames must follow certain rules. For example, they can't have spaces. If you try "92 CASH" instead of, say, 92CASH, we'll burp and ask you to try again. Also, never use ".dbs" or any of the other extensions we use in labeling files!

PRINTING TO SCREEN

Note that when you choose this option, you may scroll back and forth through the report and—if it's wider than 80 columns—left and right. Just use the Arrow keys.

NEAT PRINTER TRICK

If you print to "disk" but to a file named, simply, LPT1, your report won't print to disk after all—it will print to the printer connected to your computer's first printer port. If your printer is connected to port #2, use LPT2 as the filename.

This has limited practical application, because all the special formatting— compressed or emphasized printing—will be lost. But it does serve two functions:

- If you have two printers connected to your computer, it's a way to switch from one to the other without having to visit Program Setup and change the printer port selection there.

- If you're having trouble printing, this is one of the tests Tech Sup port uses to determine whether it's a problem with Managing Your Money (if nothing prints out to LPT1 or LPT2, it may be!) or whether our reports are working fine, but you just haven't specified the right printer codes in Printer Setup (a lot more likely).

CHAPTER 3: MONEY
THE NUB OF IT

You certainly don't have to use Managing Your Money to print your checks, and not everyone does. But one way or another, you have to pay your bills. Doing it with Managing Your Money spares you a tremendous amount of drudgery. After the first time, you never have to write out the name of whomever you're paying ... or your 18-digit account number ... or the amount of the check in English ("One hundred eighty-seven and no/100") ... or the date. In fact, you don't even have to address envelopes. After the first time, all you need tell us is the amount.

Hint: When you're setting up your accounts in Managing Your Money, it's helpful to have your last bank statement from each account you want to set up. Get your checkbook, too. Then you won't have to go hunting when it's time to enter bank balances, addresses and other information.

There are three advantages to this:

- It saves time.

- Our handwriting may be better than yours.

- Your data is "captured," and thus available for use in printing re ports and graphs, budgeting, projecting your available cash, balancing your checkbook, estimating and preparing your taxes—and more.

    Naturally, you'll still write some checks by hand; Managing Your Money makes it easy to record these, as well as your cash and credit card expenditures. But overall, once you get the hang of it, it should take you less time to be better organized; less time, not more, finally to be in control of your finances.

    By recording your transactions in Managing Your Money, you can see at any time:

- Customized reports of all your income and expenditures, organized and subtotaled by budget category and/or by payee (select Report Generator from the MONEY pulldown menu)

- Your account balances (select Money Accounts from the MONEY pulldown)

- Your actual spending versus budget, both for this month and for the year-to-date (Budget Categories) and what's left to spend

- Your cash forecast for the months or years ahead (Forecasting)

- The status of your loans (Loan Records)

- Your tax status (select TAX from the Menu Bar)

- Your total available cash and credit (select Money Accounts from the MONEY pulldown; then F4 to print: your total available cash and credit are at the end of that report)

- Your up-to-the-minute net worth (select NET WORTH from the Menu Bar)

- And more.

PART I: WHERE DO I BEGIN?

For many users, MONEY is by far the most important part of the program. Here you can design budget categories that fit your finances; set up your checking, savings and credit card accounts (among others); spend, receive and transfer money; set up Quick transactions and Alert transactions; record loans you owe (or own); forecast your available cash; print checks, invoices and reports—even pay bills electronically without having to write checks at all.

If you like, you can dive right in. Just select Spend Money from the MONEY menu and "write a check." We'll first ask you to set up a checking account and then proceed to let you enter the data.

But to get going in an organized way, you may wish to follow these steps. It won't take long, and you'll be building a good foundation for years to come.

STEP #1: SELECT THE OPTIONS YOU WANT

Select Optional Features from the FILE menu, and then Money Options. Press F1 for HELP in making your choices and then the Action Key to accept them. (Remember that none of this will "take" if you quit the program without saving, so it's a good idea to press Ctrl-S from the Menu Bar once you've changed any options.)

The Action Key is either Enter or F10; the screen will tell you which. You may change the Action Key at any time. To do so, go to the FILE menu, choose Program Setup, then Action Key. Type E for Enter or F for F10.

The simplest thing is to just stick with the settings Managing Your Money comes with and skip to Step #2 now.

But if and when you do want to tinker, here are your choices:

- Warn if transaction is over- or under-allocated. With this option activated, we'll warn you if you ever fail to fully allocate a transaction. This is helpful when you're assigning a transaction to multiple budget categories. It will not warn you if you later change the amount of a transaction and fail to reallocate it.

- Warn if something to send to CheckFree. This option only appears if you have activated the CheckFree electronic bill-paying service (under CheckFree on the MONEY menu). If you say "Yes" here, any time you have something to send CheckFree and try leaving the program without doint it, we'll warn you. We'll let you leave anyway or transmit first.

    We find out whether you have something to transmit by looking through your MONEY records. If you have a lot of data and find that it takes too long to quit the program, you can say "No" here and we won't warn you. If you do, you'll have to remember to transmit any time you change anything related to CheckFree—create a transaction or merchant, change anything in your CheckFree setup (such as your address or account), or write E-Mail.

- Five-year Budgeting. Several years ago this feature inspired a Salt Lake County commissioner to impose five-year budgeting on the County. The practice helped the County build reserves and retain an Aaa bond rating, while keeping taxes level for six years. If you take the time to project your finances into the future, you may wind up with triple-A finances, too. (Meanwhile, I subsequently persuaded that county commissioner, Bart Barker, to leave Utah and come work for me.)

- Graphs. Unless your equipment can't handle graphics, you'll almost surely want to say YES.

- Accounts Payable and Accounts Receivable. Activating this puts Payables and Receivables on your MONEY menu. We ask you for your last invoice number so we can use it when you print invoices.

- Where to start the cursor. On the Spend and Receive Money screens, we fill in the date and, if applicable, the check number, and so normally start the cursor down on the Payee or Payor field. But if you tend to enter your transactions a batch at a time, covering several days, you might prefer to have us start the cursor at the top, in the Date field, so it's easy to change.

- Reset Date. When you're entering a stack of Spend or Receive transactions, we'll continue using the last date you entered until you change it, if you say NO to this option. If you say YES, we'll drive you nuts changing the date back to today after each one. (But that's handy if you use Managing Your Money to pay most of your bills, only occasionally entering a transaction, such as a hand-written check, with a prior date.)

- Display Running Balance on Quick List. As you go down your Quick List marking transactions to execute, we show how your account balance will be affected. This is very handy, but can slow things down on older machines. If you find speed is a problem, try answering NO to this option.

- Alert Transaction warning days. How far in advance, if at all, should we remind you of transactions on your Alert List? Enter 0 if you don't want us to remind you until the day you've scheduled the transaction to be made.

- Base TAX projections on which year's figures? Normally, you'd choose THIS YEAR. But we can pass a future year's budgeted figures from MONEY to TAX instead. (It's wise to switch this option back after using it, lest you forget and not notice, weeks from now, that our TAX estimate is based on a future year's budget.)

- Change your fiscal year (F6). You almost surely don't want to do this! Most individuals and businesses file income taxes based on a calendar year. But if your business uses a fiscal year that ends in June, say, reflect that here when you begin using Managing Your Money. For details, press F1 for Help after you press F6.

- A word about Close Out Past Year. The first time you start Managing Your Money with a date from next year, we'll add Close Out Past Year (COPY) to your FILE menu. Press F7 to find out more. (Once COPY appears on the FILE menu, F7 will no longer appear here.)

- Change data set status (F8). You probably don't need this, either. Your Active data set is the one for the current year; inactive sets are for prior years and don't allow you to enter transactions with this year's date. If you inadvertently answered this question wrong during Installation, just change it here. Changing this back and forth has no effect on your data.

When you're done with Money Options, press the Action Key to save your changes.

STEP #2: SET UP YOUR MONEY ACCOUNTS

By "money accounts" we mean primarily your checking, savings and charge accounts. But you may also want to set up one or more cash accounts (His and Hers?), portfolio-linked CMA accounts, home-equity accounts and perhaps even "noncash" accounts for things like frequent flier miles, depreciation, or your gift of a fur coat to the Salvation Army (see page 340: "Noncash Items").

IMPORTANT!

Here's the best way to get into synch with your bank or credit card company:

First, on the Add a Money Account screen, enter the balance from your last statement—usually positive if it's a bank balance, negative if it's a credit card balance—in the field where we ask for "last statement balance." That way, you and they agree on where things stood November 25th (say).

Now, select Spend and Receive Money from the MONEY menu and enter all the transactions the bank doesn't know about yet—the ones made since November 25th, and the ones made prior to November 25th that hadn't yet hit your statement. That's it! It's like handing a baton smoothly from the old way you used to keep track of your checkbook to this new, swifter runner called Managing Your Money.

To start, it's fine to set up just one of your accounts. You can always add the others later.

Setting up accounts is easy, and it's all explained in HELP:

1. Select Money Accounts from the MONEY menu.

2. Press F5 to add your new account. Any HELP you need is just a keystroke away: F1.

INCLUDE IN CASH FORECASTING?

At the bottom of the screen we ask whether to include the account in Cash Forecasting. Normally you'd say Yes. If you say No, Managing Your Money's cash-forecaster will know to ignore its balance when it projects your available cash. It will still figure into your Net Worth— you'll still be rich. It just won't show up as ready cash in MONEY's cash projection.

You'd do this for, say, a savings account you've vowed never to touch til the tots turn twenty. In reality, the cash is there; but, to avoid temptation, you'd rather not think of it that way when you select Forecasting from the MONEY menu.

If you set up a home equity account, you'd almost surely want to say No. Otherwise, we'd show you deep in the red each month, with the $40,000 you'd borrowed against your house deducted from your available cash. Yet you actually have 30 years to repay that $40,000, so it's not exactly a pressing drain on your wallet.

The same logic holds for credit card accounts if you're one who leaves the balance outstanding more or less forever, and only pays the interest. Just say No!

In short: Say No for any account whose balance—positive or negative— you want Cash Forecasting to ignore. This would be any account whose balance doesn't really affect the amount of cash you can lay your hands on: a bank balance you're determined not to draw on; a home equity or credit card account balance you're not planning to repay any time soon.

But you don't have to deal with this now! (Or ever, really.) You can edit a bank or credit card account at any time. If you're just starting with Managing Your Money, press on!

STEP #3: SET UP YOUR BUDGET CATEGORY NAMES

You don't have to assign your income and expenses to categories, but being able to is one of the key benefits of using a computer to manage your money. And Managing Your Money makes it very simple. Even if you don't plan to use the program for budgeting, you'll still want to be able to list and total your expenses by category, for tax purposes.

1. Select Budget Categories from the MONEY menu. You'll get this screen:

2. Press F1 and read HELP. I won't take your time repeating it here.

3. To save you time, we've started you off with a list of common budget categories. Naturally, many won't apply to you. Just arrow down the list and press F3 to delete them. For those that do apply—Clothing, say—but for which you'd prefer a different name—Apparel—just press F2 and change it. Press the Action Key when you're done.

4. Add categories we haven't thought of—Apparel-His, Apparel-Hers, Apparel-Kids. Just press F5. In fact, even if you can't think of any others you need, press F5 anyway to see what that screen looks like, and to read its HELP. It may give you some ideas on how to set up your budget.

When you add a new category, we offer you the option of tagging it with one of our tax categories right away, or postponing that until later. I suggest you postpone it and concentrate on one job at a time. For now, just get your budget categories the way you want them. Later, you can run through all of them and assign tax treatments (i.e., tell us that Church Donations is a "Charity Contribution"). Postponing this little chore will actually save you time. That's because any new category you create without assigning a specific tax category is automatically assigned the "Not a Tax Category" tag. And for many of your budget categories, like Apparel, that's exactly right! So you'll only need to change the ones you add that do have tax consequences, like Church Contributions or Royalties or Baby-Sitting Income.

We give you a Memo field so you can record the assumptions you used to set up your budget ("includes gas and repairs but not insurance").

BUDGETING FOR SAVINGS

At the bottom of the Add Budget Category screen, we ask whether to include this category in Cash Forecasting and whether to include it in Profit & Loss. The first question is the same one we asked on the Add Money Account screen.

- You don't have to deal with this now (or ever).

- But in case you do want to deal with it, you'll see we've already done a lot of the thinking for you, in the budget categories we've started you off with.

  A budget is a spending plan. Money shelled out for rent or groceries is spent. But what of money shelled out for a savings certificate? Or for 100 shares of stock? Or to pay down the balance of your mortgage? It's not really spent, it's just moved from one of your pockets—(your checking account)—to another—(your savings account or brokerage account or the equity in your home).

  Yet some of us, understandably, want to budget for savings as well as for spending. Managing Your Money has a neat trick to accommodate this.

- Include in Cash Forecasting? The answer for almost all categories is Yes, because almost all kinds of expenditures, whether for flowers or savings bonds, cut into your available cash. Answer Yes for any expenditure that cuts into your available ready cash.

  Still, you might have a handful of categories you want to tag "No." We'll exclude them from our calculations of available cash in Forecasting (on the MONEY pulldown menu). You might do that if you set up a category called NONCASH CONTRIBU-TIONS because you planned to give $500 worth of old clothes to charity each year and wanted TAX to reflect it. Clearly, giving away clothes will not lower your available cash, so it shouldn't be reflected in Cash Forecasting. Likewise, if you planned to stick $50 a month in a cookie jar, and set up a budget category called COOKIE JAR, you might also answer No, because that cash would remain available to you (unless the cookie monster got it). Answer No for any category that does not reduce your available cash.

- Include in Profit & Loss? Answer Yes here for any spending that makes you poorer—CLEANING or MORTGAGE INTEREST or CLUB DUES. But answer No for any "spending" that just shifts money from one pocket to another—SAVINGS or MORT-GAGE PRINCIPAL or LOAN PAYMENT. (Paying down a loan reduces the amount of cash in your pocket, but doesn't make you poorer. You have less cash, but you also have less debt.)

  With Income categories, answer Yes to all those that make you richer, like SALARY, DIVIDENDS and GIFTS FROM DAD. But answer No to any that are really just transfers from one pocket to another, like IRA WITHDRAWAL. (When you take money from your IRA, it doesn't make you richer.)

GROUP THE "NO'S" TOGETHER?

While you're at it, you might consider grouping all your savings-oriented budget categories together, by putting the same character at the start of their names.

If you start them all with a Z (Z-RAINY DAY FUND), all your savings-type expenditures will be grouped alphabetically. The expense ones will sit just above the line for *NET PROFIT* (unless you have a category for ZEBRAS). Thus it will be easy to see that, while your budget shows a net profit of only $350, say, that's after putting aside $2,000 for your IRA, $3,000 for a rainy day, $12,000 for mutual fund purchases, and paying down an additional $1,582.38 on your mortgage.

To see what your profit really was, press F6 on the Budget screen and we'll exclude those categories you said not to include in Net Profit. Note, however, that with printed reports, all categories are included in the calculation of net profit, even if you've used F6.

What's the point of all this? We let you exclude categories marked "No" from the Income, Expense, and Net Profit totals. That way, if you're budgeting income of $100,000, spending of $60,000 and savings of $40,000, we won't show you just breaking even, we'll show you making a $40,000 profit. (To see this, select Budget Categories from the MONEY menu. F6 gives you the choice of All categories or only those included in Net Profit—the ones tagged Yes.)

EASIER THAN IT SOUNDS

To summarize:

1. Leave most budget categories the way they are. Just say "Yes."

2. For categories that don't make you richer or poorer, answer "No" to "Include in Profit & Loss?" (e.g., "spending" on shares in a mutual fund).

3. If a category doesn't even change the amount of cash you have available, answer "No" to "Include in Cash Forecasting?"

   You can ignore all this if you want. But to make it easy, we've started you off with some "No" categories we thought you might want to use. Feel free to delete them or to add others or to fiddle with them at any time. To see which categories are tagged Yes and No, press F7 until you see the Status screen.

   If you follow those steps, you'll be able to use F6 on the Budget Categories screen to exclude from its totals those items that don't really make you richer or poorer.

STEP #4: MAKE BUDGET ESTIMATES

You don't have to do this right away. In fact, if you don't want to make up a budget—or don't need to live within one—you don't have to do it ever!

But most of us benefit from having a plan and being able to track our progress against it. MYM makes this very easy, too. And entering budget estimates means our TAX section can make sensible projections. So, when you're ready:

1. Verify the budget categories we start you off with. Point to the first budget category on your list (the one right after our summary To-

tal Income line) and press F2. Change its name if you like, and check to be sure you're satisfied with the tax treatment we've assigned it (displayed next to "Tax Category"). If not, press F6 to change it. We'll only show you the income-type tax categories for income budget categories and expense-type tax categories for expense budget categories. Select the category you want and press the Action Key to accept it.

While you're here, you can also add a Memo (press F2 if you need more room) and tell us whether to include this category's totals in Cash Forecasting and Profit and Loss (see Budgeting for Savings, above) in case we've guessed wrong.

Then press the Action Key to save your changes.

2. Delete those that don't apply. Back on the Budget Categories screen, press F3 to delete any of our sample categories that you don't want.

3. Add new ones of your own. You'll doubtless think of things we forgot. From the main Budget Categories screen, press F5 to add new ones.

> Hint: Page Scrolling Through Your Budget Categories
>
> When viewing the details of a budget category, you can move straight to the next without having to return to your list. Just press the PgDn key. But return to your list as often as you like: you'll see your budgeted *NET PROFIT* at the end of the list grow and shrink as you enter your estimated income and expenses.

4. Make budget estimates. Now point to the first of your budget categories again and press the Action Key to make up its budget—how much do you receive from Alimony each month? (But first see Long-range Budgeting, below.) Press F1—HELP for tips and shortcuts.

When you're satisfied with this first category, press the Action Key to save your changes, and visit the next category—and the next and the next. (Of course, you're welcome to visit them in any order you want. And you needn't do this all at once.)

You might find it easier to check the tax category for each budget category first (F2 from the Budget Categories screen). Use PgDn to move to each successive category (PgDn saves your changes before moving on). When you're done, go back to the top, press the Action Key and set the budgets, again moving from category to category with PgDn.

> NOTE: If you have no idea what you spend, or if you're not keen about taking the time to make up a budget, there's an alternative. Forget it for this year. Just enter your receipts and expenditures as the year unfolds, allocating each transaction to a budget category. Next year, you'll know at a glance what you spend on things. And we'll make up your budget for you, if you like, as part of the Close Out Past Year (COPY) process. Just tell us to use last year's budget or last year's actuals as this year's budget—inflated or deflated by any amount you choose. Or, if you delay COPY through much of next year, you can use this year's "actuals" yourself in setting next year's budgets. We display them right on the screen (press the Action Key from the Budget Categories screen).

LONG-RANGE BUDGETING

Before you start entering your budget estimates, you will probably want to turn on our five-year budgeting option. (Select Options from the FILE menu, then Money Options.) If you do, our budget shortcuts will automatically fill in most of the numbers for you at the same time as you're doing this year's budget. Your cash forecast will extend a full year or five years into the future; and if you like, TAX will be able to estimate your taxes for that future year.

HINT: ALPH*BET!ZA+^ON

There's a way to impose more than just alphabetical order on your budget categories. Say you wanted to group together all the categories pertaining to each of 5 rental properties. You could put an asterisk (or any other non-alphabetic character) in front of all your rental property categories, followed by a 1 for all those categories pertaining to the first property, a 2 for all those pertaining to the second, and so on. Instead of a category called "Maintenance-123 Elm Street," you might use "*1-Maintenance" or "*Elm-Maintenance." Managing Your Money will group all the asterisks together. And within that overall group, each property will have its own little subgroup.

Or you could begin all your household categories—groceries, clothing, family car—with a hyphen ("-") to group them at the beginning of your Expenses list, making it easy to eyeball them all at once for a quick review.

Grouping items together this way may make your data easier to enter and analyze.

To exploit the possibilities here, it may help you to know how a computer "alphabetizes" non-alphabetic characters. Sing this, if you can: ! @ # $ % & * ( ) * + , - . / 0 1 2 3 4 5 6 7 8 9 : ; < = > ? @. Only then do you get to A through Z.

IMPORTANT NOTES:

- You needn't finish the job of setting up your budget before proceeding to Step #5. We're not slave-drivers. You can always add new budget categories or enter your budget estimates later. But unless you're very rich or genetically frugal, do make a budget soon: it's the first step in any successful financial plan.

- Do not enter budget estimates for conventional mortgage or automobile loans. We do that for you as part of entering the loans in Step #5, below.

- Next year, creating your budget will be a snap. We'll do most of the work for you. (See NOTE, on previous page.)

- Read HELP as you encounter each new screen.

STEP #5: SET UP YOUR LOANS

There are basically three kinds of loans: mortgage loans, that follow a standard "amortization schedule" (where the monthly payment stays constant, but is almost entirely interest at first and principal at the end); interest-only loans (where all the principal is repaid in a lump at the end); and all others, which we call special loans (including nonstandard mortgages, rule-of-78 loans, and crazy loans you make to your brother-in-law).

- You can enter all three kinds of loans in Managing Your Money.

- As part of the process, you can (and should) set up a Quick List or Alert List transaction for each, as I'll explain.

- The loans can be money you owe—or money owed you.

- It's fine to come back to this later, if you're eager to get going.

There's no need to enter all your loans now. Just remember not to make budget estimates for your mortgage payments, because we do it for you— precisely—when you set up the loan.

Managing Your Money's ability to handle mortgage-type loans (which includes most automobile loans) is particularly amazing. Once you tell us the basics, we'll create the proper Quick List or Alert List transaction for you and enter precise budget estimates. Then, if things change—you make a principal prepayment, say, or the interest rate on your mortgage declines—we recalculate everything automatically and even readjust your budgeted principal and interest payments.

We don't work that magic on special or interest-only loans—but we do work on them, so be sure to set them up and create their Quick List or Alert List transactions here. We won't fill out your budget for you; but we will remember the categories to which you want to allocate the interest and principal from these loans, make it very easy to record payments (in whatever amount), and, when you do, update the outstanding balance of the loan, and hence your net worth, accordingly.

ENTERING A NEW OR EXISTING LOAN

Setting up a loan is easy. Just follow these steps and tell the butler to hold your calls. When in doubt, read HELP.

1. From the MONEY menu, select Loan Records.

2. Press F5 to add a new one and fill in our blanks—except for the interest rate, if it's a mortgage-type loan. (If it's a special or an interest-only loan, you can fill that in, too.) Where we ask for the Payment, enter whatever monthly payment the bank actually demands, less any escrow payment for taxes or insurance, which are entered separately.

The Purpose field is just for your records. It doesn't really matter which purpose you choose. The Type field is important, though, because it determines how we handle the loan. If it's a conventional mortgage— including a typical adjustable-rate mortgage—tag it "Mortgage." Do the same with most car and other standard loans the bank calculates like a mortgage. But if it's a $50,000 mortgage payable in some unconventional way—$10,000 a year, say, for five years, plus 10% interest on the unpaid balance—tag it "Special."

Don't worry too much about the distinction between a "Special" and an "Interest-Only" loan. Basically, they're the same, except that with an interest-only loan we save you a few keystrokes because we know the payment isn't likely to involve principal.

In fact, with special and interest-only loans, don't worry too much about anything. We don't really care how many payments remain or when you took out the loan or what the interest rate is. This is mainly for your record keeping.

But with mortgage-type loans, we do care, because we need to get our "amortization schedule" as closely as possible in synch with your bank's. That way, we can make up precise budget estimates and readjust everything automatically when you pay extra principal or when the interest rate changes.

If it's a new mortgage-type loan, just enter its origination date in the Date of Loan field. But if it's an existing loan, you can do it either of two ways, whichever you find easier:

- If there have been no twists and turns in the interest rate along the way, and no principal prepayments—if, in short, it's been a plain vanilla situation—you can enter the original date of the loan, the original number of payments (360, if it's a 30-year mortgage) and the original amount. Then, after pressing the Action Key twice to record the loan, just point to it and press F2 to edit it. On that screen, enter the actual number of payments you've made to date—presumably, 12 times the number of years you've had the loan. Press F6 and we'll update everything for you and even write a little essay at the bottom of the screen. At the top of the screen we'll tell you the date through which the loan is paid up based on the number of payments you entered. If we show the wrong date, change the number of payments and press F6 again. Or ...

- Enter today's date; the amount of the loan that remains outstanding; and the number of payments that remain to be made. If you don't know any of this, your bank will tell you.

3. Now press the Action Key. We will freeze the screen and—for mortgage-type loans only—calculate what we believe to be the accurate interest rate for a loan of this size, term and monthly payments. This may vary slightly from your bank's figure, because different banks use slightly different methods of calculation.

4. If you're not happy with what you've entered, just press F6 and we'll "unfreeze" the screen to let you make changes. Otherwise press the Action Key again to add this loan to your list.

    If at that point you decide to make a change, just point to the loan and press F2 to edit it, or F3 to delete it altogether and start again. Read HELP if you're having trouble. And remember: if the interest rate we show varies slightly from the bank's stated rate, it's nothing to worry about; it's just (mathematically speaking) our saying tomay-to when they say tomah-to.

5. Even if you are happy, as you likely will be, point at your new loan and press F2 to take a look at it. If it's a mortgage-type loan, you can have some fun changing the "payments already made" (and anything else) to see what effect that has on the essay we write at the bottom of the screen. Just press F6 to have us recalculate—and then ESCape when you're through playing around, so you don't accidentally save the bogus scenario you were playing with.

6. Back on the Loan Records screen, there's one last chore. Press F6 or F7 to link this loan with an Alert List transaction or a Quick List transaction. In order for us to keep track of your loan balances properly, you must record all loan payments with one of these linked transactions.

    Which to choose? If it's a mortgage-type loan, I'd choose Alert List: F6. (Should you later wish to switch your mortgage from Alert List to Quick List, just delete the Alert List transaction— Alert List from the MONEY menu—and then come back here and create the Quick List transaction instead.) For interest-only and special loans, choose Quick List: F7. (You have no choice— we'll beep if you press F6.)

When we create your transaction, we'll ask what bank account you ordinarily use to make the payment. An Alert transaction is linked to a specific bank account; a Quick List transaction can be used with any account (tag it "Global").

Optional: Fill in the address and Memo if you like (you'll need an address if you plan to print checks and mail them with window envelopes). Fill in the loan escrows, if any. Press F7 if you're a CheckFree customer and want to make loan payments that way.

Now press the Action Key and we'll ask you to designate the budget categories into which you want us to dump the Interest and Principal from this loan, along with the escrows, if any.

Because home mortgage interest gets special tax treatment, it's important to have a special category for that—"Home Mortgage Interest." For other loans, you might assign them all to a single "Other Loan Interest" category. Or use categories such as "Automobile Interest," "Student Loan Interest" and "Rental Prop Interest"—or separate ones for each of the rental properties you own ("620-Interest" for your property at 620 Hyacinth, but "126- Interest" for the one at 126 Ocean Boulevard). Set this up any way you want.

Likewise, you might want to dump the Principal portion of your various loan payments into categories like "Equity in My Home" and "Automobile" (since by paying off the auto loan, you're essentially paying for the automobile); or generic ones like "Loan Repayment" or even (since paying off loans is a form of saving) "Saving." It's up to you.

If you haven't yet created the budget categories into which you'll want to dump the interest and principal from this loan (and escrow, if any), you can add them on the fly when you get to the screen where we ask you to choose. Just press F5.

Whatever budget buckets you choose for the interest and principal of your various loans, remember: with mortgage-type loans, we fill in the budget amounts for you automatically. Don't do it yourself, or we'll both be doing it. (No great harm, but that would essentially double your budget estimates for these loans, and thus throw them way off.)

When you're happy with the budget allocations you've chosen, press the Action Key to record this transaction, which will now be "linked" to your loan. Whenever in the future you use this Quick or Alert transaction to make a payment, we'll know to update the status of your loan. The loans will be indicated on the Quick List with an M, I or S (for Mortgage-, Interest-only- or Special-type loans) to the right of the Last Use column. (If you make the payment any other way—manually, say, on the Spend Money screen—we won't know about it, and won't update your loan. So always use a loan's Quick or Alert transaction to make its payments.)

DELETING A MORTGAGE

When you delete a mortgage-type loan, any Quick or Alert transaction you created for it will also be deleted, and the amounts we allocated to your budget categories will be pulled back out of those categories so you can start fresh. (But no actual payments you recorded will be deleted or pulled out of your Budget Categories. Delete them, if at all, one by one from the Check Register screen.)

> WARNING! Let US Readjust Your Budget!
> If you were to lower your budgeted Interest and Principal budget amounts manually (maybe the loan fell through and you're not taking it after all) and then deleted the mortgage, we'd go ahead and "pull the allocations back out of those categories" anyway, not knowing you already did it by hand—and that could leave you with negative budget amounts for those categories.

PRINTING YOUR LOAN'S PAYMENT SCHEDULE

Once you set up a mortgage loan, just point to it on the Loan Records screen and press F2 to view it in detail. Then press F4 and we'll print its amortization schedule—the month-by-month figures for the breakdown of principal and interest. (For a customized amortization schedule that includes twists and turns in the interest rate and principal prepayments, select Loan Amortization from the ANALYZE menu. It will let you play "what if" to see how your loan would look if, say, the interest rate changed in each of the next four years and, in year #2, you decided to pay off $1,000 extra in principal.)

IF OUR PAYMENT SCHEDULE DOESN'T MATCH YOUR BANK'S

It's possible, when you set up your loan, that our amortization schedule may not precisely match your bank's. Some banks have unconventional ways of calculating compound interest. Like most banks, we calculate interest based on a 360-day year. (Some banks think a year has 365 days!)

Or perhaps the figures matched until you sent in a prepayment (see page 320: "Principal Prepayments") or there was a change in the interest rate (see page 321: "Interest Rate Changes").

If the discrepancy is insignificant, as it is likely to be, we'd suggest you ignore it. When you do your income taxes, you can report as interest the amount your bank reports; but for budgeting and tax planning throughout the year, so what if our figures and the bank's disagree by a few pennies, or even a few dollars?

If the discrepancy is significant, or you prefer to enter each month's principal and interest precisely, then you will have to set up the loan as a Special Loan and enter each month's principal and interest from the amortization schedule the bank provides.

> Hint: Deleting a loan and reentering it is easy. But before you delete one, point to it on the Loan Records screen, press F2 to view its detail, and do a Print Screen. You'll have the loan information for reference as you reenter the loan and won't have to search for the original loan documents from the bank.

HOME EQUITY LOANS

These can be treated one of two ways. If you've borrowed the money in a lump and don't plan to borrow more, just set it up as a Special Loan. In setting up the Quick transaction that goes with it, allocate the interest you'll be paying to "Home Mortgage Interest" (assuming it will qualify for the home-mortgage interest deduction, as most do). Whenever you make a payment, we'll ask how much of it, if any, was principal and how much interest. (If you plan to pay only interest most of the time, set it up as an Interest-Only Loan and you'll save a few keystrokes each month.)

If, instead, you plan to raise and lower your outstanding balance frequently—to use this loan more as a fluctuating credit line than as a single long-term loan—then don't set it up as a loan at all. Select Money Accounts from the MONEY menu and set it up as a Home Equity Account. You'll be able to write checks against it, make payments toward it, reconcile your statement from it—the works. It's really like a huge credit card account (the balance is almost always negative), except that by treating it separately, we are able to break it out in your Net Worth so it doesn't look as if you owe $80,000 on your MasterCard.

BIWEEKLY LOANS—AND "BIWEEKLY" LOANS THAT REALLY AREN'T

To enter a biweekly mortgage—one of those increasingly popular loans where you wind up making 26 half-monthly payments a year (and so in effect make 13 monthly payments each year instead of 12 and pay the loan off way early)—just choose "Biweekly" as the loan's Payment Frequency. Managing Your Money knows all about biweekly loans, and will handle the whole thing fine. (But as HELP explains, you must enter the number of payments as if it were a standard monthly mortgage—360 payments for a 30-year loan—and let us recalculate it when you press F10 and add it to your list.)

That's what we mean by "biweekly."

FAKE BIWEEKLY LOANS

On the other hand, if you have a regular mortgage on which you make 12 months' worth of payments a year ... but the payments are taken out of your biweekly paycheck ... don't try to set it up as a biweekly mortgage. It's not. It's a regular monthly mortgage which you happen to pay in a funny way.

Because it's paid in a funny way (funny to us, anyway), we can't update it automatically by means of a Quick transaction linked to this loan, so don't create one. Instead, treat this as what it really is: a deduction from your paycheck (see page 308: "Step #7—Set Up Your Paycheck"). The Quick transaction you set up for your paycheck should reflect your estimate of how much is taken out for mortgage principal, mortgage interest and escrow each time. Rather than try to enter the breakdown of these three precisely, approximate it—say, $300 interest, $50 principal and

$50 escrow, if that's about what it is—and rely for the exact amount at tax time on the notice your bank will send.

As for the loan itself, set it up as a regular monthly mortgage, and occasionally update it by pointing to it on the Loan Records screen and visiting it with F2. There you can just change the number of Payments Made to reflect the current number. It's easy to know what payment you're up to, because at the top of that screen you'll see: "You're paid up through June 1992" (say). If it's now August 1992, and your employer has been dutifully taking the mortgage payments out of your weekly or biweekly paycheck, just update the loan as of two more monthly payments.

LOANS YOU MAKE TO OTHERS

You may think of loans primarily as things you owe. But if you own any—someone owes you money—this is the place to enter them in Managing Your Money, complete with Quick or Alert transactions and budget allocations. Just tag them as Lent rather than Borrowed. We'll treat them like any other loans, only we'll know that payments are grins, not winces, and that outstanding balances make you richer, not poorer.

The checks you write to make these loans you could allocate to an expense budget category called Loans I've Made, which would dump into "Not a Tax Category." When you received payments, you would presumably allocate the interest portion to a taxable Interest income category and the principal to a non-taxable Loan Repayments category.

For information on working with your loans once you've set them up—things like mortgage prepayments, interest-rate changes, and the like—see page 319: "Step #9: Paying Down Your Loans."

STEP #6: SET UP YOUR QUICK LIST TRANSACTIONS

Managing Your Money has three data-entry shortcuts to speed entry of your income and expenses:

- Quick List
- Payee Search
- Alert List

They're not mutually exclusive, by any means, but once you get going you may find yourself leaning more heavily on one or on another. It's a matter of personal preference. The purpose of all three is the same: Once you've entered a transaction, we don't ever want you to have to type its details again. Sure, the amount might change ... and perhaps the Memo. But ordinarily, we'd be able to fill in almost everything for you.

This section of the manual concerns just the Quick List. Step #8, beginning on page 314, describes the other two shortcuts—as well as how to use the Quick List.

With the Quick List, you can build a list of the people you occasionally pay and those who occasionally pay you. Once it's set up, you can go down the list and just place an X beside the 7 transactions, say, out of the 100 or 200 on the list, that you want to record—the florist, the dentist, the phone bill, your paycheck, and so on. Change the dollar amount if it's different from last time (it usually is) ... and change anything else if you need to (but you usually won't) ... and that's it!

We then record those 23 transactions just as if you'd typed in all the names, addresses, memos, dates and amounts in English. And we automatically allocate the transactions to your budget categories. I'll go into more detail in "Shortcut #3: The Quick List" and in "How I Pay My Bills," but basically that's all there is to it.

Now, how do you set up Quick List transactions? Either of two ways:

1. You can go straight to the Quick List screen and do it there. Select Quick List from the MONEY menu (or Alt-Q from the Check Register) and press F5 to create new ones—Quick Spend, Receive, or Transfer transactions.

2. Or—easier—you can add transactions you've already entered just by pointing to them on the Check Register and pressing F6.

In other words, you needn't spend a lot of time creating a list out of your head (though you're welcome to do so). You could just go about paying your bills the first month and then point to transactions on the Check Register and press F6. Presto—they're added to your Quick List. (No harm if you accidentally make duplicates. If you notice a duplicate on your Quick List, just delete it. Or leave it there; no harm done. In fact, if you execute the same transaction often—such as ATM fees—more than once during a session you might want to list it here several times so you can quickly check off four of them.)

The only kind of Quick transaction you must create on the Quick List screen is a Transfer—there's no other way to do it (if you create it with F6 from the Check Register, it won't be a Transfer). Just press F5 and type T to select Transfer (assuming you have more than one account set up).

Once you get going, almost all your bill paying can be done by ticking off transactions on the Quick List. But no rush. Build the list at your own pace—or not at all. Some of you may in fact choose to use Payee Search and the Alert List instead. Others will wind up using all three. It's just a matter of personal preference.

- But the Quick List is the only place to record payments on Special and Interest-Only loans, if you want us to update those loans automatically, as described above, in Step #5.

- And the Quick List does have some very nice features.

"THIS ACCOUNT" VS. "GLOBAL"

When you create a Quick transaction from the Check Register, we normally assign it to the checking (or savings or charge or cash or CMA) account you're working with. We display this message: "Added to Quick List. (This account only.)"

But you may actually want to use many of your Quick transactions in a variety of accounts. Sometimes you pay Sears with a personal check, sometimes with a Discover Card, sometimes with your Sears card, and sometimes with cash. That's four accounts right there.

No problem! On the Quick List list screen, F7 lets you display and work with "All" your Quick List transactions, regardless of the account they're assigned to.

You can also make a Quick transaction "Global," meaning it works with any account. This is useful if you run businesses on the side or have separate his and hers checkbooks.

When you create a Quick with F5 from the Quick List, press F8 and choose Global from the the top of the account list. Or, if you're creating the Quick transaction from the Check Register, press Ctrl-F, choose Global, then point to a transaction and press F6.

SPLITTING QUICK LIST TRANSACTIONS OVER MORE THAN ONE BUDGET CATEGORY

Not only can you set up a Quick List transaction to pay the phone bill each month, but if you allocate it 70% to the category you call Phone-Business and 30% to Phone-Personal (with F9 on the Add Quick Transaction screen), Managing Your Money will remember that split and allocate all future payments in the same proportion.

To change those proportions at any time, just return to the Quick List transactions screen, highlight the one you want, and press Alt-F9 (or F2 and then F9). After making your changes, press the Action Key. We'll remember whatever new proportion you enter.

> NOTE: In entering a new Quick List transaction, you must allocate 100% of it to budget categories—even if one is called "Unallocated" or "Miscellaneous"—in order for us to follow the same proportions for future allocations. If you allocate $70 of a $100 expenditure to Groceries and leave the rest unallocated, we'll dutifully remember that Groceries was your only allocation—and thus allocate everything, not just 70%, there. Our Quick List transactions don't remember under- or over-allocations.

STEP #7: SET UP YOUR PAYCHECK

The one Quick List transaction that can throw people for a loop is their paycheck. It's confusing, because it's not a simple thing like your $30 cable TV bill. With your paycheck, you are receiving money (your gross pay)—and spending it (the deductions)—all at the same time. So in setting up this transaction, you should allocate your gross pay to an income budget category (Salary) and the deductions to various expense categories.

Let's step through it. To enter a "Quick List transaction" for your paycheck:

1. Select Quick List from the MONEY menu (or press Alt-Q from the Check Register).

2. Press F5, then R, (or simply Alt-R) to add a "Receive Money" Quick transaction.

3. On the screen that appears next, enter the name of your employer.

4. In the Amount field, enter the actual net amount of your take home pay—the amount of the check. Say you're paid $1,000 a week, but that after deductions the actual check is for $623. Enter $623.

5. Add a memo if you like.

6. Now press F9 to allocate the paycheck to budget categories and scroll down to the income category called "Salary" (or whatever you've chosen to call it).

7. Tab into the Allocation column and enter the gross amount from your pay stub ($1,000 in this example), which is likely to be substantially more than the actual amount of the check.

8. Scroll down to an expense category, like "Taxes: Federal," and type the amount that was withheld. Notice that our message about how much of your paycheck remains to be allocated changes when you enter a number and move to the next field. You are that much closer to allocating the whole thing.

9. Now go to the other expense categories that apply—Taxes: FICA, Taxes: State, if that's taken out of your paycheck, Health Insurance, and so forth—entering the proper amounts for each. When you're all done, you'll have allocated your gross pay to "Salary" and all the deductions from it to their proper expense categories. There will be nothing left to allocate. It's easiest to just press F8 on the last category and we'll allocate the rest to it.

10. Press the Action Key to record what you've done.

11. Note the name of the account showing at the very top of the Quick List screen. If you deposit your paycheck in this same account each time, that's all there is to it. It's been added to your list of Quick List transactions for this account. If this is the wrong account, or if you sometimes deposit your paycheck in a different account, point to your newly created transaction and press F2. Then press F8 and reassign the account, or make it "global," for use with any account.

From now on, whenever you're working with the Quick List, just place an "X" beside your paycheck and we'll record receipt of the check, add it to your account balance, and dump the proper amounts into your budget categories.

IF YOUR PAYCHECK VARIES FROM WEEK TO WEEK

Say you're on commission and no two paychecks are alike. Then what do you do? Well, you can still use this Quick List transaction. At least you won't have to reenter your employer's name. Instead, you'll enter the correct amount of your check and then press Alt-F9 (or F2, F9) to enter the gross pay and deductions. This will still be faster than entering each paycheck manually, because you'll be able to page down the list of categories, immediately spotting those with allocations from the previous paycheck. And because some of them won't change (the $17.37 a week they deduct, no matter what, for health insurance), you'll have a little less to type.

IF YOUR PAYCHECK IS AUTOMATICALLY DEPOSITED IN MORE THAN ONE ACCOUNT

We can't record it in a single Quick List transaction. Instead, split it into two Quick List transactions: one you would use to record 90% of your paycheck (say) as a receipt in your checking account; a second to receive the remaining 10% to your savings account. You'd allocate each of the two transactions to your Salary income budget category. As for your deductions—income tax, FICA and all that—you could split them proportionately among the two separate transactions, but it would be much easier and just as good to allocate all the deductions to the larger of the two.

Or set up a Quick List "Receive" for 100% of your paycheck and a Quick List "Transfer" to transfer 10% of it over to the second account.

IF YOU BELONG TO A SALARY REDUCTION PLAN

With a 401K or 403B Salary Reduction retirement plan, you may be paid $1,000 a week, but have $70 of it shielded from income tax by being siphoned off to a retirement plan.

1. In Money Accounts on the MONEY menu, create a new account (called, say, RETIREMENT FUND). Specify IRA/Keogh/401K as the account Type.

2. Create two Quick Receive transactions for your paycheck.

The first will receive your salary, less the salary reduction amount, into your checking account (or wherever you deposit your paycheck). Set it up as a normal paycheck, but the amount you allocate to your SALARY budget bucket will be your gross pay ($1,000, in this example) minus the salary reduction ($70, so you would allocate $930 to SALARY). All your normal deductions go in this transaction.

The second Quick transaction will receive the salary reduction into the RETIREMENT Money Account you just created. Press F8 on the Quick List to switch to that account first. Create a Quick Receive transaction for $70 and allocate it to an income category you call 401K INCOME and that you tag "Not a Tax Category" (because no tax is due on this $70). You have thus allocated $1,000 to two income categories.

That takes care of allocating your paycheck. And as your retirement funds pile up, Net Worth will automatically know about it.

(The only problem with this—nonproblem, really—is that Social Security tax is based on your gross salary including the otherwise nontaxable Salary Reduction portion. So if you should visit our Self-Employment Tax screen in TAX, it is likely to burp when you call up your salary numbers from MONEY. You may get a message saying that your Salary numbers don't seem to jibe with the FICA that's been withheld—that too much has been withheld from your $930-a-week. Ah, but what TAX doesn't know is that it was actually being withheld, properly, on the full $1,000-a-week. This burp is harmless. Ignore it.)

IF YOU WANT TO KEEP TRACK OF ITS INVESTMENTS

If you have a "self-directed" retirement plan (one where you can invest the money in stocks, bonds, mutual funds—however you like), you may want to manage those investments in PORTFOLIO.

In that case, set up an IRA/Keogh/401K-type portfolio in PORTFOLIO, with a name like "My 401K at Work."

There's no automatic way to deposit money straight from your paycheck in MONEY to a portfolio in PORTFOLIO, so, instead, just do this:

When you enter your paycheck every couple of weeks, enter it in a MONEY IRA/Keogh/401K account as described above. But when you get a new quarterly statement showing your 401K status, "Spend" everything in that MONEY account (payee: "401K Investment," budget category: "Transfer," tax category: none), and manually add that amount to the cash balance of the Portfolio account. Then use it to buy whatever your statement shows you actually did buy that quarter.

Say your plan allows you to split your investment among four separate vehicles, as many do—typically, a government bond fund, an insurance-company fixed income fund, a stock market mutual fund, and stock in your own company. Well, each time you got a statement showing what had been done with your 401K contributions, you could visit PORTFO-LIO and buy the appropriate number of "shares" (if it's company stock or a mutual fund) or "units" (if it's something else) in each one.

Say you were putting this year's contributions into the insurance-company fixed income fund. (Why? But that's another story.) If the latest statement showed that you'd acquired $358 more of it, you could say you bought another 358 units at a price of $1 each in an "other"-type asset, or a "bond" (what a GIC most resembles), called "Aetna-GIC" ("guaranteed income certificate") with the symbol: AETNA-GIC. Periodically, when your statement arrived showing the interest that portion of your 401K had earned, you could go to PORTFOLIO's Record Income screen and enter this interest payment.

But please note that there are other perfectly fine ways of accounting for your 401K, depending on the level of detail you want. Don't feel you have to do it precisely as outlined above.

PART II: NOW THAT YOU'RE ALL SET UP ...

Now that you're all set up, you can start using the program for real.

GETTING STARTED IN MID-YEAR

All well and good, you may be thinking (at least that's what I hope you're thinking), but what about all the transactions that have already occurred this year?

YOU HAVE THREE CHOICES:

1. Ignore them. If it's October or November or December, that makes a lot of sense. Begin using Managing Your Money to write your checks, but wait until next year—which is only weeks away—to expect it to organize everything.

2. Go back through all your expenditures for the year and enter them (or perhaps just the deductible ones). If it's January or February or March, that's no big deal. Even if it's later in the year, you may find this kind of fun—and a good way to learn the program.

   Reallocate. If you change the actual amounts for a category and later want to put things back the way they were, go to the Budgets and Actuals screen (press the Action Key from the Budget Categories screen) and press Alt-A. We'll wipe out any amounts you've entered by hand, find all the transactions allocated to this category, and recompute your actuals for each month. If you have a lot of data, it can take a while because we have to look at each transaction.

3. Don't go back and record your transactions for the months gone by, but, on the Budget Categories screen, press the Action Key to visit each of your categories in turn (use Page Scroll—PgDn—to page through them fast) and enter estimates of your expenditures so far this year in the Actuals column. Start using the program for real from now on. (To unlock the Actuals column, which we safeguard from accidental changes, press F8 first.) If you're switching to Managing Your Money from another program, just use the old program to print a budget report and then enter the budget numbers here.

   If you choose door #2, and thus may be undertaking to spend the rest of the afternoon entering hundreds of transactions, remember: save your work every so often—return to the Menu Bar and press Ctrl-S—lest a power failure or some other mishap wipe it out. It's no different from saving your work on a word processor or anything else: it's crazy not to.

STEP #8: SPENDING OR RECEIVING MONEY

1. Select Spend or Receive from the MONEY menu or press Alt-S or Alt-R from your Check Register. Here's what the Spend screen looks like:

2. Look at the top of the "check" or "receipt"screen. Is this the account you want to work with? We always take you into the account you were working with last. If it's not the one you want, just press F8 to select it. (F8 appears only if you have more than one account.)

Note that in addition to its name, we display the account's balance, so you know where you stand.

3. In entering a transaction, it's easiest to TAB from field to field:

Number: If you assign a check number, we'll remember it—and assign them incrementally from then on. You can always type over the check number we supply, but ordinarily you won't have to.

- If you do type over our guess, we'll start incrementing from that number. But we'll only make it the new "Last Check Number" for this account if it's higher. In other words, if our little counter was up to 1310 and you typed 1343 as the check number, we'd reset the Last Check Number accordingly.

- But if you made it 1187—to enter a check from your spouse's book of checks, which are lower numbered than yours, we'd only reset the counter temporarily, while you were on that screen. That way, you could keep entering his or her transactions in sequence but then, when next you returned here, be back at 1311. To get back to 1311 even without leaving the screen, just press "F7-Revert to Last Check Number." You'll only see this option when you have, in fact, typed a lower number than the one we're up to. It's our Back-to-the-Future feature.

- To reset an account's Last Check Number—typically, because you accidentally typed in a check number that was too high, and the Last Check Number counter believed you—you need to visit the housekeeping screen for that account. Just select Money Accounts and then point to the one in question and press F2. Now you can just type over the Last Check Number we show. That resets the counter. Press the Action Key to record the change and get back to work.

- To get rid of numbers altogether—in your credit card accounts, for example, which don't use them, just blank out the Last Check

Number altogether. From then on, we'll leave that field blank, too. (Monkey see, monkey do.) If you should later enter a check number by mistake, and get us counting again, just return to this housekeeping screen and blank it out again.

- There are no "check numbers" on the Receive screen; only on Spend.

- CheckFree users: When you choose this payment method, the check number field vanishes. You cannot assign CheckFree check numbers.

   Date: We supply today's. Type over it, if you like, and we'll keep using the new one you enter until you leave the screen.

- If you'd rather we reverted to today's date after every transaction, tell us in Money Options (select FILE's Optional Features). This might be best if you tend to enter "historical" transactions singly, rather than a batch of them at a time, and don't want to have to bother changing the date back when you do.

> **Hint:**
> To go back or ahead just a few days, it's fastest to use our Alt- and Alt+ shortcuts. With your cursor in the Date field, just hold down the Alt key and press a few minus or plus signs. (You don't actually have to press the Shift key to tell us you mean "plus" in this instance. We'll know.) Alt+ and Alt- also work on the check-number field—or any other numeric field in Managing Your Money.

- We normally start the cursor on the Payee or Payor field, on the assumption that you'll only occasionally need to arrow up to the Date or Check Number fields to change what we've entered for you. But if you'd like us to start the cursor on the Date field each time instead, perhaps because you are entering a batch of historical data, just tell us in Money Options (select FILE's Optional Features).

- If you are a CheckFree user and specify "CFree" as the payment method, we automatically advance today's date four business days.

   Payee/Payor: Whomever you're paying or, on the Receive Money screen, whoever is paying you.

Amount: On the Spend screen, enter as little as possible. On Receive, you can go as high as $99 million and change, and we hope you do.

Category: When you TAB into the Category field, "Not Allocated" will be showing. If you like, TAB right on to the next field—you don't have to allocate income and expenses if you don't want to. But especially for transactions that are taxable or tax-deductible, it's kind of crazy not to. Just use the Up and Down Arrows to scroll through your list of categories or—much faster—Speed Scroll to the one you want. Type G and you're at Groceries (or Gasoline, anyway). Ordinarily, the first letter or two are enough.

Note that once you begin scrolling through categories, to the right of the Category window you'll see either "Income" or "Expense", which is particularly useful if you've got two categories called "Beach House," say—one for the expenses of running it, and another for the income from renting it. If you type "Bea" on a Spend transaction, we'll assume you mean the Expense category and skip the Income one.

If you'd prefer to see your whole list and not just our little one-line window ... or if you want to split the allocation over more than a single category (up to a maximum of 15) ... or if you want to set up some new category you hadn't thought to include ... just press F9 (and then F5 if you need to set up a new category).

By: TAB into this field and, if we're not displaying the proper payment (or receipt) method, just press the first letter of the one you want (or press Spacebar to go into the choice box, scroll down to it and press Enter.) We'll normally guess the most likely method for each type of account— "Check" for a checking account and "Direct" for a credit card account, for example.

Check is the obvious method for a checking account.

CheckFree will be a payment option only if you've activated CheckFree, this is your CheckFree account, and you're entering a Spend transaction. If you select it, we'll add this transaction to the list of items to be transmitted to CheckFree. Because CheckFree transactions require at least four business days to complete, you will have to use a future date. To spare you that trouble, we automatically advance the date four business days (unless you've advanced it even further).

Payable or **Receivable** will be an option only if you've chosen it on the Money Options screen (under Optional Features on the FILE menu). If you select it, the transaction won't show up on your Check Register. Rather, it will be shunted off to your Accounts Payable or Accounts Receivable list, waiting for the day you choose to execute it from there.

Note that if you select Payable, a new field pops up for the "Due Date," which we then display on the Payables screen to help you decide when to make the payment.

Direct would be for items that get taken out of or deposited into your account through some sort of special debit or credit—if, for example, your utility bill is automatically debited to your bank account or your Social Security check is automatically credited through the magic of EFT (Electronic Funds Transfer). This is also the method to use for credit card transactions.

Phone is for those of you whose banks offer bill-payment-by-phone. When you record those payments in Managing Your Money, you can tag them as "phone" payments.

ATM is for transactions done through an Automatic Teller Machine.

Address: I ordinarily bother with these only when I'm going to be printing a check and no reply envelope has been included. (The address will show through my window envelopes.) But you might also want to use it for recording credit card receipts, where one of the things the IRS will want to know is where you had this purported business lunch.

Memo: This could be as simple as your account number or as complex as a detailed accounting of how you arrived at the amount of this payment. Only the first line will print on your check, but pressing F2 opens up room for 31,999 more lines of text, should you have a lot to say. Of course, you can leave Memo blank.

4. When you're ready, press the Action Key to record the transaction. (Remember to return to the Menu Bar and Ctrl-S from time to time to save your work).

USE MEMO FIELD CODES FOR "SUBCATEGORIES"

Don't miss the power of memo search in the Report Generator (on the MONEY menu). It lets you include in your report only transactions that have a certain "character string" (any combination of letters or numbers) someplace in the memo. Thus, if you ever wanted to do reports of money you'd spent on Billy only, and you put a "BBB" someplace in the memo in all those expenditures, the Report Generator could isolate and total only those.

(I chose BBB because it's not likely to pick up other non-Billy items you don't mean to include, like the one with the memo about "Bubble bath for Bobby's birthday." You can use any codes you like, including things like $$ and *Bill* or anything else. You could simply search on "Billy," but that wouldn't pick up any with only the word "Bill." And you could simply search on "Bill," but that would pick up the memo on your purchase at B. Dalton of that Paul Erdman novel, The Billion Dollar Sure Thing.)

For those of us who like to tag our expenditures two or more ways—by rental property, say, and by type of expense and by who actually spent the money (you or your spouse)—memo search is thus a very handy way of having your cake and eating it, too. The budget allocation for this expenditure might be, simply, "Rental Property Expense." But on the memo line, you could have things like "623-Br" to flag it as an expense on the property at 623 Broadway; "Plumb" to let you extract all your plumbing expenditures for a report someday; and "::" to show it was money you spent yourself, versus ";;" for money your spouse spent or ",," for money your daughter spent.

Don't worry about any of this now! I just wanted to alert you to the possibilities.

STEP #9: PAYING DOWN YOUR LOANS

Remember the linked Quick List or Alert List transaction you created as you established each new loan? (If you didn't do it for some of your loans, select Loan Records from the MONEY menu and create them now. Don't worry: we won't let you make duplicates.) You'll find them all on either your Quick List or Alert List, patiently waiting to be used to record payments. (You can tell they were created on the Loan screen by looking at their "Type" in the middle column of the Quick List transactions screen. Where most Quick List transactions are of the "V" type, for Variable, loan transactions are "M," "S," or "I"—Mortgage, Special or Interest-Only.)

To record a loan payment, you should always use its linked transaction. That way, we can keep those loans—and your budget and your tax estimation and your net worth—all up to date automatically.

If it was created as a Quick List transaction, just place an X beside it and change the amount, if it's changed (as it might with a Special Loan where the amount varies from time to time, or with a mortgage loan on which you're prepaying principal). When you're through with the Quick List, press the Action Key.

On Special Loan payments we'll then ask you how much of the payment was for interest and how much for principal. On Interest-Only Loan payments, we'll ask you to confirm that the full amount of the payment was indeed interest. On Mortgage-type loans, we won't have to ask anything. We already know the principal-interest-escrow breakdown, and we assume any extra you've decided to pay this month is a principal prepayment and adjust all your figures accordingly. It's that simple.

Even so, there are some out-of-the-ordinary events to consider:

LATE PENALTIES

Well, I hope this one is out-of-the-ordinary. From time to time, you may be hit with an extra interest charge for paying your mortgage late. To keep everything in balance, don't simply change the amount of your Quick List transaction from $708.14 (the regular amount), say, to $723.14 (the amount you owe with the late penalty), because we assume any extra payment is a principal prepayment. The check we print will be for the right amount, but your loan amortization will ever after be slightly off.

Instead, record your normal mortgage payment (and print the check if you use Managing Your Money to print checks), and then record a separate spend transaction, allocated to Mortgage Interest (or "Mortgage Penalty Interest" if you're a super purist), for the amount of the extra interest (and print a second check).

Or, if you'd rather not print two checks, first record your normal mortgage payment and then, on the Check Register, point to this new one and press F2 to edit it. Increase the amount to include the late penalty and allocate that extra amount to your Interest allocation. Now print the check.

Late penalties often represent an outrageous rate of interest, even if relatively few dollars. That, coupled with the inconvenience of having to record two transactions instead of one, is yet another reason to try to pay on time!

PRINCIPAL PREPAYMENTS

Okay. You're sending in an extra one-time $5,000 principal payment along with your 67th regular monthly payment. How do you record that in Managing Your Money? Simple:

- Quick List transactions. Go to your Quick List and enter the actual amount you're paying—$5,873.13, say, instead of the normal $873.13. When you go back to check the status of that loan after you've executed the transaction, you'll find that we've credited you with the extra principal and recalculated the number of payments remaining. (Paying off principal hastens the pay-off date of the loan.) What's more, we automatically adjust your budgeted principal and interest figures to match the new status of your loan.

- Alert List transactions. If you linked this mortgage to an Alert List transaction, select Loan Records from the MONEY menu, point to the loan and press "F8—Prepay Principal on an Alert Loan Transaction." Instead of adding the additional principal to a regular Alert List loan payment, we create a separate transaction. This extra payment goes straight to your Check Register, without passing go and without stopping at the Alert List, and uses the next check number in sequence. You can then write out or print the check. (If the loan payment is being made via CheckFree, this extra payment will still be a regular check.)

FANCY LOAN AMORTIZATION

For some fancy footwork on mortgage loans that involve multiple principal prepayments (one-time or periodic) and a series of interest rate changes, select Loan Amortization from the ANALYZE menu. We'll take all these mind-bogglingly complex factors into account and print a customized amortization schedule. We can also show you the difference between a monthly and biweekly mortgage (where you in effect make 13 months— payments a year). We won't carry the results to Loan Records (we'll account for the changes when you really do prepay principal or have a rate adjustment). But ANALYZE's Loan Amortization is a great planning tool.

INTEREST RATE CHANGES

When the rate changes on an adjustable rate mortgage loan, select Loan Records from the MONEY menu. Highlight that loan with the cursor, press F2, fill in the new rate, press F6 to recalculate your new monthly payment and the Action Key to save the modified loan. We'll adjust all your budgeted principal and interest amounts to reflect the change. (If the new monthly payment is off slightly, come back and adjust the interest rate a hair until, through trial and error, you get the payment you want. Your bank may be rounding things off slightly differently from the norm. What it calls a 10.5% loan might to us seem like a 10.502% loan.)

ESCROW AMOUNT OR LOAN-NAME CHANGES

If taxes or insurance rates go up and the monthly escrow amounts your bank requires change, delete the linked Alert or Quick transaction (with F3) from the Alert List or the Quick List. Then return to Loan Records, point to this loan, and press F6 or F7 to create a new Alert or Quick transaction. Enter the new escrow amounts as you create the new transaction.

You can change the name of the loan itself just by typing over it on the Loan Records screen. But that won't change the payee name on the linked transaction. To do that, press F2 and F6 as just described. In these days of daily bank mergers, this could come in handy sooner than you think. (If it's set up for payment by CheckFree, you'll find that you can't change the name when you press F6. Instead, delete it on the Alert List or the Quick List and then return to Loan Records to create a new one.)

TO GET BACK ON TRACK IF YOU'VE LOUSED UP YOUR LOAN

If you somehow mis-enter or otherwise louse up the recordkeeping on a mortgage loan, you can delete it (see page 302: "Deleting a Mortgage"). But how do you reenter it—properly this time—in midstream? After all, since you first took it out several years ago as a simple 30-year $75,000 loan, the interest rate has switched four times and you've made three different small partial prepayments.

Rather than try to reconstruct all that, do this. Simply enter the loan for what it is now: a 243-payment (if that's how many the bank tells you you have left) $68,329.88 loan (if that's the outstanding principal as of the last payment) at 10.625% (if that's the current interest rate). Unless your bank is strange, entering the loan this way, odd as it may feel in a world of round numbers, should get you back on track.

> NOTE: We Can't "Un-update" Loans
>
> One of the things we can't do automatically is "un-update" your loan if you should record a Quick List loan payment and later, for some reason, delete it. So if you find you've somehow recorded one payment too many (that is, one more than you've actually made), adjust things by making your next loan payment without using its Quick List transaction (and thus without updating it), to get back in step.

ALLOCATING LOAN PROCEEDS

If you borrow $10,000 in cash from the bank, you record two things: the receipt of $10,000 in your checking account, or wherever you park the money (select Receive Money from the MONEY menu to record the receipt of funds); and the establishment of a new $10,000 loan (select Loan Records from the MONEY menu to record the new loan).

But to what budget category do you allocate the $10,000 proceeds? And what if it's not quite so simple, as in the following example?

FROM CONCORD, CA:

"I will be buying a new car soon. Should I consider the loan proceeds as 'income' and the loan payments, 'expense'? And what about the money

I'm taking out of my savings account for the down payment? How will all this affect my net worth?"

Let's start with the easy part—your net worth. Enter the car as an asset in NET WORTH (see Chapter 8) and adjust its value each year as it depreciates (unless it's one of those 1923 Stutz Bearcats that appreciate). Enter the loan in MONEY. Its outstanding balance will automatically show up as a liability in NET WORTH and decrease with each monthly payment.

Your net worth will increase by the market value of the car—but decrease by the amount of the loan and the down payment you withdrew from your savings account. Net result: a small decrease, I'm afraid, reflecting the fact that a car generally loses value the minute you take it off the lot.

Now, what about the loan proceeds?

Scenario A: You never even see the money. It goes straight from GMAC (say) to your dealer. All you see is the payment book.

In this case, there's no need to receive any cash. Just set up the loan in Loan Records, along with a Quick List transaction. When you're asked how you want to allocate the principal and interest on the loan, allocate principal to an expense budget category you might call "Auto Equity" (which is also the budget category into which you'd dump the money you withdrew from your savings account for the down payment) and interest to one called "Personal Interest."

Scenario B: You actually get a check for $10,000 which you deposit in your bank account, then write a $10,000 check to your Jaguar dealer.

Allocate the check you receive to "Loan Proceeds" (Not a Tax Category). Allocate the check you write, if it's really a strict auto loan, to the same place: "Loan Proceeds." When you allocate an expenditure to an income bucket, we automatically make it negative—so the money you spend on the car will lower your $10,000 in loan proceeds back down to $0. (If you don't want a new category for just a couple of transactions, use your Miscellaneous category. Or don't allocate these Receive and Spend transactions to categories at all.)

Then set up the loan as described in Scenario A.

(There are other perfectly acceptable ways to record loan proceeds. If you've been doing this differently and you're happy, we're happy, too.)

STEP #10: PRINTING CHECKS

You certainly don't have to, but it makes a lot of sense to print most of your checks with Managing Your Money. Otherwise, you're entering information twice: once, when you write it by hand on the check and then again when you note it on the check stub and/or record it in Managing Your Money. What's more, why should you write out the amount of the check in English and the date? We can do it for you! Why even write out the name of the payee or address an envelope? As described in Step #8 (page 313), if it's someone you've ever paid before in this account, or whom you've added to your Quick List, Payee Search or the Quick List will do all that for you— and print your account number, or anything else you've included, on the memo line.

1. Select Print Checks from the MONEY menu (or Alt-P from the Check Register).

2. Press F8 to select the checking account you want to work with, if we've guessed wrong.

3. If this is the first time you've printed checks with Managing Your Money, press F9 to let us know what kind of checks you'll be using. Just point to the proper style and press the Action Key.

   It may require a little trial and error to get set up properly the first time, or when you change to a new check style or printer (which is why we have F6 on the Print Checks screen to print "line-up" checks). But it shouldn't be hard to get things in synch, even if you're using checks other than the ones we list. Press F6 on the Select Check Format screen to make adjustments or customize a format that works for you. HELP behind that screen explains how.

4. Press F7 and look over the Check Printing Defaults. Change any you like and press the Action Key. You shouldn't have to visit this screen often, either.

   Unless you're tight for space on your hard disk, you almost surely want to answer NO to the questions about deleting the address and memo after printing. You almost surely DO want to use pre-numbered checks. If you're hand-feeding one check at a time into the printer, you'll want to PAUSE between each one. And if you're using single-sheet laser checks, you'll want to say YES to "formfeed after each check." If you're using continuous-form checks, you'll want to say NO.

5. Back on the Print Checks screen, tell us whether to print Today's Date on the checks, or to stick with whatever dates you may have used when you entered the transactions. And be sure to tell us the Starting Check Number—the number of the first blank check in your printer. Finally, tell us which checks you want us to print if we haven't guessed right (you can scroll through your transactions on the screen).

   Until you get comfortable with printing checks, you may want to print just one check first. For example, if you're printing checks 3347 thru 3355, you might initially instruct us to print only the first check—"3347 thru 3347"—to make sure it lines up properly. Then print the rest.

6. Print a line-up check if you like (F6). Then print your checks (Action Key).

> Tip: Use Blank Paper for line-up checks
> Don't waste blank checks on line-ups. They're expensive! Where possible, use blank paper and hold it up to the light with the blank check behind it.
>
> For tips on making sure the check numbers in the program match the ones on your checks, see Step No. 6 on page 139. I'll walk you through the process of printing checks, and tell you how to order checks, next under "How I Pay My Bills."

HOW I PAY MY BILLS

It's not practical to print a single check (unless you have a sheet-fed printer or an old printer you use only for checks), so I just write those out of my wallet and make a note to record them next time I'm in the program. (With "duplicate" checks—the kind that make their own copies without carbon paper—you don't even have to record your checks in a check register.)

What is a real time-saver is to use the program to pay lots of bills all at once. I keep a manila folder next to my computer. When bills come, that's where I toss them. Likewise, receipts, brokerage confirmation slips and business cards I want to record. Every couple of weeks, I power up and clean out the folder.

Anytime I write a check (or record one I've had to write out of my wallet), I always set it up as a Quick List transaction. I figure that if I'm paying whomever it is once, I'll probably have to pay him again someday. By now, I have 433 payees on my Quick List and only occasionally have to take half a minute to add a new one. So here's what I do:

1. I put my bills—and receipts for bills I've already paid by hand—in a stack, face up, like a deck of cards.

2. I speed scroll to the Quick List transaction for each one in turn, typing an "A" in the "Mark" column, to the right of the first, a "B" to the right of the second, and so on. In most cases, I type in a new amount. (With a few I needn't do even that—it's the same as last time.)

SHORTCUT: MARK FROM A TO Z

If you often pay more than 26 bills, note that there are more than 26 "letters" in a computer's alphabet—see page 296 for a computer's conception of alphabetical order.

Marking them "A, B, C" instead of all X's means they will print out in the same haphazard order I happen to be doing my bills, so the first check will go with the first bill, the second with the second, and so on. Marking them all with X's is fine, too—the checks will print out in alphabetical order. That's nice and tidy, but it means hunting around for which bill goes with which check. Or sorting the bills in alphabetical order.

For those checks I've written out of my wallet, I type the actual dates in the "Last Use" column and enter the actual check numbers at far right.

For those bills I pay by CheckFree, I don't have to do anything special, because the "By" column of the Quick List already remembers this preference (though I can always change it).

3. I press the Action Key to record my work. At this point the transactions are recorded, as far as Managing Your Money is concerned (provided that I save my work).

4. I frequently return to the Menu Bar and press Ctrl-S to save what I've done. This isn't required, but prudence is my middle name. (Previn is my middle name, actually, but that's another story.)

5. I select Print Checks from the MONEY menu.

6. I tell Managing Your Money which checks I want to print, if it hasn't guessed right, and the actual starting number of the first one in my printer. (I've gotten a lot better at getting them into their little sprockets unmangled.) This is important, because it allows us to match our check numbers to the real ones on your checks. If we've tentatively numbered your checks 400-415, but 400 and 401 go into the trash, we will actually wind up printing those payments on checks numbered 402-417. When you tell Managing Your Money that 402 is the first actual check in your printer, it knows to renumber 400 as 402, 401 as 403, and so on. That way, your check numbers in Managing Your Money will match your check numbers in the real world.

   (Should you ever gum this up, you can simply press F2 on the Check Register to visit each of the transactions in turn and renumber them yourself. With Page Scroll, going from one to the next takes just a minute.)

   I leave "Use Today's Date?" set to Yes, because the day I print them is a perfectly reasonable date to use. I may have entered the payment in Managing Your Money a week ago and been lazy about printing a batch of checks. But this feature redates the batch to today. If you prefer, answer No, and we'll use whatever date, past, present or post, you entered for each check.

7. Under Check Printing Options (F7), I answer "No!" to the questions about deleting memos and addresses after the printing is done. It can be quite helpful to have the memo available for inspection on the screen. And as for addresses, if you should louse up a print-run and have to do it over again, you'll find to your annoyance that, if you've answered "Yes" to deleting them, they're gone. Out print your checks the second time, but with no addresses to show through your window envelopes. So I choose "No."

If I backed up my budget.dbs file onto 360K floppies, instead of 1.44MB's, and hence risked running out of room one day if I took up too much space for thousands of addresses, I'd choose "Yes" and be more careful with my print runs.

I answer "Yes" to quality print mode, "Yes" to pre-numbered checks (almost everyone has these), and "Don't Pause" when printing. (See below for notes on sheet-fed printing.)

8. I turn on the printer.

9. I don't bother with line-up checks anymore, because by now I've learned how far in to feed the first check. But if I wanted, I could press F6 to print one. If the printing started too high or low on the check, I'd know to feed the checks in a little farther or less far. (And I'd enter the new "starting check number," now that I were ready to start printing for real.) It helps to make a mark on the printer to line up the check the next time.

10. I press the Action Key and watch my 23 checks come chugging out while I put stamps on the reply envelopes (and on window envelopes for those bills that come without reply envelopes).

11. When the printing's done, I rip them out of the printer—but not the memo half of the last check (I use business-style checks). I could rip out that little tail-end, too, if it were important (it never is), but I leave it as a "leader" to help me feed the checks in next time.

12. I rip the little sprocket runners off the checks all at once, sign them (checking to be sure an extra zero hasn't crept in somewhere), rip them apart and stuff them in the reply envelopes. I don't bother to rip off the bottom half of the check; I include it just as most businesses do.

Although everything is neatly synchronized, I do try to keep my eyes open, having once dropped an envelope off the edge of my desk and found that I had thus placed the check for American Express in the Book of the Month Club envelope, Book of the Month in Care, Care in Visa—and so on. This led to a lot of swearing, envelope reopening and Scotch taping, which I have since managed to avoid.

13. I drop them in the mail.

Note that printing checks is little different from printing any other report, except that the paper you use is more valuable. Printing reports—or checks—in no way affects the data on which they're based. Whether you print some of them, none of them or nine of them twice, your underlying numbers and records will remain unchanged. (The exception: If we re-number checks for you, as explained above.)

Furthermore, if you did get everything tangled (and it's hard to imagine how you could), you could just choose Revert from the FILE menu and start all over again. I've never had to do this.

Finally, trust me when I tell you there's a learning curve here. What will at first require some time and concentration should quickly become an efficient process. Your first try won't be faster than paying bills by hand. But soon you will be a pro and it should all be quite slick. And having done it this way, all the data's now available for rapid reconciliation, analysis, report generation throughout the year, and tax preparation early next year.

WRITING CHECKS BY HAND

If you prefer to pay your bills by hand, you can still save lots of time by recording the transactions on the Quick List transactions screen as you go. Just use Speed Scroll to jump to each payee as you write out the check, or use Payee Search (F6) on the Spend Money screen. It goes very fast and saves your writing out a check stub for your checkbook.

ORDERING THE CHECKS YOU'LL NEED

MECA Forms, a division of MECA Software, can provide high-quality computer checks, forms and supplies at competitive prices. The checks are custom-designed for Managing Your Money and are guaranteed compatible. You can get continuous-feed checks for a dot-matrix printer or sheet-fed checks for a laser or other page printer.

You don't need permission from your bank. You don't need to send a sample of the checks you're currently using. All you need do is call MECA Forms toll free at 1-800-992-2951. Or use the MECA Forms brochure that was included with Managing Your Money. MECA Forms promises to process your order immediately and ship standard items within four to six days.

You can order either personal-size checks or business-size. Managing Your Money works fine with either, but I recommend business-size. You can also order window envelopes. They're a big time-saver: just print and sign your checks, put them into the envelope so the mailing and return addresses show through, and mail.

MECA Forms also offers a complete line of personal and business forms and supplies, such as mailing labels, invoices and Rolodex cards designed to work with Managing Your Money.

To offer you a choice, MECA also endorses Deluxe Corporation as a supplier of compatible Managing Your Money checks. Their service is also excellent. To order from Deluxe, call 1-800-328-0304 and ask for Managing Your Money-compatible checks.

WARNING: USE HIGHER NUMBERED CHECKS

To avoid confusion when ordering, please specify a beginning check number well above the check numbers of the personal checks you currently use. That way, your computer generated checks will all be big and professional; those you write out of your wallet will be the familiar smaller ones you already have; and you'll be able to tell at a glance from the check number which is which.

PRINTING JUST A FEW CHECKS AT A TIME

A great advantage of laser sheet checks is the ease with which you can print them without having to switch back and forth between regular paper and your checks on many printers. With laser, ink jet and most newer dot-matrix printers, you can just feed them in manually while leaving your regular paper loaded.

PRINTING CHECKS WITH A LASER OR OTHER SHEET-FED PRINTER

If you have a sheet-fed printer, like a Hewlett Packard LaserJet or DeskJet, check-printing is terrific. Just remember to answer "Yes" on the check-printing screen where we ask if you want us to send a formfeed after each check. (A "formfeed" tells your printer there's nothing more to be printed on this page, so go ahead: feed it through and get ready for the next page.)

MECA Forms offers sheet-fed checks. But if you have some continuous-form checks you want to use up first, just rip off their sprocket strips and separate them before printing instead of afterward. Because of the perforations, you may have to feed them into the printer manually, to avoid jams, rather than stacking them in the paper tray. When you run out of this batch of checks, buy the sprocketless laser kind that come already separated (MECA Forms Style 4922xx business-size or 4923xx personal-size). They work fine in the paper tray.

PRINTING CHECKS THE FIRST TIME

Once you decide which type of checks you want to use—personal or business, with a stub (voucher) or without—you'll need to tell Managing Your Money, so we know where to print everything. From the Print Checks screen, press F9 to select a check format. Highlight your check style on the screen and press the Action Key. You're ready to print your first check!

> NOTE: Edit Check Layout
> If we're printing the name of your payee in the wrong place even after you've loaded the correct check style, press F9 on the print-checks screen, point to the type of check you use, press F6 and move things around. Read help for instructions. If you're using personal-size checks, see below.

PRINTING CHECKS IN "QUALITY" MODE

We give you the option, when you go to print checks, to print them in "quality" mode. If you choose "Yes" but we don't seem to be rising to the occasion, select Program Setup from the FILE menu and then Printer. Is the right printer selected? Then press F7. Are there strings of numbers entered on the lines for "Near letter quality on" and "off?" If so, are they the right strings? (Check your printer manual.) We will accept on these lines any setup strings you think will make your checks and reports look good, including those your printer requires for bold-faced or emphasized printing.

> NOTE: Laser Printers
> You can choose "No," because you're already in quality mode. Or choose "Yes"—it shouldn't make any difference, unless you've chosen to use Quality mode to mean something else.

MY CHECKS PRINT FUNNY.

"The numerical amount of my check looks like it's going to fall off the right side of the check. If it were for a larger amount—$10,000.00, say, instead of $9.31—it really would fall off the edge!"

No, it wouldn't. If you've changed the default setting to "right-justified," the larger your number, the further to the left we begin printing it. Just press F9 from the Print Checks screen, point to your check style and press F6. You can change it to "left-justify" this amount instead. Try it that way if you prefer.

I CAN'T GET THE DATE TO LINE UP.

That may be because the date is anywhere from 8 to 10 characters long. A format that looks good when it's 10 characters (12/25/1991) may look less good when it's 8 characters (1/1/1992). But feel free to press F9 and F6 from the Print Checks screen and experiment with the placement of the date.

THE PRINTING STARTS FURTHER AND FURTHER DOWN ON EACH SUCCESSIVE CHECK I PRINT.

This can happen if you've instructed us to load the wrong printer setup—e.g., Epson LX instead of Epson LQ.

But a few people have found themselves accidentally adding a phantom line to their checks. We'd then print 18-line checks instead of 17-line checks, and the printing would start one line too low on the second check, two lines too low on the third, and so on.

If this ever happens to you after you've changed the check format (F9, F6 from the Check Printing screen), here's what you're doing wrong. You've got checks that are 60-columns wide and you've told us to place the memo field, say, starting on column 12 (12 spaces from the left margin).

That would be fine, only the memo field is 50 spaces wide—whether you use its full width or not. You have it running from column 12 to column 62. Even though that 62nd column is blank most of the time, your printer jumps to the next line to "print" it, anyway. You don't notice it, because the extra character is a blank. The solution is simply to move the memo line, or any other information field you have running past column 60, a few columns to the left, so it won't overflow to the next line.

One user writes: "With your new default, the numerical amount falls off the edge of my personal-size checks. Using your routine to modify the format, I moved the numerical amount 10 spaces to the left but received an error message saying it conflicted with the amount in words. Does this mean the amount in words could overlap the numerical amount?" Yes. "Then I moved both to the left three spaces and it worked."

A little trial and error, in a program such as ours, works wonders. It's the price of flexibility.

STEP #11: A STEP TOO MANY

If you're still with me, you've covered a tremendous amount of ground. And I should think you've had it up to here with steps. Fair enough. No more steps for now. But there are a few more topics you'll probably want to read about in this chapter:

RECONCILING A MONEY ACCOUNT

One of the more tedious money-management chores—so much so that many of us don't do it—is checkbook reconciliation. Yet only if you reconcile your checkbook will you know for sure your records (and the bank's) are accurate. Managing Your Money can make it fast, easy and almost fun (even if, the first time, it requires a little tinkering).

Summary: Enter information from your bank statement at the bottom of the Reconcile Account screen, have us sort your transactions by check number and then mark on the screen those transactions that have cleared the bank. Everything will then reconcile (unless you need to enter something you forgot, or correct something you misentered, or call the bank to point out an error it made). When it does, press the Action Key to complete the process. That's it.

The Full Detail Method (optional!): Select Reconcile Account from the MONEY menu (or press Alt-E from the Check Register). Look at the top of the screen to make sure you're in the right account (you can change it with F8). The "Last Reconciled Balance" should match the beginning balance on your new bank statement. If necessary, go to Money Accounts from the MONEY menu and set it right (highlight the account and press F2 to modify it, then press the Action Key to save your changes). Then come back to the Reconcile Account screen.

At the bottom of the Reconcile screen, enter the ending balance from your current bank statement, and any interest, finance charges and services charges that appear on the statement.

Now go back up to the top of the transaction list (Ctrl-PgUp) and mark the transactions that appear on the bank statement. To make this easy, we display only transactions you haven't reconciled previously; and you can use F9 to sort them as your bank does. (Re-sort at any time if you're hunting for a specific transaction.)

Start at the top of the list, placing an "x" next to each transaction that appears on your bank statement. If you find a transaction that's not in Managing Your Money, press F5 to add it (or Alt-S, Alt-R or Alt-T). If you find an error in a transaction, press F2 to fix it. To check or change only its budget allocation, press Alt-F9.

We track the total of the In and Out transactions as you mark them, and tell you how far out of balance you are. It's fun to watch the numbers change until—yes—you're in balance! (The numbers will be correct only if you've filled in the amount fields at the bottom of the screen first.) Next to "Reconcile on Statement Date," put the statement date.

When you've marked all the transactions on your bank statement, your account should be in balance—and we'll tell you so. When you give the word, we'll put a check mark next to all the cleared transactions on your Check Register. If your balance still doesn't match the bank's, press F1 for Help finding the problem.

HANDLING YOUR CREDIT CARD ACCOUNTS

There are a variety of ways to handle credit card transactions with Managing Your Money. You should choose the one that fits your needs.

THE FULL DETAIL METHOD

You can set up a separate charge account in MONEY for each of your cards. (Select Money Accounts from the MONEY menu, press F5 to add a new one, and type cha in the Type field so we know it's a charge account. Unless the bank owes you money, be sure to enter a negative balance.) Then, as you charge things, bring your receipts home and record the charges in their respective accounts (Visa, MasterCard, etc.) and allocate them to budget categories. You'll have a running balance for each account. When the statement comes each month, reconcile it as you would your checking account.

When you write a check to pay off or pay down one of your cards, you are spending money in your checking account and receiving it into your charge account. You can do it:

- in two steps (record the check in your checking account, then go to your charge account to "receive" the same amount);

- or in one step (select Transfer Money from the MONEY menu or Alt-T from the Check Register);

- or in one even faster step (set up a Quick List Transfer transaction so that, thereafter, you can just mark it off the list as you're running through your other payments).

But however you do it, don't try to allocate the payment to budget categories, because you'd be double counting. Under this "full detail method," you recorded your various charges throughout the month and allocated them to expense categories. Now, you're just transferring some cash from one of your accounts to the other. No additional expense has occurred. There's nothing new to allocate.

A LITTLE SHORT CUT

Perhaps you're not concerned with the running balance on your cards. You figure that, at worst, every once in a while a waiter will tell you you've bumped up against your limit—whereupon you'll proffer the next card in your deck. If so, rather than setting up 13 different charge accounts and posting transactions to them as incurred, you might prefer to lump all your charge transactions into a single account called "Charge Cards" (or keep American Express separate, say, but lump all your gasoline cards—it's up to you).

Lumping all your charges into one account is less precise—and not for everyone—but easier. When individual credit card statements arrive, glance over them to be sure you weren't hit with somebody else's charges, but don't try to reconcile each one. Just enter the finance charge, if any, as a "Spend" transaction (allocated to Personal Interest Expense)—or don't even bother with that if the amounts are small and you can stand the imprecision. At the end of the year, all 14 of your creditors will dutifully inform you of the cumulative interest you were charged (which doesn't much matter anymore, since it's no longer tax-deductible).

A LITTLE BETTER SHORT CUT

Even if that strikes you as appallingly sloppy, this may make sense. It applies whether or not you lump all your charge accounts into one.

Rather than record all your transactions throughout the month more or less as they take place, record them all at once, directly from the monthly statement when it arrives. In fact, just throw your monthly statements into the folder you keep by the computer and tend to this at the same time as you clean out the rest of the folder—pay your bills, print your checks, record brokerage transactions, and so on.

You can enter a separate spend transaction for each item on the statement or—a shorter cut—"spend" the entire amount in one transaction ("Visa Payment") and allocate it over a variety of budget categories. The calculator (Ctrl-N) will make short shrift of adding up the various items that aggregate to each of your budget categories. Or perhaps you'll tot up only deductible expenditures, dumping the remainder into your "Unallocated" category—it's up to you! If you want to explain any of the charges, use the Memo field (pressing F2 to expand it, if necessary).

> NOTE: Charge account balances are ordinarily negative. Bear that in mind when entering your initial balance.

HOME EQUITY ACCOUNTS

See page 303 under Step #5, "Home Equity Loans."

EXPENSE ACCOUNTS

Though it can't fill out your company form, there's a simple way to use the program to help you with your expense accounts.

Set up an Expense budget category called "Reimbursable Expense" (or, if you submit expense accounts to several employers, set up one for each). Then, whenever you record an expenditure you plan to add to your expense account, dump it into that budget category.

When you're ready to prepare your expense report, select Report Generator from the MONEY menu; press F7 twice; mark just the budget category called "Reimbursable Expense" and press the Action Key to save your selections and back up. Now choose the dates your report should cover, select Budget & Tax Category Reports and press the Action Key. When you see the transactions you want, press F4.

I WOULD SUGGEST YOU PRINT TWO REPORTS:

Use the Allocation Report Format screen to specify that the first report's transactions be arranged by Budget Category (even though they're all from the same category, this causes us to print a grand total), followed by Date and then Payee. (Include, also, the Amount and Memo.) Put a Y on the first two lines in the right column so we include both a grand total and a day-by-day subtotal.

Now print a second report just like the first, only put Payee on the second line of the Report Format screen and Date on the third. Switch 'em. Now we'll subtotal by payee. (We could do that in the first report, too, if you put a Y beside the third line, too, but chances are you wouldn't like the resulting clutter of mostly meaningless one-item subtotals.)

If you get into the habit of entering your expenses in a format that matches your employer's needs, you can take this a step further. Say you precede all hotel charges with an "H-"—"H-Airport Marriott," "H-Universal Sheraton,"

"H-Cambridge Hyatt." And all airline charges with an "A-" and all meals with an "M-." When we print our report (the second one), you'll get neat groupings of your hotel, air and meal expenses.

There are a variety of ways to play with this depending on your needs, but this should give you an idea of the possibilities. (Note that you can save the customized report formats you come up with. There's no need to re-invent them each month. Press F6, enter a name at the bottom and press F5.)

However you choose to format the report, out will come all your Reimbursable Expenses for the months you specify. If you print them "to disk," ordered by date (see page 283: "Printing to Disk"), you'll quickly be able to add any needed detail that wasn't already in the memo. Just use our word processor (Ctrl-W) to call up the report you save.

If your company accounting department is at all flexible, it should welcome your neatly printed report, allowing you to staple it to the standard form with the simple notation: "See attached."

Naturally, this all makes most sense for people who have already chosen the Full Detail Method for charge cards described on page 335—I'm not one of them—and for whom, therefore, most of the entries they'll need for the expense report will already have been recorded in Managing Your Money.

AND WHEN YOU'RE REIMBURSED . . .

If you do adopt a system like this, what you could do when you received an expense check would be to receive it into your checking or savings account (wherever you actually deposit it) but allocate it not to an income category, like "Expense Reimbursement," but to your "Reimbursable Expense" expense category. Whenever you allocate income to an expense category, we automatically make it negative. So by doing it this way, the figure for this budget category would rise when you were owed money and fall back to zero when you'd been reimbursed.

(You'd probably want to set your monthly budget for this category at zero, as you expect no net out-of-pocket expense, and have it dump to the "Not a Tax Category" tax barrel—although if your employer ever failed to reimburse you, you could presumably claim the shortfall as an unreimbursed employee business expense.)

More detail? If your expenses aren't fully reimbursed and you need to file a Form 2106 with your taxes, you'll need to account for meals and entertainment separately from your other exenses. In this case, create an Income category, "Expense Reimbursements," and two Expense ones, "Reimb. Expense-Meals" and "Reimb. Expense-Other." Tie them to the three Form 2106 Tax Categories we provide.

You can be as elaborate as you want. One user we know, who takes about a dozen trips a year, has one income and two expense categories for every trip. He places a period at the beginning of each category, so they all sort to the top of the list, and he abbreviates the name of the city he visits. If he visits the same city more than once, he numbers them. His second visit to Washington, D.C., last year produced the Income category ".DC2 Reimbursements" and the Expense categories ".DC2 Meals, Entertai" and ".DC2 Other Expenses."

In short, many people will be best served doing their expense reports the same way they always did. But for some, Managing Your Money may help to organize the process.

MEDICAL EXPENSES AND REIMBURSEMENTS

You can handle medical expenses and reimbursements in much the same way. Set up a budget bucket for medical expenses, dumping, naturally, to one of the Schedule A medical tax barrels, and allocate all your medical expenditures there. Allocate your reimbursement there, also.

Whenever income is allocated to an expense category, we automatically take it to be negative. Say you spend $100 on a medical bill and then got a $90 reimbursement. By allocating that income to the same expense category, the total we'd show, and pass through to Schedule A in TAX, would be $10—the amount of your unreimbursed medical expenses.*

*The "Annual Total"— we show on the budget summary screen may not reflect this negative amount until the following month. Say it's July and that in May you spent $500 on reimbursable medical expenses but received $200 of reimbursements. Our annual total would show $300, just as you'd expect—the $500 expense less the $200 "negative expense." So far so good. But now, still in July, you receive the remaining $300 reimbursement you were waiting for. You'd expect, once you entered that negative expense, to see an annual total of zero. Yet until August rolled around, we would still show it as $300. Why? Because for the current month "July" our Annual Total figure is always based on the greater of your budgeted amount (probably zero, in this case) or your actual amount (LESS than zero, in this peculiar case). Once the month is over, we use the actual amount (negative $300) in figuring the Annual Total, so from then on it would look exactly right.

If you'd like a way to keep track of your reimbursements, to be sure they're really coming as they should, and if you've activated our Accounts Receivable option (select Optional Features from the FILE menu, and then Money Options), do this:

When you pay a medical bill, go also to the Receive Money screen and enter there the name of the reimbursor and the amount for which you expect to be reimbursed. In the "By:" field, select "Receivable." This tells us you haven't actually gotten the cash, but that we should add this item to your Accounts Receivable list.

You may wish, also, to note the number of the check and/or some other features of the bill, including the invoice number, for identification purposes. In other words, instead of calling the payee, "Blue Cross," you might call it, "Blue Cross re:#2405" and put the invoice number and "2/14 Appendectomy" in the memo.

Then, when the reimbursement arrives, select Receivables from the MONEY menu and record it on that screen.

NONCASH ITEMS: CHARITABLE CONTRIBUTIONS, DEPRECIATION, PARTNERSHIP LOSSES

In MONEY you can set up a thing we call a "noncash" account. This allows you to enter transactions that affect your taxes but involve no cash—and to do so without lousing up your Cash Flow projections in MONEY or affecting your net worth in NET WORTH.

Just select Money Accounts to set up a noncash account (or several, if you'd like one for depreciation and another for donations of old clothes and a third for partnership income and expense). Ignore the "cash balance" displayed for this account on the Money Accounts screen. We know it's not really cash. If it bothers you, you could always spend or receive the exact opposite amount to set the balance to zero; but you may find it helpful always to be able to see at a glance, for example, the total of your noncash tax deductions—for that's presumably what this figure will represent.

CHARITABLE CONTRIBUTIONS

If you give $2,300 in stock to the Red Cross, "write a check" for that amount in a noncash account, allocating it to your "Charitable Contributions" budget bucket. Even though it's in a noncash account, you might want to make the payee, "Red Cross—STOCK!," so that in printouts you're reminded this was not a contribution of real money and to include the backup you'll need to satisfy the IRS. The memo line in this case might read, "100 shares, Wrather Corp. common, vsp 3/4/1978." (VSP is short for "versus purchase," so you and your broker and the IRS know which Wrather shares these were.)

(If you do give shares, then go into PORTFOLIO, locate this tax lot on the Display Assets screen, and press F2 to edit it. Simply lower the number of shares you originally purchased by the number you've given away—you softie—and, on the comment line, note something like, "Excludes 100 shares given to Red Cross 12/25/1991.")

DEPRECIATION

For depreciation, simply visit your noncash account and write a "check" for each depreciation charge you want to record, dumping, presumably, into depreciation budget buckets that dump, in turn, into the appropriate Schedule C, E or F tax barrels.

We don't automatically calculate depreciation schedules for your equipment, nor update them as you start each new year; but once you've devised your depreciation schedule for a particular item, you might set it up as a Quick List transaction. Make the first four letters of the payee DEPR, say, so all your depreciation items will be grouped together—DEPR-Mack Truck, DEPR-Answering Machine, and so on. If you like, you could append the year of acquisition, too—"DEPR-Mack Truck —88." In the memo area, note whatever else you need to know, including the depreciation method (straight-line, etc.) and the actual numbers for the years to come. That way, next year you can just mark all the DEPR's on your Quick List, updating those where the amount has changed (the correct amount will be sitting a keystroke away on the memo line). I actually have an annual reminder in The Reminder Pad that reminds me to do this in January of each new year.

Note: Depreciation Is for Business Only
If you don't know anything about depreciation, you're lucky. It applies only to people who run their own businesses. And since the first $10,000 worth of business equipment you buy each year—fax machines and the like—may ordinarily be "written off" all at once

> (consult your accountant, TaxCut, or a tax guide about "Section 179 Property")—you may not have to know anything about it even if you do run a small business.

So the fact that the central air conditioning unit in your home is depreciating each year is of no consequence to Managing Your Money.

Otherwise—if you own rental properties, for example—you will want to create budget categories for depreciation. Say you just bought a $275,000 building which you may depreciate over 27.5 years. That means you get to deduct $10,000 of depreciation each year against the rental income from the building. (I'm simplifying. Check with your accountant about how much depreciation you get to take the first year, how to depreciate some of the things that came with the building, and how much of the purchase price you cannot depreciate because it represents the value of the land.) To be sure TAX knows about this each year, you'd want to "Spend" that $10,000 each year ... but not with real cash, because it's just a bookkeeping entry. That's why you spend it in a noncash account.

Rental property depreciation will ordinarily be assigned to a Schedule E tax category. Farm depreciation, to Schedule F. Any other depreciation, like the depreciation on the mainframe you just bought for your consulting practice, to Schedule C.

PARTNERSHIP GAINS AND LOSSES

To record $5,300 in partnership income that's being reported to the IRS, even though the sons-of-guns never sent you a nickel, let alone $5,300, just "receive" the income in your noncash account. It will show up in your budgets and (assuming you've set up a category called Partnership Income dumping into the Schedule E tax barrel) on Schedule E in TAX.

Early each year you can "spend" your estimated tax losses or gains from each partnership, writing a noncash "check" to, or recording a noncash "receipt" from, each. Then, as estimates of your losses shrink or grow (mine generally grow), you just go back into this noncash account and edit the transactions. Your TAX estimates will always be up-to-date.

You can also do a variation on the Quick List transactions scheme described above for DEPR, only this time, enter on the memo line of the Quick List transaction the year-by-year profit and loss estimates from the offering brochure.

Note that to account for partnerships properly, you'll also need "Not a Tax Category" budget buckets for "Partnership Cash In" and "Partnership Cash Out," because sometimes you actually do get cash from a partnership, even though that's not what the IRS goes by in taxing you; and often you have to send cash to keep the partnership afloat, even though that's not what you get to deduct. (These real cash transactions are naturally recorded in your real checking account.)

TRANSFER MONEY

Once you've set up more than one Money Account, you can select Transfer Money from the MONEY menu (or Alt-T from the Check Register) to move funds between them. Say you wrote a $500 check on your checking account and mailed it to your savings account. Rather than visit Spend Money to write the check in your checking account and then Receive Money to receive it in your savings account, Transfer Money will create both transactions at once. From then on, the two transactions are linked—change the amount in one, we'll change it in the other.

You can make the transfer by check, ATM, phone, direct or even CheckFree, if you're a CheckFree user. And you can set it up to be a one-time or recurring transfer.

You can also create Quick Transfer transactions (F5, T) on the Quick List or the Alert List.

FROM CHAPTER 4: TAX

A TAX ESTIMATOR

This section of Managing Your Money estimates your tax liability based on 1991 or 1992 tax brackets and rules (your choice). It doesn't give any significant tax advice. But many users find it valuable for figuring their estimated quarterly tax liabilities (if any) and for making decisions that have tax consequences.

To see how it works, just press F1 for HELP behind the Form 1040 screen—and as you encounter each screen thereafter.

HOW SHOULD I PROCEED?

1. Select Form 1040 from the TAX menu. Form 1040 is the main TAX screen, and will automatically reflect changes you make in the others.

2. Press F7 to update the entire TAX section with the proper numbers from elsewhere in the program. Bang. In a single keystroke, if you've entered your budget in MONEY, you'll have a pretty decent estimate of your Federal income tax. Or press F8 if you'd rather update only those starred (*) on this screen.

3. Press F1 for an explanation of exactly what the numbers we pull in represent: your actual transactions so far this year, plus your budgeted income and expenses for the remainder of the year.

4. ESCape to the Menu Bar and select Tax Tables and Parameters to see whether we've loaded the right ones for your filing status (single, joint) and tax year (1991 or 1992), and to see how to change them (Merry Widow, unMarried with Children, Divorce Court). Please also read the next section: "What If the Tax Laws Change?"

   Shortcut: From the Form 1040 screen, you can reach any schedule, A-F, simply by pressing its letter. And you can move among these six schedules the same way.

5. Visit each schedule in turn and read its HELP for a further explanation of what we've done. Change anything you like. Visit the Form 1040 Worksheet, Self-Employment Tax form and the Alternative Minimum Tax screen as well. These schedules and other screens also have an update key that pulls information from MONEY. Many of them have places to fill in some information manually, too.

WHAT IF THE TAX LAWS CHANGE?

In most respects, you should be able to change right along with them. Just select Tax Tables and Parameters from the TAX file menu.

Plus Plan members will be apprised, where possible, of changes they should make to reflect changes in the tax code. It is also our intention to include updated tax data with each annual update to the program.

> Hint: Managing Your Money comes to you with the save area empty. If you load User-defined tables before you press F8 to save some, we'll dutifully replace all the real TAX numbers with blanks. No harm. Just use F7 to reload 1991 or 1992.

What-if: If you want to play some games—to enter the Brazilian tax brackets, say, in case that minor bank fraud you masterminded seems about to unravel—go right ahead. Then, if you can get a couple of Senators to ravel it back up again for you, just go to the last field on the screen (Ctrl-L), press the Spacebar, choose 1991 or 1992 (the numbers TAX never forgets), and press F7 to reload those tax tables.

The Save Area: Note, in fact, that because TAX never forgets these numbers, you can always recover them-but that changes you do want to make to the 1992 numbers, should Congress make changes, will be wiped out if you should ever reload 1992.

That's why we provide a "save area" for your changes. Just press F8 to save your "user-defined" tax parameters. Should you ever lose them, whether they're only slightly different from the numbers we provide or wildly different (because they're Brazilian), Ctrl-L to the last field, choose User-defined, and press F7 to load them back again. Your numbers will stay there until you overwrite them by using F8 to stick some different set of tax parameters into the save area.

IMPORTANT!

- There's more on the Tax Tables & Parameters screen than meets the eye (or that will fit on one screen, anyway). To change things like the threshold for medical deductions, the Social Security tax rates, and so on, press PgDn to see the next screen and PgDn again to see the third.

- If you do switch from 1991 to 1992, or vice versa, or if you do make changes to the Tax Parameters, be sure to visit each of the TAX screens that may have been affected by your change-such as the Self-Employment Tax screen-so that the change can take hold. You needn't do anything on those screens; just visit them for an instant and return to Form 1040.

ESTIMATING A FUTURE YEAR'S TAX

Form 1040 will ordinarily pull in your current year's numbers, but FILE's Money Options screens lets you pull in your budget estimates for next year instead-or even for any of the following three years if you've activated our five-year budgeting option.

Naturally, the answers we give will be iffy at best, in part because no one knows what crazy things Congress may do, and few of us can budget accurately five months into the future, let alone five years. Still, you may have occasion to play with this, for next year's taxes if not 1996's. And you're free to change the tax laws temporarily, as described above, to craft what you consider the most likely scenario.

After you've changed the year in Money Options, be sure to change it back before you try to estimate this year's taxes.

ESTIMATING BASED ON ACTUALS-TO-DATE

Ordinarily, it makes sense to estimate your tax liability based not only on the income and expenses you've recorded so far, but also on your budgeted income and outgo for the rest of the year.

But if you would like to see what your tax would be only on the income and deductions that have actually been recorded to date, there's an easy way to do it: Quit the program and then start it up again with a date in December. Lie to us. Tell us it's New Year's Eve.

Now go to TAX and update all your figures as of "today," December 31st (chortle, chortle). We will dutifully use your actual numbers for all the months that have gone by-namely, all but December (see below). Except for December, your budgeted numbers will be ignored, just as you requested.

THE DECEMBER MESSAGE

The first time you enter the program in December each year (even if you're just faking, as suggested above), we pop up a special message, with a choice: Do you want TAX to look at "actuals only" for December in each budget category or, when the budgeted numbers are higher, to use those instead? In this case, you'd choose to look at "actuals."

(Once it really is December, you'll have a chance to switch this choice as often as you like. Look on FILE's Options menu. It will either have its own listing or be included in the COPY option.)

WARNING! If you do try this, be sure to Quit without saving when you're done. Otherwise, you could accidentally find yourself wiping out Reminders or confusing some other aspect of the program.

W-4 CALCULATOR

Form W-4 — "Employee's Withholding Allowance Certificate" — is a good example of how the IRS can make simple concepts excruciatingly complex. We attempt to make the process painless.

Just select W-4 from the TAX menu and go through the questions. We'll tell you how many allowances to claim on your real W-4.

FROM CHAPTER 7: PORTFOLIO

PORTFOLIO AT A GLANCE

This is a full-fledged portfolio management system. Most of it is self-explanatory. But here, as a reference and overview, are some of the features, and how to reach them, that may not be obvious from glancing at the Menu Bar:

Buy Assets
- Buy Multiple Lots of an Asset: Alt-F5
- Cover a Short Sale: F7

Sell Assets
- Regular and Partial Sales, First/Last-Acquired Sales
- Sell Short: F7

Update Prices
- Update Prices, Yields or Special Codes
- Update the Index You Compare Yourself to
- See or Change the Meanings of Special Codes: F8
- Change an Asset's Symbol: F7
- See All Tax Lots of a Given Symbol: F2
- Sort by Name or Symbol: F9

Record Income
- Dividends, Interest, Return-of-Capital Distributions, Automatic
- Reinvestments

Split Stocks
- Stock Splits and Stock Dividends (but not dividend reinvestments—see HELP)

Portfolios
- Set Up a New Portfolio: F5
- Revise or Delete a Portfolio: F2 or F3
- Analyze Your Brokerage Commissions: F7
- Quick-Edit Commissions: F7, Action Key
- Transfer Assets Between Portfolios: F6
- Disaggregate All Aggregated Assets (careful!): F8

Display Assets
- View or Change the Particulars of an Asset: F2
- Delete an Asset: F3
- Print Unsold, Sold or Short Assets (as sorted): F4
- Rotate to Show Current Value, Name or Original Cost: F7
- Sort by Symbol, Value, Purchase Date, Gain, Maturity, Appreciation: F9
- Work with Unsold Assets, Short Assets, Sold Positions or Good-Til-Canceleds: Action Key
- Aggregate Multiple Lots of a Single Asset: F6
- Disaggregate Asset: F2

Analyze Assets
- Capital Gains Analysis: F6
- Capital Gains Advice and Sale Candidates: F6, Action Key
- Select Specific Symbols for Analysis: Action Key, F7, ActionKey
- Appreciation Display: Action Key, Action Key, select Appreciation, Action Key
- Yield Display: Action Key, Action Key, Select Yield, Action Key
- Yield Summary Analysis: Action Key twice, select Yield, Action Key, F7
- Special Codes (by Percent) Display: Action key twice, select Special Codes %, Action Key
- Performance vs. Index Display: Action Key twice, select Performance vs. Index, Action Key
- Graph by Risk, Recommendor, etc.: Action Key twice, select criteria, F9
- Aggregate Display: Action Key twice, select Aggregation, F9

View Income
- View Your Dividend and Interest Receipts for the Year

Financial Reminders
- View Automatically-Generated Reminders

Bullishness Index
- A Good Day to Buy? To Sell?

Managing the Market (if activated)
- Updates Prices Over Your Phone Line

Report Generator
- Customized Reports in Addition to the F4 Reports Everywhere Else
- Schedule D: Select in place of Matching Assets, then Action Key
- Delete Old Sold Assets: Alt-F3

ALT-KEY SHORTCUTS

To make navigation more convenient for experienced users, we've provided some shortcuts:

- Display Assets is PORTFOLIO's Grand Central Station, just as the Check Register is in MONEY. From here you can press Alt-B to Buy Assets, Alt-S to Sell the Asset you're pointing to, Alt-R to Record Income, and Alt-U to Update Prices. And when you press ESCape, you'll be back looking at the portfolio you were working with (press F8 at any time to switch to another).

- From Buy Assets, Alt-S will take you to Sell Assets, and from Sell, Alt-B will take you to Buy. This is handy if you're entering a batch of buy and sell transactions all at once.

WHAT EXACTLY IS A PORTFOLIO?

A portfolio is any collection of assets you care to lump together. Typically, each separate brokerage account will be set up as a separate portfolio. If you keep track of a stamp collection, you could say it's part of your Merrill Lynch IRA portfolio—but presumably it would make more sense to set up a portfolio all its own, called, perhaps, "My Stamps." You might group all assets in your 401K into one portfolio. Mutual funds can be grouped together in a portfolio called "My Mutual Funds," or each given its own private portfolio, or grouped by fund "family"—Fidelity, Vanguard—you're the boss.

We'd like to record all your assets here, or at least most of them—stocks, bonds, rental properties, certificates of deposit—you name it. Portfolios are simply "file folders," if you will, to help you organize these assets into logical groupings. You may designate four different kinds of portfolios: Taxable, IRA/Keogh/401K, Hypothetical or CMA.

> **Hint:** Set up CMA's even if you don't have any
>
> You can use CMA as the "type" for a taxable portfolio even if it doesn't officially have check-writing privileges. The advantage is that you'll then get a record in MONEY of all the dollar Ins and Outs of your portfolio—the dividends you've recorded, the proceeds of sales, and so on. And you'll be able to record the transfer of funds from your checking account to this portfolio in one fell swoop in MONEY. You'll have a Check Register record of all the inflows and outflows. It's a neat trick. (You wouldn't want to do this for Hypothetical or IRA/Keogh/401K accounts, however, because then we'd treat them like real, taxable CMAs.)

- Most portfolios are taxable. A regular brokerage account, for example (or your stamp collection), you'd tag taxable. This would be true even if it contained some tax-free bonds, because while the interest on those bonds may not be taxed, the gains and losses realized when you sell them are taxable.

- If it were one of those brokerage accounts that allow you to write personal checks against it—a so-called cash management account (CMA)—you'd tag it CMA. We'd treat it just like a taxable account, only we'd know to link it to your corresponding CMA account in MONEY. Managing Your Money can keep track of up to 9 such linked accounts.

- If it were an account under the shelter of some sort of retirement account, you'd tag it IRA/Keogh/401K. We'd be sure to include it in our calculation of your net worth (and also in the Retirement Planning section of ANALYZE). But we wouldn't tell TAX about any of your gains or losses or dividends, because they are not taxable.

- If it were a play-money account, or one that for any other reason you didn't want us to count in figuring your taxes or net worth, you'd tag it hypothetical. (PORTFOLIO's Report Generator will print a Schedule D for a hypothetical portfolio, in case it's a real one you're tending for someone else. Or you may exclude it (with F6 on the Report Generator screen). Your choice.

Once you've created a portfolio, you can't go back and change its type—from taxable to CMA, say, if you've begun writing checks on your brokerage account. But if you need to, there's a way (see the last page of this chapter).

THREE STEPS TO GET STARTED

To get going with PORTFOLIO, there's a three-step process: first you set up at least one portfolio; then you fill it with the assets it already contains; then you adjust its cash balance.

STEP #1: SETTING UP YOUR PORTFOLIO

In order to list your stocks and bonds (and whatever else) in PORTFO-LIO, you must first "Add a Portfolio" for us to put them in.

1. Press Alt-P from the Menu Bar, select Portfolios from the PORT FOLIOS menu and press F5.

2. Read HELP and set up a portfolio. Don't bother with the "Initial Cash Balance"—for now, leave it blank. We'll adjust it in Step #3.

CASH MANAGEMENT ACCOUNTS

Many of you have the kind of checking accounts that are tied to broker-age accounts. So do I. They're funny animals because they are part check-ing account—MONEY—and part portfolio—PORTFOLIO.

Managing Your Money allows you to set up as many as nine of these spe-cial, linked accounts—CMA1—CMA9. Tag an account "CMA1" in MONEY and we automatically create its counterpart in Portfolio (on the PORTFOLIO menu).

> NOTE:
>
> It doesn't matter which you set up first, the Money Account or the Portfolio. But it's a little easier to set it up first as a Money Account, because then there's nothing else to do. The CMA is added in PORTFOLIO automatically. If you set it up first as a Portfolio, we burp and take you to fill out the Add Money Account screen before proceeding. n

Once your CMA account is set up, buying a stock or bond automatically reduces your cash balance in PORTFOLIO—and in MONEY. Selling a stock or receiving a dividend raises both balances. Meanwhile, paying the rent in MONEY automatically decreases your balance there—and in PORTFOLIO. The balances will match perfectly in MONEY and PORTFOLIO, but not be double-counted in NET WORTH.

SUGGESTION: MONEY MARKET MUTUAL FUNDS—CMAS

Your CMA probably "invests" cash balances in a money market mutual fund. As a practical matter, rather than recording these as mutual fund shares, and having to buy and sell shares (always at $1 per share) every time the slightest thing happens, your life will be much simpler just counting those "shares" as cash, which they essentially are. Once a month, when your statement arrives, just select Receive Money from the MONEY menu and allocate the receipt to your Interest Income budget category.) Because it's a CMA, the receipt in MONEY will automatically be reflected in your PORTFOLIO balance as well.

SUGGESTION: MONEY MARKET MUTUAL FUNDS—NON-CMA ACCOUNTS

For a regular brokerage account that sweeps cash into a money market fund, you could do this: First, "buy" 1 share of an asset called "MONEY FUND" or some such for a penny. The idea is simply to get something with that name in your portfolio. Thereafter, whenever you want to record money market interest income, select Record Income, point to MONEY FUND and record receipt of this interest. Your cash balance and budget allocations will fall right into place.

STEP #2: ADDING A NEW ASSET

Now that you've added a portfolio, back up to the Menu Bar and select Buy Assets—or just point to the portfolio and press the Action Key and F5.

Here's where you build a profile of the asset—as pictured on the preceding page. One nice feature is that you won't have to do it over each time you buy the same asset. (Some things will be new—the price, commission, date and number of shares, as well as any comment you care to make—but the other characteristics you've assigned will appear automatically.) Fill in as many of the blanks as you can. You can always add or change something later. Here's how:

Symbol: Wherever possible, use the actual stock, bond, mutual fund or option symbol of your purchase. (Consult your broker, Standard & Poor's Stock Guide or the Dow Jones News/Retrieval Service.) If you're compiling a portfolio of rare stamps, or including them in some other portfolio, assign any symbols you'll find easy to remember. Just be sure not to use a stock symbol. "GI-1945" is fine for your GI Joe 1945 commemorative, but "GI" alone is Giant Industries.

> Hint: For easier updating
>
> If you get your price quotes from the newspaper, you may wish to lead off all New York Stock Exchange names with an asterisk (say), all American Stock Exchange names with a hyphen, all NASDAQ names with a period—and so on. Then, when you select Update Prices, press F9 to sort them by name. Using these little prefixes, your assets will be grouped and listed in the same order as you find them in the paper, which makes for easier updating. (See page 296 for "alphabetical order.") On the other hand, if you do follow enough different securities to make this scheme helpful, we hope you'll consider automating the process with Managing the Market instead.

Name: Use any abbreviations you want, though the ones you find in the stock pages of the newspaper may be easiest. We pay no attention, other than to include the name when we print your Schedule D.

Number of Units: If you're buying a stock or mutual fund, just enter the number of shares.

You may enter fractional shares. When you do, the "4.237" you type will seem to be rounded to "4" on most of our displays—but we'll know! The correct number of shares is in memory; there's just not room to display it. To check us (or find out just how many shares you do have), select Display Assets and press F7 once or twice.

Stand-alone money market mutual funds, used essentially as checking or savings accounts, should be set up as Checking or Savings accounts in MONEY. But if they're tied to your brokerage account and you don't write checks against them, handle them as described in the "Suggestions" on pages 349–351. Or, if you do write checks against them, handle them as the cash component of a CMA account as described there, too.

If you're buying bonds, multiply the number of bonds—and divide their purchase price—by 10. This conforms to the manner in which bond prices and yields are quoted by your broker and in the paper: as a percentage of their $1000 face value. Instead of saying you bought 1 bond for $1000, enter 10 at $100.

Say you bought "100,000 face of Connecticut-13's-of-2001 at 112," as a broker might put it. In English, that means you bought 100 State of Connecticut bonds, each with a face value (like all bonds) of $1,000. But that you paid 112 cents on the dollar for each—$1120 per bond, $112,000 in all. And that, because they're "13s," they pay 13% interest on their face value—$130 a year (though paid semi-annually)—until they are redeemed for $1000 each in the year 2001, unless called earlier.

You'd enter 1000 as the number of units, 112 as the price, and 13 as the yield.

If you're buying options (a put or call on 100 shares of stock), enter each one as "100" to conform to the way prices are quoted. Instead of saying you bought one Nike call for $350, which you did, say you bought 100 at three-and-a-half (3.5). (See page 385: "Puts and Calls.")

If you're buying futures contracts, also called commodities, the same reasoning applies. Don't say you bought one contract on 5000 bushels of beans, say you bought 5000 units at $7.56 each—the price per bushel. That way, you'll conform to the way prices are quoted. (And it will also bring home the enormity of the risk you've undertaken.)

If you're buying precious metals, enter them by the ounce, because that's how prices are quoted.

If you're buying stamps or coins or art, enter each separate item as "1" unit unless the price is so high ($80 million) that you have to pretend it was actually "100 Van Gogh" at $800,000 each.

If you choose to enter Real estate here (see page 384), and you're buying a $2,500,000 house, enter 1000 units at $2500. (Or simply list it as an asset directly in NET WORTH.) You can't enter 1 unit at $2,500,000 because there's not enough room on the screen to allow prices of more than six places (plus three decimal places) and still display all the information we want.

Mortgages you own, and any other loans due you, could be recorded as bonds, of a sort, in a portfolio here (call it "Loans I Own"), but most users will find it more sensible and effective to enter them in the Loan Records section of MONEY.

If you're buying a $10,000 certificate of deposit here (see page 327), enter it as a bond, which is essentially what it is. But because you won't be looking up its price in the paper, you needn't bother with dividing it into 10 units to conform to the way bond prices are quoted; just enter 1 unit at $10,000. This could be in a separate portfolio you set up called "My CD" or as part of a larger one called "All My CD's"—whatever way suits you best. Every month or quarter, just up its price to its new, higher value.

If you own savings bonds, see page 382.

If you're keeping track of frequent flier miles, enter them—in a "hypothetical" portfolio—as 2490 units (nautical miles) for a trip to California, symbol TWAFF (TWA Frequent Flier, as distinguished from TWA the stock), price $0.02, if you agree with me that each mile is worth about 2 cents. You'll see an aggregate number of miles for each of your airlines in the aggregate format of our portfolio analysis, and even a rough estimate of what all those miles are worth. (Their value is more than hypothetical, but might not impress your banker if included on your balance sheet.)

If you're buying anything else, use whatever system makes sense to you. I mention the frequent flier miles not because I see much point to keeping track of them this way (it might be easier to use a noncash account in MONEY) or much point to keeping track of them at all (what's wrong with the monthly statements the airlines all send?), but to suggest that there's more you can organize here than stocks and bonds.

Purchase Date: Use the "trade date" (the day you made the transaction) not the "settlement date" (the day your payment is due). Remember, if it's June 5, 1992 and you want to record a trade you made yesterday, you need type just the number 4. When you leave the field, we make it: 6/4/1992.

Price Per Unit: Enter the price per unit (share, ounce, bushel, etc.) as described under "Number of Units" above.

> NOTE:
>
> Remember! With bonds, you didn't buy 1 bond for $995 (even though you did), you bought "10 for $99.50". With options, you didn't buy 1 GM 40 call for $360 (even though you did), you bought "100 for $3.60".

Commission: If you don't know it exactly, take a guess or leave it blank until the confirmation slip arrives. (Note our shortcut for that: F7, Action Key on the Portfolio screen.) If no commission is involved, just leave this blank.

Yield: Tell us how much cash your asset pays per unit each year. If it pays no dividend or interest (or rent), enter zero or just leave this blank.

For a stock that paid a 30-cent-a-share quarterly dividend, you'd enter "1.20" (because 30 cents a share per quarter works out to $1.20 a share per year).

For a 12.5% bond, you'd enter "12.5" (because you'll be getting $125 in interest per bond each year, but we entered each bond as 10 to conform to the way bond prices are quoted).

For the $600 monthly rent from an $80,000 rental property you had recorded as "1000 units at $80 each," you'd enter "7.20," because that is the yield per unit per year ($600 x 12 months = $7,200 a year for the whole property, or $7.20 a year for each of the 1,000 units into which you've divided it). If you entered that property as 1 unit at $80,000, then the annual yield per unit would be "$7,200."

For mutual fund shares, your yield estimate—of necessity less precise than for a stock or bond—would include just the dividends and interest, if any, you expect the fund to pay out, per share, during the year.

Tax Status: Tell us whether income from the asset is fully Taxable (as is most often the case); Free of Any Tax (tax-free municipal bonds issued by an entity within your state); subject to Federal Tax Only (U.S. Treasury securities, like Treasury bonds and Savings Bonds, are not subject to local income tax); or subject to State Tax Only (tax-free municipal bonds issued by a state other than your own will be subject to your local income tax).

You can leave this field blank if you're not sure, or if the asset is owned in a hypothetical or IRA/Keogh/401K portfolio where the tax status doesn't matter anyway. But it only takes a second to tag GM dividends as "Taxable"—which you should do even if this particular lot of GM shares is in a hypothetical or IRA/Keogh/401K type portfolio. After all, the next 50 shares of GM you buy might be in your regular brokerage account. You may as well get GM set up in Managing Your Money properly from the start.

Type: Choose one. (Use the Spacebar to jump into the choice box; then arrow up and down to see them all. Use Enter to choose.) For a kind of asset we haven't thought of, use "Other" or "Special Coded" (I'll explain below). For a mutual fund, see page 373. For a deferred annuity, use our catchall "Savings Bond/SPDA" (Single Premium Deferred Annuity).

Accrued Interest: You won't see this field unless and until you tell us that this asset is a bond. But if it is, the confirm your broker sends may well include a charge for accrued interest. If so, just enter it here (and see page 381).

CUSIP: Every publicly traded security has a CUSIP number (Committee on Uniform Securities Identification Procedures)—even those without a regular symbol. No need to enter this if you don't want to, but especially for some of your more obscure holdings it might come in handy one day. Look for the CUSIP number on your broker's confirmation slip.

Maturity Date: Leave this blank for a stock; but if it's a bond or a certificate of deposit, it "comes due" as of some date. (For a bond that can be called early, you may prefer to use the call date.) Option expiration dates can be entered here, but you needn't bother: our Financial Reminder screen determines the expiration date from the symbol.

We use the maturity date two places: Financial Reminders, to remind you the asset is maturing, and Display Assets, where F9 offers to sort in order of maturity date. If you accept this offer, all the assets with no date specified (like stocks) will come first, but never fear: at the end of the list will be your bonds and CD's, in order of their maturity dates.

Price Objective: If you enter one, we'll remind you when you reach it.

Mental Stop Loss: If you enter one, we'll remind you when you reach it. Of course, you can also enter real stop loss orders with your broker. As you know, these assure that even if you're off in Africa and not paying attention, you will be "stopped out" of your stock, now $44 a share, if, say, it should ever drop to $39.75. That way you know that the most you can lose is $4.25 a share, even if you should come back to find the stock down to $11.

The two problems with this are, first, that if the stock should encounter some major bad news, closing at $40.25 a share one night but opening the next day at $23, your broker will dutifully sell your shares at $23. He's obligated simply to sell as soon as they dip to or below the stop-loss price you specified. So you're not entirely protected. Second, what often happens is that you do indeed get stopped out at $39.50—only to see the stock bounce back to $44 and beyond. This is called getting whipsawed. The floor of the exchange is ankle high in whipsawdust.

Risk: Short term Treasury obligations entail virtually no risk. But 30-year Treasury bonds do entail risk, because if interest rates should rocket, the price of long-term bonds (even safe ones) will plunge. All stocks entail some risk, but some entail a lot. You may certainly leave this blank, but by categorizing your assets by risk, you allow us to show you the risk distribution of your portfolio(s).

Beta: This is a measure of a stock's or portfolio's volatility relative to the market as a whole. A stock that moves with the market has a beta of 1. A ponderous blue chip that goes up or down only half as fast has a beta of one half—.5. A stock that zooms and plunges at every turn may have a beta of 3 or 4. If you care about betas—I don't—find a place to look them up and fill them in. Otherwise, settle for your own risk classification (above), which amounts to much the same thing.

Or use this box to enter Value Line rankings, if you're a Value Line fan. The heading will still say "Beta," but you and I will know. Value Line ranks stocks from 1 to 5 for timeliness. If you enter those rankings here, you will be able easily to determine, for example, the proportion of your assets ranked 1 or 2 for timeliness.

Hint: F9 to back up

If you're like me, you will use special codes a lot, both in PORTFO-LIO and in the Card File. For convenience, you'll find that F9 not only takes you into your list of special codes, but back out as well. The screen shows ESCape as the key to back up, as always; but it's even easier to tap in and out with F9.

Liquidity: Fully liquid assets are those that are readily converted to cash. Illiquid assets (a better term might be frozen) include non-marketable partnership interests, stock in a family business, "letter stock"—that sort of thing. Semi-liquid assets are those you can sell, but not right away or all at once, like 75,000 shares of some stock that normally trades just 200 shares a day, a CD that doesn't mature for another six months, a Renoir, or a parcel of land that could take a year to unload. Again, you may leave this blank; but by taking a moment to fill it in, you can then always see your assets broken out by liquidity.

Industry Group: Choose one. If you don't find anything that fits, choose "Other" or assign a Special Code (see below).

RECOMMENDOR: LIKEWISE.

Special Codes: Here's one of the things that makes Managing Your Money so flexible. We've provided 52 tags for you to assign any way you like—26 upper-case letters and 26 lower-case. Press F9 here to assign meanings to these letters—and then to refresh your memory whenever you forget. F6 toggles between the upper- and lower-case codes.

For example, you could code stock tips from three newsletters A, B, and C, so you can quickly separate and compare the performance of each. If you've set up a portfolio for your stamp collection, you could have special codes for "Commemoratives," "Plate Blocks," and "First Day Covers." You are only limited by your imagination.

Hint: An extra 40 codes

Only lower- and upper-case letter codes are included in the special codes display. But for retrieval purposes—to pull out just those assets you've tagged with a question mark, say—you can add 40 more codes by using all the numbers and symbols on the keyboard. See how we've assigned 1, 2, 3 and the question mark? Wherever we give you a chance to add, change or display special codes, we also let you see the crib sheet that will remind you what they mean. While looking at the crib sheet, you may add new codes or change the meaning of existing ones.

Hint: Multiple Lots

You've entered your first purchase of AT&T, and now you want to enter the next eight lots you've purchased. Enter the Symbol, Name and Type of Asset on the Buy Assets screen, then press Alt-F5. You can enter a whole list of purchases of that asset in short order.

To see how your assets break down according to these various criteria, select Analyze Assets, mark the portfolio(s) you want to analyze, and press the Action Key twice, the letter "S" for the special codes display, and the Action Key again.

The easiest way to keep your special codes up-to-date is the Update Prices screen. The right-hand column on the Price Update screen shows all the codes you've assigned. Scroll down through your various assets, adding, changing and blanking out codes as you go.

Index: Enter here the current level of the Dow Jones or the Standard & Poor's 500 or any other index you care to compare yourself against. (Just be sure to be consistent and use the same index for all your assets.)

If you leave this box blank, we'll assume your asset performed no better or worse than the index. Otherwise, we'll be able to give you an analysis that says, in effect, "Since you bought these 50 shares they've climbed 23.1%—versus just 17% for the Dow." And another that compares the performance of your entire portfolio against the Dow (Analyze Assets, mark the portfolio(s), Action Key twice, "P," Action Key again).

Lot Comment: What you enter here will apply to the current tax lot only (that is, not all your GM shares, just these 50). Often, you won't have anything to enter here when you first buy shares. (If I place a "market order," I enter the purchase right away and use this space to record the time I placed the order and the oral confirmation number the broker gives me, just in case for some reason the order somehow were not executed. Then, when the written confirm comes, I come back and enter the commission, edit the actual price at which the trade was done, and delete this little comment). Where the Lot Comment may be more helpful is in the months and years to come. For example, if the shares rise in value and you decide to give some of them to charity (be sure to wait at least a year and a day), you might enter a comment like this: "Owned 100 shares in this tax lot; gave 30 to Red Cross on 12/4/1992." You needn't enter any comment— but can go on at monumental length with F2 (from anywhere on the screen) if you do.

Symbol Comment: Record anything that applies to all your lots of this asset—all your GM. Perhaps you'd like to keep a running record of stock splits or your broker's excuses. You might put the latest earnings estimate, or your rationale for buying it in the first place, or the name it used to go by before it merged, or the number of shares into which it's convertible (if it's a convertible bond). Visit this field and press F2 to expand it.

When you've filled in everything you'd like to keep track of, press the Action Key to add this asset to your portfolio.

STEP #3: ADJUST YOUR CASH BALANCE

When you're all finished filling a portfolio with the assets it contains, reselect Portfolio. The cash balance we show will be negative to the tune of the cost of all the things you just "bought." (If you actually had just bought them, this is how much you'd have had to dug into your pocket to pay for them; but you already owned them, so the number we show will be wrong.) Just press F2, Tab down to "Cash Balance," and type the correct current net cash balance (or margin debt) over the one we show so that our records agree with your broker's. While you're there, note that you have an expandable (F2) Memo field for comments about this port-folio.

And what is the correct cash balance? If your broker starts to confuse you with "the credit in type 1 and the debit in type 2 and the phantom short balance," interrupt politely and ask, "Cut to the chase, Herb. If I closed my account today and transferred all the securities and short positions elsewhere, how much cash would I get—or have to send you to pay off my margin debt?" That's the number that matters. Chances are, if your account is at all complicated by short sales or not-yet-settled transactions, let alone futures contracts, your broker won't know. For all his or her fancy computer screens, he'll have to call someone in the back office who can actually make heads or tails of this. But it should be possible to figure out who owes whom without actually having to close out your account and transfer the securities to see.

From now on, whenever you buy things, we'll automatically lower your cash balance by the amount of the purchase; whenever you sell, we'll automatically dump the net proceeds into your cash balance.

- When your cash balance is positive, it's just that: a cash balance. When it's negative, because you owe the broker money, that's called a margin balance. Buying stock "on margin" is like buying a TV "on time" (well, sort of). You're putting up only part of the money now and borrowing the rest.

  If you actually do send your broker a check one day, or every time you make a purchase, add this cash influx to your cash balance on the Portfolios screen (point to the portfolio, press F2 and type over the balance). Likewise, subtract an amount equal to any cash withdrawals you make.

- Adding to and subtracting from your cash balance is easy if it's all round numbers. Anyone knows that $5,000 plus $2,500 equals $7,500. But for real world situations, you'll find Ctrl-N handy. Just position the cursor on the portfolio cash balance in question; press Ctrl-N to summon the calculator and then F6 to pull the current cash balance down into it. Now just add or subtract the amount of your deposit or withdrawal, press Enter twice, and you're done. Try it!

- If you'd like an "audit trail" of these additions and subtractions—a written record of when you added or withdrew cash and where that cash came from or went—use F2. That is, while still on the Portfolios screen, with this portfolio highlighted, press F2 and jot down your entry in the memo area—"March 3, 1992: withdrew $5,000." Pressing F2 again will expand that little area into a huge blank page, on which you can set up a little table and watch it grow over the years as you add notations.

  (Of course, if you set this up as a CMA-type portfolio, its checking account side in MONEY will reflect all the inflows and outflows automatically. The only thing is that, because CMA's are all considered by Managing Your Money to be real and taxable, you wouldn't want to use one for a hypothetical or tax-deferred portfolio.)

The Portfolio memo area is also a good place to keep running notes on dealings with your broker generally. What instructions have you given him or her? What assurances has he or she given you? Who's the branch manager?

- If this is your butterfly collection and not your Paine Webber account, it presumably has no cash balance, positive or negative. Just blank out the number we show and—unless you keep cash in your lepidoptery kit or have burdened your collection with a butterfly-now-pay-later loan—just reset it to zero whenever you make a purchase or sale.

MANAGEMENT FEES

If your monthly brokerage statement shows some fees apart from those tied to a specific purchase or sale—an IRA "management fee," for example—do two things. First, subtract this charge from your cash balance, just as your broker did. But then select Spend Money and, in any account, "spend" zero dollars, but press F9 and allocate the amount of the management fee to a budget category like, "Investment Fees," which gets dumped in the Schedule A "Investment Man. Fees" tax barrel. The payee for this odd transaction should be whomever you paid the management fee.

- If you have told us to warn you if a transaction is over or under allocated (Money Options under Optional Features on the FILE menu), we'll warn you when you enter this transaction. Just tell us that yes, you really did intend the allocation to exceed the transaction amount.

  Because you spend zero dollars, we don't lower your bank balance. But because you allocate the amount of the fee to the proper budget category, it will show up on Schedule A of TAX and in MONEY Report Generator reports of your deductible expenses. (Unfortunately, investment management fees are counted as "miscellaneous deductions," which currently are deductible only to the extent they exceed 2% of your adjusted gross income.)

YOUR FINANCIAL REMINDERS

Select Financial Reminders and we remind you:

- when an asset has met or exceeded the price objective (if any) you set when you recorded its purchase;

- when an asset has fallen to or beneath the mental stop loss level you set;

- when your holding is about to go long-term (not that it much matters as of this writing, because the tax code no longer gives much benefit to long-term capital gains);

- when options are nearing expiration;

- when bonds or CD's set up as bonds are nearing maturity.

Be sure to select Optional Features on the FILE menu, and then Portfolio Options, to match our work habits to your requirements! Don't miss "F6 - Alter Financial Reminder Criteria" on that screen. (And don't forget to record your changes with the Action Key, and then to save your work before you leave the program— preferably as soon as you get back to the Menu Bar, with Ctrl-S.)

RECORDING DIVIDENDS AND INTEREST

To record a distribution from an asset:

1. Select Record Income from the PORTFOLIO menu.

2. Point to the asset that's thrown off the income. If you have this asset in more than one portfolio, be sure to choose the right one. But within a single portfolio, it doesn't matter which one you point to! Any tax lot will do.

3. Press the Action Key.

4. On the window that pops up, tell us the date you received this income (it must be this year; see page 373 for a note on recording prior years' dividends), the amount, and then the "Status."

   - I received cash means GM sent a check that you want us to put in one of your MONEY accounts.

   - Broker held for me means the check went to your broker, and we should add to your portfolio cash balance accordingly. This option will not appear if you're recording a dividend in a CMA portfolio. That's because dividends your broker receives for you in a CMA are just like getting cash and having it instantly direct-deposited to the checking account side of the CMA—so that's just what we do. Choose "I received cash" as the status for all CMA income you receive.

- Automatic Reinvestment means there was never any check at all Instead, your dividend was used to buy new shares.

5. When you've filled in these three fields, press the action key. We need to ask more questions.

6. On the Record Dividends and Interest screen that appears next, you can record receipt of:

   - Dividends

   - Return of Capital distributions (also known as liquidating dividends—see HELP)

   - Mutual fund capital gains distributions

   - Regular Interest

   - Tax-free interest (from municipal bonds)

   - AMT interest (subject to the alternative minimum tax calculation but not regular income tax)

   - Reinvested dividends and distributions

Usually this is all quite straightforward, but there are some fine points.

Ordinarily, stocks will simply throw off ordinary dividends, bonds will throw off interest, and mutual funds will throw off some combination of things you'll be advised of by the mutual fund. Change anything we may have guessed wrong.

7. After filling in the appropriate fields, press the Action Key. If this is a hypothetical or IRA/Keogh/401K portfolio, that's all there is to it. You're done, ready to record another dividend or interest payment or else to go on about your business.

   But if it's income in a real, taxable portfolio (which includes all CMA portfolios), there's one more step. When you press the Action Key, you will get yet one more window. Just what you can tell us on this window depends on the kind of portfolio the asset is in (regular or CMA) and the kind of dividend this is (cash, broker-held-for-me or reinvested).

- At the top of the screen, you'll see which MONEY account is currently active and also the current balance in that account.

  Below that, you'll see the kind of distribution you're getting ready to execute—tax-free, "Schedule B" (meaning that some or all the income should be reported on Schedule B of your tax return) or "Schedule D" (meaning that the capital gains portion will show up on Schedule D).

  Don't be concerned if the Amount shown on this screen is $0.00. If this is income "Broker Held for Me," or that was "Automatically Reinvested," then there's zero cash to be deposited in one of your MONEY accounts—which explains the zero amount. But we bring you here anyway so you can allocate the income to budget categories, for tax purposes. (There's no cash to deposit, but there may be income to keep track of and report to the IRS.)

  But maybe you did receive cash. If you received it in a non-CMA account, F8 will appear. Press it to select the MONEY account into which you deposited the dividend check. (If it's a CMA portfolio, F8 won't appear; we'll assume the cash went straight to the MONEY side of the CMA, as in fact it did.)

- We also allow you to select the proper budget allocation for this income. Just speed scroll to the proper Income category—DIVIDENDS, most likely, or BOND INTEREST or CAPITAL GAINS DISTRIBUTION.

  If you haven't set up the one you want, press F9 and then F5 to add one. (Note that the tax treatment of your dividend and taxable-interest categories will be pretty obvious. They both should be linked with "Schedule B" tax categories. But if you set up a budget category for capital gains distributions, you won't find a corresponding Schedule D tax category with which to link them. That's OK; just leave it unlinked as "Not a Tax Catgeory," because PORTFOLIO and TAX automatically know how to treat them. The budget category(ies) you set up for interest that's free of federal tax should be tagged—naturally—"Not a Tax Category.")

Hint: Partially Taxed Interest

Interest from U.S. Treasury securities is subject to Federal but not local income tax, and income from tax-free municipals may be subject to local income tax if they're issued outside the state you live in. While we do not make this distinction on the Record Dividend screen directly, you may set up as many different Income budget categories as you like, dumping each kind of interest into its appropriate category, and thus keep track of each separate type of taxable income.

If the distribution you're recording combined two or more types of income—part ordinary dividend and part capital gains distribution, say—press F9 to split the amount.

When you're all set, press the Action Key. Now your part of the job is done. Here's what we do:

- If cash was involved, we deposit it in the proper MONEY account. There, you can see (and edit) it as you would any other transaction. (Changes you make in MONEY will not affect PORTFOLIO's View Income screen, however.)

- Your budget allocations will be dumped into the categories you selected.

- A record of the dividend will be added to View Income (on PORTFOLIO's pulldown menu).

- With automatic reinvestments, we create a new lot for your new shares, which we offer to aggregate with the old ones. If you accept (yes! say yes!), you can later disaggregate and reaggregate them as often as you like (see the next page).

- Amounts you specify as capital gains distributions will figure into PORTFOLIO's capital gains analysis (select Analyze Assets) and also be reflected on Schedule D in TAX.

- Amounts you specify as return of capital distributions will lower the purchase price of your shares. In other words, if you had 100 shares of a stock for which you paid $20 a share, and now record a $500 return of capital distribution, we will do what the IRS requires. Namely, we won't report that $500 as taxable income, but we will adjust the "basis" of your shares from the $2,000 you paid in all to the $1,500 they cost you after getting $500 of your capital back. Thus the purchase price shown in Managing Your Money would now be $15 a share.

VIEWING YOUR DIVIDENDS AND INTEREST

Select View Income from the PORTFOLIO menu and you'll see each distribution you've recorded—and be able to sort them nine different ways (Ctrl-L, F9). Press F4 to order up a report.

This screen breaks out the portion of each distribution, if any, you tagged "capital gains distribution" and lumps into the "Schedule B amount" column the portions you tagged ordinary dividends and taxable interest (we call this the Schedule B column, because Schedule B is where you report dividends and interest to the IRS.)

- Note that income is listed on this screen for all portfolios, including hypothetical and IRA/Keogh/401K. But don't worry: only income attributable to Taxable and CMA portfolios will have their tax data passed through to TAX.

- If you paid accrued interest when you bought a bond, you'll find that amount listed here, as negative income, and an ACC to its right (for ACCrued interest). And if you received accrued interest when you sold a bond, you'd see that income here with an ACC to its right.

- Where cash was involved, you'll also be able to see a record of your receipt in the Money Account into which you deposited it.

AGGREGATION AND DISAGGREGATION

Say you own 350 shares of GM in one of your portfolios, but that you purchased them in 9 separate lots over the years, 25 or 50 shares at a time. Or say you purchased 250 shares initially and earned the additional 100 shares over a period of seven years by reinvesting your dividends every quarter—28 additional little purchases in all. Either way, that's a lot of separate tax lots of GM to scroll through when you're trying to eyeball your portfolio. (A tax lot is any separate purchase of shares.)

Any time you want, you can lump separate lots of the same security into a single holding (it's so much easier to view your portfolio that way! ... or disaggregate it back into its individual lots (because each has its own separate performance and tax consequences).

AN ALTERNATIVE

We already offer an Aggregate display that aggregates separate tax lots of the same security. Select Analyze Assets, mark one or more portfolios, press the Action Key twice, choose Aggregate and press the Action Key again to see it. So if you haven't aggregated your tax lots, here's a quick way to see them lumped together without having to aggregate them manually.

The other reason we offer this Aggregate display: to allow you to lump together assets in multiple portfolios. Sure, you have 350 shares of GM in this one portfolio. But you have 188 in your young son's portfolio, 12 in your infant daughter's portfolio and 690 in the trust you administer for your slightly potty Aunt. The Aggregate display allows you to view two or more of these portfolios as if they were one.

To aggregate a multi-lot holding, just highlight any one of the lots on the Display Assets screen and press F6. On the next screen, choose which tax lots to lump together (usually all—F8) and press the Action Key.

To disaggregate shares you've aggregated, point to the aggregate, press F2 to view the aggregated lots, F8 and the Action Key.

You'll see when you go to sell part or all of an aggregate holding that we first ask you to disaggregate it, and tell you how. It takes just three keystrokes: F2, F8, Action Key.

TWO WAYS OF VIEWING PERFORMANCE

When you point to an aggregate holding on the Display Assets screen and press F2, we show you its individual components and give you an opportunity to disaggregate them. But we also display a measure of performance. Two measures, really—you flip between them with F7:

1. Total Cost. This is the total you've paid for all the tax lots in this aggregate—including any cash dividends you reinvested—compared with what they're worth now. If your total investment in GM was $10,000 and it's now worth $15,000, we'd show both numbers and tell you that your investment has appreciated by 50%. Of course, as we note on the screen, this is simple appreciation. It's not a very useful number, because it shows how much your investment appreciated, but takes no account of the amount of time it took. (If it took just a year, it's awesome. If it took 20, it's awful.) That's because each separate lot in this lump was held a different length of time. To see their annualized appreciation, just disaggregate them temporarily and look at the right-hand column of the screen that appears next.

2. Original Cost. Our second way of displaying your performance on this Aggregate/Disaggregate screen makes sense for dividend reinvestments only. (That makes it particularly useful for measuring the total return on Mutual Funds if you enter all the dividends and aggregate them with the original purchase.) It looks at just the cost of the original shares you bought—the 250 shares of GM in the example above—and compares that to what your GM stake is worth now (all 350 shares, including the reinvestments). For this calculation we are able to show annualized appreciation.

The complication comes if you are both purchasing new shares of GM and reinvesting your dividends. Read on.

DIVIDEND REINVESTMENTS

The aggregating we do for you when you record a dividend reinvestment (mutual fund or otherwise) unclutters your portfolio so you can see the big picture: six major holdings, say. (Disaggregated, we might eventually show dozens of separate little tax lots.) And, as just described, it gives you a way of viewing the annualized performance of the original purchase— the duck, as I like to think of it, that gave birth to all those little dividend reinvestment ducklings.

Record a dividend reinvestment as you would any other dividend, with Record Income, and answer YES when we ask if you'd like us to aggregate these new shares with the duck that produced them. We will put the new duckling under its mother's wing. You had 250 shares; now you have 253.457 (or whatever). Next quarter, just point to this aggregate when you Record Income and record the new dividend reinvestment. Now you have 257.002 shares. And so on.

But—here's that complication I referred to—what if you purchased 250 GM, recorded a few dividend reinvestments, purchased 100 more shares—and 50 more two weeks later, bringing you up to a total of 400 you've purchased, plus the extras you've gotten through dividend reinvestments, and now you get a quarterly dividend that's reinvested?

Even though you made three separate purchases of stock (plus the reinvestments), GM is not so crazy as to think of you as three separate shareholders owning three separate lots. Its computer knows you own 403.612 shares (say) and that at $1 a share dividend you're owed $403.61, but that you reinvest your dividends. So it buys you $403.61 worth of stock and sends you or your broker a notice that you have purchased 9.214 more shares. To which of your three big blocks of GM do you aggregate these shares?

From the point of view simply of uncluttering things, it wouldn't matter. You can simply aggregate all your GM in this portfolio into one big lump. Go ahead. That's fine.

But if you really want to keep track of the annualized appreciation of each separate block of GM—or some mutual fund—you've purchased, you have to do this:

1. Treat each separate block you've purchased as a separate duck. There's the initial 250 share block you bought (plus the ducklings it's accrued through dividend reinvestment); there's the 100-share block plus its ducklings—and so on.

2. When a statement arrives telling you GM or your mutual fund credited you with $403.61 in new shares, which added 9.214 shares to your total, use Ctrl-N to divvy that up proportionally over the ducks. Don't record the dividend all at once; record three separate dividends. Point to each of your three basic blocks of this stock or fund in turn and, for each, record a dividend reinvestment equal to its proportionate share of those 9.214 new shares. (If you own 400 shares total, the 250-share block would be entitled to 62.5% of the dividend. The 100-share block would get 25% of it. And so on.)

The advantage is that we will be able to show you just how each separate duck has appreciated over the years. The disadvantage is that it's more work for you and leads, eventually—if you keep buying new blocks of the stock or mutual fund—to the on-screen clutter we were trying to avoid.

How you handle this is a matter of personal preference. If you have just one block of GM or Magellan Fund whose dividends you reinvest, our automatic aggregation of the reinvested dividends works beautifully. If you have two or three blocks you've purchased over the years, you'll have to split the dividends proportionally, but it's not much work and may well be worth the effort. But if you've purchased several blocks of GM or Magellan, and if you plan to purchase more, I'd suggest you not bother with this. Personally, I would just aggregate them all into one holding so it's easy to see the forest.

Doing so renders our "Original Cost" annualized appreciation analysis meaningless. You won't be able to see how each individual duck has performed. But that doesn't mean you have no way to evaluate your stock or fund's performance. Quite the contrary: with a mutual fund, just look in the mutual fund surveys Barron's, Money, Fortune and many others publish. And with a stock, pressing F2 to view the aggregate displays the precise annualized appreciation of each duck and duckling. That appreciation won't include dividends; but if you see that one of your lots of GM has grown at a 14.3% annualized rate, and you know more or less what its dividend rate has been, you can get a pretty good feel for how that lot of GM shares has done for you.*

And remember: it's less important to spend hours determining the precise rate of gain a stock or fund has achieved in the past than to figure out which ones to hold for the future.

DISAGGREGATE PORTFOLIOS (CAREFUL!)

This can be handy if you use PORTFOLIO extensively and have many aggregated assets. With one keystroke you can disaggregate everything so

---

* You could do this with a fund, too, but it's less meaningful, becaus a fund tends to distribute most or all its gains. An outstanding fund may show little or no price appreciation over the years, because it periodically lops off the gains it's racked up and mails them to its shareholders. So simple price appreciation, exclusive of dividends, means a lot more in looking at stocks than mutual funds.

you can look at all your assets as separate lots without going to each in turn and disaggregating it. Before you do it, it's important to save your work (Ctrl-S from the Menu Bar). Then press F8 from the Portfolio Accounts screen. Don't save while your lots are disaggregated unless you want to make it permanent. When you're through looking at your disaggregated lots, choose Revert from the FILE menu. (Don't forget to Revert or you'll have to reaggregate everything by hand!)

Say you wanted to look at the tax lots with the greatest Simple Appreciation— because you were considering a charitable gift of stock and you wanted the one that would produce the maximum savings on capital gains tax. Disaggregate everything, sort by simple appreciation, pick the two or three lots you'd consider giving (it's your 20th college reunion, after all), and then Revert and go on about your business.

MUTUAL FUNDS

Mutual funds are entered in PORTFOLIO, either as part of another portfolio or in a portfolio all their own. (There's no harm in having just one asset in a portfolio.)

You enter a mutual fund as you would any other asset. Give it a symbol and then fill out our little questionnaire (for help, see page 209: "Adding a New Asset").

Under type of asset, you can say "Common Stock," if that's what the fund invests in, or "Bond," if that's what the fund invests in, or "Metals/ Collectibles," if it's one of those hyperinflation-is-around-the-corner gold funds. You can, in addition, give it a special code to indicate it's a mutual fund. Or, if you insist, you can simply tag it "Mutual Fund." We've added that asset type because so many people did insist, but to me it makes only marginal sense. To me, an aggressive common stock mutual fund is not even remotely the same type of asset as a government bond fund. But you paid a lot of money for this program, so suit yourself.

A mutual fund's yield is ordinarily less certain than that of a stock, but you can certainly make an estimate of the dividends and interest you expect the fund to pay out, per share, during the year. (Capital gains distributions would not normally be thought of as "Yield," but again, suit yourself.)

When you do get a distribution from the fund, whether paid in cash or reinvested, there should be a statement showing how much of it represents income, how much long-term capital gain, and how many new shares, if any, were purchased. Select Record Income from the PORT-FOLIO menu, highlight the fund (see the discussion above about which lot of shares to highlight, if you have more than one) and then press the Action Key to enter the transaction. We'll record the capital gains distribution, if any; "purchase" the new shares (if the dividend was automatically reinvested); aggregate those new shares to your original purchase (the duck from which all these little ducklings come); and dump the taxable dividend portion into your Dividends budget bucket.

ENTERING PRIOR YEARS— DIVIDEND REINVESTMENTS

Once you begin using Managing Your Money, we handle mutual fund reinvestments easily, as described above. But what if you own some mutual fund you originally purchased in 1967 that, by now, has accumulated no fewer than 276 quarterly dividend reinvestments? How do you enter that in Managing Your Money?

You have two choices:

1. Simply enter all the shares in a lump—all 72.817 your mutual fund statement says you now own. As the purchase date, enter the date of purchase of the original shares or today's date or some date in between—especially while there's no distinction for tax purposes between long- and short-term gains, it doesn't much matter.

   (But the cost you enter does matter. To avoid cheating yourself at tax time when you eventually sell, the cost you record should include the total of all those dividends you reinvested. They represented actual cash on which you paid tax over the years, even though you used the cash to buy more shares; don't accidentally pay tax on those dividends again when you sell! They are not a capital gain; they are part of your cost.)

   If the shares are in an IRA, Keogh or 401K account, then none of this matters, because taxes are not an issue.

2. Enter each lot of shares as the separate purchase it was. First enter the 25 original shares you bought, then the 2.191 shares purchased with your first dividend reinvestment, then the 1.844 shares you

purchased with your next, and so on. Treat each one as a separate purchase. When you're done, to avoid having to look at all of them separately, point to the first one—the original duck—on the Display Assets screen and press F6, F8 and the Action Key to aggregate all the others to it. (To be sure the first one really shows up first, and thus becomes the duck, first press F9 on the Display Assets screen to sort them by Purchase Date.)

Note that this can only be done by recording purchases, not by using the Record Income screen. Managing Your Money allows you to enter purchases from prior years, but not dividends.

SHORTCUT: SELLING MULTIPLE LOTS

We've given you some easy ways to sell the shares you want without having to target each of 30 separate little tax lots separately. (Select Sell Assets, point to any one of the lots—it doesn't matter which—and press the Action Key to see your choices. If these are tax lots you've aggregated, you'll first have to press F2 and take a moment to disaggregate them.)

It's also easy to get an average of all your purchase prices. Just aggregate them temporarily on the Display Assets screen and look at the "Initial Price" column of the Current Value display. Or use the Aggregate Display in Analyze Assets (Action Key twice, Aggregate, Action Key) and, on the way to this display, tell us to include in our analysis only those assets purchased before or after a certain date. That's helpful if you are indeed trying to average your short- and long-term holdings separately.

WHEN YOU SELL: WHICH MUTUAL FUND SHARES ARE WHICH

Basically, you have four choices for tax purposes when you sell some, but not all, your shares in a mutual fund. (If you sell all of them, you just separate those that are short-term from those that are long-term, if tax law changes to treat them differently, and report the total gain or loss on each group.)

1. You can identify specific lots to sell by their date of purchase when you give instructions for the sale. (Do this in writing and/or be sure the dates show up on your confirmation slips.)

2. You can assume, as the IRS will, that the shares you bought longest ago are the ones you're selling now. Report each lot as a separate purchase-and-sale.

3. You can add up the cost of all the lots bought over the years, divide that by the total number of shares you hold, and consider that average the per-share cost of all the shares. If 200 of your shares have gone long-term and 100 not, the 250 you sell (say) are deemed to be the ones you've held the longest. Thus the gain or loss on 200 would be long-term and on 50, short-term.

4. You can divide all the shares into two groups, long- and short-term. Average the cost of each group and instruct the fund from which group the shares to be sold should be taken. (Again, be sure the dates show up on your confirmation slips.)

At this writing, the long-term holding period is a year and a day, but—for now—there is little practical difference between the tax treatment of long- and short-term capital gains. Even so, you'll want to decide whether to sell the shares in which you have the biggest or smallest profit or loss, so the selling features we offer should be helpful. And should long-term gains one day again receive favored treatment, you'll want to be able to show just which tax lots you've sold and which remain in your portfolio.

WHAT DISTRIBUTIONS DO TO FUND PRICES—AND TAXES

When you buy mutual fund shares and then sell them, your profit or loss is ordinarily treated like any other long- or short-term gain or loss.

On top of that, if the fund makes a distribution while you hold the shares, whether you take that distribution in cash or reinvest it in more shares, you're liable for your share of the ordinary income and long-term capital gains that distribution represents—even if you've only held the shares a few days. Never mind that it was an entire year's worth (say) of capital gains and dividend income that was distributed.

It may seem great to get a $5 a share distribution, but bear in mind that the price of the mutual fund shares will automatically fall by the same $5. It had an asset value of $60 a share; it distributed $5; now it has an asset value of $55 a share. So not only would that $5 distribution represent no windfall to you (what you got from the distribution you lost in the value of the shares), you'd have a tax bill, to boot.

None of this matters for fund shares sheltered in an IRA, Keogh or 401K. But for a taxable account, it's wisest to buy shares that do not have large undistributed gains. (When in doubt, call the fund to find out.)

Of course, the tax bomb that can fall on your head after just a couple days— ownership is neutralized if the shares are sold soon thereafter. You paid $60; got (and had to pay tax on) $5 in long-term capital gain distributions; but now could sell the shares for $55 and a $5 short-term loss.

Indeed, that can be so attractive that the IRS put a stop to it. People were purposely buying right before a big distribution, part of which would be lightly taxed as a long-term capital gain, in order to sell a day or two later to take a loss all of which would be deductible against short-term gains and up to $3,000 in ordinary income. So the IRS ruled that short-term losses on mutual fund shares must be treated as long-term up to the amount of the long-term capital gain distribution received. Of course, until some preference for long-term gains is reinstated, it makes no difference. But this is a manual for all seasons.

Two final notes:

1. Some funds may be sitting on capital losses from prior bear markets. That works to your advantage—if they learn to make gains— because future capital gains distributions will be free of tax until the loss carry forwards are used up.

2. None of this tax stuff is nearly as important as just choosing a good no-load fund whose shares will go up.

CERTIFICATES OF DEPOSIT

You can enter your CD's in one or more portfolios here, or as assets directly in NET WORTH, or as savings accounts in MONEY.

- If your CD is at a bank, it's really a Savings Account. Set it up as a savings account in MONEY and, to record the receipt of interest on it, just enter a Receive transaction, with "June Interest on Banc One CD #1040622" (say) as the Payee and Interest Income as the budget allocation.

- If it's in an IRA or Keogh account at a bank, you'd do the same thing, only set it up in MONEY as an IRA/Keogh/401K type account.

- If you hold CDs in a brokerage account, treat them as bonds in that portfolio, along with your other stocks and bonds. That's essentially what CDs are: bonds that never change in price. On the Buy Assets screen, you might want to designate them "semi-liquid," because of the penalty for cashing them in early. When you get a notice of interest having been credited, you'd record that on the Record Income screen, and designate it "Broker Held for Me." When you sell, remember that you are selling it for its principal amount only — the $100,000 you paid for it, say. That way there's no capital gain. Rather, you've already recorded that "gain" when you recorded the interest it earned.

There are other ways of handling CDs and you should feel free to devise your own method.

You may wish to use Reminders—Ctrl-R—to enter a quarterly reminder, if this is a 90-day CD, reminding you of its impending maturity.

TREASURY SECURITIES

Treasury notes and bonds are issued with maturities of up to 30 years and can be treated pretty much like any other bonds you buy or sell (though you may wish to Special Code them in order to look at them separately). Since the interest they pay is local-tax free, choose "Federal Tax Only" as the Tax Status.

Treasury bills, on the other hand, are short-term obligations more on the order of certificates of deposit—except that the issuing bank is the Federal Reserve. I'd enter them along the same lines as CD's, described above.

TAX-FREE BONDS

Unless they're hypothetical, or you've made the mistake of buying them for your IRA, they go in a TAXABLE portfolio. Remember, by taxable, we simply mean a portfolio not sheltered by law from taxation. You could have a taxable portfolio made up entirely of tax-free bonds; just indicate "Free of Any Tax" on the individual bonds. Interest on most such bonds is tax free; but profits made selling them are not.

(It's a mistake to buy tax-frees for a tax sheltered account simply because you're wasting their tax advantages in an account where tax is deferred anyway, and because you could generally have gotten a higher yield in your IRA from something else.)

Our special Yield Summary Analysis (Analyze Assets, Action Key twice, Yield, F7) does a nice job of breaking down yields by taxability.

ZERO-COUPON BONDS

Zero-coupon bonds pay no interest but, as a consequence, don't cost much. All they promise is $1,000 at maturity (like any other bond), so the more distant the maturity, the less they cost.

Zeroes are often used to fund an IRA. You'd never want to own them in your own name, because even though they pay no interest, the IRS taxes you tax as if they did. (It "imputes" interest based on the appreciation built into the bond as it climbs from what you paid for it to the eventual $1,000 at maturity.) But if you buy zero-coupon bonds for your IRA, enter them along with any other assets in that IRA portfolio. If you paid $3,000 for $15,000 of World Bank zeroes due February 1, 2005, you'd enter them like this:

Symbol: WB 0s05

Name: World Bank 0s of 2/1/05

Units: 150

Price: 20   (Remember, to conform to the way bond prices are quoted—in cents on the dollar—we don't enter 15 bonds at $200 each, we enter 150 at $20 each.)

Yield: Enter either "0," which is technically correct, or the yield to maturity of the bond (which you should certainly know when you buy it, and can calculate with ANALYZE's Yield to Maturity, if you don't).

Every so often, you can call your broker and ask for a quote on your bonds and update the price—but these are not the kinds of things you buy to look at in the paper every day.

In fact, they're not the kinds of things you buy to sell, because if you do call your broker to sell them, his firm will grin broadly and take a big bite out of the sale price for its trouble. (The commission is trivial; it's the spread between the "bid and the asked"—often 5% or more on a small lot of zero coupon bonds—that kills you.) Best to buy with the intention, at least, of holding on to maturity.

CAPITAL GAINS ON ZEROES

There's one non-problem with all of this. We do not handle capital gains of zeroes properly. It's a non-problem because assets under the umbrella of an IRA or Keogh are not subject to capital gains tax anyway. The Capital Gains Analysis in PORTFOLIO is obviously meant for only those of your portfolios that are taxable (so check off only those when you tell us which portfolios you want to analyze).

A ZERO-COUPON BOND IN A TAXABLE PORTFOLIO

If you did buy and sell a zero-coupon bond in a taxable portfolio, we'd show the profit (or loss) as a capital gain (or loss), when, in fact, it's more complicated than that. What actually happens with a zero is that each year you pay ordinary income tax on the imputed interest (the amount by which the bond would appreciate if it compounded steadily from where you bought it to $1,000 at maturity). But in the real world, long-term interest rates fluctuate. Say you bought a zero-coupon bond at $100 knowing that it would compound at 11.5% a year to $1,000. Three years later, interest rates in general had declined dramatically and when you went to sell the bond, you got $250 for it. The difference between what you actually got—$250—and the amount to which the IRS had expected it to grow at 11.5% compounded—about $143—represents a long-term capital gain. Managing Your Money, on the other hand, would show the gain simply as the difference between the $250 you got and the $100 you paid.

The one kind of zero-coupon bond that can make sense for a taxable portfolio, and so will require an adjustment to our capital gains calculation when you sell it, is a municipal zero. Municipal zeroes carry the same tax exemption as any other municipal bond, so there's no imputed tax to pay on their accretion. But when you sell them, your taxable gain should be lowered (or your loss increased) by the amount the bond "should" have appreciated in the time that has elapsed since you bought it. (If you own any municipal zeroes purchased before March 1, 1984 you qualify for even more favorable tax treatment. Ask your broker or accountant.)

ORIGINAL-DISCOUNT BONDS

Issued at a discount from their maturity value, gains in their value are taxed as capital gains or losses only to the extent their appreciation exceeds or falls short of the compounded annual return that was built into the bond at issuance by virtue of the discount. That annual return is supposed to be reported as interest income each year, even though you didn't receive it.

BONDS BOUGHT AT A PREMIUM

You have a choice with bonds you buy at a premium. If you pay $1,250 for a bond that will be redeemed for $1,000 ten years from now, you can either give it no special treatment (in which case Managing Your Money handles the capital gain or loss realized when you sell the bond or it's redeemed), or you can "amortize the premium" (in which case you'll have to make some adjustments). Unless big bucks are involved, amortizing the premium is probably not worth it. But if it is, you'd take that extra $250 per bond and write it off as an ordinary deduction against income over the ensuing 10 years. Say you held the bond until it was redeemed for $1,000. Instead of showing a $250 long-term loss, as Managing Your Money would, you would show no loss at all, because the "basis" of the bond had gradually been written down from $1,250 to $1,000 as you took the deductions. If this could be meaningful to you, check with your accountant. And note that on municipal bonds, the law says you must amortize the premium if you want any tax benefit from the premium—you can't take a capital loss on the premium when you cash the bonds in.

BONDS: ACCRUED INTEREST

With bonds, in addition to a brokerage commission, you may have to pay accrued interest. You pay $10,000 for the bonds, say, $50 in commission, but $321.07 in accrued interest. This is not part of the purchase price. It's a payment you've made to the seller representing his pro-rata share of the next semi-annual interest payment. It won't be much if you buy the bond right after an interest payment has been made, but it will be a lot if you buy it with just a few days to go until the next payment. (When you sell the bond, the same thing is done for you: your share of the next interest payment is automatically added to your proceeds.)

Only when a bond is "trading flat"—it's in default, and future interest payments are iffy—is no adjustment for accrued interest made.

When you record the purchase or sale of a bond in Managing Your Money, we ask for the accrued interest paid or received, if any, and then do two things:

1. We keep a record of it in View Income. (Note the "ACC" we put just before the Portfolio or Status column; and note that the last F9 sorting option is "Accrued Interest.")

2. We allocate the amount to whatever budget category you tell us to. You might want to stick with your regular "Interest" category, or it could be a category you set up called "Accrued Interest."

At the end of the year, select View Income, use F9 to sort by "Accrued Interest," and print out a list to attach to your tax return with the notation "Accrued Interest." Accrued interest paid is a legitimate deduction against the interest income you will be getting from these bonds. Otherwise, you'd pay tax on the full six month interest payment when, in effect, you might really only have received a couple of weeks' worth.

(If you pay the accrued interest this year and don't receive your interest payment until next year, you may have to delay taking the deduction until next year, to match the two. If significant sums are involved, consult your accountant.)

> NOTE: Accrued interest received when you sell your bonds is taxable income.

SAVINGS BONDS

EE Savings "Bonds" are not bonds in the conventional sense. They're not denominated in $1,000's, they don't pay semi-annual interest, and you can't buy or sell them by calling your broker. If you own a bunch, you might set up a portfolio called Savings Bonds and enter them this way:

Purchase date: whatever it was.

Quantity: 1 (or whatever number of bonds you actually bought).

Price per unit: $37.50 (or whatever price you actually paid for each bond, not the face value, which is twice as high).

Commission: none (your bank or employer-sponsored payroll savings plan is supposed to do this for free).

Yield: 6% or any other number you feel most accurately estimates the long-term yield you'll receive. (EE Bonds guarantee a minimum of 6% if held five years, but are tied to 85% of the average five-year Treasury rate during the time you own them, and so might ultimately pay more than 6% if held to maturity.)

Tax Status: I guess you'd say "Taxable," because eventually the income is taxed ... but since it can be deferred for many years, as in an IRA, you might set up this portfolio as an IRA/Keogh/401K type. Or perhaps you should say "Free of Any Tax," because the interest on bonds purchased after 1989 may be entirely tax free if those bonds are eventually redeemed to pay tuition. (Certain income restrictions apply.) Up to you.

Asset type: Savings Bond. Note that by tagging them this way, they'll show up on their own line in Retirement Planning on the ANALYZE menu and amongst the extracted assets of Your Net Worth—if you have them in a taxable portfolio. (If you have them in an IRA/Keogh/401K portfolio, they'll be included under the overall "IRA/Keogh/401K" heading on the Retirement Planning and Your Net Worth screens.)

Price Objective: This is sort of meaningless, but you could enter the face value of the bond if you like. I'd leave it blank and use the Lot Comment line to record the face value and serial number of the bond.

Once a year, you could go to the price update screen and add 6% to the price of each to reflect the appreciation (or even more if it looks as if they'll wind up yielding more than the minimum). You could add an annual reminder to Reminders (Ctrl-R): "January 15: Don't forget to add 6% to Savings Bonds!"

Of course, if you buy a new bond each week, this could all be quite time consuming. Here's a possible shortcut.

Give all the $37.50 bonds bought in '89 the same symbol and name; likewise all those bought in '90, etc. (You'd be able to tell them apart by the purchase dates and, in the comment line, by specific serial numbers.)

Under the symbol "SB89 37.50" would go all the purchases of that type bond. All the $500 (face value) bonds you bought for $250 in 1989 could have the symbol "SB89 250." And so on.

By grouping them that way, you could adjust their prices in batches, averaging them all as a class. For those purchased in the year just ended, you might raise the price by 3%—assuming you'd owned them an average of half a year. For prior years, you'd increase the price by the full 6%, or even by the 6.9% they were recently earning according to the government's formula (though you're only guaranteed 6% to maturity: the rest depends on what happens to interest rates in the future).

This would be simpler, and would also fit nicely with the Aggregation we can do for you (see page 368: "Aggregation and Disaggregation").

REAL ESTATE

Real estate you own may be entered directly in NET WORTH as assets under an aggregate category you might call "Real Estate," or under a couple of different categories you called "Homes" and "Rental Properties."

Or enter it in a portfolio you set up here, called "Real Estate." The sum of the value of the properties gets pulled into NET WORTH under the extract heading "Real Estate." And by recording the properties here, you can include them in PORTFOLIO analyses, too.

For help setting up such a portfolio, please see page 351: "Setting Up Your Portfolio" and then "Adding a New Asset."

Meanwhile, use MONEY's Loan section to enter each of the mortgages (see page 297: "Set Up Your Loans"). With the Quick List transactions feature of MONEY, monthly mortgage payments take just a few keystrokes. The proper amount of each month's interest, principal and escrow will automatically hit the proper budget and tax categories in MONEY and TAX, and NET WORTH will reflect the slight decrease in the amount you owe.

TO UPDATE THE VALUE OF YOUR REAL ESTATE...

If you've entered each property as an asset in PORTFOLIO, just visit Update Prices every so often and adjust the price manually. Otherwise, if you've entered your properties directly in NET WORTH and skipped entering them here, just go to NET WORTH, visit each one, and update its value there.

SHORT SALES

When you think a stock is going to go down and want to profit if it does, you can either buy a put (see below) or you can sell it short. Selling a stock short means getting your broker to borrow some, selling it, and then minutes, months or even years later buying it back ("covering" it), to return it. If it costs less to buy it back than you got when you sold it, you've made a profit. But if you sold it short at 60 and had to pay 80 to buy it back, you've got a loss. Plus, when you're short a stock, you don't get it's dividends, you have to pay those dividends. So it's a very risky game— even more so when you consider that most of the time, the stock market trends up.

If you do sell short, just select Sell Assets and press F7 to record the transaction. Note that your cash balance will not be affected by this sale, as for a normal sale. Only when you cover the short and close out your position will the profit or loss it produced be added to or subtracted from your cash balance. But in viewing your gains and losses in this portfolio (Analyze Assets), gains and losses from ongoing short sales are included.

To view your various shorts, select Display Assets and use the Action Key to display your shorts. (The Action Key displays Unsold Assets, Sold Assets, Short Positions and Good-Til-Canceleds in rotation.) To cover one of your shorts, press F6. (Or select Buy Assets and press F7 there, which will take you to this same display.)

To record a dividend on a short sale, select Record Income, point to the short, and press the Action Key. We'll force you to enter the amount as negative and then debit your cash balance (just as your broker has), reduce the taxable dividends we tell Schedule B in TAX about, and show this payment with a minus sign on the View Income screen. But to avoid problems with the IRS, it's best at tax time to report the full amount of dividends received and then, on a new line, clearly show this negative amount as "Dividends PAID on short sales."

Your short sales will not show up as "sold assets" until you've covered the short sale and closed out your position. Up to that point, they're kept separately as short sales.

PUTS AND CALLS

Puts and calls are options (not obligations) to sell or buy 100 shares of some underlying stock at a specified price (the "strike price") up until some expiration date. You buy a put if you think the stock is headed down. You buy a call if you think it's going up. Believe me, the less you know about this, the better.

If you buy a put or a call, just enter it like any other asset. Say you bought one GM put for $350. You'd enter that as 100 units at $3.50 each, because puts and calls are quoted in terms of the 100 shares of stock they give you the right to buy or sell. Run through the rest of the screen filling in the blanks. (For "Risk," enter "Speculative.")

If you sell your put or call, you handle that on the Sell Assets screen, just as if it were 100 shares of a little stock called "GM April 90 Put" or some such.

If it expired worthless, you'd "sell" it for zero dollars as of the expiration date. (At least you save on commissions.)

If you exercise a call, that means you paid $600 (say) for the right to buy 100 shares of GM at 80 and, by gum, you're going to do it. When you do, enter the GM purchase price as 86 (the $80 per share you paid, plus the $6 per share you paid for the call) and note in the comment field what you've done, including the price and purchase date of the call. Then staple the confirmation slip showing your purchase of the call to the one showing your purchase of the stock (and/or make a note on your monthly statement). Then delete the call from your portfolio (F3 on Display Assets)—you don't own it any more.

Note that you don't "sell" the call in Managing Your Money, you delete it, because you didn't sell it. No taxable event has occurred. Note also that when you delete it, your cash balance will rise by the $600 you paid for it, as if you never had bought it in the first place. But that's fine, because by recording 86 as the purchase price instead of 80, you'll in effect be paying that $600 all over again, so your cash balance will be just what it should be. Note, penultimately, that I'm including commissions in this $600 example of the purchase price of my call (actually, it was $550 for the call and a $50 commission). You should, too. And note, finally, that when you eventually sell your 100 shares of GM, your profit or loss will, correctly, be figured on that $86 purchase price we used, not the $80 exercise price.

If you exercise a put, forcing the poor fool who sold the put to take 100 shares of IBM you bought the right to shove down his throat at $160, say, you run through a similar routine (though I'm yet to meet anyone who's ever exercised a put). You staple the confirms together and/or make a note on your monthly statement. You record the sale price not as $160, but as $160 less the price per share you paid for your put. You make a note on the comment line of the stock just before you sell it, stating that the sale price reflects this put you bought at such and such price on such and such date. Then you delete the put from your portfolio, because you don't own it anymore. (You won't be able to View/Edit the Lot Comment line after the sale, but you will be able to include it in a report with PORTFOLIO'S Report Generator.)

If you write (sell) naked calls—sell calls without owning any of the underlying stock—you are crazy, because that means you've sold someone the right to buy from you shares of stock you don't own. Shorting stocks is risky enough; shorting calls is far worse because your maximum gain is the premium you are paid for the call. If the stock drops 100 points you don't make $10,000, as you would if you had shorted 100 shares—you make the few hundred dollars you were paid for selling the call. But if the stock should rise 100 points instead, you lose the same $10,000 you would have lost shorting it.

If you insist on doing this crazy thing, you'd enter the call you sold as a short sale. The sale price might be 6, if you were paid $600 for the call, and if you got really lucky and IBM tanked, you might be able to "cover" your short for zero, if the option expired worthless. Otherwise, you'd cover it at whatever price you eventually had to pay to extricate yourself from this mess. If IBM went to 250, you could buy back the call for around $9,000. Or, if you waited until the call were exercised, you'd have to go into the market and buy 100 shares at $250 (which you'd enter as $244, to reflect the $6 you got by selling the call) and then sell them at $160 a few seconds later, as you had promised you'd do, for a net loss of $8,400.

If you write (sell) naked puts, you're a little less crazy, but only if you really wouldn't mind owning 100 shares of IBM at 95. Here is the stock selling at 110, and you're thinking, Gee, if it ever got down to 95 I'd sure want to grab 100 shares. And then you're thinking, Well, that being the case, I may as well be paid a few hundred dollars while I wait. If it never gets down to 95, the put I've sold expires worthless and I get to keep that money. If it does get down to 95, and the stock is "put" to me, I still get to keep the money, which lowers my cost per share even further. (So when you record the purchase in Managing Your Money, you show the purchase price not as $95 but as $90, say, explaining why in the comment line, deleting the put from your portfolio of shorts, and stapling the confirms together.) Of course, if it gets down to $95, you may not want it after all, or other stocks may have become even more attractive, but there's no point crying over spilt milk.

The danger in writing naked puts is that you write them on more stock than you can afford to buy, assuming not all the stocks you've done this with could possibly go down that much, let alone at the same time. For that to happen, one man told me in the summer of 1987, the market would have to drop, like, 200 points in a day. He was already ahead more than $1 million from writing naked puts, he told me, three months before the crash. (He lost it all, and a lot more.)

If you write covered calls, you are less crazy still, though not as smart as some brokers who see an endless stream of quarterly commissions would have you think. Writing a covered call means you already own 100 shares of IBM (as opposed to a naked call, where you don't own them) and you don't mind selling someone the right to buy it from you at 130. The stock's 110 now, so if it rockets to 250 in a month (which would never happen anyway), you make the first 20 points of profit, you keep whatever dividend may have been paid, and you keep the premium you were paid for writing the call. Not terrible. If, more likely, IBM just gradually edges up over the years, you get all that gradual gain, all the dividends, and a nice premium every quarter for writing a new covered call. The flaw in all this is that your gain is limited but your loss is not. If IBM should edge gradually down instead of up—or fall precipitously—years of better than average returns with this strategy could turn to losses. (You'd lose less having written the calls than not writing them; but might have lost less still never having started with these shares in the first place. In the long run, only your broker wins with options, even covered calls.)

In any event, we have no fancy way to link the calls you sell and the underlying shares you own. Record your sale of the call as a short sale; record your ownership of the underlying 100 shares of IBM as a normal purchase. If the call you've shorted expires worthless, or you buy it back to cover it at some price, record this as an ordinary short-cover. If instead the call is exercised and your 100 shares of IBM are "called away from you," record the sale of those shares, but include in the sale price the $6 a share (or whatever) you were paid (after commission) for the call. Note this on the comment line of this lot of IBM shares; staple your confirmation slips together; and delete the short sale from your portfolio of shorts. You are no longer short a call on IBM—it's been exercised.

> Hint: An unfancy way to link them
>
> If we have no fancy way to link the call you wrote with the 100 shares of stock that underlies it, we've nonetheless got an unfancy way. Say you own 100 shares of GM and you now write an October 80 call against them. Just buy—for a price of zero—100 shares of a "stock" you give this symbol: GM-OCT-CVD. The GM- part should assure that it shows up on your screen right after the actual shares themselves, like a shadow; OCT means October; but, most important, CVD would be your own shorthand, everywhere, for "covered." This "asset" would have no value or substance—it's just a reminder. Likewise, on the short-sale screen, short a call (at $0) with a symbol just like the real one, only with the letters CVD appended. Covered calls will thus show up in pairs: the real one, with real dollars and real price fluctuations, followed by this phantom option with the CVD suffix, just to remind you that, yes, you're covered.

If you write covered puts, meaning you're short the actual shares but also have sold someone the right to sell you the shares you'll need to cover that short, you're far more sophisticated than I am and need no help from me figuring out how to account for the transaction.

FROM CHAPTER 8: NET WORTH
ASSET ALLOCATION

Personal finance magazines often publish articles about how much of your investments to put in real estate, stocks, bonds and cash if you're young (and have time to invest for the long term) or nearing retirement (and need safety). Those general common sense articles are fine. But have you ever wished an expert were available to recommend where you should put your money?

Well, that's in effect what the Asset Allocation section of NET WORTH does.

(Recognizing the limitations of common sense magazine articles, one good personal finance magazine offers a $249 asset allocation software program of its own, based on exactly the same "Nobel-prize winning concepts" built into Asset Allocation.)

When you select Asset Allocation from the Net Worth menu, you'll get a side menu:

> About Asset Allocation
> Estimate Future Return
> Asset Mixes
> Analyze Required Wealth

Please start with About Asset Allocation and work your way through each screen, reading HELP along the way.

As you'll see, Asset Allocation is no toy. It was designed for Managing Your Money by Mark Kritzman, a past president of the Society of Quantitative Analysts, a member of the Prize Committee of the Institute for Quantitative Research in Finance, a member of the Review Board of the Institute of Chartered Financial Analysts' Research Foundation, a member of the Editorial Board of the Financial Analysts Journal, and author of Asset Allocation for Institutional Portfolios (Business One Irwin, 1990) and co-author of Quantitative Methods for Financial Analysis (Dow Jones-Irwin, 1989). He has lectured at Columbia, NYU, Stanford and Yale, and at industry seminars in the U.S., Europe and Japan. Before co-founding Windham Capital Management — which advises institutions on asset allocation and has about $700 million under management — he was a Vice President at Bankers Trust and held investment positions at AT&T and the Equitable Life Assurance Society.

> NOTE: Plus Plan members can expect to hear from Mark Kritzman periodically in our newsletter, Managing Your Money Better. Among other things, he might suggest what historical assumptions to plug into Asset Allocation, since these play such an important part in its recommendations.

When you read About Asset Allocation, you'll see I don't hold out our asset allocation model or any other as being magic. Far from it. But Asset Allocation can be an important tool in managing your money.

INDEX

O

Occupational Outlook Handbook, 230
Oil and gas limited partnerships, 168-169
Oil funds, 168-169
100 Highest Yields, 125
Open listing, 215

P

Parent Loans for Undergraduate Students (PLUS), 196
Parnassus Fund, 139
Parnership Record, The, 164, 169
Partnerships. *See* Limited partnerships
Parton, Dolly, 18
Passbook accounts, 50, 123
Passive investing, 138
Paul Revere Life, 67
Pax World, 139
Payout risk, 153
Payroll taxes, 246
Payroll-based employee stock-ownership plans (PAYSOPs), 20
P/E ratio, 141-145
Pell Grant, 193
Pension Benefit Guaranty Corporation, 248
Pension plans, 15-17, 247-252
    job hopping and, 230, 251
    vesting of, 19, 228, 251
Pension Rights Center, 19
Perkins Loans, 195
Phoenix Mutual Life, 77
Pioneer Fund, 139
PLUS, 196
Poelker, John, 241
Pools, investment, 138
Preference items, 99
Pregnancy, disability coverage for, 67
Premiums
    car insurance, 84-86

    disability insurance, 65-68
    health insurance, 80
    life insurance, 68, 74, 75
    nursing home insurance, 86-87
    reducing costs of, 64-65
    Prepayment of mortgage, 211-212
Price/earnings (P/E) ratio, 141-145
Prime rate, 2
Probate, 259
Professional Tape Reader, 143
Profit-sharing Keogh plan, 104-105
Profit-sharing plans, 19
Provident Companies, 67
Put options, 166-167

Q

Q-TIP trust, 264

R

R & D partnerships, 171
Raise, negotiating, 228-229
Rate of return, 54
Raymond James & Associates, 23, 40
Real estate
    as investment, 159-164
    rental properties, 108-109, 161
    second home, 108, 162
See also Home ownership
Real estate brokers, 214-216
Real Estate Investment Trust (REIT), 7, 164
Real estate limited partnerships, 106-107, 109, 137, 159, 163
Record keeping, financial, 14-17, 115
Redecorating, 207
Reed's Real Estate Investor's Monthly, 164
Refinancing, 209-210, 235